1

# Must Close Saturday

*Frontispiece:* Marie Burke and a gaggle of tartaned schoolgirls filling the stage for the ludicrously unghostly *Happy Holiday*

# Must Close Saturday

*The Decline and Fall of the British Musical Flop*

### Adrian Wright

THE BOYDELL PRESS

First published 2017
The Boydell Press, Woodbridge

ISBN 978 1 78327 235 8

The Boydell Press is an imprint of Boydell & Br
PO Box 9, Woodbridge, Suffolk IP12 3DF, UK
and of Boydell & Brewer Inc.
668 Mt Hope Avenue, Rochester, NY 14620–2731, USA
website: www.boydellandbrewer.com

A CIP catalogue record for this book is available
from the British Library

The publisher has no responsibility for the continued existence or accuracy of URLs for
external or third-party internet websites referred to in this book, and does not guarantee
that any content on such websites is, or will remain, accurate or appropriate

This publication is printed on acid-free paper

Printed and bound in Great Britain by TJ International Ltd.

# Contents

# Illustrations

Every effort has been made to trace the copyright holders of the illustrations; apologies are offered for any omission, and the publishers will be pleased to add any necessary acknowledgement in subsequent editions.

# Preface and Acknowledgements

**When, oh when, will the British musical gain contact with reality instead of the outmoded values of showbiz?**

*Guardian* on *The Card*

It was in 1977 that the *Guardian* took the trouble to ask Lionel Bart 'Whatever happened to the British musical?'

It was a fair enough question. Everybody who knew anything about the British musical, about which almost everybody in Britain knew hardly anything, thought it had pretty well gone down the proverbial plughole, but there probably wasn't a moment's hesitation before Bart replied 'It stopped when I stopped. It was big when Gilbert and Sullivan were doing some; when Noel Coward was doing some. It was big when I was doing some.'[1]

I wish I had seen this brilliantly concise analysis of what happened to the British musical in the second half of the twentieth century before attempting to capture the mystery in a book of 140,000 words. Bart had a point. Of course, enough British musicals have pleased and managed to run into respectable age, and by the beginning of the 1970s a more commercially keen 'international' brand of musical had (often clutching a bible) crept up on London, bringing much wider recognition and success to its creators and their products, recognition and success denied its predecessors.

'Nothing Succeeds Like Success' ran the title of one of the more intellectually inane songs in *The Card*, supposedly a period musical based on an undeservedly mutilated novel by Arnold Bennett, but effectually a collection of quasi pop-songs hung out to dry by the creators of the theme tune to *Crossroads*, and there was no denying the truth of it. Success, however, only exists because of failure. Success romps over failure, swims in clear water above the sinking depths of failure, rolls on as failure folds up, fades away, hides itself shamefaced as the curtain falls too soon, taking its creators down with the speed of a *Titanic*.

Success versus failure; these are simply, after all, labels, and the labels are slapped on with little heed of justice. Who can say if the show that runs four nights, two weeks or a few months is a failure, or the show that runs five years or seems destined to run for ever is a success? They may have been labelled wrongly. *Charlie Girl*, a catchpenny musical of the mid 1960s, survived severe critical drubbing to go on to long but very possibly ill-deserved life. Against the background of taste, invention and wit, *Charlie Girl* is a flop, but its 2,202 performances rank it a success. Three years later, *The Young Visiters* showed what could be done when taste, invention and wit were in place, but the cast were no sooner on stage than clearing their dressing-rooms. In more recent times, overshadowed by the internationalism of the product, can we say that Andrew Lloyd Webber's *The Woman in White* and *Love Never Dies* were successes because they ran well beyond the 250 performances that provide the watermark between failure and success used (arbitrarily, but that is life) in this book? As a musical, *The Woman in White* was a sad, lumbering thing, washed-up bits and bobs of Wilkie Collins via some spooky hints of M. R. James and microwaved cold cuts of Benjamin Britten, without a shred of the fun extracted from the novel in the glorious British film *Crimes at the Dark House*, with the irreplaceable Tod Slaughter up to no good at all. Unrelievably tedious as it is, *The Woman in White* is a hit, as is *Love Never Dies*, affectionately dubbed *Paint Never Dries*. Both of the little blighters clung on in the West End for dear life.

Where did failure or success lay? How worthy a success was something like *Pickwick*? Hitched to the Dickens' caravan headed up by *Oliver!*, there was nothing original or striking about it, complete with an overdose of saccharine that might have choked that wily old gentleman of English letters who wasn't averse to a few spoonfuls of literary sugar. How much more valuable, how much braver, was *The Fields of Ambrosia*, a musical about the electric chair? A sure flop if we see how many performances it lasted, perhaps an interesting flop, an adventurous flop, if we look closer. The same, of course, can be said of the shows counted, performance-wise, as successes. The purpose here, however, is with the British musical flop from 1960, a year that marks a decided shift for the genre.

Perverse as it seems, this account – this *celebration* – of the British flop musical begins, not with a bang or whimper, but with *Oliver!*, a musical whose beginning at Wimbledon Theatre in 1960 now appears so distant that it might as well have happened in the Stone Age. It seemed to have occurred to nobody before Lionel Bart to make a musical from Dickens. Francis Burnand and Edward Solomon's *Pickwick* had played successfully in London in 1889, and in 1951 Arthur Benjamin had turned *A Tale of Two Cities* into an opera for the Festival of Britain, but otherwise Dickens had rested unmolested. Of any of those working in musical theatre at the fag-end of the 1950s, Bart seems the least likely candidate for being the first to plunder the grand old man of English literature's catalogue, unleashing a stream of musical adaptations that included not only *A Tale of Two Cities* and *Pickwick*, but *Great Expectations*, *Hard Times*, *Nicholas Nickleby*, *A Christmas Carol*, *The Old Curiosity Shop* (filmed as *Quilp*) and *The Mystery of Edwin Drood*.

These were busy times for Bart. At the same time as he was thumbing through Dickens' novel of underworld Victorian London and knocking out songs for Tommy Steele, he burst into the West End as lyricist for *Lock Up Your Daughters*, and provided the songs for *Fings Ain't Wot They Used T'Be*. He seems to have had difficulty placing his adaptation of *Oliver Twist* before impresario Donald Albery took it up; one producer turned it down 'because it lacked a gimmick. He suggested an all-black cast.'[2] With the financially acute Albery at the helm there was no possibility of extravagance in its staging, and as the opening night in London approached, Albery was convinced that disaster loomed. 'I thought it was the biggest flop I'd ever had. All the backers tried to get out.'[3] At Wimbledon, the show lost £4,500 in its two-and-a-half-week stay. In such circumstances, the company and its producers – as with so many others that follow inevitably in these pages – feared they might soon be out of work. Bart had turned down writing a movie for Elvis Presley to concentrate on casting his new show.

Many of those who signed to appear in *Oliver!* knew what it meant to be in a flop. Ron Moody, cast as Fagin – despite the fact that Bart had at various times dreamed of Sid James or Max Bygraves, and Peter O'Toole for the movie – had just endured one: the London production of *Candide*, one of the worthiest of failures, blundering on for 60 performances at the Saville. Georgia Brown, cast as Nancy, had recently played in one of the most innovative British musical flops of the 1960s, *The Lily White Boys*. As for the movie, Bart told the *Daily Mail* 'I want Elizabeth Taylor as Nancy', and – as a side order – he planned on Richard Burton for Bill Sikes. Bart changed his mind the following year; now, he was planning on making his own movie, with Danny Kaye as Fagin. These wayward assertions were joined by Bart's suggestion that Spike Milligan should take over when Moody left the cast.

The musical actresses that followed Brown as Nancy were no strangers to flops either: Vivienne Martin was the leading lady of too many of them in the 1960s, including *The Match Girls*, *Joey Joey* and *Queenie*; Judith Bruce notched up *Mister Venus* (a Frankie Howerd vehicle that seriously misfired), *Man of Magic*, *Tom Brown's Schooldays*, and two American efforts, *The Great American Backstage Musical* and *Marilyn!*; the ever-welcome Nicolette Roeg, decisive and vibrant and grossly underrated, survived some mega muddles, among them *Belle*, *Two Cities* and the American *Fiorello!* Only a few weeks before being cast as the original Widow Corney, Hope Jackman had been hustled out of the Princes Theatre, where a little sermonising musical, *Johnny the Priest*, gave up the ghost after a few nights, passing away and taking with it the school of verismo musicals (or what in London passed for verismo musicals). Not one of these would have been surprised if *Oliver!* itself had flopped.

To almost everyone's surprise, the opening at the New Theatre at the bottom end of St Martin's Lane was, to put it mildly, a success. His pessimism having flown out of the stage door, Albery told the press 'The first night was the most terrific I have ever seen in my life.'[4] Theatre libraries rushed to purchase £22,000 worth of tickets. Five Broadway managements pestered for the rights. The curtain went up and down: 23 times according to some sources; 17 times according to Moody; 18 times according to Ganzl. In his indispensable history of British musical theatre, Ganzl highlights the glowing response that *Oliver!* received on this first showing, but the notices were not altogether encouraging, the London critics already badly brusied by having encountered so many apparently dismal British musicals.

In the *Guardian*, Philip Hope-Wallace described 'a sad disappointment, a very starveling musical from the workhouse' with 'a certain gutter-sparrow charm' and 'some pleasant tunefulness. But the lyrical side of it sounds fatally fast hack work and the book, rinsed from Dickens' *Oliver Twist*, is the merest strip cartoon.'[5] What was more, there was 'rampageous overacting from such people as Mrs Sowerberry, Noah Claypole and Fagin'. For *The Times*, Moody's Fagin and Keith Hamshere's Oliver were the best things of the night; neither newspaper mentioned Georgia Brown, whose remaining years would be marked by the British musical theatre's inability to make use of her talents. Meanwhile, *The Times*, although approving, could only head its review 'Hotch-Potch Musical version of *Oliver Twist*'.

Robert Muller, one of several of the most influential popular press critics of the day, came to the curious conclusion that this was 'a melange of every conceivable idiom, from comic opera to blues [with] the vivacity of a Cockney Offenbach, the grace and simplicity of early Rodgers, and a style and aptness entirely of its own'.[6] *Tatler and Bystander* appreciated that 'gusto and pathos alike, aiming at an effect of guilelessness, were put across with little of the art that conceals art. There was a curious lack throughout of the professional know-how which is the mark of the rival American product even when it is trying for simplicity.'[7] This comparison with American product had long plagued British musicals, and would go on doing so until the present day. In breaking through a barrier of success that very few other British musicals had hitherto even come within sight of, *Oliver!* seemed at once a singular achievement and a torch of hope for the future of home-grown shows. It made it to Broadway, and ran, and Georgia Brown and Judith Bruce went with it. It made it onto film, with Moody adapting his stage performance (basically not much more than a collection of old tricks he'd learned from revue – but tricks polished with the generous assistance of Vivienne Martin, with whom he worked closely on his interpretation) and a miscast Shani Wallis in lieu of the unwanted Brown. In the wings lurked Moody's ambition to stage his own musical biography of the Regency clown Joseph Grimaldi, a dream doomed to disappointment.

But *Oliver!* kept on, scarcely drawing breath. It never stopped, in revival after revival, and remains probably the only British musical written by other than Andrew Lloyd Webber that the man on the Clapham omnibus could name. He probably has little remembrance of Bart's next two works, the mammoth *Blitz!* with its many brilliant moments, and the Liverpudlian *Maggie May*. Both are sometimes casually referred to as flops, but technically were not, *Blitz!* flagging up 568 performances and *Maggie May* 501. It wasn't until 1965 that Bart collided with his first theatrical failure, *Twang!* In his case, the musical flop showed its deadliest effect by ending his career. Bart was not the first, and would certainly not be the last, to discover the power of the British musical flop. Even more savagely, his *La Strada* ran for one performance on Broadway, by which time it had anyway been stripped of almost all his songs.

By the time Robin Hood and his brave but none too merry men invaded the Shaftesbury Theatre for *Twang!* the designer who had contributed so much to the Bart works had already departed, having provided the sets for *Lock Up Your Daughters, Oliver!, Blitz!* and *Maggie May.* Sean Kenny's innovative sets for *Oliver!* marked the beginning of a revitalisation of the visual and physical quality of the British musical theatre. Way beyond Kenny's early death in 1973, is it Kenny's influence we see extended and extrapolated in such design extravaganza land-scapes as those invented for the likes of *Metropolis* and *Napoleon*? Kenny's work focused the audience's mind on design, a thing that had never particularly mat-tered to the designers of musicals by Coward, Novello, Wilson, Slade and most of those that had come before. Nevertheless, there remained a generous selection of British musicals that landed on stage looking as if they had just been emptied from a van direct from a week in Barnsley.

At ten minutes past two on the morning of 18 July 1957 PC Colin Reedman was proceeding along Theobalds Road in Holborn when he saw a man 'singing and dancing and shouting in a very loud voice'. The man almost caused an accident by running after a taxi. Later that day in the dock at Clerkenwell Court, Peter O'Toole pleaded guilty to being drunk and disorderly, explaining to the magistrate 'I had been celebrating'. He was fined ten shillings. That seems to have been the begin-ning and end of O'Toole's criminal career. The same evening he walked through the stage door of the Garrick Theatre to lead the cast of the harmless Swiss musical *Oh! My Papa!* that had opened the previous night. No matter that the audience had cheered for a full five minutes after curtain fall; the critics were unflinching in their dismissal, a fact that O'Toole was unaware of when carousing in Theobalds Road. The shock waves washed up by the British press on many a musical sub-merged *Oh! My Papa!* Milton Shulman, the critic of the London *Evening Standard*, delivered a hammer blow to its innocent entertainment.

> Grimly dedicated to charm, it dispenses it like so many thick slices of liverwurst [...] Although Paul Burkhard's music is laden with Viennese schmaltz [...] the lyrics and the book have about as light a touch as a panzer division in full retreat [...the cast] has little success looking pleasing in excruciating costumes and indulging in dance routines consisting of that combination of knee jerks and elbow waggles last seen in *Salad Days*, which I now identify as the Bristol Trot.[8]

After reading the *Evening Standard's* review of *Oh! My Papa!* O'Toole probably needed another stiffener, as two years later did Britain's unofficial playwriting Angry Young Man John Osborne, chased by an angry mob from the Palace Theatre after the opening night of his only musical, *The World of Paul Slickey.* His pursuers hadn't even bothered to wait for the next morning's notices to confirm the show's fate. The leading lady gave the booing gallery a vigorous two-finger salute as the curtain fell.

On both sides of the Atlantic, the public has long enjoyed a fascination with the theatrical flop, in whatever genre. Eric Maschwitz was no stranger to such failures, notching up some grand examples. His play *Thirteen for Dinner* ran for one night. His adaptation of Arnold Ridley's 1920's spine-tingler *The Ghost Train* into the 1954 *Happy Holiday* was an object lesson in how to turn a hit play into a clanking disaster with tunes, dismantling Ridley's plot until it was only the idea of a train thundering mysteriously through the night that remained. With scant regard to the original play, Maschwitz's version totally emasculated the charm that Ridley had worked, introducing hordes of schoolgirls and superfluous new characters. Ronald Barker condemned the show as 'a most distressing experience'. Unfortunately, *Happy Holiday* happened to be the first British musical whose songs were intended for American exploitation, but 'We shall have to do better than this or we shall become the laughing stock of Broadway.' But what else could possibly be wrong with it? Was it that the second half deteriorated into dream sequences, 'which are far less entertaining than anything Freud ever thought up'? Was it that 'the artistic despair apparently spread to everyone's bones'? Was it that Berkeley Sutcliffe provided 'dreary sets and quite [in fact, very] ugly costumes'? Was it that its leading man, comic Reg Dixon, 'was conspicuously unfunny'? Was it that 'it is difficult to believe that anyone was responsible for arranging the antics which passed for dancing'?[9]

The past is littered with such follies, of which the public generally took little notice as shows came and went, sometimes with breathtaking speed. Taking anything under 250 performances as defining the flop, we can see how many productions in 1960 failed commercially (most had already been critically censured) as *Oliver!* set its face to the future: *Joie de Vivre*, from an unfashionable Terence Rattigan play; *Call It Love?*, a bunch of insubstantial revue sketches with some tepid Sandy Wilson songs; *The Golden Touch*, a 'with-it' musical produced by the very un-hip management of H. M. Tennent; *Johnny the Priest*, a sort of *West Side Story* of London's docklands, with bibles and ping-pong; *The Dancing Heiress*, a half-baked, half-American, half-pastiche of musicals; a very silly enterprise called *The Princess*, that turned out to be a bad ballet school showcase; a biting satire on British life, *The Lily White Boys*, that probably deserves reconsideration; Slade and Reynolds's panto musical with cow *Hooray for Daisy!*; *Mr Burke M.P.*, a political satire involving politicians and chimpanzees, and *Follow That Girl*, Slade and Reynolds's somewhat unenthusiastic follow-up to *Salad Days* at the Vaudeville Theatre, making a total of ten British musical flops in 1960.

In contrast to this abundant harvest in the space of a year, there was a total of only seven British musical flops, during what may well have been the twilight years of the British musical, between 2009 and 2014: two modest offerings, *Love Story*

1  *Twenty Minutes South*, an intimate British musical flop of the 1950s. Jack Manuel, Daphne Anderson and Brian Blades sing 'I Like People'

and *Too Close To the Sun* (the first welcomed by some, the second derided); two so-so pieces, *Betty Blue Eyes* and *Lend Me a Tenor*, and – ultimately – three major productions attached to three prominent names that seemed to mark a very final end to hope for the future of the genre, Tim Rice's *From Here To Eternity*, Lloyd Webber's *Stephen Ward* and (more vulgarly and enjoyably) Harry Hill's *I Can't Sing*. These works already seem to have taken the form of footnotes in histories of their creators. Ultimately, these striking failures suggested an impasse, an end to the possibility of future successes, an apparently impenetrably thick final curtain at last grazing, if not touching, the stage.

In different circumstances, the falling-off of numbers of British musical flops may have been seen as a good thing, but less musical flops did not result in an increased amount of successful product. Those seven flops over a six-year period reflect the fact that managements were increasingly unwilling to risk new musical theatre works, depending on the continued success of the long-running international successes that continued to block new musical theatre. Those mammoths have effectively diminished the vitality of the London musical; indeed, all but swamped it. Imaginative endeavour, innovation and a rush to revival of rarely seen works has been taken over by the under-funded but thriving fringe theatres beyond the West End, the energetic little theatres underneath railway lines, where it's best to take a cushion, the lavatories have to be avoided and ticket prices do not involve mortgaging your house. It is in fringe theatre that hope resides for the continuance of the British musical, not the West End. Rising costs, the apparent lack of appropriate writers and composers (and the unwillingness of managements to search them out), and the constantly ringing tills of Lloyd Webber's *Phantom*, the never-ending barricading of *Les Misérables*, and the clap-happy invasion of juke-box musicals with established songs pushed into assemblages of libretto like currants in an Eccles cake, have all but obliterated originality and experiment. This book deals with what may well be the dying days of the truly British musical flop, but it is intended as celebration, not wake.

Apathy towards London's musical flops began to change in the mid 1960s, at a time when critics of British musicals were chief mourners at the bedside of what many diagnosed as a mortally ill beast. The protracted collapse of Lionel Bart's *Twang!*, its potential excitements accentuated by a questionable number of exclamation marks (one or two or more?), introduced a detailed account of the backstage frictions to many more of the public than the few that sat through its performances. The attractiveness of such failure centred on the musical as the ultimate theatrical *folie de grandeur*. The inappropriateness of material, the financial penalties of failure, the sheer *fun* to be had at the expense (financially, too) of the musical flop, began to excite the public consciousness in a way it had never quite achieved in the first half of the century. The wit with which the major theatre critics dealt with such productions sharpened the *grandeur* of the *folie*. Reading a condemnatory review of the latest British musical often qualified as a blood sport, and one that continues to this day. In musical theatre, as elsewhere, nothing succeeds like success, but failure has its particular subtle fascination, perhaps more notably when the *folie* is more obviously silly and the *grandeur* even more ostentatious.

Something about musicals has too often attracted those who have little or no idea of how to create them. Disc jockey Mike Read's works include his biographical trip around Cliff Richard, imaginatively titled *Cliff* (mercifully outside the scope of this book) and *Oh Puck*, his adaptation of *A Midsummer Night's Dream*. Read's only London musical, *Oscar Wilde*, appeared with little *grandeur* but much *folie* for one performance at the Shaw Theatre in 2004. The *Daily Telegraph* denounced it as 'bilge … a pitiful vanity project', an opinion echoed by John Gross in the *Sunday Telegraph*: 'To say that the result of [Read's] labours is dire would be an understatement. The storyline is all over the place, with production values to match. Characterisation is grotesque, and the sense of period is wonky: Wilde's departure for France in 1897 is signalled by the strains of "La Vie en Rose", composed in 1945.'[10] The quality of such product is seriously in doubt; what may we do but stand back and wonder at it ever reaching the stage? Vanity plays its part, harbouring a resilient band of British musicals that, seemingly insistent on destruction, forced themselves onto the London scene.

Folly would not be enough to sustain anything like academic interest in the musical flop. The British musical flop has been the stamping ground of experiment, of daring, of the stretching of good taste. Vital life has flowed through it, whether deserving or undeserving of its fate. Lost at the back of dusty drawers, its remnants unplayed cast recordings and fading theatre programmes, the ignored, the misunderstood, the forgotten, have much to tell us. Revival is all, but to be meaningful the digging must be deep. There has clearly not been enough delving into the fate of forgotten musicals (so many of them, necessarily, flops).

Many British musical flops of an earlier period have been extensively dealt with in my previous book *A Tanner's Worth of Tune* (Boydell Press, 2010). *Must Close Saturday* covers most but not all British musical flops between 1960 and 2016; it does not claim to be comprehensive. The main qualification is that they were presented in a West End theatre, although there are exceptions. Fringe theatre productions, productions of children's musicals, productions predominantly using already established songs, rock musicals, shows concocted from old pop songs, one-man or one-woman shows, revivals, revues and shows presented for fixed seasons are not necessarily covered. Some, however, do appear in these pages. Some shows that originated in other countries but were subsequently seen in London are included, generally when the West End production was significantly different from that seen elsewhere. Shows originally produced on Broadway or off-Broadway are generally excluded. Entries for each of the main productions discussed give the title in bold type followed by production details: *Title* (Theatre, date of first performance; number of performances).

I have not listed the little army of performers, writers, composers, producers, dancers, chorus members, stage managers and other busy personnel involved in the musicals that crowd this book, but I thank them all for talking to me. Among the performers, I have to thank Judith Bruce, Dora Bryan, Margaret Burton, Peter Byrne, Doreen Hermitage, Pip Hinton, Graham Hoadley, Cheryl Kennedy, Jean Kent, Vivienne Martin, Patricia Michael, Gwen Nelson, Anna Sharkey, Ronnie Stevens, Terri Stevens, Jan Waters, and Mark Wynter; among the composers, Lionel Bart, Peter Greenwell, Hugh Hastings, David Heneker, Julian Slade and Sandy Wilson.

I am fortunate to have had generous encouragement and assistance from Stewart Nicholls, who has been at the forefront of reviving interest in the British musical. My thanks are due to Vivyan Ellacott, whose on-line celebration of the British musical at www.overthefootlights.co.uk is an excellent resource. I have also deeply appreciated the encouragement and assistance of Paul Guinery, and thank Roger Mellor and Terence Dunning for their constant interest. Michael King was invaluable as technical assistant to the author. The inclusion of the many rarely seen photographs used in the book would not have been made possible without the kind assistance of Martin Phillips, to whom I am very grateful. My main debt of gratitude must be to the staff of the Victoria and Albert Theatre and Performance Archive for their friendly and ever-willing assistance, even when they gazed mysteriously at what I had summoned from their vaults and said 'You are the only person that ever asks for this stuff.'

Michael Middeke at the Boydell Press commissioned the book. My thanks are due to him and the Boydell staff for the care they have taken in its production.

Adrian Wright
Norfolk, 2017

# 1960

## 1960

*The Lily White Boys*
*The Dancing Heiress*
*Follow That Girl*
*Johnny the Priest*
*The Golden Touch*
*Call It Love?*
*Innocent as Hell*
*Joie de Vivre*
*The Princess*
*Mr Burke M.P.*
*Hooray for Daisy!*

In what by its very nature may be an increasingly dispiriting discussion of the fate of the British musical we can at least breathe a communal sigh of relief that it begins with one of the most unusual and inventive of its year, of its decade, of the last sixty years. This means that very few of the British public will ever have heard of *The Lily White Boys* (Royal Court Theatre, 27 January 1960; 45). Perhaps the Royal Court, so often labelled as the bastion of what might be called 'New Wave' drama, once wore a more jolly face. For a time, that now lost and largely forgotten art, intimate revue, rooted and thrived there. In 1955, the Royal Court even hazarded one of the most essentially British musicals of the period, concerning a music festival in a coastal town that could only have been meant as Aldeburgh, the spiritual home of Benjamin Britten. *The Burning Boat* made several stops along the road to perfection, although some of Geoffrey Wright's sinuous score deserves to be remembered; 'Swimming Against the Tide' and 'A Quiet Part of the World' have scarcely been bettered for songs of their type, but their type, lightweight British pastoral, has long been consigned to oblivion. There is certainly nothing 'New Wave' about *The Burning Boat*, where emotional reticence keeps its characters, music book and lyrics well short of the sort of explosive emotionalism that has all but engulfed the British musical. Five years later, *The Lily White Boys* pointed a way forward (yet *another* way forward) for a genre that generally attracted critical disregard and public apathy. Wasn't it time that the British musical grew up? Wasn't the fact that this new sort of musical had a distinguished director in Lindsay Anderson, and sets by a man fast becoming the titan of West End scenic design, Sean Kenny? Plus Albert Finney, on the verge of forever establishing his working-class credentials with the film of *Saturday Night and Sunday Morning*, in his only stage musical.

How times had changed. The mid 1950s had seen the rise of Julian Slade and Dorothy Reynolds with the unassuming *Salad Days*; two pianos, a tiny cast who barely qualified as singers, choreography that looked nothing like dancing – as if someone had pushed back the living-room carpet for a bit of a do – and a plot that could have been conceived under the influence of hallucinatory drugs. In the opposite corner, breathing frolicsome sophistication and a great dollop of camp, was Sandy Wilson, unencumbered by any collaborator in his equally unassuming pastiche of 1920s musicals (thank you, Vincent Youmans, for some of the ideas and several of the tunes) *The Boy Friend*. In fact, Wilson almost did have a collaborator in Geoffrey Wright, with whom he had already written the unlucky touring musical *Caprice*, but in the end Wright waved Wilson goodbye, having recommended that one of the songs might be called 'It's Nicer in Nice'.

Wilson and Slade won spurious fame in the BBC radio's *Round the Horne* as two roaringly gay men ('I'm Julian and this is my friend Sandy'), probably embedded in the memories of many who had no idea of who their progenitors were, and who had never experienced the works of either. Decades later, when a BBC Radio 3 programme *Stage and Screen* deigned to make a programme about British musicals, it crammed Wilson and Slade into the same studio for an hour's superficial excursion through their careers, much to Wilson's dislike of having his work compared to that of Slade. The BBC treated them as if they were a double act from some theatrical mausoleum, allowed out for the afternoon from Denville Hall. On that occasion, Wilson's spiky comments about his fellow composer's work made one grateful that they were not. The programme only served to further confuse the British public; which was which, was Slade Wilson or was Wilson Slade, and who had written what? By now, anyway, their careers had faded so much from view that they might have been bussed into Broadcasting House from another country. Both men paid the price of success come too early. From 1959 their pre-eminence in British musicals was overshadowed by the rapid rise not only of the verismo school but of Lionel Begleiter (alias Bart) with three substantial successes, as lyricist for *Lock Up Your Daughters*, as song-writer for *Fings Ain't Wot They Used T'Be*, and sole author of *Oliver!* Several songs from these productions became popular in a way that Slade and Wilson could only have dreamed of.

Slade and Wilson were very different talents. Wilson's background was in intimate revue, his interest in recapturing a past. Even those who had no time for *The Boy Friend* might acknowledge his capacity for pastiche. *The Boy Friend* worked. One of the very few British musicals to transfer to New York, it helped make a star of its American Polly Browne, Julie Andrews, and, more modestly, of its London Polly, Anne Rogers. Like Slade and Reynolds, Wilson pursued a highly individual style, increasingly pursuing goals that diverted him from the mainstream. His 1958 *Valmouth* outraged some and delighted others, breaking some of the bonds by which the British musical had too long been bound, even if, rather less blatantly than *Salad Days*, occasionally reverting to revue. Luxurious, faintly degenerate, breathing old lavender and lace, *Valmouth*'s fey neo-exoticism seemed to capture much of the spirit of Ronald Firbank's 1919 novella. It distanced itself not only from the gentlemanly and ladylike gentilities of Slade and Reynolds but from Wilson's earlier efforts.

An earlier piece, *The Buccaneer*, set out a sort of template for what a Wilson musical play might be, a neatly formed cousin to that much-regretted relic 'the well-made play'. Shape, wit, taste and a tidy tunefulness; no wonder that Noel Coward told Wilson he was the best of British lyricists (alongside Coward, of course). *The Buccaneer* had happy, bouncy sounds, around a slight story about the threatened closure of a boys' comic paper. To some, it mapped out Wilson's *modus operandi* in which neatness was prominent. It showed where he naturally belonged, as in a duet for Betty Warren and Eliot Makeham towards the end of the show, 'Behind the Times'. The trouble for Wilson was that he was both behind and ahead of them. His decade of success was sliced off when his sequel to *The Boy Friend*, the 1964 *Divorce Me, Darling!*, flopped. It wasn't only that public interest and taste had moved on; the British public of ten years before had more or less forgotten about Polly Browne and the giggling girls of Madame Dubonnet's finishing school. The fickle public had exercised its right not to care. Following his expulsion from London, Wilson trudged a lonely path with *His Monkey Wife* and *The Clapham Wonder*.

Slade and Reynolds were no less immune to changes beyond their control. Measured against the perceived strengths of Bart, their work struggled to find critical or commercial success. By 1960 it was as if they were writing shows for an audience that seemed to have radically shrunk, or might no longer exist. The fact that Wilson's works were 'period' musicals to an extent cushioned him against being thought of as out of touch. Slade and Reynolds, setting their pieces in an apparently modern Britain, had less defence against their critics. It was they who suffered rather more from the rise of another phenomenon, the type of British musical that we might call 'verismo', kitchen-sink, low-life. If at the movies, we'd be talking *cinéma vérité*.

Such works came and went with astonishing speed over the space of a few years, but by 1960 these too were withering. Just for a moment, it was as if the writers of British musicals had been catching up on their reading and straight theatre-going, taking in John Osborne's *Look Back in Anger* (1956) and his music-hall play that so very obviously really wanted to be a musical if it had only been brave enough, *The Entertainer* (1957); Arnold Wesker's great trilogy of real life, *Chicken Soup with Barley* (1958), *Roots* (1959) and *I'm Talking About Jerusalem* (1960); John Braine's *Room at the Top* (1957); Keith Waterhouse's first novel *There is a Happy Land* (1957), his 1959 collaboration with Willis Hall, *Billy Liar*, and Alan Sillitoe's *Saturday Night and Sunday Morning* (1958). Oddly, only one of these works has been turned into a musical. When London tackled the verismo that was already entrenched in British literature by the late 1950s, it came up with subjects and sources of its own. *Expresso Bongo* showed the way in 1958, followed by the glut of verismo that occupied 1959 – *Fings Ain't Wot They Used T'Be*, *The World of Paul Slickey* (perhaps qualifying for inclusion), *The Crooked Mile* and *Make Me an Offer* – effectively bowing out in 1960 with *The Lily White Boys* and *Johnny the Priest*. In intimate revue, it took even longer for verismo to raise its head. Waterhouse and Hall were well-qualified to write *England, Our England*, in which two Lowry-type working-class men are at the mercy of shifting social issues.

> 1st Worker:   How's your Edwin getting on these days?
> 2nd Worker:  He's in Hollywood at the moment apparently. How's your little Brenda?
> 1st Worker:   She was having lunch with Cyril Connolly, last we heard.[1]

The supposedly 'verismo' musicals of this period were essentially domestic, but, unlike much of the literature and film industry of the time setting its focus on the North of England, these works never looked beyond London. This was always a step too far for the British musical, with a particularly honourable exception that, unsurprisingly if we accept that London could not see beyond itself, was produced in Nottingham and never sent to the West End. Walter Greenwood's 1930s tale of working-class life in the Great Depression, *Love on the Dole*, was adapted by Terry Hughes, with music by Alan Fluck and lyrics by Robert Gray. This was probably Britain's finest attempt at a verismo musical, sensitively directed by Gillian Lynne, with a top-notch cast. The quality of Fluck and Gray's score was way above any of the London verismos, always relevant to characterisation, always pushing the story forward. Despite moments of much-needed jollity, it was inevitably depressing, which may have alarmed London managements. By its nature, of course, verismo *is* depressing. In the remaking of Greenwood's original, the adaptors stayed true to their task, along the way producing a score that yearns to be revived. One of its numbers, 'Beyond the Hill' was reprised at curtain fall, one of the most moving final moments in British musicals. In 1970, there was something remarkable about this show, at a time when the British musical was moving rapidly, and in the wrong direction, towards a sort of ersatz internationalism.

Meanwhile, *The Lily White Boys* was clearly the most original, the most adventurous and most challenging British verismo, even if it was almost a last gasp. *Plays and Players* was alive to it:

> Despite some faults, *The Lily White Boys* is easily the most ambitious, the most exciting and the most successful of the experimental musicals of the last ten years. And its achievements should not be looked down upon from the heights of Brecht and Weill, but should rather be looked up to from the pitifully low level of the English musical entertainment stretching back from *Salad Days* to *The Geisha*.[2]

Alan Pryce-Jones in the *Observer* applauded:

What is wholly good about this piece is that it breaks away from the normal pattern of a British musical. The gentility, the fake high spirits, the tonic-and-dominant tunes, the sub-Gilbert lyrics are a thousand miles behind. There is no reason why this should not be the start of a new theatrical form properly equipped to sharpen the edge of social comment [...] we deserve our own approach to the art of decision, and it is hardly surprising that it refuses to be full-grown at a first attempt.[3]

*The Times* took a different view under its headline 'Satire Fails in Musical':

The hard little jokes never cut deep enough to make us sit up and wonder if the society we live in is really on the verge of bankruptcy. That was the effect made by Brecht's *Threepenny Opera* even many years after the society it lashed had vanished.[4]

Time has largely forgotten Harry Cookson, the author of *The Lily White Boys*. This ranks as one of the many injustices exposed in this book. Did Cookson realise that his three distinctly unappealing juvenile delinquents were descendants of the three juvenile delinquents invented by Noel Coward to offer a few minutes of much-needed relief to his 1950 *Ace of Clubs*, a somewhat moribund effort to bring the British musical up to date? In those far-off days, the three no-gooders had popped up in a nightclub scene for no discernible reason other than to gain Coward a few laughs. Coward had never done sociology. By 1960, juvenile delinquency was no longer always considered a joke, despite *West Side Story*'s 'Gee, Officer Krupke'.

Another British musical about juvenile delinquency, *Johnny the Priest*, was already en route to London. By now, prostitution (*Fings Ain't Wot They Used T'Be*), sex change (*The World of Paul Slickey*), and radical social changes (*Expresso Bongo*) were acceptable subjects. The scatter-gun technique of John Osborne's saga of Paul Slickey had nothing in common with *The Lily White Boys*, but what hope did Cookson's play have for a commercial future when Frances Stephens, editor of the somewhat staid *Theatre World*, sat through a musical in which 'the depressive aspects far outweigh the normally entertaining'? There is much to contemplate in that phrase: 'normally entertaining'. In this, *The Lily White Boys* made no concessions, refused to pretty-up. It didn't poeticise its delinquents in the way that Sondheim had in *West Side Story*; if *The Lily White Boys* sang verse, it was blank verse. In fact, *Johnny the Priest* didn't try poeticising its delinquents' lyrics; the fact that their lyrics are so feeble led critics to discount them. In fact, they remain the more authentic because of their feebleness. Meanwhile, poor Frances Stephens, writing up her review of those lily-white boys in Fleet Street's Dorset Buildings, lamented that the authors of *The Lily White Boys* shared 'a knowledge bordering on despair in the modern manner, for all their daring, lively wit and dialogue'.[5]

Knowledge bordering on despair? It's a tempting title for a treatise on the British musical's attitude to social change. That is what propelled the lily white boys, played by Albert Finney, Monty Landis and Philip Locke, from petty crime and kicking the sticks of old ladies from under them, or coshing the unsuspecting passer-by, to the more respectable and morally acceptable corruption and ill-doing that climbing the greasy pole of success brought them. As for the lily white's girlfriends (played by Georgia Brown, Sally Ann Field and Ann Lynn), sex proved a useful tool in changing the shape of their lives. Why not? It had been three years since Harold Macmillan had assured a meeting in Bedford that 'most of our people have never had it so good', before retiring to his country estate. It seemed natural that Coward's updated three juvenile delinquents should want to become three of the 'most of our people'. No wonder that audiences leaving the Royal Court were met by a man parading a placard that warned of the dangerous leftish social attitudes they had just witnessed. What right had the British musical to interfere in such matters? What right had it to take a view? At least *The Lily White Boys* hadn't the temerity to call itself a musical! Sheltering behind its description as 'a play with songs', its chances of permeating the public consciousness were negligible. Some of it was simply bad timing; the British musical was about to ditch some of the best ideas it had had for decades.

*The Dancing Heiress* (Lyric Theatre, Hammersmith, 15 March 1960; 15) bows in as the first of the British musicals of the 1960s to exemplify many of the problems the genre faced. Not that it was really British, but washed up on the shore of the West End, one of the huddled masses yearning to be free on the golden shore beneath Miss Liberty – a musical spiced with a couple of murders set in New York in 1933. A sort of pastiche of Hollywood movies of the period, it had shreds of threads that would turn up again in various forms in the off-Broadway *The Great American Backstage Musical*, *Nite Club International* and *Murderous Instincts*. The work of Jack Fletcher and Murray Grand, and directed by dancer John Heawood, it had strong leads in Irving Davies, Jill Ireland, Lally Bowers and Millicent Martin, who had scored heavily in *Expresso Bongo* and *The Crooked Mile*. The score fastened on popular songs as their models, very much in the manner adopted by Sandy Wilson in *The Boy Friend* and *Divorce Me Darling!* Now, audiences hearing Grand's 'Life is Peaches and Cream' were nudged into remembering 'Life Is Just a Bowl of Cherries'; how could they hear 'We're Out For Money' without thinking 'We're *In* the Money'?

Producer Fred Sadoff walked out before the London opening, perhaps despairing (as many others would subsequently despair) of having a patently American piece inaccurately performed by the British. 'What stupefies me', wrote Cecil Wilson, 'with its indeterminate ineptitude, despite the dauntless radiance of Millicent Martin, is that it plainly enraptured a large part of the house.' The show was 'so clumsily inconsequential, mixing as it does a couple of murders with snatches of Astaire and Rogers dancing, a troupe of shrill showgirls, and a rare muddle of American accents, that someone seems to have dropped the script at rehearsal,

2  Jill Ireland doing a torch number in *The Dancing Heiress*

and reassembled the pages in the wrong order'.[6] The *Observer* recognised a fact that would serve for the next fifty years: 'it is reassuring to find that Americans can imitate British musicals as badly as we imitate them'.[7]

Julian Slade and Dorothy Reynolds's **Follow That Girl** (Vaudeville Theatre, 17 March 1960; 211) moved into *Salad Days'* old home fast on its heels. For many, it must have seemed this was the team's follow-up to their impossible record-breaker, although in 1957 their *Free as Air* had begun a year-long stay across the road at the Savoy Theatre, lasting a respectable 401 performances. For some, *Free as Air* seemed the same song sung over, another whimsy, at least this time avoiding dropping-out into revue, about escaping the hurly-burly of modern life, and with the advantage of a decent orchestra well orchestrated. It stopped Slade's music from tinkling, a word that critics kept handy for anything Slade wrote. *Free as Air* had given Slade and Reynolds something to do in the in-between years, but they had had six years to come up with a show that might follow *Salad Days* into the Vaudeville, a theatre that might by now have been renamed the Slade–Reynolds Institute, and where their final work, *Wildest Dreams*, would be played out.

The best they could come up with was a revamp of their very first musical that had wowed Bristolians at their Old Vic back in 1952. The critic of the *Western Daily Press* (perhaps the person responsible for letting that 'tinkling' out of the dictionary) applauded: 'Up to now we have known Julian Slade as a composer of tinkling music incidental to some of the Old Vic's classical revivals. On this occasion he emerges as a writer of popular tunes that with a little encouragement from the public could easily become hit ones.'[8] The occasion was a Christmas show Slade and Reynolds had written with actor James Cairncross and the encouragement of director Denis Carey, *Christmas in King Street*. Eight years later, it would do service as *Follow That Girl*, much altered, its location shifted from Bristol to London, minus John Neville as the young hero and Reynolds' ghostly impersonation of Sarah Siddons.

The London plot was simple enough, with enough switching between periods to suggest a light-headed J. B. Priestley had popped in to advise on time travel. Beginning in the present day with young author Tom Blenkinsop (Peter Gilmore) and debutante girlfriend Victoria (sublimely cast in the unfortunately unable-to-sing Susan Hampshire) discussing Tom's new book, the action reverts to Victorian when his invented characters come alive to sing 'Tra La La'. This got things off to a fair start, but the rest of the evening didn't get much further than such inconsequentiality, although the Victorian Victoria – fallen in love with at first sight by the Victorian Tom as a fresh-faced police constable – is pursued by a Tweedledum and Tweedledee pair of suitors, by anxious parents Patricia Routledge and Cairncross, and Tom's bereft parents Newton Blick and Marion Grimaldi. Between them they conjure up a few moments of that particular Slade and Reynolds atmosphere so difficult (if we avoid 'tinkling') to describe: the polka 'I'm

Away', the catchy title song (but isn't it a little too much like 'Peg 'o My Heart'?), and Grimaldi and company's 'Solitary Stranger'. After six years, was this really the best they could have done? Oddly, *Theatre World* fastened on 'Taken For a Ride' as the show's winner, a number that would scarcely have passed muster in a contemporary revue, although it suggested a semblance of real life as its quartet of male travel officials surrounded the deliciously turned-out Hampshire. Around her and like her, the delights of the night were principally visual, garlanded about with Hutchinson Scott's period décor.

The first night had its problems reported in the *Sunday Dispatch*, whose charitable verdict was 'one of arrested development in British musicals [...] The gallery revolt on Thursday night (and they had many sympathisers below) made it healthily plain that we, at least, have grown up since *Salad Days*, and no longer want to romp.'[9] The *Tatler* agreed: 'Kipling claimed at the end of his life that he had never tried to repeat a success. [Slade and Reynolds] might have done well to ponder the worldly wisdom of this austere rule of authorship. The replacement turns out to be a close and inferior imitation of *Salad Days* – and at curtain fall on the first night of *Follow That Girl* the gallery – more, I think, in sorrow than anger – broke through the polite applause of the stalls.'[10] Contemplating the show's 'fairy lightness', Robert Muller thought that the writers had gone 'to infinite trouble to guarantee their audiences 150 minutes of torpor [...] The composer himself is in the orchestra pit, leading a real gone sextet, and hammering away at his upright piano like a love-smitten college boy, modestly besotted on his talent.'[11]

Was kindly *Theatre World*'s description of 'one of the flimsiest musicals ever written' justified? Probably. There was nothing wrong with templates: Gilbert had constructed his best works on the frame of his early successes, as did Oscar Hammerstein II. There was no reason why Slade and Reynolds shouldn't do the same, but *Follow That Girl* lacked an essential spirit that was needed to carry it beyond its innate charm. Sometimes this deficiency blared out of the score. 'Song and Dance', a really awkward number with its double chorus and arthritic scoring, made a reasonable enough finale to Act One, but while the lyric was telling us that everyone was enjoying kicking up that song and dance, there was nothing about the telling that made us want to join in. Looking back, it seems pretty obvious that following that girl was just about the worst thing that could have followed *Salad Days'* magic piano Minnie and her troupe of gaily prancing admirers into London.

Last in the line of the verismo musicals of the late 1950s, **Johnny the Priest** (Princes Theatre, 19 April 1960; 14) was commissioned by the Players' Theatre, whose earlier verismo, *The Crooked Mile*, had undeniably created a critical stirring of enthusiasm for the British musical, but lost the producers £15,000. *Johnny the Priest* took the Players' deeper into the red, losing £25,000. In its way, this too was an ambitious attempt at a slice of real life. Now, based on R. C. Sherriff's play *The Telescope*, it was essentially a battle between Good and Evil. One of the problems was that the Good was undeniably Good: an intense young vicar, Richard High-field and his wife. The Evil wasn't so much evil as troublesome, personified by a basically decent young lad, Johnny, who, as legend has it, falls in with 'the wrong sort'. Except that the 'wrong sort' isn't really the wrong sort but teddy boys and youths who like to raise a ruckus at the youth club. None of this is on show in Sherriff's play that toured in 1957 but never reached London.

Highfield has decided to take over a failing parish in London's Docklands where an elderly vicar has been unable to meet the needs of his dwindling flock and its dissatisfied youth, but Highfield's worthy ideals are challenged when one of the boys steals a telescope and asks his help in escaping the law. Johnny isn't too much of a bad egg. He isn't *Brighton Rock*'s Pinky, or *Oliver Twist*'s Bill Sikes or Alan Sillitoe's Arthur Seaton. Johnny is young, a teenager when teenagers had almost not yet been invented. We know he cannot be a bad lad when his heart stops at the wonder of a starlit sky. This was at once simple and difficult meat for any musical. It was not made easier when some critics suggested that *Johnny the Priest* was intended as Britain's reply to *West Side Story*. In the event, there was little evidence to justify the comparison. Peter Powell, then artistic director of the Everyman Theatre, Cheltenham, who had directed *The Telescope*, decided that Sherriff's play would work as a musical, writing book and lyrics. Presumably in an effort to catch a whiff of modernity and realism, the Players' Theatre hired Norman Marshall, an exponent of 'the other' theatre, as director. His experience and knowledge of musicals was, however, limited. Antony Hopkins, whose one-act opera *Three's Company*, set in a modern office, had played as part of a double-bill at Hammer-smith in 1957, was brought in as composer. His score for *Johnny the Priest* was distinctive, but went largely unappreciated, as did (with rather more reason) Pow-ell's adaptation. His lyrics may be naïve, flaccid and (in the persistent sermonising of the Highfields) sanctimonious, but aren't they a reasonable approximation of how these characters would speak? Johnny and his mates, and girlfriend Vi (a nice ordinary girl who will hopefully make Johnny a good wife some time after the curtain has come down; will Highfield marry them? We can only wonder. Here is a musical where the curtain comes down on a predicament, not on a happy ending) can't spin the endlessly, intricate rhymes that Sondheim puts into the mouths of the workaday characters of *West Side Story*. There is no implanting of poetry on these characters.

The reviews signed *Johnny the Priest*'s death sentence. Robert Muller wrote of 'the painful inadequacy' of Hopkins' music, explaining that 'His score is cold, sexless, and devoid of style. It veers between unconvinced Slade, Ravel-and-Soda, tinny palais-de-dance, and – his true metier – modern English comic opera. Mr Hopkins can invent a tune, to be sure, but he cannot develop it into the purpose of stage musical.'[12] The last words may be true, but Muller's verdict is overwrought. Listening to the score almost seven decades later, *Johnny the Priest* contains a treasure trove of fascinating material. Irving Wardle's assessment in *The Times* nevertheless pinpointed the problem. 'Like some stiff-postured old mannequin exhumed from the basement to be replaced in the shop window clad in Bermuda shorts and stockings that glow in the dark, R. C. Sherriff's sturdily conventional three-acter *The Telescope* reappears as *Johnny the Priest*, daringly got up as an adult musical.' The original qualities of the play had been lost 'in a musical which tries to open up a modest little play into a lurid social parable [...] Instead of the fluent exploitation of an idea through dialogue, song and dance, there is a succession of dislocated episodes – gymnastic production numbers, old-style lyrical duets and undisciplined slouching linked together with grinding gear changes'.[13] In line with Wardle, Milton Shulman regretted 'the complicated rhythm of the music whooping up every naïve statement into an atonal frenzy. Nor do the lyrics by Peter Powell help very much since they are heavily humourless and achingly obvious.'[14]

What point then, in reconsidering *Johnny the Priest*? Its shelf life was short and its sell-by date is long past. As a museum piece, it might just about justify revival, but its obvious clumsiness argues against it. The original cast was grandly recorded. Jeremy Brett (heroic in his hope for better things to come in 'A Boy Called Johnny') and Stephanie Voss as the Highfields represent the hymnal parts, Johnny and Vi the stagey adolescence that already by 1960 was fraying at the edges, Hope Jackman as Johnny's mother the vulgarian voice of the working class in what orchestrator Gordon Langford recalled as the hit number of the night, 'Johnny Earn Peanuts'.

Far from being that stiff-postured old mannequin, perhaps *Johnny the Priest* attempted something that, in different hands from the management of the Players' Theatre, might have flourished. The wallpaper song 'A Tanner's Worth of Tune' is a delight, and there is the heart-stopping moment of 'Rooftops' when the unsophisticated Johnny, so hopeful of getting into the Merchant Navy, is struck dumb by a sky of stars. 'How can, how can I express, how beautiful?' he stammers to Langford's (or is it Hopkins's, for they shared the orchestration?) shimmering strings. Sherriff drove his 87-year-old mother from Esher to London for the first night but, not surprisingly, got her home to bed before attending the first-night party, the jollity of which may have been diminished when the morning papers arrived. They made another expedition the following week for the London premiere of his rather more successful play *A Shred of Evidence*.

In the meantime, Hopkins, already probably incensed by discovering that Decca had advertised Malcolm Arnold as the show's composer, publicly complained about the rough treatment the show had received from the critics. There had, however, been some appreciation, far more than that for many another, more successful, enterprise. W. A. Darlington, arguing that the adaptation was a watered-down and less effective parable than Sherriff's original, wrote 'I do not believe that so serious a play as this is good material for a musical'. But, thought Bernard Levin, 'taken for what it is, *Johnny the Priest* is musically more interesting than any such show for a very long time'. What was more, Hopkins's music was 'very close indeed to that of Mr Benjamin Britten – there is the same clean lyricism, the same ingenuity, the same handling of recitative'. Levin may or may not be correct in judging these similarities, but Hopkins had 'thrown a bridge across the absurd and arbitrary gulf that divides one kind of art from another, and for that at least he deserves praise'.[15]

*The Golden Touch* (Piccadilly Theatre, 5 May 1960; 12) had an enthusiastic firstnight reception. The next day's newspaper headlined reviews brought a rude awakening. 'Nothing Quite Charming' (*Guardian*), 'The Music Here Is Dreadful' (*Daily Mail*), 'Beatniks At It Again: Glum Musical For Squares' (*Daily Telegraph*), 'Musical With No Stars Has Verve and Charm' (*Evening News*). Insisting that its music was 'strident, insipid, imitative [and] a pompous tinkle', Robert Muller thought that it 'makes even the score of Julian Slade's *Follow That Girl* sound like a shining example of professionalism'.[16] The critic of the *Sunday Dispatch* could only have just taken his ear-plugs out, remembering how 'The mickey-taking got blunted by an absurd plot, the wit grew more laboured, the music ever less memorable, and the orchestral din – this is the noisiest musical ever – went on pounding our ears.'[17] 'The songs are loud and uncatchy,' reported *The Times*, 'and incidentally need more singing than most of the cast can manage. The book finds just that level which passes with the simple for alluring sophistication and may, perhaps, strike the sophisticated as agreeably naïve.'[18]

What had the critics expected? *The Golden Touch* (an unfortunate title, as things turned out) was librettist Julian More and composer James Gilbert's follow-up to their hugely successful 1956 *Grab Me a Gondola*, a light-headed satire vaguely based on the idea of Diana Dors and the Venice Film Festival that had made a star of its leading lady Joan Heal. For some reason, the show caught on with the public; after all, it had plenty of zest, colour and Heal's barnstorming performance, but there was nothing distinguished about its songs, even if its Shakespearean parody 'Cravin' for the Avon' became widely known among those who appreciated a bit of wit escaping from a British musical. It sounded even better to those who had never heard Cole Porter doing the same thing better in *Kiss Me, Kate*'s 'Brush Up Your Shakespeare'. Nevertheless, having got *Grab Me a Gondola* to 673 performances, Gilbert and More were a team that would have to be reckoned with, and coming fast on the coat-tails of Slade and Reynolds they had claims to be the new hope for a very different type of British musical.

On the face of it, *The Golden Touch* could not have got off to a brighter start, championed by its young producer Michael Codron, with a genuine passion for musical theatre. Codron had been encouraged by the writers' earlier success, but difficulties arose. The original director, Minos Volanakis, departed during rehearsals. This was perhaps one of the best things to happen to *The Golden Touch*, with choreographer Paddy Stone stepping into the role. Stone's efforts to make the show work were made harder because his leading lady Evelyne Ker was in a relationship with More, who resisted any attempts to tinker with the script. Stone's well-remembered irritation with Ker was reflected by some of the London critics; the *Daily Mail* thought she looked like a little bunny rabbit, and sang like one too.

There was rather more praise for its male leads, Sergio Franchi and Gordon Boyd, late of the imported Australian flop *Kookaburra* (1959) and too soon to face yet another flop, the 1962 *Vanity Fair*. Franchi and Boyd's duet 'Not Enough Of Her To Go Round' and a duet for Ker and Cec Linder 'You're So Like Your Father' were singled out for mention, although the *Guardian* decided that another number, 'Funny Thing', 'seems likely to be noticed'.[19] Praising Hugh Casson's sets and Jocelyn Rickards' costumes as 'very good', *Plays and Players* clearly detected *something* about the show that made it significant:

> British musicals, one feels, ought to work on this sort of recipe, combining the satire of an Evelyn Waugh, say, with the spectacle of Rodgers and Hammerstein. If this one doesn't reach the summit, it is a long step in the right direction and one has only to contrast this with the unlamented anaemia of *Salad Days* to realise how good it is.[20]

On its pre-London tour, the show often played to nearly empty houses. At the Piccadilly, the notice went up almost at once, leaving Codron with a loss of over £20,000. Despite its success, *Grab Me a Gondola* has never entered the repertory of British musical theatre (but what has?). Concluding that 'the British musical, at best, is marking a fairly slow time', Leonard Beaton saw that More and Gilbert had used 'the Gallic vixen of *Irma la Douce*, the modern American dancing of *West Side Story* and the business-is-business formula of *Make Me an Offer*'. If all that *The Golden Touch* represented was an attempt to bring these elements together, it isn't without merit. If *The Golden Touch* had turned up trumps, their pursuit of formula might have brought great dividends, but the show's immediate collapse scrubbed their names out. In retrospect, there seems no reason why beatniks (topical), French leading ladies, beefcake men, jazzed-up choreography (and who better to make this work than the multi-talented Stone?) and world politics should not prove a working concoction. Operetta had fed on such stuff for years, with sometimes barely discernible adjustments to a basic plot that just about propped up the songs. The stopping of More and Gilbert's progress was yet another example of no sort of British musical pleasing the critics.

Much was expected of Sandy Wilson after the interesting works he had already produced: *The Buccaneer*, *The Boy Friend*, and what had seemed to some the slightly shocking, almost ground-breaking distinction of *Valmouth*, snatched from the supposedly decadent Ronald Firbank novella. At least his contribution to ***Call It Love?*** (Wyndham's Theatre, 22 June 1960; 5), five insubstantial pastiche numbers, bore the Wilson *Boy Friend* stamp, but it was a backward step for a writer with some claim to being the potential *enfant terrible* of the British musical. In fact, he had just begun work on an adaptation of Anne Scott-James's satire on the rag trade, *In the Mink*. This would eventually join others in Wilson's bottom drawer of unproduced works that included biomusicals of Amy Johnson and Henry VIII, and *Goodbye To Berlin* from the stories of Christopher Isherwood, beaten to the finishing post by the much superior *Cabaret*.

Beside such company, *Call It Love?* was small fry. Schoolteacher Robert Tanitch's play comprised four playlets designed to demonstrate changing attitudes to romance: an 1880 proposal, a 1912 engagement, elopement in 1927 and marriage in 1960. The drab Wildean epigrams ('I always think it is a luxury to receive flowers in the country') fell on deaf ears; before the interval slow-handclapping broke out. Although at final curtain there was decent applause, there was no question of a run. Tanitch was philosophical: 'The songs, of course, were fine. I suppose it was the words that died.' Lally Bowers was praised for playing four scatty women, but the critics signed the warrant with headlines that could only sink the show. 'Even Those In the Stalls Couldn't Take It'; 'Call It Love? – I can only call for help'; 'Too Thin to stand up on its own'; 'Call It Love? No, just another West End flop.' It was all too much for *Plays and Players*. 'Call it trite, call it trash, call it a frothily over-decorated parcel of immature, unfunny sketches loosely tied together with mercifully forgettable tunes – call it what you like, it will not sway the box office receipts by one cupro-nickel sixpence.'[21] It reminded the public that Wilson was hitched to musical pastiche, a path which, soon enough with *Divorce Me, Darling!*, would bring about the premature end of his West End career. *Call It Love?* called it a day at the end of its first week.

On the heels of *The Dancing Heiress* and the follow-up to John Cranko's successful West End revue *Cranks* – the completely unsuccessful *New Cranks* – the company of **Innocent as Hell** (Lyric Theatre, Hammersmith, 29 June 1960; 13) turned off the Shepherds Bush Road for its try-out of the first musical – book, music and lyrics – by Andrew Rosenthal. The young author had begun promisingly in 1952 with a gay-themed play, *Third Person*. Refused a licence by the Lord Chamberlain, it found shelter at the 'private' Arts Theatre, but after changes to the script was allowed to progress to the Criterion. The same year, his play *Red Letter Day* at the Garrick Theatre had the advantage of Fay Compton as leading lady. There was more than enough female musical talent in director Vida Hope's company of *Innocent as Hell*, including its leading ladies Hy Hazell and Anne Francine as two old friends chasing the same man (Griffith Jones), but Rosenthal had written a 'play with music' rather than the real thing, a format that had well and truly scuppered *Call It Love?* only a few days earlier. Hazell had already scored with her Dixie Collins in *Expresso Bongo* and Mrs Squeezum in *Lock Up Your Daughters*, and would go on to excellent work in the London production of Richard Rodgers' *No Strings*, *Charlie Girl* and *Ann Veronica*. Francine had played in the Broadway

*By the Beautiful Sea* in 1954, but her biggest successes, including a notable Vera Charles in *Mame*, lay ahead. Admirers of mature actresses would have hastened to the Lyric just to see who the show had collected: Barbara Couper as Mother Cramm, Patricia Laffan (the scary 'devil girl from Mars' of bad British movie legend[22]) as Lady Parsley, and Totti Truman Taylor as the wonderfully named Isadora Hole. Of the younger cast, Barbara Evans as a man-eating South American struck a chord singing 'I Want That'. Despite these enticements, *Plays and Players* seemed more impressed by the ballets of 'coloured artists' Ward Fleming and Richardina Jackson, deciding that the show's theme 'is not an original one either for comedy or tragedy and Mr. Rosenthal has certainly brought no originality to it, although his efforts to be "different" are both obvious and painful'.[23] Sixteen years after *Innocent as Hell*'s last night, the show resurfaced as *Two of Everything* for a try-out in Manhattan.

In 1936, Terence Rattigan had made his reputation with the lightest of confections, *French Without Tears*, a play to which maiden aunts (and the fictional Aunt Edna, much mentioned in theatrical circles in later years) might safely be taken. There were probably a good number of maiden aunts at each of its 1,039 performances. A sprinkling of foreign talk ensured that only reasonably well-educated theatregoers would fully appreciate its wit. The plot revolved around three young Englishmen studying at a crammer on the Ile de Tourterelles in the Mediterranean, and the romantic entanglements that follow when Diana, sister to one of the students, arrives. A neat example of the well-made play, the very lightness of Rattigan's entertainment bore little resemblance to any of his later work. *Separate Tables*, *The Deep Blue Sea*, *The Browning Version*, *The Winslow Boy* and *Cause Célèbre* (an account of the Alma Rattenbury murder case) all speak seriously of the human condition. If a musical had to be made from Rattigan (and he had only himself to blame, adapting the play in readiness for music and lyrics), *French Without Tears*, apparently insubstantial and involving the concept of gaily striped blazers and people at French windows wondering if anyone was for tennis, might have seemed a safe bet, even if Noel Coward and his collaborators would later go for *The Sleeping Prince*, turning it into the somewhat turgid *The Girl Who Came To Supper*.

*Joie de Vivre* (Queen's Theatre, 14 July 1960; 4) had been Rattigan's intended title for what became *French Without Tears*. Now, he worked with lyricist Paul Dehn and composer Robert Stolz. The 80-year-old Stolz was almost at the end of his working life, having studied in Vienna under composer Engelbert Humperdinck and written for cabaret, films, theatre and the then popular ice shows. Some of his most prominent compositions were heard in *White Horse Inn* and the slight but delightful 1927 musical comedy *The Blue Train*, marking Lily Elsie's last London appearance. Some 33 years later, he seemed an odd choice for a supposedly bright, youthful British musical.

Director William Chappell seemed perfectly poised as the man for H. M. Tennent's production, and the casting was, at least, interesting. Joanna Rigby as Diana was undoubtedly its leading lady, but it was Joan Heal, a favourite Tennent artist, who was headlined. Heal's three incursions into the show promised a deal of Gallic and Highland fun, with a 'Scottish Can Can', ''Allo, Beeg Boy' and 'Le West End'; the idea of Heal's intervention as Chi-Chi (a character mentioned but never seen in Rattigan's original play) was a silly attempt to recreate the impact Heal had made in *Grab Me a Gondola*. From there on, Heal found success harder to come by. Leading man Donald Sinden had no ear for music. Elsewhere, names that would make their mark in future years filled out the company, among them Anna Sharkey, dancer Lindsay Kemp, Patricia Michael, and Jill Martin in the key role of Jacqueline with one of the better songs, 'The Kiss Was Very, Very Small'.

The first-night curtain fell to a storm of protest, and didn't rise again. The review headlines confirmed the worst: 'Booing at Rattigan Musical', 'Sadly I Tell You There's No Joie de Vivre in This Vivre'; 'French Without Tears Lacks Joie de Vivre'. Robert Muller suggested 'the success of the modern musical depends less on the book than on the music, the lyrics and the production, and in all these departments last night's offering failed lamentably [...] For a Tennent production, the miscasting is really spectacular [...] the saddest evening I have spent in a theatre this year.'[24]

Kenneth Tynan didn't spend the evening there; he left at the interval, but recalled 'The music, which appears to have come from some other show, is by Robert Stolz, and represents a notable retreat from the spirit of experimentalism that marked the same composer's score for *White Horse Inn*.'[25] With no such irony, *The Times* reported 'a dated idiom unredeemed by satirical intention, though burlesque would have been one of the logical approaches to be selected'.[26] Early on the afternoon of its third day, Heal's dresser telephoned her at home, warning her to bring a suitcase so that her dressing room could be cleared. Rattigan was philosophical, apparently accepting the audience and critics' verdict: 'They just didn't like the play. They thought it was a trivial, meretricious little piece, hopelessly dated.'

Perhaps the 'New Musical in Ballet and Song', *The Princess* (Strand Theatre, 23 August 1960; 44), had been a sensation when seen at the Royal Poinciana Playhouse, Palm Beach, two years earlier. Its producer Ted Kneeland offered a synopsis that began 'Our story takes place once upon a time in a little Kingdom ... somewhere familiar to us all.' The ensuing events lead us to presume it's Fairyland, although Act III Scene II menacingly moved to 'The Valley of Tears'. Apparently encouraged by Christopher Hassall, who had written up 'The Princess' in 'story-book' form, Kneeland's enormous company turned up nightly at the Strand for what seems to have been a rum do. Composer Mario Braggiotti was no stranger to London, having been the on-stage pianist for the Astaires during their run of

*Funny Face* thirty years earlier. Braggiotti completed his score in London, 'and for the past two years has lived in the magical world of entrechat, quatres and arabesques'. Dancing their way through his 500-page score were librettist-choreographer Jo-Anna, Violette Verdy as the adult princess, Pierre Lacotte and 12-year-old Claudia Cravey as the younger princess. Audiences studying their programmes discovered illuminating notes:

> To startle and excite an audience by means of bold and strange dissonance of music and choreography is indeed important, but such treatment can only be applied when the effect is justified and reconcilable with the situation. The problem is relatively simple when employing the medium of the spoken word, but in combining the interpretative arts of music, mime and ballet, subtlety is required to produce a harmonious integration. Abstract qualities, such as The Virtues, Graces and human traits, give vast scope for imaginative treatment while the ever-present danger is in carrying inventiveness too far and so defeating its own end. A delicate compromise between striking ingenuity and convention must be the aim.[27]

Forewarned, audiences at the Strand must have been in a state of extreme intellectual alert when the curtain rose. Reading the critical drubbing that followed *The Princess*'s London premiere, the management decided to offer the public a week of free seats, but nothing could save it. 'Did it really happen?' wondered Robert Muller. 'Did sopranos really sing mock arias from stage boxes? Did basses boom recitatives? Did first night scenic disasters really make the gallery break into uncontrollable merriment? The answers are in the affirmative.'[28] Peter Roberts in *Plays and Players* asked

> At whom can this 'musical in ballet and song' be directed? People who like their musicals to be musical, in the manner of *My Fair Lady* and *The Most Happy Fella*, will not take kindly to the fact that the principal singers and chorus have been unceremoniously pushed out of sight in a box where they fulfil the role of narrator. And balletomanes who have been thrilled by the choreography of shows like *West Side Story* will yawn at the classical-ballet-and-water which is used to deck out this insipid fairy story. Playgoers who have enjoyed the satire and provocative comment on present day affairs at the Theatre Workshop plays-with-music will be beside themselves with boredom as this little tale unfolds its obvious way. Who, then, will patronise this show?[29]

Its inclusion in these pages gives a clue.

Following his commission from the Mermaid to adapt Dickens's *Great Expectations* for its stage, Gerald Frow wrote music, book and lyrics for his first original play **Mr Burke M.P.** (Mermaid Theatre, 6 October 1960; 114), played for a twice-nightly season at a top ticket price of 15 shillings. Hopes that this attempt at a rollicking, contemporary satire would match the success of the same theatre's

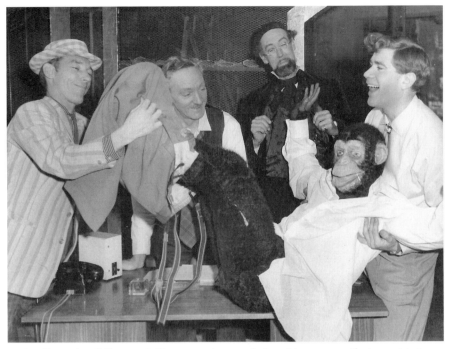

**3**  Spot the difference? *Homo sapiens* and the chimpanzee that went into Parliament. *Mr Burke M.P.*, Mermaid Theatre, 1960. L to R: Ron Pember, Duncan McIntyre, Raf de la Torre, Brian Rawlinson

long-runner and transferable *Lock Up Your Daughters*, were soon dispelled, and made more of a bitter pill when the fact of its being the Mermaid's first 'new' play was of such interest. Frow's farcical concoction favoured the ape over *Homo sapiens*. Now, the once-downtrodden animal is celebrated and promoted in a mind-bending campaign by a popular daily newspaper, propelling one of the species into Downing Street. Most critics felt the joke withered before the interval. 'Tedious Romp About Monkey Elected M.P.' headlined the *Daily Telegraph*,[30] a warning echoed by the *Evening Standard*,[31] 'At Least the Idea Was Promising', and by the *Daily Mail*'s opinion that 'Two hours of monkey business is too much.'[32] For *The Times* ('Monkey Tricks at Mermaid: Mr Burke M.P. Falls Flat'), the evening was 'as hollow as a drum and as ear-splitting as a drum can be' in a 'crude satire' with 'songs in doggerel verse' lacing a story that it thought unconvincing and unentertaining.[33] Some relief was generated by The Vipers, a musical ensemble headed up by skiffle specialist Wally Whyton, but the songs at his disposal were slight. Sally Miles' direction was 'anything but subtle. It rains hammer blows on the world of advertising and public relations, taking huge belly-laughs at the gullibility of the public'.[34] There was praise for Raf de la Torre as the titular monkey, but little recognition of the adventurousness of the Mermaid's management in presenting such a blatantly political piece so early in its commercial career. Eleven years later, Sandy Wilson would make his case for the female of the species in his adaptation of John Collier's eccentric novella *His Monkey Wife.*

An end-of-year school report on Julian Slade and Dorothy Reynolds might have read 'They have undoubted ability but their work this year has been disappointing. They must try harder.' In March, their *Follow That Girl* had been booed. How many of its audience knew they were watching a warmed-up old piece, taken out of the Bristol Old Vic cupboard and dusted off for London? Now, the pair repeated the trick for their Christmas offering *Hooray for Daisy!* (Lyric, Hammersmith, 20 December 1960; 51), which had played the Bristol Old Vic a year before. As a Yuletide offering for adults it not surprisingly had pantomime at its core. In the sleepy village of Milbury – standing in for the sleepy spires of Cambridge that began *Salad Days*, the sleepy island of Terhou in *Free as Air*, and the sleepy hamlet of Nelderham in the soon-to-follow *Wildest Dreams* – plans are afoot for the annual panto. The return of fetching young Priscilla Vernon to the place of her enchanted childhood shakes up the contented cocktail of locals, who almost to a man fall for her charms, to the consternation of the village spinster Georgina Cosens, brilliantly played for Reynolds who had kept the best of the comedy for herself. Her performance, still to be heard in recorded moments from the Bristol production, is high comedy-playing of a probably extinct order. Lisa Gordon Smith, trying to find a good word for *Hooray for Daisy!*, found it here, in her characterisation 'as a nice middle-aged widow which I shall never forget. She gives a masterly characterisation of a woman who is silly enough to fall in love with the curate and sensible enough to appreciate her own folly. This is comedy acting at its best.'[35]

During Milbury's rehearsals for 'Jack and the Beanstalk' an errant tin of baked beans erupts into a giant beanstalk up which the cast climb into regions unknown to pursue a second Act that now seems even more absurd than it must have been half a century ago. Reynolds and her husband Angus Mackay as the inevitably timid curate recreated their Bristol roles as the principal comedians, memorably exchanging insulting remarks about one another in 'Personally'. Elsewhere, there were considerable cast changes en route to Hammersmith. Bristol's miscast Priscilla, Annette Crosbie, was replaced by Eleanor Drew, the original Jane of *Salad Days* and the Naomi Tighe of the almost completely forgotten Christopher Whelen 1959 musical *School*. Peter Gilmore's romantic Stranger was replaced by Robin Hunter, and James Cairncross by Norman Jones. Others in the Bristol company that didn't make it to London included Leonard Rossiter, Peter Bowles and Patrick Garland.

If there is any surprise about *Hooray for Daisy!* it is that such a supposedly silly and seemingly insignificant piece should put up so many plaintive songs, of which 'Personally' is one. Act Two has several, from the home-sick Milbury worthies recalling their lives before the beanstalk ('It Won't Be the Same'), through Priscilla's gentle apology to her three rejected suitors ('I'm Sorry') to the faintly mournful duet for the two lovers 'Madam, Will You Dine?' The melancholia spreads through Priscilla's evocative arrival song, 'I Feel As If I'd Never Been Away'. There can be no claim for *Hooray for Daisy!* being Slade's best, with its collection of strangely angular numbers. This is music with speed bumps. Try the opener, 'She's Coming On the 4.48', 'If Only You Needed Me', 'How, When and Where', and the potentially embarrassing 'Soft Hoof Shuffle', repeated as a chorus finale extolling the virtues of Milbury's very own favourite bovine. Among alterations to the score, Drew was given 'He's Got Absolutely Nothing' (yet more melancholia) from Slade's Cambridge musical *Lady May*, while the Bristol male duet 'Let's Do a Duet' was amended for Drew and Hunter. 'You Never Know' was replaced in London by the first Act finale 'Going Up', and another company number, 'Ting-a-Ling', added for the Hammersmith production.

Charitably inclined as the *Stage* may have been, it knew the show 'must be judged on its merits which are, alas, painfully few', with a first half that was 'lamentable', and songs that might have been rejects from *Salad Days* – quite possible.[36] 'It is jolly and harmless enough in the manner of the best end-of-term school show,' wrote Peter Lewis, 'but if you expect wit, pungency, and sophistication for heaven's sake don't say I didn't warn you'.[37] The *Daily Telegraph*'s tactful verdict was that

> The authors have spared us most of the [pantomime] performance itself, possibly because they felt that the events leading up to it had already borne a sufficiently close resemblance to the same thing. The failure of Denis Carey's production to distinguish between the two is one of several weaknesses in what amounts (if that is not too strong a word) to an exceedingly modest entertainment even for this time of year.[38]

Jolly and harmless it certainly was. Perhaps the besetting sin of it was to be well-meant. No need to search for sub-text in *Hooray for Daisy!*'s final curtain speech of Milbury's Fairy Queen, as spoken by Dorothy Reynolds.

> And so our pantomime sedately moves towards its close,
> And Milbury approved.
> They praised the way each actor took his part.
> The thieving Stranger stole Priscilla's heart,
> And Mr Pewsey saw them safely wed;
> The vicar, much the same, had stayed in bed,
> But though our dreams of happiness come true,
> Our greatest pleasure is in pleasing you,
> And we've succeeded in three hours beguiling
> If you forgive our faults and go home smiling.

# 1961–1964

*'There are bound to be worse musical plays in the future. I hope I do not have to witness them'*

**Guardian** on *Vanity Fair*

## 1961

*The Three Caskets*
*Belle*
*Wildest Dreams*

With its eye on a West End transfer, the Players' Theatre mounted a revival of Gordon Snell and Peter Greenwell's operetta *The Three Caskets* (Players' Theatre, 1 March 1961; season), originally produced in a shorter version at that theatre in 1956. Now extended to provide a full evening, with new songs, and orchestrations by Gordon Langford played by the Eugene Pini Orchestra, the updating of scenes from *The Merchant of Venice* moved the action to Miss Portia Browne's residence in Belmont Square, Mayfair. It was a pretty conceit for the educated sensibilities of the typical Players' audience, but whether it would have rung a bell with the average London theatregoer is doubtful. Portia, played by Margaret Burton, was wooed in turn by Denis Martin as an Irish tenor, Robin Hunter as a black-face Morocco Joe arriving complete with 'nigger minstrel' songs, and heroic Laurie Payne (formerly a romantic presence in A. P. Herbert and Vivian Ellis's *The Water Gipsies* and the Louisa M. Alcott musical *A Girl Called Jo*) as the soldierly Honourable Percy Bassanio. It seemed an odd project in a climate already suffused with the rhythms and street-wisdom of *West Side Story*, and more so because Greenwell was one of the few British composers who had seemed to be pushing the boundaries towards modernity with *The Crooked Mile*. Coming so soon in the wake of the catastrophic *Johnny the Priest*, with its curious cocktail of teddy boys and semi-operatic *religioso*, it showed the Players' management as out of kilter with the world beyond Villiers Street. Greenwell's next collaboration with Peter Wildeblood, *House of Cards*, suffered from an identity crisis, too, unsure of what idiom it assumed. It was generally agreed that this economy-sized edition of *The Three Caskets*, despite its bright lightness, was not as diverting as it had more briefly been in 1956, when the joke had worked better because it wasn't so stretched.

While writers of opera have relished murder and its perpetrators (Italian composers practically put up WANTED posters for them), writers of musical plays have quietly tiptoed away. Stephen Sondheim's *Sweeney Todd* would ultimately give the lie to murder being a no-go area if you wanted commercial success. Beside the fact that Sondheim's work is a masterpiece, it helps that Todd (we hope) was a fiction, and that Sondheim was able to lean on bloody legend. The challenge of melding murder with musical play (not opera) music is fraught with difficulty.

Where are the barriers? A musical about the psychopathic Neville Heath, who almost ritualistically butchered two women in 1946? It might be the stuff of opera, but a musical? Terence Rattigan based his play *Cause Célèbre* on the case of Alma Rattenbury, whose teenage lover murdered her husband in 1935. The Rattenbury affair cries out for operatic treatment, but has a tempting allure to the adventurous musical theatre writer, for Alma was not only an accomplished pianist but, under the name of 'Lozanne', wrote romantic (even slushy) romantic ballads that could be sung in the front parlour. 'Night Brings Me You' was one of them, of which any musical adaptation might make use: what better title to underline Alma's passion for the young chauffeur-handyman for whom she had advertised in the newspaper ('ex-Boy Scout preferred')?

A Pathé short encapsules her, seated at a grand piano accompanying a performance of one of her hits, 'Dark Haired Marie'. Proving herself an ideal candidate for opera, Alma concludes the Rattenbury affair by being acquitted of murder but committing suicide, stabbing herself in the heart six times before falling into a river. As apotheosis, her hapless lover, George Stoner, is sentenced to death but reprieved. Then, we can consider the 'Brides in the Bath' murders by the Svengali-like George Smith, whose trial at the Old Bailey had crowds of women eager to catch a glimpse of this lethal Lothario of the closet. Helpfully, Smith had enough victims to keep a sizeable queue of leading ladies busy in any musical adaptation. And then, of course, there's Hawley Harvey Crippen, hanged by the neck until dead at Pentonville on the morning of 23 November 1910.

Dismembered remains of his music-hall artiste wife Cora, née Turner, billed on the halls as Belle Elmore, real name Kunigunde Mackamotzki, were discovered at the Crippens' London home, 39 Hilldrop Crescent. Crippen, sometime proper doctor, quack doctor, homeopathic charlatan and dubiously qualified dentist, was apprehended on board the SS *Montrose*, by which he hoped to escape from England with his young lover-cum-dental-assistant Ethel Le Neve. One of Crippen's most ardent pursuants, the Assistant Commissioner of Crime for the Metropolitan Police Sir Melville Macnaghten, would claim that 'no case has ever fascinated the British public, and, indeed, engaged the attention of the whole world, in quite the same way that the case of Dr Crippen did'.[1] None could have guessed that half a century later the musical *Belle* (Strand Theatre, 4 May 1961; 44) would have Crippen operatically duetting with Ethel on the pleasures of domestic bliss at no. 39, or a comic scene with Hawley injecting vast amounts of poison into Belle's beef tea, or Hawley helter-skeltering through his past in a ragtime patter-song 'Coldwater, Michigan'.

What made Wolf Mankowitz, already a serious figure (and there were very few of them) in British musicals, turn to Crippen? His involvement in two of the most significant 'New Wave' musicals of the late 1950s, *Expresso Bongo* and *Make Me an Offer*, had showed thoughtful, even political, intent. Both had involved collaboration with composer Monty Norman, after which both broke from their partnership with David Heneker. *Belle* wasn't classifiable as 'New Wave', wasn't, by the terms of 1961 musical theatre, at all classifiable, probably in itself a reason for its failure, but it's not difficult to see the appealing components that might have beckoned a new dawn of British musicals. Mankowitz based the show on a (presumably unproduced) play by Beverley Cross.

Cora's links to Edwardian music hall gave Mankowitz and Norman a ready-prepared canvas. The most infamous murder of its time would be framed by the plush and gilt and seedy opulence of the music halls that proliferated throughout the country in Edwardian England. How apt that one of the show's happiest choruses 'Meet Me At the Strand' should ultimately be sung at that very theatre (did Norman write it knowing that *Belle* was going there?), with plucky soubrette Nicolette Roeg delivering one of the very few moments of the show that simply offered a warm-hearted pastiche of music hall's spirit. Little else of *Belle* was as straightforward. It relished its opportunity to mingle spectacle (Loudon Sainthill's brilliant sets) with horror, knockabout comedy and sentiment, the last exclusively the province of Ethel. Norman's pastiche score roamed over all manner of styles of the period, from mindlessly patriotic anthems, 'The Bravest of Men', to nigger-minstrel routines in which a now-heavenly Cora angelically joined. None could have argued against its casting, with George Benson perfectly impersonating the little doctor, and Rose Hill, magnificently off-key, as 'Bird of Paradise' Cora.

This is a score of superb invention and decisiveness. Ethel's songs ring with truth, a truth that removed her completely from the mock-horror of everything around her. Examine her numbers: 'You Are Mine', a romantic recall of her times in the dentist's surgery with Crippen. It is all simplicity, naivety, with no trace of artifice about it. It immediately tells us what side Norman (and presumably Mankowitz) is on, for their Ethel is a total innocent. Compare her with the much more obviously conniving 'Ethel' of Caryl Brahms and Ned Sherrin's novel *Rappel 1910*. The novel leaves a question mark over Ethel's involvement in Cora's murder. The very fact that Brahms had been working on her own musical about Crippen, only to be beaten to the post by *Belle*, should heighten our interest. Norman is Counsel for the Defence. How else might Ethel throw off the ecstasy of the head-over-heels 'I Can't Stop Singing', or, at the ball after Cora's 'disappearance', allow herself 'Waltzing With You?' If there can be any doubt of Ethel's innocence it's in her final cry, 'Don't Ever Leave Me' as Crippen's fate (and hers) unfolds. *Belle* had an integrity often lacking in the British musical.

Threading through is the recurring 'Ballad of Dr Crippen', as the light-heartedness of the story leads inexorably to the execution shed. What – no happy ending? Having sat through it all, at last the audience was sent out into the night pondering on the moral dilemma surrounding capital punishment. Only six years before *Belle*, Ruth Ellis, the last woman in Britain to be handed the death penalty, was hanged for murder. Shortly before *Belle* opened, Anthony Miller was the last British teenager to be hanged. Parliamentary attempts to abolish capital punishment had floundered after the Death Penalty (Abolition) Bill of 1956. Four years on, the revue *Hang Down Your Head and Die* used that theatrical form to make a passionate plea for an end to the horror of the scaffold.

*Belle* exposed itself to a press that was both ignorant and vituperative. There was (perhaps) no doubting that the show was, in the words of its director Val May, 'a complete mess'[2], but for Bernard Levin it was 'a practically unsalvageable mess' with 'one scene of shatteringly offensive vulgarity'.[3] J. W. Lambert needed context in which the show could be placed, suggesting that *The Music Man* represented the sweet, and *The Threepenny Opera* the sour. The trouble with *Belle* was that it offered 'a diluted mixture of the two, and our latent puritanism rushes up to support our wary suspicion of any free, unembarrassed approach. We have, undeniably, qualms. The easiest way to allay these misgivings is to say that in any case the piece is thoroughly bad. This, however, is not true. *Belle* is a manufactured article, certainly, like most musicals, but it generates genuine high spirits.'[4] At least this was considered criticism, against Levin's denunciation of 'a nerveless hybrid'.[5] Robert Muller pointed thumbs down, seeing the writers' opportunity to find 'in the life and death story of Dr Crippen, some pertinent commentary on the moral values of a topsy-turvy world. But none of these elegant ideas came off in this brash, callous, and off-hand realisation [...] No doubt easily scandalised souls will claim that Mr Mankowitz went too far. The trouble is that he didn't go nearly far enough. *Belle* lacks the courage of its convictions.'[6]

Incensed by the critical reaction as *Belle* moved from Southsea and Brighton into London, Mankowitz went to war with *Belle*'s detractors, mounting a campaign to combat them. In full fig, chorus members carried a coffin to the *Daily Mail*'s headquarters, marking the fact that its review had helped kill the show. Mankowitz sent two vans to Wembley to broadcast its music to the crowds, and thousands of leaflets were distributed. On the second night, he went on stage at the Strand, telling the audience 'I do not acknowledge good or bad taste [...] There is no reason why British musicals should be in a strait-jacket. Anything is material for a musical if it is done with compassion and understanding.'[7] He went on television's *Right To Reply*, telling the critic Alan Brien that he had received hundreds of letters in support of the production.

Brien:          They don't write to me.
Mankowitz:  Well, maybe they don't read your paper, dear boy. The correspondence
                   columns of the popular papers have been running letters about this for
                   some days now.

| Brien: | Saying what? |
|---|---|
| Mankowitz: | Saying the show is great. |
| Brien: | Are you sure you haven't been rolling around posting letters in different areas? |
| Mankowitz: | That's libellous, you know. |
| Brien: | I don't care. You aren't going to sue me for libel. |
| Mankowitz: | I might. |

He didn't.

Before consigning *Belle* once again to theatrical oblivion, we can return to Caryl Brahms and the passion for Crippen's period that roars out of the highly literate pages of *Rappel 1910*. Brahms's highly fictionalised musical based on the Crippen case had been announced in the *Evening News* two days before Mankowitz and Norman announced theirs. It was never to happen. Perhaps the lyrics that keep interrupting the narrative of *Rappel 1910* are leftovers of Brahms's abandoned libretto; I think they must be. Now and then, bits of them seem to have strayed into one of her later works, *Sing a Rude Song*. It was with trepidation that Brahms went to the first night of *Belle* at the Strand, telling herself (with typical wit) that she was, after all, 'just the guide showing the paying patron around the masterpieces'. To her relief, she found it 'something quite new in English musicals – more closely akin to *Oliver!* than anything else. I was amazed at the hard tone of the London press for I left the theatre convinced that it would run a year.'[8] Sadly, Mankowitz's subsequent musicals never dared.

In their careers of diminishing returns, **Wildest Dreams** (Vaudeville Theatre, 3 August 1961; 76) was the last straw for Julian Slade and Dorothy Reynolds, things having begun so happily with the record-breaking *Salad Days*. That playful, revue-like nonsense, about a young couple coming down from university and getting married with the hope of falling in love against a background of summer skies and getting stuck with a battered old piano that magically made everyone in London dance (hard luck on the provinces) had succeeded despite some dismissive reviews. After, the team struggled on with *Free as Air*, not strong book-wise but more solid than its predecessor, and certainly Slade's best score, but the works that followed on – *Follow That Girl* and *Hooray for Daisy!* – were much less appealing. By 1961, they must have had doubts about foisting their new show on London, although audiences at the Everyman, Cheltenham, for which it was commissioned, lapped it up. *Wildest Dreams* marked the end of a collaboration that had achieved a remarkable amount over its decade; a catalogue of original works. As much could be said of very few other British writers of musical theatre except Ivor Novello, whose mainstream list of shows, from *Glamorous Night* on, were at least completely original.

The revue elements that had kept *Salad Days* together (a beauty parlour scene for Dorothy Reynolds, and a send-up of night-club singers for Reynolds, British policemen doing ballroom dancing down at the nick) were more cleverly integrated into *Wildest Dreams*, seemingly part of the plot. The title was a clue: now it was dream sequences (it had been good enough for *Carousel*), with sexually incipient schoolgirl Carol Arden summoning up a swarthy sheikh ('There may have been others I turned into mothers') in rural Gloucestershire.

The plot, mercifully of postage stamp size, could not have been less confusing. An ambitious young newspaper reporter is sent by his editor to the sleepy village of Nelderham to discover why they have not responded to a questionnaire. Ambition dictates that the reporter must expose this highly contented, almost smug, village to the public glare. This shying away from the public glare had very much been at the heart of *Salad Days, Free as Air* and *Follow That Girl*. There was just enough room on the postage stamp to have the young reporter fall in love with the sexually incipient schoolgirl played by Anna Dawson, probably the finest gamine of her period. Denis Quilley played the reporter at Cheltenham, but was unavailable when the production was remounted for London, and was replaced by John Baddeley, who had already done service in *Follow That Girl*.

The score had many felicities, not least a strutting trio for the working class in Bank Holiday mood, 'There's a Place We Know', with (most daringly for Slade and Reynolds) a nudge and wink as to what naughty things might go on there. A lilting hymn to the British countryside, 'The Days Go By', imbued with that curious Slade melancholy, and the stand-out 'Girl on the Hill', stood out. Miss Reynolds had the perhaps unenviable task of going on stage every night as leading lady, playing the ex-actress (something that Reynolds was in no danger of becoming) Harriet Gray. It hardly mattered that, on the first night at the Vaudeville, Reynolds (the Florence Foster Jenkins of the British musical) missed her entry in the final quartet of lovers, 'This Man Loves You'. This at least made the *Guardian*'s critic sit up. For him it was 'the surprise of the evening and struck like a thunderbolt'.[9] Slade recalled this as Reynolds' funniest performance in any of their works (she had been in all except *Follow That Girl*), but after the damning reviews it was she who decided their collaboration was finished.

The passing of *Wildest Dreams* marked a point of departure for the British musical to which there was no return ticket. Slade and Reynolds had overridden the crest of verismo musicals that briefly invaded London at the end of the 1950s, and just about survived the rise of Lionel Bart. In 1962, Slade was beguiled into writing the score for a major musical adaptation of a literary classic, *Vanity Fair*. It was the work that might have wrenched him from his modest, carefree talent. But just how carefree is *Wildest Dreams*? If blindfolded, would we know that it's from the same pens that wrote *Salad Days*? It may not have the inexplicable potency of *Salad Days*, although it's arguable that none of the many revivals of that show has achieved the potency of the original, but there is about it a sense of reality and passion that suggests that maybe even Slade and Reynolds had begun growing up.

Philip Hope-Wallace suggested that

**4** Ronnie Barker, Annie Ross and Peter Gilmore dress rehearsing *All In Love*, an unloved off-Broadway import to the May Fair Theatre in 1964. This adaptation of Sheridan's *The Rivals* suffered from the lack of an off-London theatre

> The latest and by no means the worst of the line of tinkly musicals […] will surely draw upon itself a furious rain of critical obloquy […] But for each theatregoer who longs for the kitchen sink with or without dustbins there must be 50 whose idea of bliss is a dainty tea with home-made cakes.[10]

The *Tatler*'s Anthony Cookman was one of the few alive to the show's sub-texts, hidden in

> a mixture of extraordinary naivety and sudden, rather unnerving flashes of worldliness […] Among all the coyness of the story and the tinkling of tunes that rarely do anything else but tinkle there is a touch of something – can it be sincerity? – which comes as a saving grace and carries a hint of why the shows that Mr Slade and Miss Reynolds concoct have an endearing effect on such a large variety of people.[11]

It is said that Queen Elizabeth II's favourite song is *Salad Days'* 'We Said We Wouldn't Look Back'. She is possibly unaware of *Wildest Dreams*.

# 1962

*Scapa!*
*Vanity Fair*

Was the nautical entertainment that preceded Lionel Bart's *Blitz!* at the Adelphi quite as dismal as reported? Did it really inspire the theory that musicals were invented to satisfy 'the need for some kind of group torture, with the audience doing a mental war-dance'?[12]

If for no other reason than that its composer had turned his own play into a musical, *Scapa!* (Adelphi Theatre, 8 March 1962; 44) deserves note. Hugh Hastings' *Seagulls Over Sorrento*, following the fortunes of four volunteer able seamen consigned to 'an island, not far from the mainland, in Scapa Flow, where a disused wartime naval fortress has been converted into a naval experimental base', had caught some sort of public mood in London in 1950, running for 1,551 performances, and getting productions worldwide. In the hostile arena into which the show was about to enter, its creators probably sought reassurance. After all, Hastings' play had been a colossal success; now, the musical version's leading man was well known from television, radio and recordings; its leading comedian might attract a 'different' audience because he was a popular radio disc-jockey, and it was that rarest of beasts, an all-male musical, a very distant cousin to Benjamin Britten's *Billy Budd*. What other all-male plays might be dealt this blow? *Journey's End*? Meanwhile, in a somewhat desperate attempt to summon spectators to the Adelphi, the company marched through London streets in full naval rig. At a gala performance, the press was on hand to see Admiral of the Fleet Earl Mountbatten inspect a cast line-up.

In selecting *Scapa!*'s four male leads, director George Carden had assembled an odd bunch. As its romantic tenor (romantic at a distance as his rhapsodising of women had to be done without one in sight) David Hughes had the voice but not the height for Hastings' originally named 'Lofty', now rechristened 'Dusty'. Hastings' verdict was that 'David was short in stature, but otherwise ideal. It was difficult to find a tall bloke who could sing and who had established a name on early television.' Although he had played opposite Ginger Rogers in a clunking television production of the British musical *Carissima*,[13] his only stage musical had been the unsuccessful *Summer Song*[14] in 1956. *Seagulls Over Sorrento*'s original Able Seaman Badger had been notably played by old-stager Ronald Shiner. *Scapa!*'s Badger was Pete Murray, more youthful but lacking stage-craft, after Anthony Newley turned down the part. The theatre programme introduced Murray as 'well known as a T.V. panellist and Compere', but his only West End experience had been in a mild R. C. Sherriff play *Miss Mabel* twelve years earlier. Hastings' verdict on Murray? 'Brave effort, but uncharismatic.'[15] Edward Woodward, conscripted to play Haggis, with the unappetising prospect of singing 'The Sound of Bagpipes', had yet to establish himself as a highly professional leading man of musicals (in the Broadway *High Spirits* and the British *Two Cities*) but had recently been noted for his 'Wisherman's Song' in the revue *The Art of Living*. Fourthly, American Timothy Gray signed on as Sprog (played in *Seagulls* by Nigel Stock). It seemed an odd assignment for Gray, who had played Broadway and co-written the score of the British hit *Love from Judy*, as well as contributing material to British revues such as *Airs on a Shoestring* and *Penny Plain*. He got some of the better numbers in *Scapa!*, including his introductory 'I Like It Here' and the rumbustious 'I Wish I Was an Orchestra'. Hastings thought that Gray 'should have had a dekko at Theodor Uppman in *Billy Budd*'.[16]

The appalling reviews sent Hastings into an emotional crisis, aggravated by the fact that Carden left Britain the day after opening night, leaving Hastings in charge of the production, and responsible for trying to pull the show into better shape. Perhaps he was fortunate enough not to see the *Queen* review of 'a quite dreadful, all-male, derriere-posturing musical [...] The tale of several sailors assigned to the Scapa Flow naval base is depressingly camped up by an unfeisty crew of boy sailors in suggestively tight trousers, ghoulishly stupid musical numbers and service jokes which should have, but did not, go out when TV first came in.'[17] Irving Wardle for *The Times* thought that whatever interest the characters had had in Hastings' play had evaporated. What was more, 'the numbers cut clean across the idiom of the play; they belong to the world of the romantic musical and thus conflict jarringly with the unromantic all-male society of the naval base. Even the dances [...] have been short-circuited into the usual pop style with an effect (e.g. a transvestite brothel cabaret) sometimes bordering on the obscene.'[18] Anthony Cookman in *Tatler* lamented 'an exceedingly ugly affair'.[19]

*Scapa!* was probably fatally scuppered by three other coruscating notices. Robert Muller in the *Daily Mail* had not been amused by a spectacle that was 'grisly, embarrassing and pretty well unendurable [...] The songs (revue ditties without charm or originality) do not carry the action forward; they interrupt it.

The long, dim naval grumble, set to music by the author himself, is an insuffera-
ble mixture of condescension, gentility and smut, with vulgar interludes of pop
heroics, and chirpy chattering from the ratings.'[20] Bernard Levin, still recovering
from having suffered the disastrous revue *Not To Worry*,[21] now realised that *Not
To Worry* had not been 'the worst show put on in the West End of London in the
past fifteen years. This musical is doubly, trebly, decuply, worse [...] The badness
of the music is matched by the dreariness of the acting, and the décor is exactly
as ugly as the production is old-fashioned.'[22] David Pryce-Jones in the *Financial
Times* abandoned the sinking ship by deciding the show 'defined the rock-bottom
of the London musical for quite some time to come' and that '*Scapa!* did give a
new meaning to those exhausted adjectives, embarrassing and futile'.[23]

S. A. Gorlinsky, who co-produced with Jack Hylton, had already weathered two
substantial flops, the 1956 *Chrysanthemum* and the Frankie Howerd vehicle (the
wheels came off) *Mister Venus*. Why had he thought well enough of *Scapa!* to risk
yet another failure? In an act of pity, Hylton waived the production's rent for its last
two weeks of lingering death. Every day during afternoon tea, the Brown's Hotel's
string trio delighted customers by playing a selection from the show, although few
of the customers could have known what they were listening to with the crumpets.
A few poorly recorded numbers by the original cast suggest that *Scapa!* may not
have been quite as awful as it was painted, but it was consigned to the oblivion that
British musical after British musical was doomed to inhabit.

At the other end of the year, an ungovernable adaptation from William Makepeace Thackeray elicited as much derision as had *Scapa!* The blame for **Vanity
Fair** (Queen's Theatre, 27 November 1962; 70) was laid firmly at the feet of its
creators: book writers Robin Miller (who also wrote the lyrics) and Alan Pryce-
Jones, and composer Julian Slade. In fact, there was so much else wrong with a
piece that, following its closure, was to be resurrected provincially in a much-
amended and much-reduced form. Pryce-Jones, author and formerly editor of the
*Times Literary Supplement*, had no theatrical background. Miller was inexperienced in musical theatre. Slade's collaboration with Dorothy Reynolds had ended
with *Wildest Dreams*, by which time his critical reputation had slumped.

The pressure for Slade was now to come up with music that equalled the epic
stature of Thackeray's novel. This it signally failed to do. Although over-stuffed with
characters, none managed to worm its way into the audience's affection. Frances
Cuka was a brave, unexpected but inaccurate choice for the viperish Becky Sharp.
In the tradition of many leading ladies of Slade's musicals (Dorothy Reynolds,
Annette Crosbie, Susan Hampshire among them) she was no singer. Perhaps the
producers didn't see this as a disadvantage. The problem was made worse because
Slade and Miller came up with such feeble material. 'I'm No Angel' must be one
of the worst introductory numbers for a leading lady; 'Mama' is a three-minute
simper; 'Rebecca' cries out for a major rethink. Gordon Boyd probably had three

of the best numbers – a decent ballad 'Someone To Believe In', an effective duet with Eira Heath in 'There He Is', and 'Advice To Women', adapted from a number originally intended for *Wildest Dreams*. But *Vanity Fair* bulged with peripheral matter. Its main draw was Sybil Thorndike as Miss Crawley, recently released from Coward's *Waiting in the Wings*, which had already fallen foul of Bernard Levin, but Slade and Miller were at their very weakest in Thorndike's items, 'Dear Miss Crawley' and 'Forgive Me'. It would be charitable to say these sounded like watered-down Coward.

The notices were dismal, leavened only by sympathetic nods to some of the cast. Gerard Fray for the *Guardian* remembered 'three endless hours', during which Slade's music and Harris's direction 'did not prevent the "novel without a hero" being converted into the musical play without anything – without anything at all except moments of bathos which followed each other so closely that the evening became simultaneously bathetic and pathetic'. Fray realised that 'There are bound to be worse musical plays in the future. I hope I do not have to witness them.'[24] *The Times* highlighted 'the tinsel banalities of the score', which even Dame Sybil could not disguise. 'It is the most ambitious score Mr Slade has written, but its main achievement is only to overcast the work of his collaborators. Its principal effect is to turn the show into a charade.'[25]

If a death blow was needed, Bernard Levin supplied it, damning *Vanity Fair* as a

ghastly exercise in theatrical necrophily [in which] The music and words alike are of a total, stunning vacuity that produces a tedium which in the end turns physical. Not since Mr Coward's *Waiting in the Wings* have I felt so bruised and stiff after a show [...] there is not a chord in the music, nor a line in the words, that does not reek of the theatrical graveyard, the barren tinkling of the one matching the empty braying of the other to perfection.[26]

# 1963

*Virtue in Danger*
*Enrico*
*House of Cards*
*Pocahontas*

Audiences turning up for the musical version of Vanbrugh's *The Relapse* could at least be confident that it would not last as long as Vanbrugh's original, which if delivered uncut would have taken four hours. Concision had been only one of the Mermaid Theatre's problems in adapting it for the musical stage, where it played twice-nightly at a running length of two hours including interval.

Another problem was that the musical was blatantly conceived as a follow-up success to the immensely well-attended *Lock Up Your Daughters* that had done so much for the Mermaid's reputation when it opened there in 1959. Why, then, didn't Bernard Miles go back to Laurie Johnson and Lionel Bart for a sequel to their hit Restoration romp? Instead, he turned to composer James Bernard and Paul Dehn. For some, the following-up *Virtue in Danger* (Mermaid Theatre, 10 April 1963, transferred to Strand Theatre; 121) was much more appealing than its predecessor, but it undeniably lacked that show's popular appeal, and attracted criticism that could much more fairly have been directed at *Lock Up Your Daughters*, at best a second-grade effort with good moments. There was a measured response to the new show's cast recording, from Michael Cox in *Gramophone*. 'The lyrics are excellent and make one wish that Paul Dehn would write more often for the light musical theatre. James Bernard's music shows great respect for the period of the play both in style and orchestration but fully exploits the rhythm and wit of more modern music.' Cox went on to praise 'a cast of real actors with real voices [...] This is undoubtedly the best English musical for many months and I strongly recommend it for its wit and originality.'[27]

*Virtue in Danger*'s casting was brilliant, with John Moffatt perfectly in period as Lord Foppington, Patsy Byrne as the socially uncomfortable but delightful Miss Hoyden, grumpy Gwen Nelson as her Nurse, and Barrie Ingham as Fashion among the leading players. The chief delight was in Patricia Routledge's sultry widow Berinthia, exemplary in 'Wait a Little Longer, Lover'. Routledge had laboured long and hard in British musical theatre, with little commercial success. Almost a protégé of Julian Slade, her early successes at Bristol Old Vic had taken her into a supporting role in *The Duenna* and *Follow That Girl*. By the time of *Virtue in Danger*, she had also survived one British musical catastrophe, *Zuleika*, and an American musical seen only in London, *The Love Doctor*. The year before *Virtue in Danger*, there were good notices for her performance in the title role of *Little Mary Sunshine*. A much better production than its off-Broadway original, it too was a West End flop.

Routledge's bad luck with musicals followed her to New York, where she became much better known for her work than in Britain, through Jule Styne's *Darling of the Day*, Leonard Bernstein and Alan Jay Lerner's *1600 Pennsylvania Avenue*, in which she played the American President's wives, through her portrayal of Queen Victoria in the Broadway-bound *Love Match* that closed on the road in Los Angeles, and in *Say Hello To Harvey*, based on Mary Chase's familiar comedy *Harvey*, in which Routledge once again gave a sterling performance. With *Say Hello To Harvey* dying en route to Broadway, Routledge's American career in musicals came to an end. It came as no surprise that the producers of British musicals had no idea what to do with her.

After a well-attended two-month run of *Virtue in Danger* at the Mermaid, the production was taken up by H. M. Tennent and moved into the Strand Theatre. It was an unaccommodating space for such an intimate piece, with its gentle instrumentation and refined playing. The comparison with *Lock Up Your Daughters* did not escape the critics. 'Once again,' reported *The Times*,

> the Mermaid has settled on an invitingly salacious classic, knocked the genuine
> bawdy out of it, substituted music and lyrics, and offered up the result as a harmless
> show for the family [with] a collection of insipidly four-square tunes orchestrated in
> the manner of Ivor Novello and repeated without variation through every stanza of

the leaden lyrics. The score neither fits the idiom of the play, nor compensates with the theatrical impact of the modern musical.[28]

W. A. Darlington warmed to the piece, although

> Not much attempt is made to preserve the Restoration atmosphere. The dresses are there, but the formal manners and speech are presented in modern pastiche. Paul Dehn [...] has wisely, I think, kept to rhythms and phrasing in which he and his singers are at ease, while being careful to avoid actual anachronisms. This enables James Bernard to keep the action swinging along with music of the same quality, which has little period colour about it but is gay and tuneful.[29]

Such lack of appreciation for a work that beamed with vigour and charm helped bring down yet another British musical. Routledge's singing of 'Let's Fall Together' was alone worth the price of a ticket.

One of the first 'international' musicals to reach London before the tsunami of that sub-genre threatened to flood London, the Italian *Enrico* (Piccadilly Theatre, 3 July 1963; 86) had a stormy crossing. Telling the story of the imaginary centenarian Enrico, here was a sort of cavalcade of Italian history, told by Pietro Garinei and Sandro Giovannini, translated and reformed into English by Peter Myers and Ronald Cass, with music by Renato Rascel, who also played the title role. Garinei and Giovannini were no strangers to London; their *When in Rome* had played 298 performances at the Adelphi Theatre four years earlier, a success helped along by its well-liked British leads, Dickie Henderson and June Laverick, she as the wife who writes a scandalous novel of which her husband is supposedly the virile Lothario. Garinei and Giovannini could still be found in London in 1978, when their *Beyond the Rainbow*, after its three-and-a-half-year run in Italy as *Aggiungi Un Posto A Tavola*, introduced West End playgoers to Johnny Dorelli. Rascel was already an Italian film and stage star, and the composer of the worldwide 'Arrivederci, Roma', but Signor Rascel's London debut as Enrico was less happy. *The Times* explained that he 'sings, dances, acts and plays the guitar, but not one of these activities rise above mediocrity, and even in the second row his voice is often drowned in accompaniment'.[30] Milton Shulman saw Rascel as 'a kind of Arthur Askey of Italy [...] an amiable little man with a mildly endearing comic style and little else. He sings and dances, too, but I hardly think they are counted among his major talents.'[31]

Rascel's responsibility as composer and star of *Enrico* was considerable, not least in having to play a role that spanned a hundred years. The son of an Italian hatter, Enrico Venutti is born in 1863, on the very day Italian independence is declared. He grows to manhood, bankrupts his father's shop, relishes seduction and socialism, makes a fortune out of selling boaters, joins the Fascists and oversees social reform. *Theatre World* detected product endorsement: 'The commercial triumphs of present-day Italy were vociferously listed in reiterative song.'[32] Luxuriously staged it may have been, but critics failed to detect much substance beneath the spectacular surface, and 'for all its incident, it manages to be singularly empty';[33] it was 'altogether a spectacular handful of macaroni – but, like macaroni, it's no use looking for something inside'.[34] Jeremy Rundall complained that 'Aside from the shattering tendentiousness of the theme, the second half of *Enrico* provides yet another example of the folly whereby musicals pack all their best material into the first seventy minutes. *Enrico* is too long by a third in any case, and the period after the interval is one of unrelieved anti-climax.'[35]

Eleanor Fazan, well experienced as a revue director, may have been the ideal choice to knit together *Enrico*'s elements, but its assembly was problematic. The opening was twice postponed, and the production closed with a loss of £80,000. The theatre programme's complex list of scenes and characters is all but incomprehensible.

Reginald Woolley's typically gloomy designs set the mood for an adaptation of Alexander Ostrovsky's play *Even a Wise Man Stumbles.* Some of the Russian playwright's works had already been musicalised, in Tchaikovsky's incidental music to *The Snow Maiden* (also metamorphosed into an opera by Rimsky-Korsakov), and Janáček's *Kátá Kabanová.* The prospect of a British musical coming from this source was interesting, but **House of Cards** (Phoenix Theatre, 2 October 1963; 27) was hustled almost grudgingly into the West End after shunting around the fringes of London following its run at the Players' Theatre. Four years on from *The Crooked Mile*, few probably remembered the hope that Peter Greenwell and Peter Wildeblood had held out for the British musical. Whatever the deficiencies of that work, the grandest of the 1950s verismo pieces, it had an ambition far above any of its competitors, and an orchestral grandeur that very few musicals to come could boast. Considered by some to have been the best British musical for years, something that might even be spoken of (or whispered) in the same breath as *West Side Story*, *The Crooked Mile* was never going to be anything but essentially British. In common with all the other 'verismo' musicals of the time, it set itself firmly in London, whereas so much of contemporary literature driving forward the 'New Wave' that tried out social realism moved its action to the North of England. That was something British musicals were reluctant to try. A fine work such as the 1970 *Love on the Dole*, based on Walter Greenwood's novel, was set in Hanky Park. What chance did it have of transferring from its run at Nottingham Playhouse? When it came to realism in musicals, London liked to stay home.

The Players' Theatre had long supported Greenwell, who for many years was its musical director. In 1955, they had produced his *Twenty Minutes South*, a thoroughly homespun piece about London suburbans, with a dainty heroine, pipe-smoking leading men, and squeaking typists dreaming of film stars, to a libretto by a Players' artiste, Maurice Browning. Directed by Hattie Jacques, the show transferred to the St Martin's Theatre for a modest run. Their thirst for British musicals enlivened by the runaway success of *The Boy Friend*, the Players' went on promoting Greenwell with *The Three Caskets or Venice Re-Served*, adapted by Gordon Snell from scenes in *The Merchant of Venice*. The score marked Greenwell as a distinctly different composer to most of those working in British musical theatre, with a natural inclination to more classically based material. In 1957, Snell and Greenwell again collaborated on another Players' production, the 'musical fantasy' *Antarctica*. Inhabitants of Snell's South Pole included the Abominable Snowman, the St Bernard dog Boris (Bernard Cribbins), a Snow Queen (Marion Grimaldi) and attendant maidens. *Theatre World* assured its readers that 'the entertainment passes 90 minutes most agreeably. Habitués accustomed to Victorian pastiche will not be disturbed.'[36]

*House of Cards* was well if not ideally cast, with fresh-out-of-RADA Patrick Mower as the beguilingly handsome but scheming Yegor Glumov, whose caustic diary, revealing his thoughts on those he uses to further his romantic and business careers, falls into their hands. In the central role of Mashenka, Barbara Evans had surprisingly little to sing, as did Mower, and neither seemed to make much impression. The quick collapse of *House of Cards* discouraged Wildeblood from continuing to work with Greenwell; he saw no future in their collaboration bearing critical or commercial reward. *Plays and Players* showed no enthusiasm for the new work. 'Peter Greenwell's music was presumably intended either as pastiche or parody – I can think of no more charitable explanation. Peter Wildeblood's lyrics had the same ambiguously familiar flavour. Whether they were intended to be gently reminiscent or bitterly mocking, however, I was never able to work out.'[37]

Listening to the score today, there is something to be said for that view. *House of Cards* is a strange melting-pot of all sorts and manner of styles, now operatic, now a point number that sounds like something Coward might have got away with thirty years before, now a 'bluesey' romantic moan, 'Somewhere There's Someone', that sounds like something rescued from a smoky subterranean night-club, now a catchy number that could have come from any bright-eyed musical comedy of the previous twenty years, 'The Trouble With Women'. There are items that suspiciously suggest they were written specifically to suit the typical Players' Theatre clientele, and to suit some of its performers; the witty 'Charity Begins at Home', superbly delivered by Stella Moray, is the obvious example. Ultimately, though, the two Peters combine to create work that in many ways is far superior to almost everything that was going on around them at the time.

For B. A. Young in *Punch*, the writers had come up with 'a bountiful score that, for all its frequently old-fashioned ring, is often very pretty and occasionally throws out a tiny suggestion of Tchaikovsky or Borodin to chime with the setting in Moscow in 1912 [...] There is one song, 'The End of Summer', which would surely have been a hit in the days before Elvis.'[38] Conversely, the *Evening Standard* thought its director Vida Hope, who had worked such magic with *The*

*Boy Friend*, 'has failed utterly to bestow her period charm on this very ordinary piece of theatre. Admittedly, she is short of material. The music [...] is unmemorable, often ugly, and the book [...] dreary.'[39] There was no denying that after *The Crooked Mile*, Greenwell and Wildeblood had taken a step back (several, perhaps). The lushness of *The Crooked Mile*, almost in spite of its Soho gangster and prostitute theme, was nowhere to be found in *House of Cards*, which at times lapsed into revue. One of the understandable reasons may have been the Players' reluctance to splash out financially as they had, to their cost, with *The Crooked Mile*. The score was orchestrated by Gordon Langford, who had previously orchestrated *The Crooked Mile*.

> In *House of Cards*, there were two particular pieces that I still think of and adore. One was called 'The End of Summer' which I still play. There was the most glorious waltz called 'The Mashenka Waltz', and I always thought that one of these days I would do a large symphonic arrangement of it, but it hasn't happened and it probably won't happen now. It's the most beautiful waltz and I think that Peter absolutely excelled himself there. Oh gosh, when I think of it now ... wonderful, wonderful.
>
> The orchestra was most unorthodox. We had something like flute and clarinet, mandolin (played by Hugo Dalton, one of the best players around), accordion, bass guitar and three trombones – now there's an unusual line-up for you. It was the attempt to get some Russian atmosphere. I was really most upset that that show didn't do better, or that it wasn't recorded, even if nobody but enthusiasts would want to buy the recording. Anyway, for my money, Peter's two best songs appeared in that show.[40]

*Pocahontas* (Lyric Theatre, 14 November 1963; 12) did nothing to enhance the reputation of the British musical for audiences who had no inkling that it was in fact American, being the sole work of Kermit Goell, providing book and lyrics for his retelling of the story of the famed Indian princess, according to *Plays and Players*, of 'mind-numbing banality'. Hugh Leonard left at the interval, but not before noticing the sets, 'a succession of quivering backdrops and plywood conifers, the like of which Irving would have thrown out of the Lyceum'.[41] The American Anita Gillette crossed the Atlantic to play the princess opposite a stiff British leading man, Terence Cooper, who assumed the dual roles of John Smith and John Rolfe (only having signed up for one) during the tour. Decca announced an original cast recording, but thought better of it. Uncaring as to whether the show was illegally British or truly American, audiences decided it wanted nothing to do with it. A question mark hovers over a third-night incident, when, ten minutes after curtain rise, Hugh Leonard observed how

> Mr Terence Cooper delighted the audience by removing his shirt and flinging it into the orchestra pit. For one insane, glorious moment, it seemed as if stylisation of a kind was about to break through, sending up all that had gone before. But, alas, the musical director [that doyenne of the craft, Philip Martell] hurled the shirt back at

Mr Cooper, who had merely been guilty of an excess of lustiness; whereupon most of those on-stage compounded the felony by sniggering.

Shortly afterwards, to impress some Indians in his role of Captain John Smith, Mr Cooper threw some gunpowder on a fire. Nothing happened, except that Mr Cooper said 'Oh, Dear!' in a slightly martyred manner; and at this point I cringed in embarrassment, murmuring a far more appropriate four-letter word.[42]

# 1964

## *Our Man Crichton*

J. M. Barrie's boy that didn't grow up, Peter Pan, is one of the most timeless in literature, and the subject of many a musical version. Other plays such as *Mary Rose* and *Dear Brutus* mark Barrie as the kindly dramatist offering characters a second chance at life. He also provided the theatre with plays on which several musicals have been based. *What Every Woman Knows*, with its indomitable heroine Maggie Wylie, has the unique distinction of having been turned into both an American and a British musical: in 1953 Broadway briefly accommodated British leading lady Betty Paul in the title role of *Maggie*; in 1977 Anna Sharkey was the West End Maggie in Michael Wild's adaptation. Christopher Hassall and Harry Parr Davies' *Dear Miss Phoebe* came from *Quality Street*, and the tartan-infused *Wild Grows the Heather*, a notable 1956 flop supposedly penned by librettist William Henry and composer Robert Lindon[43] from *The Little Minister*. There is an as yet unperformed Julian Slade musical of *Dear Brutus*. Christopher Whelen, composer for John Osborne's *The World of Paul Slickey*, also wrote the score for a Birmingham Repertory musical of *Walker London*.

Barrie's 'social' comedy *The Admirable Crichton* satirised the Edwardian class system, following the career of the Earl of Loam's exemplary manservant Crichton. The efficacy of Barrie's message had lost much of its sting by 1964; David Robinson wrote of the 1957 movie that 'Barrie's play now seems more remote than Gammer Gurton'. In the splendid environs of Belgravia, the Earl expounds a preposterous theory of classlessness, which he generously insists on enacting for one day a year. When the Earl's party, attended by Crichton and the between-stairs skivvy Tweeny, are stranded on a desert island, the relationships shift, with Crichton becoming the natural, respected leader of the shipwrecked. He is now considered proper enough to marry Loam's daughter, Lady Mary. The wedding is abandoned when a passing ship rescues the refugees. Back in England, the old order is established; Mary consents to marry a more socially suitable candidate, and Crichton reverts uncomplainingly to his previous station. 'You are the best man among us,' Lady Mary somewhat patronisingly assures him. 'On an island, my lady, perhaps,' replies Crichton, 'but in England, no.' British snobbery wins the day, and Crichton, apparently, closes the baize door on the servants' quarters.

For *Our Man Crichton* (Shaftesbury Theatre, 22 December 1964; 208), the writers had Tweeny making a last-minute escape to a new life, essentially to give

5    Millicent Martin preparing to leave for a desert island in *Our Man Crichton*

the leading lady her somewhat overwrought eleven o'clock number 'My Time Will Come'. Their decision to up the emotional stakes with Martin's determined outburst was criticised by some as being out of place, but was surely the best way to bring down the curtain on a show that often promised more than it gave. In the final minutes, it seemed that Tweeny was having her Eliza Doolittle moment, every trace of the squawky Cockney gone. In this, Tweeny emerged the victor, moving on from a life from which Crichton made no attempt to free himself. Audiences were left to decide what this told them about the British class system.

Gravitas was added by bringing in Clifford Williams from the Royal Shakespeare Company as director. Kenneth More had already played Barrie's hero in the 1957 Columbia movie of the play; *Our Man Crichton* would, sensibly, be his only musical. As Tweeny, Millicent Martin seemed like ideal casting, following critical success in *Expresso Bongo* and *The Crooked Mile*. Her line in strangulated Cockney achieved national fame as one of the *That Was the Week That Was* team on BBC television. David Kernan, cast as the twittish Ernest Woolley, had been *TWTWTW*'s juvenile lead. Much of the secondary casting was impeccable, notably George Benson's Lord Loam and Patricia Lambert (*Once Upon a Mattress*, *The Music Man*) as his daughter Mary, Barrie's intended leading lady. Here was the crux of the musical's problem: Lady Mary, billed well below the title, was demoted to support Tweeny, now inflated to the star role. The trouble was compounded by the fact that the composer and lyricist wrote numbers designed for Martin rather than designed for the character she was playing. Lambert's tasteful contribution (her 'Yesterday's World' is one of the best items in a patchy score) was especially helpful because More was incapable of recognising a musical note, groaning through their drone of a duet, 'I Never Looked For You', and otherwise being only minimally involved with the score. Michael Annals' castaway's island bore a striking resemblance to a Fortnum and Mason Christmas window display. The move to the island meant that the chorus was left ashore.

Composer David Lee and librettist Herbert Kretzmer were also *TWTWTW* regulars, having written such TV numbers as 'Lullaby for an Illegitimate Child' for Martin, although their best known composition was probably the Peter Sellers–Sophia Loren 'Goodness Gracious Me'. Their work for *Our Man Crichton* had a deal of style and charm. Martin's hectic East End complaint 'I Tries' may too obviously have been an example of the stuff Kretzmer and Lee had tailored to her style in *TWTWTW*, but lyrics and music were above average for British musicals of the 1960s. Of the comedy numbers, Kernan's silly-ass 'Nobody Showed Me How' was clearly unsatisfactory, but there was some wit and verve in 'Doesn't Travel Broaden the Mind?', and for a time it seemed that Martin and Kernan's snappy desert island duet 'Little Darlin' would become popular.

In the *Evening Standard* Milton Shulman extolled the show's virtues: 'Barrie's musty moralizing has acquired a fresh piquancy and relevance in its fresh setting. This is largely due to Herbert Kretzmer's intelligent adaptation and his pointed, edgy lyrics which give the theme a contemporary urgency and zest no longer present in the play.'[44] *The Times* considered that 'In terms of construction and staging, it is an expert piece of work. All the same one goes away unsatisfied, for the show is awkwardly stranded between Barrie's age and our own. The original play's concern with the artificiality of class barriers gives it an obvious link with the modern theatre. But what are we to make of the final return home and Crichton's descent to his former station in life?'[45] Philip Hope-Wallace, declaring Martin 'the show's salvation', described 'a middling good musical ... The music has plenty of go but not much else. The book and lyrics by Herbert Kretzmer make the point quite effectively some of the time, though Barrie's point seems pretty blunt by the end of the evening ... The result is likeable but not impressive. The sentimental songs just are not up to snuff.'[46] If the most sentimental of them was Martin's 'My Time Will Come', in a scene not sanctioned by Barrie's play, at least Kretzmer and Lee did for the ending of *Our Man Crichton* what Lerner and Loewe had already done for *Pygmalion*; pointed a hopeful way forward. As a resolve of the show's central theme, it seemed inadequate.

# 1965–1966

'This musical tribute to the musical Martians in our midst sets a new standard for idiocy'

*The Times* on *On the Level*

## 1965

*The Wayward Way*
*Divorce Me, Darling!*
*Four Thousand Brass Halfpennies*
*Passion Flower Hotel*
*Twang!*

The West End was never the right milieu for *The Wayward Way* (Vaudeville Theatre, 27 January 1965; 36), an American musicalisation of the nineteenth-century temperance melodrama *The Drunkard*. Shaftesbury Avenue was no place for theatrical trinkets. *The Wayward Way* had already played Los Angeles for six years, but never chanced Broadway; its non-musical predecessor had played LA for twenty years, making it a sort of US compatriot of *The Mousetrap*. Lightly dotted with songs by composer Lorne Huycke and lyricist Bill Howe that had no hope of lasting beyond the exit doors, the British production of *The Wayward Way*, presented by Tommy Duggan, had a season at the Lyric, Hammersmith before its London opening. It was artfully cast, with Jim Dale and David Holliday, late of *Sail Away* and *No Strings*, as leading men, playing opposite innocent heroine Roberta D'Esti. Deranged Mad Agnes was played by Cheryl Kennedy, with one of the best lyrics of the evening: 'Why do they call me dotty when Agnes is my name?' In the shadow of the greatest British stage villain of all time – who else but the inimitable Tod Slaughter?[1] – John Gower's Squire Cribbs had little to offer but a deep voice, but elsewhere the trifling felicities of the piece worked well enough, if overplaying was wanted. With the evening's tract against the consequent social evils of drink packed away, the second half was given over to an 'Olio', a series of vaudevillian turns reminiscent of a revue night at the Players' Theatre in Charing Cross.

There remained the question of style. Should the primped-up Victorian drama be played straight or served up as warmed-up cod, blatantly mocked or gently parodied or done straight-faced? Answer came there none, so much nonsense already having been written about how other shows dealt with a similar problem of period style (*The Boy Friend* aping the 1920s or *Little Mary Sunshine* aping American operetta). The main problem with *The Wayward Way* was that it was small and dramatically insubstantial. Likeable as it was, it was easy to overlook. The management pointed to the death of Winston Churchill three days before opening as one reason for its lack of publicity; frivolity, perhaps much needed, couldn't break through the public gloom. Meanwhile, W. A. Darlington, the conservative but percipient drama critic of the *Daily Telegraph*, thought it 'much relished by an exuberant audience, whose hissing, cheers and booing were last night almost as insistent as the cast's determination to leave no parodying stone unturned', but warned that if the cast 'want a long run, they must get back to the timing and polish which impressed my colleague and others at Hammersmith'.[2]

After three weeks of dwindling audiences, the cast and backstage staff offered to work for a week without pay to keep the show on. Much the same had happened three years earlier with *Little Mary Sunshine* when its star, Patricia Routledge, presented a cheque from the company to the management. Miss D'Esti rallied the troops, insisting that 'All we need now is for the public to join in our fight, and I am positive the show will run forever',[3] but Equity blocked the idea. The closing notice was posted as the curtain rose on the final Saturday night performance of *The Wayward Way*'s fourth week.

Sandy Wilson's **Divorce Me, Darling!** (Globe Theatre, 1 February 1965; 87) could as well have been titled *Hostage to Fortune*. His 1920s pastiche *The Boy Friend* had broken from its moorings at the Players' Theatre to become one of the most substantial hits of the 1950s. His subsequent career was less happy. *The Buccaneer*, a sprightly miniature based on the fate of an old-fashioned boys' comic, had played the West End for a few weeks. His ill-judged score for the ill-judged revue-like *Call It Love?* had lasted four performances. His (by many) highly praised *Valmouth*, pulled from the precious writings of Ronald Firbank, hadn't prospered commercially. *Valmouth* had already diverted Wilson on to the esoteric and camp path that would prove his career-undoing with *His Monkey Wife* (the leading man marries a chimpanzee) and the gloom-laden *The Clapham Wonder*, neither of which reached the West End.

Now, it was back to pastiche, reviving the characters and plot of *The Boy Friend*, moving it ten years on into the 1930s. A difference was evident in the title. *The Boy Friend* promised romance, or the hope of it; *Divorce Me, Darling!* spelled disappointment and disillusion. Another problem was that for much of Wilson's potential audience the essential remembrance of the 1930s was not British but American, Ginger Rogers rather than Jessie Matthews, Fred Astaire rather than Jack Buchanan. *The Boy Friend*, despite having taken much of its inspiration from American musical theatre, had nevertheless seemed utterly British. *Divorce Me, Darling!* seemed just as British, but now its pastiche made strong use of American originals. The other cause for concern was that Wilson might be unaware of the cold world's indifference to musical sequels. At least Slade and Reynolds had never attempted a follow-up to *Salad Days* (how do you follow-up on a show that had no proper plot?) but – come to think of it – it might have been interesting to discover what became of Tim and Jane's marriage, an arrangement begun when they were jobless and not in love.

No matter: *Divorce Me, Darling!*, after its modest debut at the Players' Theatre, was re-dressed with a splendour denied its predecessor, a bigger cast and spank-ingly appropriate orchestrations by Ian MacPherson. The death of Vida Hope (on whom Wilson had so heavily depended as director of *The Boy Friend*) in part robbed Wilson of the show he probably imagined. Hope's mantle was taken over by Steven Vinaver, who would be equally unlucky with the Broadway-bound *Darling of the Day* three years later, when he was dismissed as director before rehearsals began. The authentically period choreography of Buddy Bradley helped build a head of steam, but Vinaver was unable to do much to disguise the weakness of Wilson's libretto.

Audiences that had flocked to *The Boy Friend*, a show to which the British showed an apparently undying loyalty, seemed uninterested in discovering what had happened to its characters after the curtain fell. A second instalment of *The Boy Friend*, ten years later? Wilson's faith in the British public was misguided. Besides, his treatment of the 1930s differed wildly from his treatment of the 1920s. His fictional characters were now used as puppets to impersonate famous figures of the period: Patricia Michael's Polly Browne became Gertrude Lawrence, and her boyfriend (now husband) Tony had metamorphosed into Noel Coward, pre-sumably because Wilson had incorporated a pastiche of the *Private Lives'* balcony scene. Bobby Van Heusen was reborn as Fred Astaire and madcap Maisie as a sort of manically tap-dancing Elsie Randolph, with Irlin Hall as a Martha Raye type. Joan Heal, half-heartedly billed as the show's star, coped with playing a revived Madame Dubonnet who had unconvincingly become a cabaret star along Marlene Dietrich lines. What was more, Wilson flooded the stage with a seemingly unend-ing parade of characters in a bewildering sequence of non-events. Lost among it all were happy numbers that had no lasting power with that massive, ageing but fickle audience that had long ago flocked to *The Boy Friend*.

The return of Polly and Co. was saluted by a press generally sympathetic to Wilson's self-imposed predicament. *The Times* considered the full pleasure 'of shows of this kind are open only to those who can view the modern pastiche against a vivid recollection of the productions of the period itself'; furthermore, at various moments 'one is in the situation of viewing the show in double perspec-tive – both against its period and against its predecessor'. There was more: 'the quality of writing is not high'; 'Mr Wilson has used the loose construction of his musical comedy as a pretext for poor construction himself'.[4] R. B. Marriott decided that 'nothing is quite good enough' in a plot that 'becomes a bit of a bore [...] In fact, despite moments of gaiety, scraps of neat parody and a couple of good numbers [it] is not to be compared to the witty, deft, light-hearted show that ran for years and made Mr Wilson's name in the theatre.'[5] The headline of

Harold Hobson's *Sunday Times* notice, 'Trouble with reality' summed up the central difficulty.

Wilson's tilts at the critics were several. Citing Herbert Kretzmer's review, Wilson retaliated: 'I didn't like the tunes in *Our Man Crichton*.[6] I was bored to tears.'[7] As for Bernard Levin: 'I didn't expect such virulence. He was filthily rude.'[8] Levin had complained of a first act 'relentlessly incomprehensible', remembering 'the dreadful screeching for top notes in which almost all of a very poor cast indulge' and 'the even worse acting', not forgetting 'the awful childishness of the book and the weakness of most (not all) of the lyrics'.[9] On a kinder note, the *Illustrated London News* suggested 'some of us feel that this awkward decade did the thing better itself'.[10] *Divorce Me, Darling!* was the last of Wilson's West End career.

*Four Thousand Brass Halfpennies* (Mermaid Theatre, 18 July 1965; in repertory) never established itself as a Mermaid favourite, probably reeling from its generally terrible reviews. Very much an in-house production, the adaptation of John Dryden's *Amphitryon* was by the theatre's creator Bernard Miles, whose version of Henry Fielding's *Rape Upon Rape* had found great success as *Lock Up Your Daughters*, establishing the Mermaid as a theatre from which vibrant British musicals might emerge. The husband of Miles's daughter Sally, Gerald Frow, had been sole writer for the 1960 Mermaid musical *Mr Burke M.P.*, and would go on to be part-devisor of another Mermaid hit, *Cowardy Custard*; now, he was credited

**6**  Sally Miles singing the Caduceus Song, with Ronald Cunliffe, and James Bolam as Mercury in *Four Thousand Brass Halfpennies*

as lyricist. During his tenure at the theatre, Bernard Miles's keen ambitions for the musical play had him hiring some interesting composers, among them Laurie Johnson, Nick Bicât, James Bernard and – for *Four Thousand Brass Halfpennies* – Kenny Graham. The obituaries of this idiosyncratic jazz composer of distinction seem to have overlooked his commission from Miles. Giraudoux had turned the legend of Amphitryon into the 1929 play *Amphitryon 38*, signalling Giraudoux's belief that this was the 38th time the legend had been retold. Some thought the English translation of Giraudoux's play heavy-handed; after sitting through the musical version, *Theatre World* remarked that if Giraudoux's version was heavy-handed, 'the treatment given the legend at Puddle Dock was heavy on all fours' when 'Most of the songs were hobbling and trite [...] Altogether the performances stirred memories of pierrot troupes and concert-parties long laid to rest.' Furthermore, not many of the songs 'were much help but this did not matter as there were no voices'.[11] The strong cast included James Bolam as Mercury, Freddie Jones as Jupiter, diminutive Denise Coffey as Phaedra, and Esmond Knight as Amphitryon. Brightly updated designs by Trewin Copplestone suggested the piece might have allegorical references to our own times, but the often savage reviews didn't seem to recognise them, noting that 'the singing is appalling and the acting a little better', with Graham's music denounced as 'suggestive of the sounds made by a rat in trying to extricate itself from a bedspring'. Unhelpfully but perhaps mercifully, the show was well hidden within the repertory season into which it had been slotted. Frow and Graham had little better luck with their earlier musical from Dumas, *Three Musketeers*, originally produced at Margate in 1962, and the next year in repertory at the Lyric Theatre, Hammersmith.

If Wilson's sequel distanced itself from the present by thirty years, ***Passion Flower Hotel*** (Prince of Wales Theatre, 24 August 1965; 148) suggested that its up-to-dateness was its reason for being. Here was the British musical that longed to swing along in tune with a London that would soon officially be known to be swinging. The permissive promise in Wolf Mankowitz's adaptation of Rosalind Erskine's novel was of a daringly modern musical about the sexual attitudes and hormonal ups and downs of modern-day adolescents, the girls of Bryant House ('finishing') School and the boys of Longcombe School. Here was a score from young British men of the moment: composer John Barry and lyricist Trevor Peacock, both debuting in musical theatre. 'The John Barry Sound' was already a thriving brand guaranteeing driving, strongly rhythmic pop music. With a book from Wolf Mankowitz, whose stated aim in the 1950s had been to establish a distinctive 'school' of British musicals, attention focused on the titillating aspects of Erskine's novel, in which posh girls open a brothel in the basement of their finishing school, and turn their gymnasium into a strip club. With the publicity suggesting that the show offered more than the Windmill's stationary nudes ever could, it was not surprising that young males, who often made up a substantial part of the audience, emerged bitterly disappointed. Too much of *Passion Flower Hotel* resembled one of those anodyne sex films that the British film industry had by now been reduced to churning out. On stage at the Prince of Wales, all people got was a lot of childish innuendo, the occasional glimpse of a suspender top, girls in hockey skirts, and a final curtain that came down with one of the girls looking to be 'finished'.

The stars were no more than youngsters, many of whom would go on to interesting careers. There wasn't a decent singer among them. The girls of Bryant School included Pauline Collins, Jane Birkin, Karin Fernald and Francesca Annis, while the boys ('excruciatingly bad' according to *Queen*[12]) of Longcombe included Nicky Henson, Bunny May, Jeremy Clyde and Bill Kenwright. Any characters over the age of 22 were consigned to the sidings. Directed by veteran William (Billy) Chappell, the only father figure among them, and choreographed by 22-year-old Peter Gordeno, the amalgam was a little odd, with Barry's throbbing score relenting now and again to make way for ballads: for Annis 'How Much of the Dream Comes True?', and for Fernald and Clyde the touching 'Something Different'. Only one number, the rackety 'What Does This Country Need Today?', made an attempt at social comment, a reminder of the more intelligent stuff Mankowitz had once been involved in, but ultimately *Passion Flower Hotel* had too many ineffectual songs.

*Queen* suggested that 'It should have been either witty or very rumbustious, and could have got away with either. For example, it might have sent up "adult hypocrisy" or "the public schools" but this is probably demanding too much from a book which is unredeemed by honest vulgarity, let alone wit.' Moreover, the show 'ignores everything we've learnt about what makes for a successful musical, from *West Side Story* on. The songs don't do anything to advance the plot, neither do they set a mood.'[13] Hugh Leonard for *Plays and Players* decided that 'There is much talent behind this show, but it has all the signs of having been cast in desperation, hacked asunder with insensitivity, and stuck together again on the morning of the opening night',[14] while Eric Shorter for the *Daily Telegraph* complained 'the story, though it chugs along brightly enough [...] ultimately has the demoralising effect of seeming to make sex dull'.[15] Many paying customers agreed, irritated by a show that had not been aimed at the age group it was supposedly representing. Rejecting its dishonesty, cheap-looking sets (surprising what you can do with plywood) that looked as if they'd been hammered together, and the appalling amplification, walkouts during performances were not uncommon. As *The Times* had warned, 'The lightness and sympathy which might have made all this acceptably funny seems to have been sacrificed for the sake of middle-aged sniggers.'[16]

By the mid 1960s Lionel Bart was the most prominent creator of British musicals, commercially if not critically unassailable. Not the least of his achievements was to have contributed to or solely written a string of shows that were in every way British: *Lock Up Your Daughters* (330 performances, and revivals), *Fings Ain't Wot They Used T'Be* (897 performances), *Oliver!* (2,618 performances, a Broadway run and an endless afterlife in revival), his World War II tribute *Blitz!* (568 performances), and his Liverpudlian tale of tarts and dockers *Maggie May* (501 performances). By 1965 there was the distinct suspicion that Bart was riding for a fall; if he'd enjoyed a long run of good luck, it was about time it ran out.

Decline and fall came with yet another truly British subject in **Twang!** (Shaftesbury Theatre, 20 December 1965; 43). Bart's standing was enough to win a contract with Brookfield Productions on the evidence of two songs (probably without so much as a verse) and a couple of lines suggesting some sort of a plot, but thereafter everything that could go wrong did. Discarding the idea of adapting Victor Hugo's *The Hunchback of Notre Dame*, Bart turned to Robin Hood. Now, Bart intended to remake Nottingham's hero as a cross between Errol Flynn and Bugs Bunny. He began collaborating with the American humourist Harvey Orkin, who had never worked in theatre; Orkin was one of the few that stayed the course, credited at the end of the endurance test as book writer. Joan Littlewood, who had directed *Fings* for Theatre Workshop at Stratford East, volunteered to direct the new show, her first excursion into West End commercial theatre. Discouragingly, Bart recalled that 'Joan doesn't think much of the things I've done that she didn't stage; she walked out at the intervals of *Blitz!* and *Oliver!* and thought *Maggie May* was a right load of old rubbish.' The production team included Paddy Stone, who had choreographed *Maggie May* and directed *Little Mary Sunshine* in London, the Establishment designer Oliver Messel (marking a clear break from Sean Kenny, who had been an essential component of Bart's earlier shows), and Kenneth Moule as musical director.

Dissension broke in from the start, with endless changes during Littlewood's chaotic rehearsals, the company playing cowboys and Indians in the morning, and performing ad-lib operas after lunch. The floodgates of chaos were wide open. Arguments between Stone and his dancers were commonplace, as were complaints about Messel's unworkable costumes, with chorines complaining that their garments were wrongly cut at the crotch, and too heavy. Littlewood told the cast to wear them inside out. Alfie Bass, cast as Will Scarlett, departed. Littlewood demanded the script be rewritten, and wrote a new one. Bart recognised little of his original in it. The inexperienced producer, John Bryan, who had never worked in musical theatre, asked for assistance from Bernard Delfont. Littlewood demanded that the entire company support her. Stone and his dancers didn't want to, but reluctantly agreed. At one time, three different versions of the show were being rehearsed: Bart's, Littlewood's and Stone's. Littlewood banned Bryan from rehearsals. Moule had a breakdown and was replaced as musical director by Gareth Davies.

On the first night at Manchester, James Booth's line 'Oh, we suffer for the cause, my God, we suffer' was answered by cat calls, and Barbara Windsor remonstrated

7   James Booth as Robin Hood in *Twang!*, the musical that brought down
Lionel Bart

with the audience. There was no curtain call. Anticipating disaster, the national press travelled to Manchester, and wrote damning reviews. Booth admitted that 'I do not intend to carry on in a part that is damaging to me.' Littlewood walked out again. Allowed back into the theatre, Bryan brought in Burt Shevelove as rescuing director-cum-show doctor. He told Delfont 'I can only promise I can make it less bad.' Furious at the actions of the men involved, Littlewood threatened to go back to face them 'and their pale pink egos'.

At last, Littlewood departed for good. Denis Norden was hired to write jokes that might pep up the script. An exhausted cast ploughed on through continuing rewrites and cuts. Scenting catastrophe, Delfont withdrew his support, but consented to the show opening at the Shaftesbury, itself a mixed blessing, with the theatre's reputation as a freshly dug grave for many of the musicals it took in. Delfont's producing partner Arthur Lewis said 'Do you know what it's like, bringing this show into London? It's like giving a crazy man £30,000 and having him flush the notes down the toilet one by one.' Even at the last post, the Shaftesbury premiere was postponed, but the critics were eventually let loose.

J. C. Trewin regretted that 'Mr Bart, I feel unhappily, has had only a rough idea of his piece. Though there had been advance stories of provincial chaos, we had hoped for a possible surprise in London. No Luck: it was a sad night [...] The thing indeed is as hollow as a dead tree, and its company's loyal professionalism cannot aid it.'[17] For Jeremy Kingston in *Punch* it was 'a witless and dull thing', but *Queen* 'found it not nearly as bad as all that. It isn't good [...] it's slow, woolly, disorganised, with an unclever book and music almost entirely lacking in the brassy vigour (albeit derivative) which we've had in the past from Bart. But it doesn't begin to compare in awfulness with *Charlie Girl* or *Passion Flower Hotel*, and in some ways it beats the Palladium.'[18]

Ignoring the advice of Noel Coward not to invest in his own work, Bart was spending £4,150 a week to keep the show on. 'I am educated by this production,' he said. 'The show was stabbed in the back from the beginning, but I cannot reveal who did it.' The closing notice was posted on 14 January 1966, a date that effectively marked the end of Bart's West End career as writer and composer. In his remaining years, he made the ill-advised decision to sell his *Oliver!* rights, and was reduced to something related to penury, although *Oliver!* has seldom since been off the stage. Back at the Shaftesbury, Shevelove's parting words to the company were pinned on the stage door message board: 'We all stood on tiptoe, for a long time, and nobody gave us a kiss. How sad. Love, Burt.'[19]

# 1966

*The Match Girls*
*On the Level*
*Strike a Light!*
*Jorrocks*
*Joey Joey*
*Man of Magic*

If good intentions were enough, the first decent British musical of the year would have taken the laurel. The previous year the British public had had to make do with a string of light-hearted nonsense: a sent-up Victorian melodrama, a not much appreciated soufflé recalling the 1930s (but not terribly relevant if you were a 1930s coal-miner or on the Jarrow March or living in a Peabody building), a sort of sex musical that never achieved more than half cock, and a show about Robin Hood that might have served if you couldn't get a ticket for the panto. Blessedly, the musical flops of 1966 were rather more interesting than the success of 1965, *Charlie Girl*, blithely casting off its awful reviews to survive into an ill-deserved long life, whereas *The Match Girls* (Globe Theatre, 1 March 1966; 119), hopeful as it may have been of commercial success, at least hadn't blatantly aimed at it.

The strike over conditions at the Bryant and May factory in 1888 had helped nudge Victorian Britain into an awareness of the industrial conditions in which vast numbers of employees worked. The white phosphorus used in the manufacture of matches could cause phossy jaw, an excruciating and corrosive disease that affected gums and teeth and could result in brain damage and, if untreated, death. With the support of the campaigning humanitarian Annie Besant, the girls at the Bow factory set up a committee and struck for better conditions and pay. Within a week, they had won many of their demands. Here, at last, was a theme through which the British musical might thrive in a youthfulness, vigour and invention; a musical that seemed to involve something resembling ideas.

The breakthrough wasn't achieved by West End managements or producers, but by the tiny Leatherhead Repertory Company in November 1965. Actor Bill Owen seemed a good enough choice as its librettist. Ten years before, he had written book and lyrics for *Caste*, from Tom Robertson's Victorian play, played Sam Gerridge and organised the choreography. His association with Robertson's socially conscious play was well matched by Owen's working relationship with the socialist Unity Theatre in King's Cross, outside which he would park his Rolls-Royce, and for which he wrote *The Match Girls* as a play, produced in 1947. It was obvious that Owen had the passion and sense of social justice that the writing of *The Match Girls* demanded. Ultimately, it was the jazz-affected music of Tony Russell, with whom Owen began collaboration in 1959, and the heavily choreographed direction of Gillian Lynne, that pointed a way forward. After some cast changes, with Gerard Hely taking over from Eric Flynn as the docker Joe, and replacing Anna Barry with Marion Grimaldi as Annie Besant – like Besant, Grimaldi had once been a member of the Fabian Society – the show moved to London.

Its star in all but name remained Vivienne Martin as the leader of the match girls, Kate, but the part was underwritten. Lynne's hugely energised production nevertheless provided a splendid opportunity to see some of the best of the female repertory company of musical actresses and dancers that British musicals could offer, among them Cheryl Kennedy, Julia Sutton and Judith Paris, with male dancers including Ray C. Davis, Neil Fitzwilliam and Jan Colet at the forefront of the item that stole the show, 'The Hopping Dance'. For Grimaldi, coming across as a pallid campaigner, there was little to do but rise to the occasion of a stirring aria 'I Long To See the Day', and nothing much to do for Hely except look brawny. Owen's libretto failed to explore character and situation, accentuated by the total lack of any stage conflict between the match girls and the factory owners. The struggle was depicted, but the cockney japes too often threatened to overtake the show's serious intent, and Martin was denied the chance of a sufficiently meaty number of her own, having to make do with the ineffective 'Comes a Time'.

'If this musical hasn't turned out to be an actually tiptop show,' wrote Jeremy Kingston, it was 'better than average' despite the 'generally banal' dialogue, with Russell's music 'intelligent if not, at least on first hearing, always tuneful'.[20] For Bernard Levin, ultimately 'there just isn't enough talent in it to carry it to success'.[21] The *Daily Sketch* curiously thought the score the best since *West Side Story* (what could it have been thinking?), *Queen* found Martin 'spunky, tender, wholly convincing',[22] but the *Illustrated London News* complained of a libretto that 'totters along on stilts [...] throughout, there is this friction between truth and falsity. Though Mr Owen's intentions are absolutely sincere, he has not fulfilled them in his book and lyrics.'[23] *The Match Girls* at least showed the dangers of attempting to fashion a jolly British musical from social misery. Another example was already on the way.

On the coat-tails of *Passion Flower Hotel*, a show directly aimed at 'swinging' London, **On the Level** (Saville Theatre, 19 April 1966; 118), may have been *about* the young, but were they turning up at the Saville after a day's shopping in Carnaby Street? Like *Passion Flower Hotel*, *On the Level* had the air and airs of being targeted at the middle-aged, or at least of being aware that its audience would be made up of such. *The Times* wasn't deceived by Ronald Millar's book and lyrics that seemed to offer a New Age musical hurtled along by high energy and vitality, supposedly reflecting what was going on when the audience, probably exhausted by three hours of *On the Level*, walked back into real life.

> The sight of middle-aged showmen sycophantically clambering on board the bandwagon of youth is one of the most contemptible the theatre at present has to offer [...] this musical tribute to the musical Martians in our midst sets a new standard for idiocy [...] The idea seems to be that in a show about youth, youth is all people want to see. Who cares about plot, character, melody or even variety of spectacle? Again and again, clad in shrunken trousers and hideous thigh-length sacks, the boys and girls rush on to stamp their way through Ron Grainer's deafening and undistinguished pop numbers.[24]

**8** Chorus boy Bobby Bannerman falsely arrested by Phyllida Law in a
publicity shot for the musical intended to beguile 1966's swinging London,
*On the Level*

Millar and his composer were the unlikely creators of *On the Level*, their previous work *Robert and Elizabeth* having proved their brilliance at recreating Victoriana with a modern twist from a clanking psychological and romantic drama *The Barretts of Wimpole Street*. London had taken to it, and its stars Keith Michell and June Bronhill as the poetic Robert Browning and Elizabeth Barrett. No such welcome awaited *On the Level*, loosely based on a French scandal of a few years earlier, when students in Marseilles got to see the answers before sitting their examinations. The high professionalism that had made such a success of *Robert and Elizabeth* was maintained, retaining Wendy Toye as director, Malcolm Pride as designer, and giving *Robert and Elizabeth*'s Henrietta, Angela Richards, her first female lead. For a time, *On the Level* also had a star name in Leslie Phillips, but he left after the Manchester try-out – a baptism of fire, with a first night that lasted three and a half hours – where his role was cut down (Phillips told the press it was 'a potted version of my original part'[25]). He was replaced by the less starry Barrie Ingham, and nearly an hour was cut from the show.

*Robert and Elizabeth* had been immeasurably helped by its stars, and the casting of distinguished straight actor John Clements, and subsequently barn-storming Donald Wolfit, as Elizabeth's creepy father; *On the Level* reached London with no stars, although for a moment it seemed as if it might be about to create one in Sheila White, for whom Millar and Grainer wrote the only song to achieve much of a presence outside the Saville, 'Bleep Bleep'. Elsewhere, the score was serviceable without being memorable or tuneful, although Richards' 'Strangely Attractive' was just that, and her appealing boyfriend played by Gary Bond hymned 'My Girl At the Dance'.

The critics were undecided. Peter Lewis detected 'Action, but no brains and no talent. The result is witless, tasteless, pointless, tuneless and will not do at all.'[26] Milton Shulman decreed that 'Not since *Salad Days* has such idiocy been served up in an English musical.'[27] Conversely, *Punch* applauded 'blindingly exciting numbers [set to] Ron Grainer's swirling, loud beat music. Some of the frenetic dancing continued long after I'd have thought it humanly possible for dancers to fling their bodies about [...] *On the Level* may turn out to define for the theatre the young pop London scene for 1966,'[28] a view endorsed by the *Illustrated London News* for whom 'this is a musical both ingenious and impetuous. It fizzes with energy'.[29] J. Roger Baker denounced 'the latest, and most cold-blooded attempt to cash in on the Cult of the Young [...] Grainer's music disappointed me greatly. The through-composed numbers in *Robert and Elizabeth* seemed to indicate that this country had at last got someone to take the musical seriously. But here we are, back to ternary form, and deadly with it.'[30]

The young shoppers of Carnaby Street didn't bother turning up at the Saville, suggesting that *On the Level* had all along really been nothing more than a more noisy than usual British musical written for the middle-aged. For many, Grainer's next London score, *Sing a Rude Song*, was another disappointment from a composer who clearly had better to give.

*The Match Girls* had barely clocked out before the next shift at Bryant and May took over in the second musical of the year – as if one hadn't been enough – about their plight. *The Match Girls* had relished its general gloom, with its opening number about the 'phossyjaw' that horribly disfigured and killed the workers. When *The Match Girls* kicked up its heels in the factory yard during a raffle or went off to dance in the Kent hop fields, they were alleviating the grim realities of their lives. The cockney banter, the knees-up, was no more than an emotional response to the unbearable, a veneer on everyday horrors. The attitude of the creators of *Strike a Light!* (Piccadilly Theatre, 5 July 1966; 30) was very different, although its authors probably only pointed out the difference because the rival set of match girls had beaten them into London. By golly, this set of match girls had a totally different attitude to their plight. They had made a musical of it, and were determined to be chirpy throughout.

Librettist Joyce Adcock and composer Gordon Caleb had been working on their show for six years, meanwhile collaborating on two musicals, *Hannibal's Highway* and the 1965 *Dearest Dracula* staged in Dublin.[31] Adcock was at pains to explain that at the time of the Bryant and May strike phossy-jaw was uncommon, and that '*Strike a Light!* is not a musical about misery, disease and squalor. It is a musical about courage, vitality and hope.'[32] If this was supposed to put a distance between the new show and its predecessor, it overlooked the fact that *The Match Girls* had been about those things too. Things were hardly helped by John Taylor contributing a few songs to a score that was forgotten as soon as the show was packed away.

The casting was more stellar than for *The Match Girls*. Jeannie Carson was now figurehead of the indomitable females, returning to London years after her triumphant performance in the quasi-British *Love from Judy*, after which she had left England to pursue a successful American career.[33] Fourteen years on, London seemed to have forgotten that here was one of the finest musical stars it would create. As the elder stateswoman of the show, Evelyn Laye proved no more successful at portraying the formidable Annie Besant than had Marion Grimaldi in *The Match Girls*. The allure of the theatrical grande dame was a little too much in evidence, but anything approaching characterisation was asking a bit much of Laye, and conveying intellectual thought on stage is a stretch for any actor. The whiffs of *Bitter-Sweet* that wafted on from the wings suggested little of the steely socialism of the Fabian Society. The inclusion of John Fraser, one of Britain's most handsome leading men, seems to have made little impression; his only, lonely musical. Attracting more interest was the feisty hands-on-hips Josephine Blake as a termagant of the match girl crew. A semblance of reality was welcomed in Disley Jones's industrial sets.

Making her first-night entrance, Laye was given an ovation of several minutes, but, ominously, a production of *An Ideal Husband* was already scheduled to move into the Piccadilly, a much less propitious home than the Globe that had housed *The Match Girls.* The notices for *Strike a Light!* were generally unenthusiastic. Terry Coleman in the *Guardian* complained 'How little is even attempted [...] it's enough to speak cockney and be facetious. Say "virgin" or "silly cow" or "oh, me bloody feet" and it brings the house down [...] The music is rowdy and mindless, like the stuff they use as background to not very good documentary films, and not one melody sticks in the head.'[34] Arguing that poverty was 'a singularly inappropriate subject for a conventional West End musical', Frank Marcus found Caleb's music 'pleasant' and David Scase's production achieved 'a nice flow', for 'within its limits, *Strike a Light!* was an honest, unpretentious and successful piece'.[35]

After opening night, its producer Alexander Bridge confessed that 'The result has been a shock. The critical notices produced only a handful of people at the box office. The first night was very exciting and enthusiastic, and we were all very confident. But the critics now have enormous power and the public reaction to their notices is very immediate.' *Strike a Light!* had 72 people on its payroll, and needed £5,000 a week at the box office to break even. For its last two weeks every member of cast was paid a generous £15. Something of a death blow to *both* match girl musicals was dealt by Milton Shulman who told readers that 'of the two I preferred *The Match Girls* and I didn't like that much. It, at least, seemed seriously involved with its theme. *Strike a Light!* merely uses this Victorian incident as an excuse for some trite sentiment and some mundane production numbers.' As for Laye, she 'would be much more at home at a flower show than in a picket line'.[36]

In retrospect, the next flop of the year shines beacon-like, beckoning us back to a type of production that we may now only hopelessly dream of, but by 1966 critical reaction to British musicals had established a reputation for disdain that would do much to accelerate their decline. *Jorrocks* (New Theatre, 22 September 1966; 181) was surely the finest British musical flop of the year; David Heneker considered it his best score. It was: cleverer, more stylish and witty than his greatest successes *Half a Sixpence* and the much inferior *Charlie Girl*, and vastly superior to the Heneker show that followed, *Phil the Fluter*. Its hero was John Jorrocks, the Falstaffian tea merchant who in 1845 takes up the Mastership of the Old Handley Cross Hunt, stirring up the locals, upsetting social divisions, but restoring the Hunt to its old glory, and earning his place in the Elysian fields. Those fields would of course be echoing to the sound of the chase, for fox-hunting was at the very centre of the R. S. Surtees books from which the show was made.

Presented in London by Donald Albery, whose production of *Oliver!* had closed two weeks earlier at the same theatre after 2,618 performances, *Jorrocks* inhabited much the same orchestral sound world, partly because of Albery's control over orchestra size. In fact, the new show was much grander than its predecessor, brighter and wittier. The verdict of *Plays and Players* was predominantly negative, claiming that Beverley Cross's book 'seems to subscribe to the belief that musicals are no more than out-of-season pantomimes in which plot development, character drawing and literate dialogue are not only intrusive but a positive burden to audiences'. Peter Roberts conceded that ultimately the show provided 'an undemanding and not too painful evening. But it is an anachronism in its techniques and presentation: a little more daring and the presumption of an audience with minimal intelligence might have made it worth seeing. The genre is dying, but not on its feet.'[37]

It had a more appealing central character than Fagin in Jorrocks, well cast in Joss Ackland. There seemed no reason, either, why Cross's adaptation and Heneker's music and lyrics, marred here and there by the sort of items that often blotted the composer's work (here they were 'We'd Imagined a Man' and 'Once He's In He'll Never Get Out'), should not stand comparison to Bart's. Compared to much of the stuff around in 1960, the score bristled with good things, from Belinda's skipping entrance song (Ackland wanted it cut) to 'Love Your Neighbour', 'A Little Bit Individual' and 'You Can Rely On Me'. No one could say that *Jorrocks* had no tunes, although none of them caught on outside the theatre. After *Jorrocks*, British musicals didn't get much cheerier, and if in doubt Jorrocks himself was front stage leading the company in rousing encomiums to hunting, describing 'The Hounds of John Jorrocks' or 'The Sport of Kings'. Even on earth, Jorrocks was now usually accompanied by what passed for a heavenly choir, ready to hail 'The Happiest Man Alive'. Happy was a word that springs to mind with *Jorrocks*, despite the show being about defenceless animals being ripped to pieces for the enjoyment of rich people on horseback. *Jorrocks* made much, too, of Surtees' comedy, with the brilliant Thelma Ruby as Jorrocks' long-suffering wife, and Paul Eddington as Captain Miserrimus Doleful, superbly duetted in 'I Well Recall the Day'.

The welcome for *Jorrocks* was considerable. *The Times* headed its review 'Irrepressible Jorrocks off to a spanking gallop':

> It's a big improvement on their previous musical *Half a Sixpence*. For one thing, it is tightly made. Mr Cross has not lost his way in the byways of Surtees (as Wolf Mankowitz did in *Pickwick*) but taken a firm plot following Jorrocks' rise from the tea trade to command of the Handley Cross hunt, and his triumph over his class enemies in that snob-ridden spa [...] The writing, in fact, never relapses into mere routine (a common fault of British musicals); and, apart from a couple of insipid romantic numbers, this is equally true of its music.[38]

For the *Sunday Times* it was 'an outstanding triumph',[39] for the *Evening News* 'one of the most endearing musicals you'll run to earth in a long day's hunting',[40] and the *Illustrated London News* forecast 'a long gallop ahead of it. It glows with warmth and enjoyment, and Val May's direction keeps it in period and avoids the usual musical-play routines.'[41] Alternatively, Philip Hope-Wallace summed it up as 'all just rather colourless and unambitious',[42] while the *Sunday Express* thought Heneker's music 'pleasant and even hummable, but the show lacks individuality'.[43] Its subject matter left the show open to vociferous reactions from pro- and anti-hunting parties, some of whom attended performances, and did little to help *Jorrocks* to a long life. The original cast recording – all that remains – is a joy.

If only the next of the year's shows had got into the recording studio! Ron Moody's *Joey Joey* (Saville Theatre, 11 October 1966; 23), a biomusical about the Regency clown Joseph Grimaldi, had been hanging around a long time. It had surfaced four years earlier as *Joey*, 'a pantomimic harlequinade', for a seven-week season at Bristol's Theatre Royal, with Moody and Jan Waters as Mr and Mrs Grimaldi. Did Moody ever read the notice in *Theatre World*, a generally kindly journal? It sounded a warning that he might have heeded. 'It is hard to believe that the dull creature we saw in the first act [...] would ever have survived the vociferous criticism of early nineteenth century audiences [...] weak and indecisive Grimaldi may have been, and something of a snob to boot, but he *must* have had, at some point in his career, the vital spark that made Ron Moody a star in *Oliver!*. That point was omitted here.' The blame was laid at Moody's door, for 'He attempted too much. One wished that someone could have advised him [...] to leave the playing of the title role to someone closer in temperament to the authentic clowning tradition.'[44]

Contemporaneous with Grimaldi, one of the towering figures of British Regency theatre was Edmund Kean, the subject of the American biomusical by Robert Wright and George Forrest, whose adaptations made up from the opuses of classical composers – *Song of Norway* from Grieg, *Gypsy Lady* from Victor Herbert, *Magdalena* from Villa-Lobos, *The Great Waltz* from Johann Strauss, *Kismet* from Borodin, and *Anya* from Rachmaninoff – have sometimes been underrated. Of their three original works, *The Love Doctor*[45] was a notable fiasco in London, and, despite great success on Broadway, their grandiloquent *Grand Hotel*, co-written with Maury Yeston, was a West End failure,[46] but the 1961 *Kean* was an almost monumental achievement. It had the advantage of an intelligent book by Peter Stone, incorporating material borrowed from Alexandre Dumas and Jean-Paul Sartre. As a musical biography of a long-dead actor, *Kean* was light years away from the timid *Joey Joey*. Moody should have been forced to sit through every one of *Kean*'s 92 Broadway performances in 1961. That would still, of course, not have prevented *Joey Joey* from flopping.

Considering the low level of intelligent content in the flood of biomusicals that crashed into London in later years – among them *Phil the Fluter, Thomas and the King, Winnie, King, Matador, Leonardo, Lautrec, Napoleon* – *Kean* was the rarest of the rare. Unlike *Joey Joey*, it had the advantage of a genuine Broadway star in the god-like Alfred Drake, to whom London had given obeisance in *Kismet* a decade earlier. Might *Kean* have done better in London? Wherever it happened, it was caviare to the general. Stone, Wright and Forrest explored their subject, set him in a perspective, presented a complexity. While Moody made do with looking morose in motley and sharing his misery with 'The Life That I Lead' (a sort of sub-Anthony Newley sob song), Drake grappled with a book that had Kean as deeply mentally troubled, sexually and artistically adrift, not knowing if he was man or shadow. How much better, he asked, things would have been had Shakespeare written him 'a role called Kean'. But everything about the American show shone, its sharp professionalism, brilliant orchestrations, questing libretto, drilled chorus only serving to show up Moody's more lacklustre assemblage. Not only all that, but Wright and Forrest came up with an original signature number for Kean, 'Sweet Danger', that was almost as good as any of the tunes they'd snatched from the classics. *Kean* dared much and failed; *Joey* dared nothing and failed anyway.

Moody's score was inoffensive and not lacking in a charm enhanced by Alfred Ralston's orchestrations, with two of Grimaldi's actual routines, *Typitywitchet* brought in as an opening number, and the rowdy *Hot Codlins*, with Moody manfully hoping to involve the audience in community singing as if they'd just sat down to the pierrots on Brighton sands. Two saving graces of the affair were designer Timothy O'Brien's evocation of Regency London, a bewitching background for Grimaldi's 'Run Across London', and Tazeena Firth's costumes, but in front of them the antique humour that may well have had Sadler's Wells' audience in stitches in 1819 met with stone-faced response over 150 years later. What hope, then, in resuscitating the spirit of the father of clowns, wound into a few words by his exemplary biographer Richard Findlater, describing how 'A great clown such as Grimaldi leads us into that kingdom of the imagination where all men are equal before the vast practical joke of creation. He asserts, in the face of death, the comedy of living [...] And he himself stands as a symbol of rebellion, a Lord of Misrule, the beloved enemy of law, and order, and mortality.'[47] Where was the vaguest hint of any of this in *Joey Joey*?

Moody's show opened in Manchester as *The Great Grimaldi*, where it was obvious it wasn't working. The possibility of bringing in Larry Gelbart to revamp the script had given way to hiring Keith Waterhouse and Willis Hall, but this last ditch attempt to rescue the project did little to improve things. Do what they could, nobody seemed able to locate a plot. There was nothing wrong with the casting, its main pleasure being Vivienne Martin, well-equipped with some attractive numbers. Surrounding her were principals rarely seen in musicals, including the ex-D'Oyly Carte comedian Peter Pratt as John Kemble, and two excellent drolls in the lugubrious Gordon Rollings as Grimaldi's Pantaloon, James Barnes, and chubby comic Joe Baker as Tom Ellar.

Renamed *Joey Joey*, the show was unhelpfully posted to that outpost of the theatrical empire, the Saville Theatre. The *Daily Telegraph* left it 'feeling that the spirit of Grimaldi had altogether evaded this earnest attempt at reincarnation', conceding that 'In a rather uninspired way book, lyrics and music all served their purpose',[48] while Philip Hope-Wallace grudgingly decided that 'on its own unambitious level the musical gets by in a raucous way'.[49] For *Plays and Players* 'Most of the book comes in the first half, and very tedious it is [...] in the second half things brighten up considerably'.[50] Finding Moody wanting, J. C. Trewin described 'an amiable period piece that has no sense of period and lives only on the energy and good nature of all concerned'.[51] In agreement, the *Evening News* thought it inevitable that 'the very thing that made [Grimaldi] unique [...] will almost certainly escape his impersonator. As a musical, *Joey Joey* is well below par, but the flavour of the past is captured by backcloths and side flats and with breathless knockabout.'[52] Indeed, the acrobatic harlequinades, performed by Johnny Hutch and his troupe with such delight, remained in the memory when all else faded. The producers Bernard Delfont and Arthur Lewis posted the closing notice on the first Saturday. The show on which Moody claimed to have worked for 17 years was over in just over two ill-attended weeks. His immediate response was to tell the press he was retiring from the stage, but by Christmas he was scaring children as Captain Hook in the traditional Scala Theatre's *Peter Pan*.

**9**   'Life is a game we are bound to play.' Grimaldi's words brought back to life in Ron Moody's disastrous *Joey Joey*

The closing moments of *Joey Joey* had Grimaldi and his son Joey, planned to follow in his father's footsteps, happily looking to a bright future as 'Father and Son'. The truth was different, and might have made for a better basis for the show. Grimaldi retired, a broken man. Joey had long been a burden to him, having to be supported through bouts of madness. An upturn in fortune saw him cast as Scaramouch in *Don Juan* at the Queen's Theatre, but Joey damaged himself falling through a stage trap (perhaps in just such a harlequinade as proved to be the chief joy of *Joey Joey*). Falling into delirium, Joey died shortly after his 30th birthday.

Grimaldi's lieutenants, too, faded from view. Faithful Jack (John) Bologna retired to Glasgow, taught dancing and blacked up as assistant to 'Anderson, the Wizard of the North'. Grimaldi's Harlequin, Tom Ellar, prematurely aged by physical exertion and mercury poisoning, hit hard times and was refused employment in the great theatres at which he had once played. Reduced to picking up 'a few halfpence by giving them a song or a dance, or a tune on my guitar', he eked out his career in such dives as the Standard in Shoreditch and a public house in Shadwell. William Makepeace Thackeray lamented seeing the old man at Bow Street after being charged with appearing at a penny theatre, dressed in tattered motley. A few days before his death in 1842, Ellar got himself a job at a respectable theatre, the Adelphi, but it was too late. Things went badly with James Barnes, too, crowned as 'the prince of pantaloons' in one of his obituaries. Charles Dibdin hailed Barnes's creation 'as completely original as Grimaldi's Clown'. Yet all these characters did when resurrected for *Joey Joey* was sing and dance, do some feeble jokes and stand around while Moody took centrestage.

Grimaldi's end was no happier. Steeped in melancholia, he died two weeks after his last appearance at Sadler's Wells. Never mind that *Figaro* wrote a scathing tribute, recalling his heavy drinking: 'we cannot make out how he is any more lost to us now than he has been for the last ten years [...] we cannot look upon his death as a national calamity'. There was about as much mourning for *Joey Joey*.

The Harry Houdini biomusical **Man of Magic** (Piccadilly Theatre, 16 November 1966; 135) had all the hallmarks of a Harold Fielding product. The handsomest, most mellifluous musical actor in London, the American Stuart Damon, was now promoted to leading man after good work as a secondary lead in Fielding's *Charlie Girl*. Essentially the lynchpin of the evening, Damon was a strong presence, and got some of the best moments of the score, not least 'Suddenly' and his roaring duet with his leading lady, 'When I Conquer the World'. The writers and producers of British musicals did with Damon what they usually did with first-class performers – ignored them. Just as veteran Anna Neagle had been drafted in to boost the appeal of *Charlie Girl*, veteran comic actor Stubby Kaye, his reputation long ago established through *Guys and Dolls*, was brought in as comedy relief. This accentuated one of *Man of Magic*'s several difficulties; the comedy was painfully unfunny. You could only sympathise with Kaye having to get through the abominable 'Kester's Crystal Cabbage' and 'Take Your Medicine' eight times a week. These numbers marked the lowest point of the score by Wilfred Josephs, masquerading here as Wilfred Wylam. This was regrettable, for much of the score suggested he could have written assuredly for musical theatre.

For Judith Bruce, cast as Houdini's wife, Bess, *Man of Magic* was the first major musical in which she created an original role, having taken over from Pat Kirkwood in *Wonderful Town,* Nancy in *Oliver!* (London and Broadway) and from Georgia Brown in *Maggie May.* She had also spent a disastrous time with Frankie Howerd as the love interest in *Mister Venus.* Now, as in the later *Tom Brown's Schooldays,* her numbers lacked distinction: the so-so 'The Man That Captures My Heart' leading on to two po-faced ballads, 'Like No Other Man' (in fact one of Josephs' most musical moments) and 'This He Knows'. The good news was that between them Damon, Bruce and Kaye made *Man of Magic* convincingly American, with Bruce displaying a voice that was continents away from the warblings of many a leading lady. Before London, the originally cast Joan Miller was replaced by Doris Hare in the role of Houdini's momma. It was perhaps unhelpful that director Peter Ebert, most experienced in opera, could not disguise the modesty of the enterprise, a small list of main characters and a small ensemble.

Moving to London after its Manchester try-out, the show had a top ticket price of 35 shillings, down to a bargain 8/6d in the Upper Circle. The 'musical fantasy suggested by incidents in the life of Harry Houdini' had book and lyrics by John Morley and Aubrey Cash. As actor, Morley had played in various British musicals including *Follow That Girl* and worked at the fringes of musical theatre for many years, writing for London Palladium pantomimes, for the foxy puppet Basil Brush, for the Players' Theatre, and collaborating with Sandy Wilson on an unproduced musical about Amy Johnson. Twelve years after *Man of Magic* he collaborated with Gyles Brandreth on a book, *The Magic of Houdini,* which claimed to reveal the tricks behind Houdini's illusions.[53] Less involved with musical theatre, Cash went on to write for the TV soap opera *Crossroads* and the screenplay of the British sex-film *Adventures of a Plumber's Mate.*

Much of the interest in *Man of Magic* centred on its recreation of Houdini's illusions, restaged by Timothy Dill-Russell, who switched with Damon just before Houdini was lowered into a tank for the famous Chinese Water Torture sequence. Puppetry reproduced Houdini's escapades at Brooklyn Bridge, and Bruce was strapped to a table to endure an oncoming buzz saw. Such diversions were undoubted highlights of the show, but didn't save it.

The critics were in agreement that after a promising beginning *Man of Magic* went off-song. Peter Lewis enjoyed the first half but 'After that, conviction goes out of the show. The music, interesting up till then, turns banal and one begins to feel one has been here rather too often.'[54] B. A. Young concurred: 'The first quarter of an hour put me in such a euphoric mood that I really believed we might be in for another *Oklahoma!* but then things began to go wrong: there were long patches of threadbare sentiment and unfunny humour [probably one of those appalling Stubby Kaye numbers] that let the show go off the boil.'[55] Felix Barker thought that the most mystifying trick of the night was 'the complete and bewildering disappearance of this bustling, colourful show into thin air [...] The hard-won success of the earlier part of the evening promptly evaporated before our very eyes in confusion, anti-climax and schmaltzy sentiment.'[56]

There was praise enough for the principals, for Damon 'who has a good rich singing voice, carries out the illusions and escapes plausibly [and] Judith Bruce is vivid and charming as Bess',[57] while B. A. Young saw 'a really splendid romantic hero in Stuart Damon – warm, handsome, lithe, with a pleasing baritone voice which he wields with a minimum of dependence on electrical chicanery. It has a delightful heroine in Judith Bruce. It has that most endearing of comics, Stubby Kaye.'[58] Fielding had picked his trio with care, but the general effect of *Man of Magic* failed, as it were, to pull a rabbit out of the hat, a trick that Houdini would have considered elementary.

# 1967–1969

**‘So wholesome, so naïve, so worthy that one feels rather like a villain in a Victorian melodrama for disliking it so much’**
*Evening Standard* on *High Diplomacy*

## 1967

*Queenie*
*Mrs Wilson's Diary*

In the 1960s, transatlantic collaboration in the writing of British musicals was rare. *Queenie* (Comedy Theatre, 22 June 1967; 20) was rarer still, the only British musical written in rhyming verse by perhaps the unlikeliest of poets, Ted Willis, best known as the creator of the long-running TV series *Dixon of Dock Green* ['Evenin' all.']. Purportedly inspired by Willis's 1948 play (and subsequent 1958 film about a working-class family's struggle, *No Trees in the Street*, *Queenie* bore some resemblance to a TV series Willis had created in 1964, *The Four Seasons of Rosie Carr*, a sort of family saga with Rosie starting off as barmaid. By 1967, Rosie had become Queenie Swann (Vivienne Martin), London publican of 'The Queen of Sheba' and widow, courted by a little collection of suitors, from which she finally selects ex-sailor barman James (Kevin Colson) as mate. After scrapping his first draft, Willis was encouraged to continue by impresario Arthur Lewis. Lewis was probably responsible for linking Willis up with two American musicians. Dick Manning's credits included writing the Perry Como hit 'Hot Diggity' and in 1944 composing the first musical to be performed in full on American television, *The Boys From Boise*. Marvin Laird was already known as a Broadway arranger from 1965, and would go on to later success as a composer with the off-Broadway *Ruthless!* in 1992. Meanwhile, Manning and Laird worked at setting Willis's lyrics, sent on tape from his home in Chislehurst.

Directed by Lewis and designed by the prolific Hutchinson Scott, Willis's piece first played at Guildford as *The Ballad of Queenie Swann*, before being presented in London by Lewis and Bernard Delfont. It was strongly cast, with Queenie's lovers played by Colson, Bill Owen, Simon Oates and Paul Eddington, Eddington taking many of the reviews as a punctilious undertaker (*Lady* thought him 'the most amusing thing in an unpretentious night'[1]), with attractive juveniles Cheryl Kennedy and Neil Fitzwilliam. Almost incidentally, *Queenie* was yet another half-hearted attempt to establish Vivienne Martin as a British musical star. Her progress had been interesting, from understudying and taking over from Dora Bryan in

Vivian Ellis and A. P. Herbert's *The Water Gipsies* twelve years earlier, through her takeover as Nancy in the original *Oliver!*, and leading roles in *The Match Girls* and *Joey Joey*. Martin had a resilience, an edge and quality that should have been better appreciated, as here in her three solos, 'I Can't Help Remembering', 'This Is the Meaning Of Love' and 'How Does He Look In the Morning?' One reviewer noted her budgerigar brightness, but too often her talents were undervalued.

Despite reservations, the critics were not unkind. Philip Hope-Wallace was 'kindly disposed towards it but found it in the end monotonous – telescoped, in a healing memory, into some two and a half hours of cockney yowling and fairly engaging high spirits'.[2] Under the headline 'Self Indulgent Musical Has Lots of Charm' *The Times* described the music as 'cosmopolitan and, though not annoy-ing, hardly memorable',[3] while the *Illustrated London News* considered that 'the "ballad" apart, this is a simple-hearted cockney musical piece'.[4] *Lady* decided that 'the ingenuity can defeat itself, because one loses the thread of a speech in waiting anxiously for the rhyme. But the entertainment [...] has a certain zest [and] the score keeps a rattling liveliness.' *Punch* had much fun rhyming its response: 'The rudest word throughout, I think, is "kiss", and all the dialogue's in verse like this.' There were twenty musical numbers, 'several of which are passable in parts and might, with plugging, get into the charts.'[5] Alas, the arrival of Queenie Swann into London, bright and appealing as it was, roused negligible interest. Being tucked away at the back of Leicester Square didn't help.

Based on the popular 'Mrs Wilson's Diary' entries in *Private Eye*, **Mrs Wilson's Diary** (Criterion Theatre, 24 October 1967; 175) was 'an affectionate lampoon' of Prime Minister Harold Wilson and his wife Mary, here called Gladys. Written by Richard Ingrams and John Wells, it had rudimentary music by Jeremy Taylor linking together a patchy evening of mild knockabout mockery with Bill Wallis's PM and Myfanwy Jenn particularly endearing as Mrs W. The staff at 10 Downing Street is faced with a threat of an American invasion after Harold has criticised the Vietnam War. It is a matter of priorities, and Harold prefers dressing as a boy scout, meeting with his guru, and planning to murder hard-drinking George Brown, from whom Gladys has to hide the Wincarnis, taking her attention from her obsession with Vim. More of a revue than a musical, there were moments of vague pungency, as when Peter Reeves as Gerald Kaufman sang 'What would they think, those socialists of yore / If they could see what they were fighting for?' With Theatre Worskhop 'nuts' Stephen Lewis, Bob Grant, Howard Goorney and Sandra Caron among its small cast, Joan Littlewood's production, originally seen at Strat-ford East, proved a popular draw, seizing the political moment. 'Why Should I Worry?' sang Harold cheerfully at the close of Act One, faintly but perhaps know-ingly recalling Laurence Olivier's 'Why Should I Care?' in *The Entertainer*.

# 1968

*The Dancing Years* (revival)
*Mr and Mrs*
*The Young Visiters*

It wasn't often that London managements looked over their shoulders to the
past years of the British musical; if they
did, all they seemed to catch a glimpse of
was *Oliver!* Returning to a musical is not
always a happy experience, particularly if
you happen to have written it. One wonders what Ivor Novello made of ABPC's
pathetic attempt at filming his *The Dancing Years* in 1950. He must at some point
have girded unwilling loins and crept into a darkened cinema to see what a dog's
dinner had been made of one of his greatest stage successes. The plot, or what
passed for one, had come to him when he'd seen Miliza Korjus in the 1939 movie
*The Great Waltz*. Blinking at daylight as he left the cinema, he had wondered
whether Roma Beaumont, an actress then touring in his *Crest of the Wave*, could
pass as a twelve-year-old girl called Grete. Since no absurdity was impossible
in a Novello show, of course she could. On *The Dancing Years*' opening night at
Drury Lane in 1939, Beaumont's singing and capering of 'Primrose' was one of the
numbers that stopped the show (it may be coincidental that, two years before, she
had played Primrose in a tour of *Primrose Time*).

The success of Novello's hit was interrupted by the outbreak of war, but the
company gathered its skirts and toured before returning to London in triumph,
reopening at the Adelphi in 1942 and running for 969 performances through
the close of the war. With its soaring Viennese-flavoured melodies, Mary Ellis as
Maria and its composer-creator as the struggling composer Rudi, *The Dancing
Years* was a perfectly appropriate diversion for war-distressed audiences. But what
of Novello, probably unsuccessfully disguised behind dark glasses and unshaved,
just having sat through the film version (come to that, why hadn't they asked him
to be in it?). What did he make of Dennis Price's Technicolor impersonation of
him, the ridiculously bad choreography, the characterless twitterings of its leading
lady Gisèle Préville? Perhaps he regretted that he'd never come up with a decent
plot. Would he have agreed with Leslie Halliwell's opinion that it was 'lamentable
[...] precisely the ingredients which worked so well on stage seem embarrassing
on film'?[6] London had last sat through the show at the Casino in 1947, with Barry
Sinclair another inadequate substitute for Novello, Jessica James as Maria, and
Nicolette Roeg as Grete.

Two decades on, Novello's legendary reputation had barely survived his death
in 1951, and a revival of *The Dancing Years* (Saville Theatre, 6 June 1968; 52) did
little to right the wrong. Novello would have known that his popularity had never
much dimmed in the provinces, but was now the moment to attempt a resurgence
of his operetta in London? The shoots of hope had been noted. John Hanson's
resuscitation of *The Desert Song* had taken everyone by surprise by becoming a
hit at the Palace. Now, across the road from the Saville at the Cambridge Theatre,
Hanson was back, lifting an obviously empty Old Heidelberg mug to *The Student*

**10** 'My dearest dear'. June Bronhill and a lederhosen-less David Knight recreating Novello's dancing years at the Saville Theatre in 1968

*Prince*, in a revival that would do a good deal better than the Novello revival at the Saville, and therefore escape attention in these pages.

The obvious ace in the pack of the Saville's production was its star, June Bronhill, an unarguable case of perfect casting. One of the very few singers at Sadler's Wells Opera to break through the public consciousness with her performances in Offenbach operettas and her bewitching 1958 Merry Widow, Bronhill had gone on to wider popularity with her affecting Elizabeth Barrett Browning in *Robert and Elizabeth*, after which British producers and writers hadn't a clue what to do with her. She would certainly have enthralled the audiences that Mary Ellis had originally thrilled at the Lane, but that was in 1939, and this was 1968, when the production values awarded the revival were unimpressive. There was, too, one major problem the management could not overcome: Novello was dead. This is the killing fact at the heart of anything that has since happened to his work. His very presence in his schmaltzy romances was the one essential component, the thing that, above all else, the customers had come to see; without him, the works seem hopelessly diminished. Now, it fell to the hapless David Knight to wear the mantle and (never wise) the lederhosen, and he did all that could be expected of actors put into such an impossible situation and obliged to expose their knees.

Audiences at the Saville didn't get such value for their money (a top price for tickets of 35 shillings; 8/6d. for the Upper Circle) as in Novello's time. Joan Davis's direction couldn't hide a prevailing tiredness. The *Guardian* complained of cramped scenery and an unsophisticated orchestra in a show of 'poor man's Lehár, a jog-trot round the merry widow country'.[7] *Punch* gazed at 'wobbling backdrops of vanished Vienna' and an 'idiotic story of thwarted love'.[8] Exempting Bronhill, the *Sunday Times* asked 'Why insult the public you aim to please? As tatty as a third-rate touring company at the end of its tether, this production is also painfully under-cast.'[9]

It was, too. Moyna Cope was no booming Olive Gilbert (it didn't matter that Miss Gilbert wasn't much of an actress; she was always in good company in a Novello show), and Cathy Jose had no chance of becoming another Roma Beaumont, never mind the gaping void where Novello had once bestrode the stage, almost defying audiences to snigger at his inventions. His original script had bravely brought the Nazis into the frame, throwing the shadow of an anti-Jew totalitarian regime across the proceedings, but this uncomfortable component had been forgotten at the Saville, freeing audiences to listen to Bronhill's ravishing vocals and stare at those knees. It left unexplained why such reminders of operetta's past should be treated so tawdrily. Another example, *The Maid of the Mountains*, was not too far off, its shuddering backcloths, papier-mâché mountains and job-lot costumes even then en route to Cambridge Circus.

Having bestowed his blessing on the creators of *Mr and Mrs* (Palace Theatre, 11 December 1968; 44) Noel Coward poured scorn on this adaptation from two of his plays, *Fumed Oak* and *Still Life* (better known in its film version as *Brief Encounter*). John Taylor's book, music and lyrics took rough hold of Coward's delicate originals, turned *Fumed Oak* into a curtain raiser 'Mr', and served up an updating of *Still Life* as main course 'Mrs', shackling them together and catapulting them, kicking, screaming, thumping and bawling, into the West End.

Promoted as 'A sparkling new musical for all seasons – the perfect family show' (odd, because the original plays had no such intention), *Mr and Mrs* opened with a top ticket price of £2. The casting was medium rare, its leading man John Neville (once alongside Richard Burton the great hope of British drama), its leading lady the patently non-singing Honor Blackman (James Bond's Pussy Galore and *The Avengers*' Cathy Gale). Third-billed was the Lancastrian comedienne Hylda Baker in her one London musical, bringing her unique grotesquerie and malapropisms (loathed by Coward) to the moaning mother-in-law in 'Mr', and the railway station buffet manageress in 'Mrs',[10] with dance-band singer Alan Breeze (of the BBC's *Billy Cotton Band Show*) as her amorous station porter giving a rumbustious performance despite his chronic off-stage stammer.

Taylor's work had featured in the Dora Bryan revue *Six of One*, in collaboration with David Heneker for *Charlie Girl* and as the composer of additional songs for *Strike a Light!*, but *Mr and Mrs* was his main London *oeuvre*. The damning reviews were expected after a shaky first night during which the audience applauded the line 'All this is going to be demolished tomorrow'. The drastic rearrangement of Coward's plays seems to have been the work of director Ross Taylor (credited with 'adaptation') or Taylor. Whoever was responsible, the musical turned two fragile playlets into one hulking, stomping Frankenstein monster of a show. Felix Barker thought it 'a terrible warning of how subtle and dangerous it is to puff things up. Sarcastic bursts of laughter punctuated scenes which should have been moving. This was not pleasant: yet one could not blame the audience for finding them [presumably the love duets for Neville and Blackman] over-sentimental'.[11] Preferring 'Mr' to 'Mrs', Philip Hope-Wallace disliked this treatment of Coward's love story, now with 'the addition of music, some of it very weary rinses of umpty-tum, some of it screaming pop of the feeblest kind [of which 'The Electric Circus' with its deafening disco insistence, was a prime example] managing to overlay the simple sentimentality'.[12]

The *Sunday Times* remarked Taylor's 'distrust of Mr Coward's slight but touching story' in a production 'swamped by its competing accessories, and even at times made ridiculous'.[13] Succinctly defining Taylor's dilemma, Michael Billington wrote that 'By juxtaposing amiably old-fashioned romantic numbers with modern "rock" he suggests that he is out to attract admirers of both John Hanson and *Hair*, but the result is a musical mish-mash'.[14] Neville and Blackman battled on after discouraging notices that reported 'only bigger voices could really carry the songs',[15] and that 'Mr Neville sang – how shall one say? – gallantly, perhaps. So, in her fashion, did Miss Blackman'.[16]

**11**   Nothing like a dog audition for getting some press coverage. Honor
Blackman and John Neville go walkies before the first night of *Mr and Mrs*.
Most inappropriately, Hylda Baker is in the background

There was never the suspicion that Taylor would be a driving force in the British musical, but the supreme brashness and vulgarity of *Mr and Mrs* demonstrated an extraordinary virility. Blown out of proportion, it exploited its source material as the excuse to fill one of London's largest houses with an exuberant disregard for taste, in some vain hope that 'the perfect family' it was supposed to have been written for would crowd into the theatre. Its main delights were the unashamedly confident orchestrations of Taylor's in-your-face songs and, above all, the gloriously inappropriate Baker, outrageously interpolating her ancient comedy routines into the muddled goings-on, and mangling Coward's dialogue to magnificent effect. The *coup de th*éâtre was Baker giving a masterclass in physical comedy by coming down a long flight of steps in ill-fitting high heels. It is quite possible that *Mr and Mrs* was, for whatever reasons, enormously enjoyable.

Compared to *Mr and Mrs*, **The Young Visiters** (Piccadilly Theatre, 23 December 1968; 63) was a masterclass in good taste and charm, and without doubt one of the most attractive British musicals of the 1960s. The turf would have said that its hurdles were comparable to the Grand National's Becher's Brook. For a start, the title was incorrectly spelt: shouldn't this be *The Young Visitors*? (No. Its original author wasn't so hot on spelling.) And opening two days before Christmas: so, this was obviously a show for *children*? A show for children who couldn't spell? And at the Piccadilly, whose ghostly doors had a reputation for welcoming in many a musical disaster before spitting them out without delay? Some of the major problems of the show were grammatical. No matter that trying to capture the spirit of Thackeray's *Vanity Fair* had meant sleepless nights for Julian Slade in 1962, or how Wildeblood and Greenwell struggled to reshape Ostrovsky's *Even a Wise Man Stumbles* in 1963; their problems were as nothing to those faced by Michael Ashton in adapting *The Young Visitors*.

Some of the blame lay with J. M. Barrie, without whom the novel by little Daisy Ashford would never have been published. Born into a colourfully unconventional middle-class family, Daisy became an author at the age of eight in 1889, reciting stories to her father who wrote them out in fair copy. At the end of World War I, a Mrs Devlin (the now married Daisy Ashford) lent her friend Margaret Mackenzie a twopenny notebook in which she had pencilled 'The Young Visiters, or Mr Salteena's Plan'. Forgotten for thirty years, its author thought the story had something about it, as did Mackenzie, who showed it to the writer Frank Swinnerton, who in turn interested the publisher Chatto and Windus. Ashford's novelette, complete with its unedited spellings and grammar, appeared in 1919, with a preface by Barrie, whom many suspected of having written it as a spoof. He hadn't. *The Young Visiters* was an immediate bestseller, the *Daily Mail* celebrating 'the book over which half London is laughing, the other half having to wait while more copies are being printed'. Ashford ended her writing career at the age of thirteen.

She was at the musical's first night, acknowledged by the audience at final curtain. It had risen on the explanatory number 'Daisy Ashford's Written a Book', with young Daisy informing the audience that she had written a book with a start and a middle and an end (Samuel Beckett it wasn't). At her back, Peter Rice's sets evoked pages from a Victorian child's storybook. The distinct atmosphere of Ashton's book and lyrics was perfectly matched by Ian Kellam's witty, agile and (as few of the critics appreciated) memorable score. (Just how *many* scores *are* memorable after one hearing? It's a constant complaint made by critics, certainly throughout the period covered in this book.) The skill throughout *The Young Visiters* is to lock the songs into a cohesive and precise naivety, a sort of preserved childishness, a sense of heightened innocence. It's there in song after song after the lights go down on young Daisy and the characters appear: the preposterously socially ambitious Alfred Salteena, and the apple of his eye, the 17-year-old Miss Ethel Monticue, a little minx eagerly hoping to catch a wealthy mate and scale the social ladder. We can only sympathise with Mr Salteena's wish to meet the 'Prettiest In the Face', or his keen vision of 'My Young Visiters and Me', while Ethel's ridiculously ardent arias seem exquisitely in line with her aching determination to get on.

The other, perhaps greater achievement, of Ashton and Kellam's terrific score, marred only by the interruption of faceless numbers by Richard Kerr and Joan Maitland (for goodness knows what reason), is to dramatise the moment, to make something real and human from such obviously juvenile material. It's this that distinguishes *The Young Visiters* from almost every other British musical. It's only because the show was lucky enough to get an original cast recording that we can still appreciate how Ashford and Kellam (Kellam especially) turn the last quarter of an hour of the score into something approaching the intense, as number after number builds to the glorious final curtain.

As it nears its end, *The Young Visiters* reaches a sublimity that very few other British musicals have attained. We travel through Ethel's tragic explanation that Mr Salteena has been in love with 'The Girl I Was', to Bessie Topp, one of Salteena's servants, admitting 'I'm Not Beautiful'. Ashton's lyric doesn't demand grandeur, but Kellam's music insists on it, and the settings work superbly. It gets better. Happy nuptial knots are tied in 'Better For Marrying You', and then the score spills out its heart with 'In Love With the Girl I See'. Is there a more effective curtain in British musicals of the 1960s? I don't know it. As if this all isn't enough, for the curtain call there's a return of young Daisy, celebrating the fact that her story, with its start and a middle and an end, is over and done. What better tellers could there have been than Alfred Marks's utterly respectable Mr Salteena, Jan Waters' beautifully characterised Ethel, and the support of Vivienne Ross and Anna Sharkey as below-stairs' soubrettes, Ross getting the best of the deal in one of the score's standouts 'First and Last Love', and her second act scene with Salteena.

For the *Daily Telegraph*, John Barber regretted that 'the fragrance fades in a large auditorium, which demands something more than funny spelling and a quaint child's-eye view of the polite Victorian world. Its paper-thin characters are left with far too much distance to go in its paper-boat plot [...] I do not doubt at all that this mild but perfectly professional little divertissement will give pleasure, but [...] it never generates theatrical excitement.'[17] Jeremy Kingston approved, only complaining that 'the production strives for bigness when intimacy would be more appropriate [...] The music is unmemorable but the lyrics are lively.'[18] For *The Times*, it was a 'jolly evening' but missed 'the full, almost frightening social impact of the book'[19], while J. C. Trewin, a great admirer of Ashford's novel, considered it 'In 1969 the richest of dodges, even if little could be so resolutely out of key with the current stage.'[20]

# 1969

*Two Cities*
*Ann Veronica*
*High Diplomacy*
*The Stiffkey Scandals of 1932*
*Phil the Fluter*

The starting pistol for the assault on Charles Dickens' novels had been sounded by Lionel Bart's *Oliver!* nine years earlier. Although not eclipsing the number of musicals inspired by J. M. Barrie, and the handful of musicals inspired by H. G. Wells (*Half a Sixpence, Ann Veronica* and the provincial *Mr Polly*), Dickens provided musical fodder from such works as *Great Expectations* (in more than one version, none of them for London) and *Nicholas Nickleby*. Not surprisingly, the darker novels, *Bleak House, Little Dorrit, Our Mutual Friend* and *Dombey and Son*, escaped musicalisation, with perhaps one exception, Dickens' fiction of the French Revolution, *A Tale of Two Cities*, from which *Two Cities* (Palace Theatre, 27 February 1969; 44) was fashioned. Reaching London at a cost of £110,00, with a top ticket price of 40 shillings, it had lost its co-star en route. Joy Nichols, cast as Madame Defarge, had been top-billed opposite its leading man on the pre-London posters. Anthony Dawes, playing Stryver, began every day wondering who or what had been replaced. Edward Woodward, the new Sydney Carton, had already starred in the Broadway *High Spirits* and was well known to British television audiences from the spy series *Callan*. Nichols was replaced by Nicolette Roeg, injecting much-needed grit into the proceedings with the nattiest number of the night, the 'Knitting Song'. For the young lovers, director Vivian Matalon chose the Australian Kevin Colson, late of *Queenie*, and Elizabeth Power.

The adaptation around which the songs were written was by Constance Cox. What she thought of it remains a mystery. Her name had been almost synonymous with BBC television versions of Dickens, and her name on the credits helped lend *Two Cities* a dash of gravitas. The gravitas vanished the moment the conductor picked up the baton. Reactions to the music of Jeff Wayne and the elementary lyrics of Jerry Wayne were generally less enthusiastic, wrapped as the evening was around the start of Dickens' book, as the chorus solemnly intoned 'The Best of Times', with the final curtain falling (in the nick of time to avoid decapitating its star) as Carton mounted the scaffold with his swan-song 'It's a Far, Far Better Thing'. As the lovers, Colson and Power had an effective duet 'Two Different People', while Woodward's standout ballad 'Only a Fool' was theatrically thrilling in the most obvious way. Meanwhile, attempts to inject humour by introducing Carton as an 'Independent Man' proved highly embarrassing. It got worse, with the full-throated Woodward having to extol the show's heroine as a 'Golden Haired Doll'. The set piece was inevitably the storming of the Bastille. As imagined by choreographer Jaime Rogers 'this bloody event comes out looking as if the French mobs tried to kick their way through the Bastille after taking a detour through Oklahoma'.[21]

Irving Wardle wrote: 'Not content with reviving authentically antique musicals,[22] the Palace has now turned to the modern facsimile trade [...] Apart from the speed of its scene changes, its style is strictly pre-1930; and it seems less an adaptation of Dickens than a musical extension of that long running melodrama *The Only Way*.'[23] The *Guardian* suggested that Dickens' novel 'deserves better than this rinse-through, with a big, beef-cake baritone, Sydney Carton, and a Madame Defarge in high heels and a ginger golliwog hair do',[24] as the *Illustrated London News* could 'hear the clock moving backwards with a resolute clang'.[25] John Barber in the *Daily Telegraph* thought it 'a valiant attempt to put the clock back to the days of *Lilac Time* and *The Vagabond King*. It should please theatre-goers of simpler tastes, especially those who have regretted recent American attempts to bring sense and realism into the popular musical theatre.'[26] Whatever its qualities, *Two Cities* generated little enthusiasm among theatregoers, and was summarily dismissed.

*Ann Veronica* (Cambridge Theatre, 17 April 1969; 44) endured the fate of many a British musical of the 1960s: an unsympathetic critical dismissal and the same number of performances as *Two Cities*, but in its way this was as splendid an effort to mount a lush production as the genre had seen during the decade. H. G. Wells' 1909 novel celebrated the faltering but irreversible emergence of the New Woman, emancipated enough to make up her own mind what to do with life. Following on the success of the musicalisation of *Kipps* into *Half a Sixpence*, and with H. G.'s son Frank Wells as co-writer of the book with Ronald Gow, the new Wells musical held promise. The score, music by Cyril Ornadel and lyrics by David Croft, made no concession to modern trends in musicals, and wasn't over-bothered with a genuine period feel (at a picnic, the chorus girls sang about 'getting laid'). Croft was already at work on another, unproduced, musical, *The Maker of Heavenly Trousers*, set in 1930s China, when production of *Ann Veronica* began. Ornadel and Croft had collaborated since 1948. Four years later some of their songs were included in the London revue *The Bells of St Martin's*,[27] and in 1956

**12** As the star of *Ann Veronica*, Mary Millar resists the charms of Mr Ramage (Arthur Lowe); she may be wondering why her name is billed way below that of its intended leading lady Dorothy Tutin

they collaborated on the Cicely Courtneidge vehicle *Star Maker*.[28] Ornadel's 1963 London success, *Pickwick*, owed much of its run to its star, Harry Secombe.

*Ann Veronica* started off with a genuine star of its own, a very considerable one from the legitimate stage, Dorothy Tutin, but, exposed to the demands of Ornadel's music, Tutin reconsidered after the opening night at Coventry's Belgrade Theatre, asking that one of her numbers, 'If I Should Lose You', be cut. Faced with the option of rethinking the score or replacing the star, the management decided she should go. To what extent Ornadel was instrumental in her removal is not made clear from his autobiography, but this was a mistake from which *Ann Veronica* never properly recovered. Tutin was replaced by her understudy, Mary Millar, a seasoned player but patently not in the same class as Tutin. Overnight, the leading lady's name fell from above the title to far below it.

Two very considerable assets remained: Arthur Lowe and Hy Hazell. Their names had been noticeable by their absence from the title page of the Coventry programme, but it was they who had from the beginning contributed the star performances. Hazell had by far the best of the material, including 'Maternity', despite more lyrical anachronisms, while Lowe at least had one of those drunk scenes of which he was a master. The score too often sounded pedestrian, with the heroine's arias inclining to the insipid – the exception being the frenzied 'Sweep Me Off My Feet' – despite an effective title song with its insistence that 'It's the end of an age'. Which, if you happened to be singing about *Ann Veronica*, it probably was. On the credit side, Peter Rice's attractive design, the superb orchestrations of Ornadel and Bobby Richards, a convincing Peter Reeves as Mr Capes, and the singing of Millar, which Tutin could never have matched, aimed for the best.

The reviews were far from encouraging. Laurence Dubie for the *Guardian* thought it lacked 'any theatrical surprise or excitement. There is no inner momentum to make it "work". The dated staging, with the chorus bouncing down to the front of the stage and adopting statuesque poses waiting for the applause ... does not help.'[29] *Lady* praised 'good passages; but the musical play is an artificial medium and the narrative stiffens',[30] a view confirmed by the *Illustrated London News*: 'Here and there a useful libretto, now and again pleasant music, but all, I fear, in a despairing cause.'[31] Recalling its disastrous first-night stage management, with resistant scenery and long stage waits, Herbert Kretzmer pronounced it 'heavy handed and humdrum'.[32] Michael Billington had moved on from noting 'a besetting ordinariness about Cyril Ornadel's music and David Croft's lyrics' to recording 'the noise during the simplest of scene changes, [suggesting that] the dockyard at Chatham was being busily dismantled'.[33] In London, takings at the box-office dwindled to £27 a day, and *Ann Veronica* retired with an estimated loss of £75,000. Croft and Ornadel never collaborated again. Remembering the show's closure, Ornadel wrote 'There is nothing so loud as the shattering sound of a flop musical – the agony of having to start all over again, the terrible personal knowledge that the music was just not good enough, the deep disappointment of personal failure. It was all too much for me. I became ill with pneumonia.'[34]

Moral Re-Armament's policy of sermonising around worldwide goodwill through musical theatre, following the successful run of *Annie* in 1967, continued with **High Diplomacy** (Westminster Theatre, 5 June 1969; 172), music once again by William L. Reed, now collaborating with George Fraser, *Annie's* librettist Alan Thornhill, and Hugh Steadman Williams. Now, the scene was set 'in and around the Peace Palace, where a top-level international conference is being held'.[35] According to the writers, that conference, presumably a vague parody of the United Nations, was attended by delegates who bore all the traditional, almost pantomimic, characteristics of their race, propped up at the table during open season for easy laughs from a British audience. The suited males make no progress on reaching an agreement about world peace until the appearance of a woman called Candida. She is clearly no relation to Shaw's *Candida* with her radical ideas about relationships between men and women, but owes something to early Christians' perception of salvation and purity. The name suggests the colour white, which the leading character of *High Diplomacy*, as played by the black Muriel Smith, was not. Here, Candida is a woman who turns up thirty minutes after a musical begins, an apparently 'ordinary' woman from 'the Precarious Isles', mistaken by the politicians for the delegate who will make the vital difference to the conference. Of course, she's no ordinary woman; being the Westminster Theatre, and being Moral Re-Armament, she manages to chat with God during a thunderstorm.

Peter Roberts in *The Times* realised that 'It would be pleasant to think that this musical's jaundiced evocation of the democratic processes of international debate could be so easily resolved, or that a musical could be sustained on such slender material.' The show 'did little to disprove the growing conviction that 1969 is not to be a vintage year for the musical'.[36] *Lady* sat through 'neither a good musical nor an effective sermon, though it has – most valuably – the voice and the relaxed presence of Muriel Smith'.[37] Milton Shulman's thumbs-down pronounced it 'all so wholesome, so naïve, so worthy that one feels rather like a villain in a Victorian melodrama for disliking it so much. Judged by any reasonable West End standards, *High Diplomacy* is almost embarrassingly bad.'[38]

The clumsy titles of many of its numbers confirm Shulman's dismissal; who was walking out of the Westminster Theatre humming the tunes of 'Give 'em What They Want – Tell 'em What To Do' or 'If I Don't Do It, Nobody Else Will'? It seemed extraordinary that at the end of the 1960s such cack-handed lyrics could still gambol, but Thornhill and Reed's success with *Annie* had persuaded them to continue along fustian lines. Smith, the one selling point of *High Diplomacy*, had once been the American star of *Carmen Jones*, who had established herself as a London favourite in Rodgers and Hammerstein's 'Katisha' roles as Bloody Mary in *South Pacific* and Lady Thiang in *The King and I*. Smith's political convictions made her the ideal match for the ideals that *High Diplomacy*'s creators advocated: she had turned down Samuel Goldwyn's offer to star in *Porgy and Bess* because she disagreed with its attitude to blacks. What on earth was *High Diplomacy* like when Smith was indisposed? Lagging behind her in *High Diplomacy* came Donald Scott, a takeover Captain von Trapp in both the Broadway and West End *The Sound of Music*, and Patricia Bredin, whose career had struggled after *Free as Air* twelve years earlier. Patrons were accorded the most courteous of welcomes by the polite front of house staff arriving for *High Diplomacy*, but there was always something of the Sunday school about the Westminster. The high moral standards demanded by the management did not always act to the theatre's advantage.

\*

*The Stiffkey Scandals of 1932* (Queen's Theatre, 12 June 1969; 12) promised something quite distinctive; a basically documentary treatment of the Rector of Stiffkey, Harold Davidson (even late for his defrocking at Norwich Cathedral), his downfall brought about by his questionable link with the 'working girls' of Soho. Five years earlier, its authors, David Wright (book) and David Wood (music and lyrics) had used this format for their groundbreaking revue about capital punishment, *Hang Down Your Head and Die*.[39] The circus setting of that show 'stands firmly and impressively as a creation in its own right, whether or not you may be drawn to the fact of capital punishment, for or against',[40] leading R. B. Marriott to declare *Hang Down Your Head and Die* the best new show in London. Prior to the Oxford staging, the Lord Chamberlain had blue-pencilled 45 minutes of the script, including scenes describing the execution of the American spy Ethel Rosenberg, 'male bestiality' (as the press described it), biblical references, and new lyrics written to the Victorian street ballad 'Sam Hall', the last words of a criminal on the scaffold. By the time *Hang Down Your Head* reached London, many of the

**13**   Loved by her supporting cast, idolised by millions, let down by her writers and apparently ignored by the British public, the great Betty Grable's only London musical, *Belle Starr*, was critically mauled. Even Walter Cartier as a prancing sheriff couldn't save her

excisions had been reinstated. In a class of its own, this revue was in some ways a natural theatrical cousin to the television series *That Was the Week That Was*, in its treatment of social issues. Public opinion (*Punch* suggested that the public was as keen on hanging as it was on cricket) was heard throughout the piece, in taped remarks specially recorded in London pubs. The achievement of *Hang Down Your Head* was acknowledged in the headline of Levin's review: 'Brilliant: These People Do Honour To The Theatre and To Themselves.'[41]

Could the same documentary-based approach work for *The Stiffkey Scandals of 1932*? The stranger-than-fiction saga of Davidson's hectic weekday life among London prostitutes, the pyjama parties at his quiet Norfolk rectory, the gutter press photographs (probably doctored) showing him with a naked woman, his lurid trial, and his final phase as a fairground freak, focused against his previous life as a music-hall act in scenes that skittered between Stiffkey Parish Church, Liverpool Street Station, Blackpool (where Davidson was exhibited along the Golden Mile as if he were a monstrous curiosity) and Skegness Amusement Park (where he met a biblical death at the paws of a lioness). Was Harold the last Christian to be thrown to the lions?

*Queen* remembered a musical with 'a nice sense of period, some good performances, notably that of Charles Lewsen as the luckless vicar, and some cutting things to say about our still very much alive predilection for self-righteous peeping tommery. Too cutting, perhaps, since apparently nobody wanted to see it.'[42] For the *Illustrated London News* 'The evening, in spite of a professionally swift production by Patrick Garland in projected settings, could not transcend the dull vulgarity of its material. At curtain fall, a voice from the gallery shouted "Rubbish". The verdict was inescapable, and the play has vanished.'[43] Not before a dream sequence when Davidson is found guilty by the ecclesiastics and opens a paper parcel he has been nursing all evening, taking from it a pair of dancing shoes and going into 'When My Dream Boat Comes Home'.

*Lady* sighed: 'Now that the musical about the Harold Davidson case has ended at the Queen's, I can merely regret that it was ever done.'[44] The *Guardian*'s Philip Hope-Wallace endured a 'long dreary evening' enlivened by the apotheosis of Davidson's death scene, 'but of drama otherwise there is not a scrap. The court hearing is interminable. The lyrics and the music are of a poverty which is really staggering.'[45] In the *Daily Telegraph* John Barber struggled 'to imagine a more bizarre entertainment'.[46]

A more hopeful note was sounded by the *Stage*, whose critic R. B. Marriott had been unimpressed by Annie Ross, Terri (Terese) Stevens and Lewsen, although 'The music makes one believe that David Wright might well do much better with a more inspiring script to drive him.' Ahead of the production, the *Stage* in an editorial note celebrated the fact that 'The tragi-comedy of the Revd Harold Davidson, the first Christian for ages to die in a lion's den, and maybe the last ever of the line, should provide material, touching, amusing, stark, fascinating, socially significant, to make an outstanding British musical. Now, perhaps others in the field of musicals will be attracted by subjects of equal interest and colour.'[47]

This hope was, like many of the Revd Harold Davidson, forlorn. The general reaction to the *Scandals* was in tune with the *Daily Telegraph*'s reaction when it was televised: 'One wonders in the end whether there was artistic justification for presenting a musical about so sad and peculiar a person.' Of course there had been, but for many the show went where musicals were not meant to go. In 1997, it resurfaced in a revised version at Norwich Playhouse as *The Prostitutes' Padre*, promising Jimmy Thompson, author and star of the 1959 flop *The Quiz Kid*, as the nimble rector, but Thompson abandoned the production before opening night. The Norwich production could hardly have been more dismal, but could not obliterate the suspicion that the rector's story might yet make a good musical.

A musical built around the rise and fall of the charity Kids Company, announced for the Donmar Warehouse in 2017 is, in its way, a remote descendant of the Harold Davidson musical, relying heavily on official documents of the period: the documentary musical lives again. Its most colourful character will no doubt be Camila Batmanghelidjh, whose name may yet be remembered in song. The show's title, *The Public Administration and Constitutional Affairs Committee Takes Oral Evidence on Whitehall's Relationship with Kids Company*, may not be catchy, but may take the British musical in yet another new direction.

Harold Fielding's disregard for the finer feelings of the British musical continued with one of the most dispiriting products of the period, ***Phil the Fluter*** (Palace Theatre, 13 November 1969; 123). Noting that the Palace had recently endured 'flop, flop, flop[48] and now was faced with *Phil the Fluter*, *Punch* denounced 'the book, oh the book, dim and careless [...] falls below even the low standard typical of life-story musicals. Idiotic love interest – the hero in an instant switching his love from one Fitzmaurice daughter to her sister – minimal career interest and padding that goes on and on. However memorably the three Percy French songs, a show with a storyline as faint as this compels boredom.'[49] The *Daily Telegraph* found a 'theatrical bran-tub into which every possible ingredient has been poured with minimal regard for logic or internal consistency [...] I shall always think of this as the show that threw in everything bar the kitchen sink.'[50]

For Milton Shulman, the Percy French biomusical was 'as close as one can get to a formula musical without actually hiring a computer to do the job [...] David Heneker's songs are relentlessly conventional but usually tuneful. The only response to the book by Beverley Cross and Donal Giltinan is ouch. The death rattle of jokes misfiring is one of the less happy aspects of the evening.'[51] In agreement, *Tatler* confirmed that 'the result of this mixture as before is a curiously witless, tactless, pointless entertainment redeemed only by some of the music of Percy French [...] and by the work of a superbly eccentric dancer called Fred Evans [...] I disliked *Phil the Fluter* intensely.'[52]

What was it about British musicals, at least *this* British musical, that inspired such strong reaction? Perhaps at the back of it was the feeling that the British musical might be in a better state than it was. What was the point of it? For decades it had stood, or crumbled, in the shadow of its American counterpart, despite occasional industrious attempts to establish a style, a voice, an attitude, a purpose, that might alter its course. Focusing on *Phil the Fluter*, the spotlight fixes on Fielding's assembly of the show as producer. He had already brought Rodgers and Hammerstein's *Cinderella*, Meredith Willson's *The Music Man* and Coward's transatlantic liner *Sail Away* to London before assembling new British musicals, starting with the 1963 Tommy Steele vehicle *Half a Sixpence*, the only one of Fielding's British musicals to cross the Atlantic. It marked the beginning of a long association with David Heneker, whose reputation as a composer was tied to kitchen-sink musicals of the 1950s. Fielding made sure that *Half a Sixpence*, written for pop-singer-turned-actor Tommy Steele, was bigger. It set Fielding thinking that building a pop singer into a West End musical might not be a bad idea; when the next Heneker show *Charlie Girl* came along it was Joe Brown, a friendly scruff-haired bovver boy with no bother. That time round it worked even better than it had in *Half a Sixpence*. There seemed no reason why the same trick shouldn't work again for *Phil the Fluter*, so the pleasing, fresh-faced Mark Wynter was signed to play French.

The Hit Parade element, presumably included to attract an audience under pensionable age, needed balance, a weighting of age and experience. It wasn't apparent in *Half a Sixpence*, but Hugh and Margaret Williams's not-much-praised script for *Charlie Girl* meant that Fielding had to find a British actress of advancing years who would bring in the older audience. The list of possibilities can't have been long, but Jessie Matthews seems not to have been on the short list. Anna Neagle, long held in affection by the British public, was the perfect choice, her elegant *Spring In Park Lane*-type of gracious dancing ideally suited to the job in hand. She might have been just as suitable for the elderly female star role in *Phil the Fluter*, but now Fielding signed another elderly star, Evelyn Laye.

With Wynter and Laye in place, all that *Phil the Fluter* needed was a comic in the wake of *Charlie Girl*'s Derek Nimmo. Stanley Baxter was one of the biggest names in British television, but musicals had never been his thing, and his presence became another destabilising element. In *Phil the Fluter* he discovered that a Harold Fielding musical (perhaps, any musical) wasn't his thing. The numbers Heneker handed him were ghastly. Heneker was already hampered with having to write a score for a show about Percy French; it seemed only polite to include some of French's compositions. Of course, audiences knew French's songs before walking into the theatre, and couldn't remember Heneker's when they walked out. Heneker was on a losing wicket.

*Phil the Fluter* originated with a radio play by Donal Giltinan that was successfully transformed into a musical, *The Golden Years*, that ran successfully in Ireland. Fielding hired Heneker and Beverley Cross (the team behind *Half a Sixpence* and *Jorrocks*) to turn *The Golden Years* into a London spectacular, with Wallace Douglas directing as he had for *Charlie Girl*, but the disparate elements didn't appeal. Baxter and Wynter's material was well below par, with the ever-theatrical Laye getting the standout number of the night in 'They Don't Make Them Like That Any More', perfectly summing up her special place in British theatre. Heneker thought 'How Would You Like Me?' a good enough number to reuse later in *Peg*. Throughout, Cross's attempt to build a plot around French's life was complicated without any danger of becoming interesting.

At the end of the 1960s the reputation of the British musical was at one of the lowest points in its history. The decade had seen the fade of Sandy Wilson, with his last West End offering of *Divorce Me, Darling!*, and the total eclipse of the plein-air musical in Slade and Reynolds's *Wildest Dreams*. *Twang!* had served Bart a fatal blow. David Heneker's impact in the 1950s as a composer of works with some claim to social significance had successfully ridden a career throughout the 1960s, but his tide turned with *Phil the Fluter*, after which he moved on to less ostentatious projects. Monty Norman, successfully linked with Heneker through the 1950s, had run into muddier waters in the early 1960s with the much-maligned *Belle* but remained nailed to the mast of working on musicals that attempted to move the British musical forward. His integrity was poorly rewarded.

# 1970–1972

'It is both tedious and saddening to watch that high-minded headmaster Dr Arnold making up to a cabaret-voiced matron'
*Sunday Telegraph* on *Tom Brown's Schooldays*

## 1970

*'Erb*
*Mandrake*
*Sing a Rude Song*
*Lie Down, I Think I Love You*
*Isabel's a Jezebel*

The new year marked a real shift in British musical flops, slightly more encouraging to anyone who wanted to see them progress than to those who had money invested in them. Along the way there was a lot of rather dreadful rudeness that would have seemed unthinkable to creators of musical theatre even five years before.

The 1960s had seen a few shows vaguely connected to Trade Unionism: *The Match Girls* and its successor Bryant and May *Strike a Light!*, and the 1967 Moral Re-Armament *Annie*, a surprise long-runner at the Westminster Theatre. *'Erb* (Strand Theatre, 7 April 1970; 38) was another attempt to interest audiences in social issues. Ronald Harwood, who would turn J. B. Priestley's *The Good Companions* into a rather dull musical four years later, acquired the rights to William Pett Ridge's 1903 novel. Harwood suggested that Trevor Peacock should write its music, book and lyrics. He seemed the perfect choice. Although Peacock had written the lyrics for *Passion Flower Hotel*, he couldn't read or write music; it was up to arranger Gareth Davies to turn Peacock's tunes into a score for the show's debut at Manchester University Theatre in 1969.

Ridge's 'Erb, properly Herbert Barnes, is a richly Dickensian character, Bermondsey-born. Cockney socialist hero, Labour Party enthusiast, park orator and humanist, he is a parcel carman on the railway, earning 23 shillings and 6d a week, and reading John Stuart Mill for light relief. Ridge, a prolific novelist in the line of Dickens, was himself a humanitarian, having established the Hoxton Babies Home in 1907. Like 'Erb, Ridge's ideal was to see the world 'better and brighter', in line with the Bryant and May girls, Pickwick and Annie Jaeger. So it was that 'Erb created the first trade union for van drivers.

*'Erb* was well received at Manchester, with Braham Murray directing his first musical. The show was taken up by producer Michael Pilbrow's offer of a London transfer, but by the time it opened in London it had survived many changes.

**14**   The answer was almost certainly 'No'

Murray had resisted Pilbrow's insistence that the actress Deborah Grant, playing 'Erb's girlfriend, be replaced by a better singer. The small band that had played in Manchester grew to a sizeable pit orchestra, albeit playing in shirt sleeves. Murray regretted that 'What had seemed a fresh, original show in Manchester was to London just another Cockney knees-up musical'.[1] On opening night, the critic Felix Barker arrived ten minutes late and slept until the interval.

'As a musical, the narrative reaches the theatre with an exhilarating direct-ness and simplicity,' wrote J. C. Trewin,[2] but for John Barber it was 'sad to see Mr Peacock's talent so elaborately and emptily over-extended'.[3] Philip Hope-Wallace found it 'clean, friendly in a rather flaccid and even childish way, and now and again picks up a little jollity with a whiff of the old turn of the century Music Hall'. As for Peacock's impersonation of 'Erb, it was 'open and sincere and won respect in a dogged way, but hardly enough, I would think, to carry this innocent and plucky example of the English folk musical to a long success'.[4]

Critics had a rich time of it with the hapless *Mandrake* (Criterion Theatre, 16 April 1970; 12). John Barber considered it 'unsure of its own style. To disguise a formula that the authors seem to feel is outdated, the text is bespattered with off-colour jokes and the dialogue riddled with permissive gags about pregnancy, chastity belts and so on, and a startling collection of four-letter words.'[5] 'Nobody alive now dare ask for good taste' wrote Philip Hope-Wallace, 'but this ...'.[6] Most prospective customers needed only to read the review headlines: the *Daily Mail*'s 'A Show for the Crude and the Tone Deaf', or the *Daily Telegraph*'s 'More Impudence Than Wit in Musical', while the verdict on the songs was not encouraging – 'tinkling and not memorable' (*Punch*), 'indifferent' (*Daily Telegraph*), 'tiddly' (*Evening Stan-dard*); numbers that 'mimic every style imaginable and are ghastly' (*Daily Mail*). There was a song about urination, a love song for Sarah Atkinson that ended with 'fuck' and such lyrics as 'I hope I can cope / With my urge to grope'.

Originally directed by Val May for the Bristol Old Vic in 1969, *Mandrake* was redirected for London by Edward Carrick, and publicised as 'a bawdy new musical'; a bastard crossbreed of the 1969 *Canterbury Tales*, for which Chaucer's sauciest passages had been plundered for such richly *double-entendre* numbers as Nicky Henson's 'I Have a Noble Cock', and every supposedly fashionable, and sometimes naked, musical since *Hair*. Based on Machiavelli's 1520 play *Mandragola*, *Man-drake* had book and lyrics by Michael Alfreds and music by the esteemed musical director Anthony Bowles. In sixteenth-century Florence, Callimaco (Paul Shelley) lusts after Lucrezia (Sarah Atkinson), drugging her with mandrake, which will encourage her love-making, with the extra advantage of making her want to kill the first man she has sex with. Perhaps not surprising for a score by a man who had spent most of his professional life conducting other people's, Bowles seems to have assimilated all sorts of influences. When the show was revived for off-Broadway in 1984, a kindly review in the *New York Times* considered it 'the kind of musical that

Cole Porter might have written had he survived into the age when actors could casually toss around four-letter words'. Indeed, one of the numbers, 'She Never Knew What Hit Her', was reminiscent of Porter's 'Let's Do It', while 'The Waters of the Spa' recalled the style of Sondheim's 'A Weekend in the Country' from *A Little Night Music*, which had opened in New York in 1973.

Roy Kinnear as Ligurio and Margaret Burton as Sostrata were the stars of the London production. It was another disappointment for Burton, the original (but replaced for the West End) leading lady of *Twenty Minutes South* and, again for the Players' Theatre, the Portia of *The Three Caskets*, although she had got an astonishingly long run out of the Moral Re-Armament's *Annie*. Irving Wardle saw her Sostrata as a Florentine Hylda Baker; Philip Hope-Wallace remembered how Burton 'swooped about as a mischievous matron, in the manner of an inferior Hermione Baddeley'.[7] Other attempts at musicalising Machiavelli's play include the 1974 Washington production *The Mandrake*, a Canadian radio version titled *Mandragola*, another adaptation that played off-Broadway in 1976, and the American Folk Theater's 1987 version *Whores of Heaven*. With the distance of time and the persistence with which composers of musical theatre have pursued its original source, *Mandrake* sounds intriguing enough to warrant a revival, which it may yet get, with the tut-tutting at allusions to sex toys of 1970 forgotten, but *Mandrake* was no sooner planted in Piccadilly Circus than it was uprooted.

Rudeness was in the air. ***Sing a Rude Song*** (Garrick Theatre, 26 May 1970; 71) was yet another show that sat unhappily in the 1970s, when it seemed better suited to either of the previous two decades, although even then it would have benefited from different writers. What was it about Ned Sherrin and Caryl Brahms's musicals that denied popularity? Too much cleverness? And did Alan Bennett's name on the credits of a musical about the most famous music-hall artist of all time merely compound the feeling that a considerable collection of intelligence had resulted in a musical that didn't work? Brahms and Sherrin had long been industriously working at the coalface, in 1962 having perhaps their most substantial success with the retelling of the Cinderella story by four black performers using traditional music, *Cindy-Ella*. That work had a charm that none of their subsequent pieces sustained, and none achieved much success. Adapted by Brahms and Sherrin from the Brahms–S. J. Simon novel, *No Bed for Bacon* with a score by Malcolm Williamson had a run at Bristol Old Vic in 1959 before being briefly revived in 1963. Anthony Bowles had provided music for the Brahms–Sherrin musical *Shut Up and Sing*, the tale of two rival gangs, performed by RADA students in 1960. This seemed to mark unusual territory for Brahms and Sherrin, being a story 'of resilient cockney youth … These kids take their fun where they find it … in consciously aping all that is worst in the seamier side of American life.'[8] Their 'concept and lyrics' for *Liberty Ranch!*, an adaptation of Goldsmith's *She Stoops To Conquer*, was produced at Greenwich in 1972, and four years later

**15** The spirit of a little-bit-of-what-you-fancy-does-you-good somehow evaded Ron Grainer's score for the Marie Lloyd biomusical *Sing a Rude Song*, despite the presence of the chirpy Barbara Windsor, facing up to Denis Quilley

a Dickens musical seen at Stratford East, *Nickleby and Me*, had music by Ron Grainer, the composer for *Sing a Rude Song*. Another show, *The Mitford Girls*, reached London in 1981.

*Sing a Rude Song* had its beginning nine years earlier as a Ted Willis project for 'a sort of biographical Black and White Minstrel Show, without the Black and White'.[9] At the Ivy restaurant, the writers consulted the aged Clarice Mayne, once a great music-hall performer, who had known Marie Lloyd and offered them an impression of her. They interviewed Ada Reeve at 'The Hoop' in Notting Hill Gate. Two years on, the project had changed into a show in which Cleo Laine would play Marie. A year later, Brahms and Sherrin took the idea to Joan Littlewood, who listened to the songs and went away, after insisting that she wanted Barbara Windsor as Marie. The impresario Peter Bridge expressed interest but alarm at its commercial prospects. The name of Georgia Brown was mentioned as the ideal reincarnation, but Marie's daughter, the unstarry Marie Lloyd Junior, preferred Petula Clark. A blowback from Stratford East came when it announced *The Marie Lloyd Story*, written by Daniel Farson, with a score made up from new songs and some of Lloyd's original numbers. Denied the sumptuousness heaped on *Sing a Rude Song* by its directors, Sherrin and Robin Phillips, the Farson–Littlewood version nevertheless had the advantage of vastly superior songs that sprang directly from their subject and her period, and an appropriately rough-hewn star in Avis Bunnage. At the Garrick, audiences had Barbara Windsor, already experienced in musicals via *Love from Judy*, *Fings Ain't Wot They Used T'Be*, *Twang!* and the Danny La Rue cross-dressing *Come Spy With Me*.

Windsor's suitability was questioned by some, John Barber deciding that 'Miss Windsor is a limited actress',[10] and the *Sunday Express* complaining that 'As talented as Barbara Windsor is, her particular pint-sized magnetism [...] is hardly sufficient for a successful impersonation of the Queen of the Music Halls.'[11] The piece itself failed to generate much enthusiasm. Peter Lewis for the *Daily Mail* wrote that 'In its broad way, it is cheerful undemanding entertainment. But hardly a worthy biography of a star.'[12] Barber was unmoved, because 'Little is made of this rich material except for a lachrymose scene of parting, or a self-pitying bout of drinking. The emotions are not engaged.'[13] The last of Grainer's London scores, following *Robert and Elizabeth* and *On the Level*, pleased the *Evening Standard*, being 'full of gay, lilting, tuneful melodies that achieve the unique feat of sounding reasonably modern without clashing with the period'.[14] Michael Billington suggested that 'the final effect is one of a slightly dissipated and unfocused exuberance'.[15]

In her autobiography, Windsor blamed the collapse of the show on the fact that the West End transfer was delayed three months after its Greenwich opening, and 'the tide had changed in British theatre, as it does from time to time, and we'd been left stranded'.[16] The reasons for its demise may have been more complex. The casting of Bee Gees pop-singer Maurice Gibb as one of Lloyd's husbands was ill-advised, and as another of her husbands the excellent Denis Quilley was ill-served. Compared to the way in which Lloyd's songs had miraculously survived in popular culture ('Don't Dilly-Dally' and 'A Bit of a Ruin That Cromwell Knocked About a Bit' and 'Oh, Mr Porter!'), the numbers in *Sing a Rude Song* didn't cut the mustard, and were immediately forgotten, while Avis Bunnage roused the Stratford East audience into joining in with old favourites that had never been forgotten on a sweet Saturday night at the Rose and Crown. With the distant soundings from the failures of other British biomusicals, notably *Joey Joey*, came the reminder that recreating long-dead stars of Britain's theatrical past was seldom a ticket to West End success.

Goodness knows how or why the sole work of the 22-year-old Ceredig Davies, *Lie Down, I Think I Love You* (Strand Theatre, 14 October 1970; 13), got into mainstream London. In the £60,000 production, originally involving the writer John Gorrie whose name vanished before opening night, the average age of the cast was 22, too. In the streets of London, student protest was in the air, so perhaps it was inevitable that someone would add airs to such youthful uprisings. Davies's plot had a group of students planning to put a bomb on top of Broadcasting House, with Ray Brooks as the students' gay landlord. Nude scenes, filmed in the grounds of a Stowe public school, were projected on stage; the school subsequently regretted giving permission. For Michael Billington, the show couldn't conceal the fact that 'what we're really seeing is an updated version of the Gang Show minus Ralph Reader's peculiar logistics'. The catchpenny attempt to write an anti-establishment musical that filled the stage with students was quickly done with. As Billington reported, 'That perennially ailing patient, the British musical, last night suffered a mild relapse [...] Admittedly the body showed spasmodic signs of life throughout the evening but there was no evidence of any activity whatsoever above the neck.'[17]

At least there *were* stirrings within the British musical. Five years after the confusing frivolities of *Twang!*, it looked as if writers and producers were moving on, if not always in the right direction. There was no way that a young audience was going to be pulled into a show about Marie Lloyd, something so artificially created that it bore no resemblance to life as lived at the beginning of the 1970s. For that matter, it had borne precious little resemblance to life as lived by Marie Lloyd in the 1870s; in its way, *Sing a Rude Song* had been just another musical for the middle-aged, middle-of-the-road clientele that went to the theatre for an unthreatening night out. At least *Lie Down, I Think I Love You* was an expression of something youthful. It reached out. Youthfulness was at the back of two of the hits running in London in 1970, the 'nude' revue *Oh! Calcutta!* and Galt Mac-Dermot's *Hair*. MacDermot's latest show, 'a new musical fable' entitled *Isabel's a Jezebel* (Duchess Theatre, 15 December 1970; 61), was more modest but no less daring. William Dumaresq's libretto, based on a Grimm fairy story, gave Isabel a sea-living lover, with whom she spent most of the evening either having sex or discussing the problems of having children, abortion and baby-killing, conveyed in tryingly repetitive dialogue. Dumaresq went on to collaborate again with Mac-Dermot in the Broadway-only *The Human Comedy*, whose laughter stopped after 16 performances.

During previews for *Isabel's a Jezebel*, audiences were known to grow restive. There was heckling, with cries of 'Get it off the stage', and walkouts. Two days before opening night the leading lady quit, to be replaced by her understudy. One of the players V-signed the discontented audience as the curtain fell. The first night was postponed for last-minute adjustments and cuts, but by the time the show opened there were still 39 numbers to face. The critics in general were in a more sympathetic mood than some of the paying customers. The *Sunday Telegraph* thought much of it 'achingly memorable, distinguished by Mr. MacDermot's throbbing music and the very fine visceral singing of Maria Popkiewicz'.[18] Philip Hope-Wallace praised its 'flair and vigour. It belongs to your grubby and yowling school of *Hair* [...] rather than the indecent, unfunny school of *Calcutta*.'[19] For Michael Billington, the book was 'unmitigated drivel [...] like a millstone around the neck of Mr MacDermot's often highly inventive score',[20] a view encored by John Barber's appreciation of 'a composer so strong, both harmonically and rhythmically, that he could set a catalogue to music – and here he has done so. His use of counterpoint, of background choruses and recitative passages keeps the air tingling and the limping show on its feet.'[21]

# 1971

*Maybe That's Your Problem*
*Romance!*
*Ambassador*
*His Monkey Wife*

The Roundhouse was at once the right and wrong place for Raspberry Enterprises' production of *Maybe That's Your Problem* (Roundhouse, 10 June 1971; 18). The West End proper wasn't ready for a show about premature ejaculation, but the 'alternative' reputation of the reformed railway engine shed in Chalk Farm was probably the best option, despite its size that dwarfed the relative modesty of *Maybe That's Your Problem*. The book told of hero Marvin (Douglas Lambert), cursed with 'an impatient groin'. No wonder his cockney girlfriend sends him to a psychiatrist, from whose couch emanated a series of flashbacks, including a nightmare sequence about sexual perversion and permissiveness, a ballet about the deadly sins, a Womens' Lib meeting, gay issues and a Passover scene. There was no shortage of Jewish humour in Don Black's lyrics, some of which may or may not have helped explain the hero's penile dysfunctioning. An Anglo-American collaboration, the show seemed to many more off-Broadway than out-of-the-West-End, with its book by Lionel Chetwynd and its music by Walter Scharf.

John Barber reported that it 'provided only tame and soft-centred entertainment' with Scharf's music 'competent without being memorable. The book and lyrics [...] veer uncomfortably between sophistication and slush.'[22] For the *Guardian*, Caryl Brahms praised John Cameron's stunning orchestrations, but 'there is something going from oasis to oasis in this crass, wayward but often oddly jolly, permissive entertainment',[23] while Michael Billington thought that 'all one can do is lament that an often lively and tuneful score by Walter Scharf has been tethered to a book of such mind-blowing witlessness'.[24] The fact that no director was credited in the programme hadn't helped. Nevertheless, some sort of immortality was achieved when Roy Castle and Dilys Watling recorded some numbers, as did *Maybe*'s leading lady Andee Silver.

Whatever its deficiencies, at least the writers had tried to twitch the British musical into new life. The theatre programme showed a cartoon of a nude male, a scattering of musical notes covering the area from which his problem emanated. Could this be the Great Britain over which Edward Heath and his Conservative government were ruling? No wonder *Maybe That's Your Problem* couldn't get into the West End. What would the middle-aged audiences touring Shaftesbury Avenue make of such stuff? But it's one of only a small handful of shows in 1971 that seemed aware of social shifts; what was to follow later in the year showed an almost wilful refusal to pay any regard to reality beyond the stage door. Poor old Marvin certainly had an embarrassing problem, but so did society, with increasing industrial disputes, a first-ever postal strike that went on for weeks, the freeing up of divorce laws (for the first time records showed that there were over 100,000 divorces during the year) that reflected swiftly changing attitudes to the church, marriage and sexual behaviour, Education Minister Margaret Thatcher ending the free supply of daily milk to schoolchildren, and Enoch Powell advocating the repatriation of immigrants. How was the British musical to respond to the fast-changing social scene? Could it? And would it if it could?

All trace of having written *Romance!* (Duke of York's Theatre, 28 September 1971; 6) has vanished from the official list of works by John Spurling, but it cannot be denied that this mini-musical, with songs and direction by Charles Ross, announced as 'A drawing-room comedy musical play – charming and elegant' did once occupy the West End. Ross explained that 'Our show is sophisticated. The characters do not swear and they do wear pretty clothes. We have in fact, everything except a French window. But there is much more depth than at first appears, and an element of satire.'[25] Swimming against the current tide in musicals, Ross's attempted turning back of the clock recalled what Alan Melville had tried to do for musicals in 1959 with his and Charles Zwar's *Marigold* – an unashamedly costume-pieced Victorian romance – intended as an antidote to the aggressively 'modern' musical. Melville, like Ross a specialist in intimate revue, had tried the same thing with that specialised genre in *All Square*, an attempt to banish all thought of *Beyond the Fringe*, taking revue back to its earlier manner, cloaked in glamour. Neither of Melville's efforts met with commercial success. Ross had already burned his fingers with a ham-fisted 'modern' musical of his own, *Harmony Close*, with second-drawer music by Ronnie Cass, but this, too, failed to ignite much enthusiasm. Its modernity had been ersatz, a string of old-fashioned revue ideas stuck together among a vague plot about life in a London mews.

London was also the setting for *Romance!*, in which a well-to-do business man (Bill Simpson, best known for his television appearances in *Dr Finlay's Casebook*) and his wife (Joyce Blair) embark on affairs with, respectively, a secretary (Roberta D'Esti) and a fit young waiter (Jess Conrad). Dissatisfied with their liaisons, husband and wife reunite. Simpson's 'teeth-grating'[26] debut in musical theatre went unappreciated and unrepeated. The *Evening News* decided that 'The necessary light-hearted charm is missing. The show lacks either gay Lonsdale cynicism or the wide-eyed Julian Slade whimsy promised by the tum-tee-tum music [...] it must be an almighty send-up, but a send-up of what?'[27] Backed by what Ross described as 'tiny angels', *Romance!* closed at the end of its first week, with Simpson admitting that 'You can't do all the things that I do and not fall flat on your arse sometimes.'[28] Reviewing *Harmony Close*, Philip Hope-Wallace had written that 'The celebration of London as a place of charm is indeed the most novel and interesting sociological aspect of this pleasant, fleet-footed little piece ... It should do well,' but Ross hadn't made *Harmony Close* into a commercial success, and couldn't make *Romance!* one either.

A few days before *Ambassador* (Her Majesty's Theatre, 19 October 1971; 86) opened, Howard Keel told reporters 'It's a period piece'. He'd done a lot of those. 'Very tender. Maybe it's not got the realism of *West Side Story* [correct] but it's got something. Tenderness, delicacy – so the flow must be just right. That's very difficult.' It was. When he'd first been offered *Ambassador*, he turned it down. He had just finished playing *The Most Happy Fella* in mid-West America. The Manchester opening of *Ambassador* was cancelled because he had a bad throat, and its eventual first night in Manchester had been 'instant shit'.

There was much *more* romance in *Ambassador*, adapted from the Henry James novel *The Ambassadors*, than in *Romance!*. The show was stuffed with it. The only good reasons for bothering about it were Keel and Danielle Darrieux, and the romance was middle-aged. This was an obstacle that some, but not all, musicals have overcome. Both performers brought qualities in very limited supply in British musicals of the 1970s, Keel a solidly friendly and masculine Hollywood gleam, and Darrieux the sort of French glamour that had long vanished, possibly even in Paris. Having made 90 films in her home country, she had never played London but had taken over from Katharine Hepburn for a three-month engagement on Broadway in *Coco*. The pity now was that the material was not better, with *Ambassador* bearing many marks of an under-par Broadway show, which it eventually, with many tweakings and its two mature stars still intact, became.

James's story centred on a dull but wealthy Massachusetts man, Lambert

Strether (Keel). Strether stands safe on the sidelines of life, living by the clock, to the second. Forced out of character, he travels to Paris charged with rescuing frisky young Chad Newsome from the clutches of Marie de Vionnet (Darrieux), or possibly from the arms of her daughter Jeanne (Isobel Stuart). In many ways, the Paris setting was the show's undoing. It opened up apparently irresistible opportunities for its adaptors to spend much of the evening trying to be as French as possible, and – even worse – trying to be witty about it. No tired cliché went unused. The book writer, Don Ettlinger, was a newcomer to musical theatre, making linear mincemeat of James's novel. Unsurprisingly, Irving Wardle appreciated newcomer Don Gohman's music, which 'supplies a welcome distraction from the book which conforms to the rock-bottom standard from which this genre so rarely escapes'.[29]

The more experienced Hal Hackaday had already written lyrics for a friendly Broadway musical about the Marx Brothers, *Minnie's Boys*. As with many a more genuinely British musical, there was far too much dross in *Ambassador*'s list of songs: either attempting to create character as in 'A Man You Can Set Your Watch By' or 'It's a Woman', or in such feeble comedy numbers as 'What Can You Do With a Nude?' and 'You Can Tell a Lady By Her Hat'. And when the sets for Massachusetts wheeled away into the wings at Her Majesty's to be replaced by what designer Peter Rice thought people might recognise as Paris, the cardboard recreations emphasised the unreality of it all, despite Stone Widney's direction and the musical staging of Gillian Lynne.

Keel's comforting presence on stage offered something many modern British musicals lacked, and in his life-affirming anthem, the musically uninteresting but proficient 'All of My Life', he allied sensitivity with undeniable manliness. He allowed audiences to relax. Festooned with male dancers, Darrieux had her finest moments in an entrancing entrance number 'Surprise', and 'That's What I Need Tonight' – obvious standouts in an evening that had them in short supply – but attracted less critical praise than her leading man. The supporting players failed to make much impression, despite the inclusion of veteran Ellen Pollock, the glorious Margaret Courtenay (wasted as the underwritten Amelia Newsome), and Richard Heffer as a song-less Chad. Stuart made her West End debut as Jeanne with 'Love Finds the Lonely' and 'Mama', lost in a score that was pleasant but undistinguished.

*Tatler* readers were probably not rushing for tickets to see

> an appallingly underwritten and hopelessly wooden musical which becalms its case in a sea of sickly sentiment. The acting is seldom less than embarrassing, the chorus are motivated by a kind of benign inefficiency, the songs are deeply unmemorable, there is a breath-taking lack of heart, soul or talent and one has the definite impression that the whole thing may be taking place under 40 feet of water [...] what one longs for most of all is to be let out of the theatre.[30]

New York had to go through a revised version all over again the following year, but the American *Ambassador* closed up at the end of its second week.

*

On the fringes of London theatre, Sandy Wilson's adaptation of John Collier's novella, *His Monkey Wife* (Hampstead Theatre Club, 20 December 1971; season) had its admirers, but the public to whom such work appealed was not of the clamouring variety. That public, that had flocked with anticipation of innocent enjoyment to *The Boy Friend*, was now offered a story about an English school-teacher who marries a chimpanzee that becomes one of Charles B. Cochran's leading ladies. Robert Swann (the Ashley of Harold Rome's *Gone With the Wind*) was the admirably cast hero, Bridget Armstrong (*Follow That Girl, Fiorello!)* was perfection as his totally selfish girlfriend, and June Ritchie (*Gone With the Wind*'s brilliant Scarlett O'Hara) an astonishing chimp. Why weren't British writers and producers falling over themselves to write a musical for her? Some of Wilson's numbers might just as well have come out of *The Boy Friend* (try 'Haverstock Hill' or 'Doing the Chimpanzee' or 'Leave It All To Smithers'), and most of the others had a fragility that endangered their preservation. Neatly put together, *His Monkey Wife* confirmed Wilson's integrity but placed him even further beyond the pale with London managements.

# 1972

*The Londoners*
*The Maid of the Mountains*
*Tom Brown's Schooldays*
*Trelawny*
*Pull Both Ends*
*Smilin' Through*
*Popkiss*
*Stand and Deliver*
*I and Albert*

Lionel Bart's career spluttered to an ignoble end with the Broadway one-performance *La Strada* in 1969. When the show opened in New York in December, the audience heard only three songs from Bart's original score; by now, the show was fleshed out by other hands, although a subsequently released demo recording suggests that Bart's original was not without merit. Three years later, there was a touching reminder of his past glories in *The Londoners* (Theatre Royal, Stratford East, 27 March 1972; 63); it took him back to the theatrical roots from which he had blossomed into the British musical's hottest property. Stephen Lewis's play *Sparrers Can't Sing* had been directed by Joan Littlewood at Stratford East in the early 1960s before briefly transferring to London. Like much of her work, it seemed tailored for the theatre in which it played, a fun palace originally built to entertain dockers, costers and railway navvies. Lewis's play, about three local families whose slum terraces are about to be torn down and occupants rehoused, belonged to the people who looked to that theatre as a focal point of survival in what was by now a desert of demolition and concrete redevelopment. Its title tidied up for a wider public who presumably would not understand what 'sparrers' were, the Elstree movie *Sparrows Can't Sing* (a big mistake, the correct spelling damns the effect) nevertheless caught much of the genuine atmosphere and style of Littlewood's Theatre Workshop, probably because Littlewood directed

**16**  The desolation surrounding the Theatre Royal Stratford East in 1972 seems strangely appropriate for *The Londoners*, exemplified here by the show's youthful lovers Martine Howard and Ray Hoskins

the film and gave parts to some of her best loved 'nuts', James Booth, Barbara Windsor, Brian Murphy, Avis Bunnage, Fanny Carby, Murray Melvin et al.

When, after a notable absence, Littlewood returned to helm Stratford East, it was to direct a musical version of Lewis's play; a sort of renewal of commitment to the principles to which the theatre had clung during her stewardship. *The Londoners* seemed perfectly at home here, in a theatre that had never lost its rackety, music-hall ambience, safely beyond the reach of Shaftesbury Avenue. The air of innocent jollity was unforced, and in the interval you got jellied eels and mussels. On stage, many of the original play's 'nuts' had been brought back for the musical, now joined by Martine Howard and Ray Hoskins as a pair of young lovers.

There's no mention of any song titles in the theatre's programme. It's as if the songs by Bart hardly mattered any more, but that would be wrong. They were crucial. No matter how many composers of British musicals put on the cockney for a knees-up, there was always something intrinsically phoney about them. Those tattered but determinedly cheery urchins in *Barnardo*, the lusty East End match girls in *Strike a Light!*, almost every stage cockney that ever darkened a British musical by sticking their thumbs under their waistcoats and shouting 'Oi' – none convinced us for a moment, unless Bart was about. But now, did Bart think so little of his own work that he was content not to have his songs listed? From the critics who wound their way to Stratford East, some of whom had probably played a part in Bart's downfall by damning *Twang!*, came notices that sounded a mourning note, as if (too late) they regretted his demise. The *Evening News* thought 'the first tremulous shades of *Oliver!* haunts it'.[31] For Michael Billington, there was 'a genuine feeling for the disruptive effects of change on traditional social values [...] *The Londoners* may not be the tidiest or most disciplined show in London; but, like Marie Lloyd, it has a heart as big as Waterloo Station.'[32]

Rough at the edges and pretty well everywhere else *The Londoners* may have been, but its gutsiness, its attempt to mirror reality, its Littlewood quality of being 'felt', was something the West End could not and never would achieve. To the present day, cockneys in West End musicals put their thumbs in their waistcoats (unless it's their braces) and do as Mother Brown did, not as Bart, courtesy of Littlewood, did. They even occasionally shout 'Oi'. Apparently, Bart wrote very little new material for *The Londoners*, but could always come up with something, even when drunk. At some point, he took over Stephen Lewis's role, and sang his own song 'Mirror Man', accompanied by the pleasingly tin-pot Bob Kerr's Whoopee Band whose instruments included motor-horns, saw, teapots and kazoos. One of the most effective moments came when that redoubtable fog-horn of an actress Rita Webb as the Grandmother sang the title song through the window of her condemned house. That alone sounds like a moment that no one genuinely interested in the beating soul of the British musical should have missed.

Bart was reunited with Littlewood for the 'candy-floss entertainment' **Costa Packet** (Theatre Royal, Stratford East, 5 October 1972; 65), co-writing with fellow

Littlewood 'nuts' Frank Norman (with whom Bart had collaborated on *Fings Ain't Wot They Used T'Be*) and Alan Klein, whose pop musical *What a Crazy World* was first seen at Stratford East in 1962.

'The people who saw *Maid* in 1917 and came back again in 1942 out of nostalgia are now dead and buried, and this production is no more than their memorial service. R. I. P.'[33] *Plays and Players'* harsh verdict on an old favourite was surely unfair. Attempts to reinstall operetta to the contemporary stage had in recent years enjoyed some unexpected success, with both *The Desert Song* and *The Student Prince* reaching London (both, admittedly, with the box-office advantage of John Hanson as their star) and achieving rewarding runs in the face of a good deal of critical carping. Revival of *British* operetta proved less resilient. Within ten years, that bastion of what the British considered to be light opera, the D'Oyly Carte Opera Company, would be in murkier water than that treaded by either H.M.S. Pinafore or those pirates from Penzance. Operetta had been briefly embraced by Sadler's Wells in the late 1950s, but Offenbach and his like could never imbed themselves in the British psyche. British operetta had reached a full stop with Ivor Novello, still working up a head of steam in the early 1950s with his farewell flourish *King's Rhapsody*, but Novello was milk-and-water stuff compared to the vibrancy of European operetta, part of a tradition that still flourishes with extraordinary vigour. Touring versions of operettas could still be found roaming the provinces – in 1964 Bryan Johnson was student prince-ing in what passed for old Heidelberg as Prince Karl Franz opposite the innkeeper's niece of Janette Miller – but in London, no. June Bronhill had given hope to the 1968 revival of *The Dancing Years*, but Novello's work was not easily revitalised. Neither, it seemed, was the work of Harold Fraser-Simson and his collaborators in **The Maid of the Mountains** (Palace Theatre, 29 April 1972; 96). Strangely, the first night of this £80,000 revival (perhaps to soften the critical impact) was a Saturday, with a bargain top price of £2.50. What could there possibly be to complain about?

Although London audiences had by now got beyond expecting leading ladies to be wheeled on stage on papier-mâché rocks (Maria's entrance for the Palace's *The Sound of Music*), there was some sympathy when the 1972 Maid spent much of her time standing among rock formations that still seemed made of the same stuff, backcloths fluttering in the background. The maid and her operetta colleagues were used to such conditions, having been kept alive on tour, sustained by meagre budgets. Papier-mâché rocks and unconvincing skies were the life blood of these bloodless revivals, but few other home-grown operettas had given as much pleasure to people as this tale of the mountain-dwelling Teresa, with her passion for swarthy brigand Baldassare and his band of lovable ne'er-do-wells; 'obviously all homosexual', joked *Plays and Players*; 'not one of them lay a well-manicured finger on her'.[34]

Daly Theatre's production of 1917 enraptured audiences, running through the closing months of the Great War to 1,352 performances. Said to be the one London show that every returning British serviceman wanted to see, it was inextricably linked to its maid, Jose Collins, and only closed when she could no longer face performing it. She was rapturously received at its final night, despite having completely lost her voice. At one time there were fourteen road companies going up and down the country performing the *Maid*. Its setting may have been some unspecified European mountainous range known to have been the backdrop to several eighteenth-century operas, but its atmosphere hovered somewhere around the hillier regions of Eastbourne, for the *Maid* is essentially a British piece. Or is it? What, anyway, is it to be essentially British? Here and there, Fraser-Simson's music sounds as if it's caught a whiff of Emmerich Kálmán, and in its famous waltz song there is a distinct (and intended) acknowledgement to Lehár's waltz song from *The Merry Widow*. Unarguably, the *Maid* is full of glorious sounds.

At the Palace, Frederick Lonsdale's original script had undergone tweaking by its 1972 producer/adaptor Emile Littler, and the temptation to leave the score as heard in 1917 was resisted. It was almost *de rigueur* that some material would be rejected and songs from other sources brought in to plug the gaps. Sadly, these were not by Fraser-Simson, although there was a wealth to choose from; it is highly doubtful that the producers even considered plundering any of the many other Fraser-Simson scores. The multi-talented James W. Tate and his fellow lyricists had contributed four numbers to the 1917 production that sat beautifully alongside Fraser-Simson's items, providing some of the best songs, 'My Life Is Love', 'A Bachelor Gay', 'A Paradise for Two' and, in blatantly musical comedy vein, 'When You're In Love'. Sensibly, these were retained in the new revival. Unfortunately, Littler dragged in 'Pedro the Fisherman' from the 1943 *The Lisbon Story* (almost 30 years out of period) and 'The Song of the Vagabonds' from Rudolf Friml's 1925 *The Vagabond King*.

There was no question of overlooking Fraser-Simson's thematic waltz-song 'Love Will Find a Way', surely one of the most ravishing melodies in British musical theatre. Despite going on to write many more operetta-like pieces, it is for *The Maid of the Mountains* that he is best remembered. The show was seen again in London in 1921 (with Collins, her voice restored), 1930, and in 1942 when the maid was Sylvia Cecil, Coward's soprano from *Pacific 1860* and *Ace of Clubs*. That revival reached 224 performances, although *The Times* confessed that without Collins 'there is no pretending that the entertainment is the same thing'.[35]

The maid for 1972, Lynn Kennington, had already done service as one of *The Sound of Music*'s many nuns worried about Maria, and as Adriana in the unsuccessful Drury Lane revival of *The Boys from Syracuse*, as well as touring with John Hanson in his 1964 version of *The Maid of the Mountains*, in which he no doubt kept the maid's best numbers to himself. That production had Douglas Byng as the comedic General Malona. Now, that role was taken by the exuberantly vulgar Jimmy Edwards in splendid form, a great balance to the wonderfully muscular

Kennington, whose Maid exulted in swooping vocal gymnastics, and could surely not have been bettered if theatrical effect was wanted. As Baldassare, Gordon Clyde seemed perfectly in period with the demands of the piece, and sounded like the sort of performer who was no stranger to papier-mâché rocks and quivering backdrops.

There was little surprise that in 1972 such an aged operettary musical comedy could expect little critical respect in London. There were exceptions. 'I wouldn't have missed it for worlds,' wrote John Barber, the production proving that 'good pop is indestructible'.[36] Hailing a 'musty relic', Milton Shulman decided: 'Perhaps for audiences of a very advanced age, catching faint echoes of tired jokes through their ear trumpets, *Maid of the Mountains* may still be a nostalgic change from the telly.'[37] The *Tatler* was adamant:

> To think that here and now, in the middle of 1972, a production of this nature is actually occupying the stage of a major London theatre is frankly chilling [...] it is in fact hard to think of anyone short of God who could possibly have helped the show rise above its own kitsch awfulness: when a musical is as old as this one, so old in fact that anyone with happy memories of it can reasonably be accused of senility, there is a lot to be said for letting sleeping doggerel lie.[38]

Indeed, the only exception to this rule may be the deservedly immortal *Show Boat*, a work revived as late as 2016 in a glowing production at the New London Theatre that drew ecstatic reviews but failed to attract audiences.

It was all very well to suspect that **Tom Brown's Schooldays** (Cambridge Theatre, 9 May 1972; 76) happened in the train of *Oliver!* merely because producers and writers sensed success in filling the stage not with happy hours but with hordes of pubescent schoolboys. What else, after all, suggested this was a suitable case for musical treatment? Nothing. Perhaps, in the style of amateur productions, the boys' grandparents, aunties and uncles would be clamouring for tickets at the box-office, forming untidy queues in Cambridge Circus to see this adaptation of Thomas Hughes' Victorian novel. Overhead lay the vague cloud of being yet another British musical supposedly intended, in some unspecified way, to appeal to the mythical family audience that the managements of British musicals were constantly in search of. If *Oliver!* was one of the reasons for forcing Hughes' book into a musical strait-jacket, it suggested that the writers and producers had little intention of forwarding the British musical. Still, Peter Coe seemed an appropriate director. He, after all, had directed the original London *Oliver!*, creating a show with which present-day audiences are quite unacquainted, Bart's little piece having over the years been exaggerated to absurd proportions.

But what audience *was* this new show for? Its content was oddly balanced, its adult and unconvincing romance acted out against the sound of Hughes turning in his grave. The highly unlikely sexual attraction between the morally tight-lipped

Dr Arnold, usually with his nose in a (or *the*) good book, and his matron Mary Penrose, was patently absurd, and made even more so by matron's outbursts of Shirley Bassey-like proportions. In such ways did the composers of British musicals resemble Victorian body-snatchers. There was something absurd, too, in Roy Dotrice, allegedly unable to recognise a musical note when he heard one, piously declaring from the pulpit of Rugby School that he had been enjoying 'A Vision Of Youth', and even more worryingly for the headmaster of an all-male school, demanding to be told 'What Is a Man?'

It was almost worth sitting through such baloney to hear Judith Bruce's incisive delivery of matron's heart-achy ballads, even if she seemed as confused as Dr Arnold, asking 'Where Is He?' when we knew jolly well he was in the pulpit having yet another of those worrying visions of youth, apparently acceptable to educated Victorians but rather more dubious in 1972. Shouldn't matron, anyway, have been doing some light bandaging or checking that all was well in the boys' dorms after 'lights out'? Never mind that Judith Bruce was one of the finest leading ladies of the period, with a Vivien Leigh-like poise and professionalism.

The wisest decision of the evening was probably not to inflict a duet on Dotrice and Bruce, or – more fairly – to land Bruce with having to cope with Dotrice; that would probably have sent them both to the sick bay. The writers attempted to divert attention from this far from torrid relationship between scholar and state-registered nurse by introducing stomping gypsies working up a frenzy about 'The Ballad of the Great White Horse', and a group of happy but pitifully uneducated yokels, ably led by the always welcome Ray C. Davis, mummersetting their way through numbers that had nothing to do with anything in the world except having a bit of a knees-up, 'Three Acres and a Cow' (trouble with numeracy), 'Warwickshire Home' and the children's nursery-like 'One For Your Nose'.

For W. Stephen Gilbert, 'the adaptation hadn't been thought through', and lacked 'a Fagin, a Bumble, a really memorable ditty and the smell of a hit about it', although Bruce's 'Shirley Bassey-ish voice brings a touch of class to the proceedings'.[39] The *Sunday Telegraph* decided that 'One would need to be exceptionally keen on small boys to get much pleasure out of this weird concoction, [...] it is both tedious and saddening to watch that high-minded headmaster Dr Arnold making up to a cabaret-voiced matron.'[40] *The Daily Telegraph* had already decided the show was 'punctuated by unfortunate throwbacks to old musical comedies at their worst', but there was praise for the boys, all of whom were 'splendid, both in casting and direction'.[41] Just how bad some thought the show is clear from the *Illustrated London News*, whose critic admitted 'I preferred *Maid of the Mountains*.'[42]

Saddled with the role, script and lyrics at his disposal, Dotrice ('one of the four or five finest actors of his generation', according to *Plays and Players*[43]) brought dignity to a role that in lesser hands would have been excruciating. Bruce, placed on stage below her idol's pulpit with her back to the audience so that she might mouth Dotrice's words at him as he warbled overhead, was the other ace in the production's hand. For co-librettists Joan and Jack Maitland, the Hughes adaptation was a rare moment in the West End sun. The extent of Joan's earlier association with the libretto of Lionel Bart's *Blitz!* remains something of a mystery, but *Tom Brown's Schooldays* was 'the culmination of the most gratifying work she has ever undertaken'.[44] Her involvement with the show was consolidated by it being co-presented by her personal manager, Joe Vegoda. The Maitlands' lyrics were set by Chris Andrews, a successful composer of pop music who had written hits for Sandie Shaw and Adam Faith. His musicalisation of *Tom Brown's Schooldays* was his only British musical.

Julian Slade's career had skidded from his collaboration with Dorothy Reynolds after the reception for *Wildest Dreams*. Despite, or perhaps because of, possibly being their seminal work (more adventurously scored and more organic than the record-breaking *Salad Days*), it sealed the critical derision that had gathered momentum through their subsequent works. Reviewing *Wildest Dreams*, Robert Muller railed at 'the petty, priggish, piffling, platitudinous, philistine awfulness of the whole thing'.[45] Beneath the headline 'Fantasy Saved By Sincerity – Commonsense with the Sugar', *The Times* remembered 'lots and lots of tinkling, indistinguishable songs. Does it all sound unbearable? Well, it ought to be, but somehow it is not. Improbably enough, it has a disturbing quality of sincerity of being meant, which carries one, albeit unwillingly, over some of the bits.'[46] On the rebound from *Wildest Dreams*, Slade unexpectedly fell in with a major musicalisation of Thackeray's *Vanity Fair*, co-written with Alan Pryce-Jones and Robin Miller.

Whatever the qualities of Slade's work with Reynolds, one of their achievements had been to write a series of completely original pieces; everything of Slade post-Reynolds depended on adaptation. One of the provincial scores that kept Slade's name alive after *Vanity Fair* had been *Out of Bounds*, from Arthur Wing Pinero's *The Schoolmistress*, for the Bristol Old Vic. It was Bristol that had given Slade his first chances, and continued supporting him. When the theatre underwent substantial restoration in 1972, it appropriately turned to Slade for celebration in another Pinero adaptation, this time from his utterly theatrical *Trelawny of the Wells*, adapted by Aubrey Woods with assistance from George Rowell, and directed by Val May.

The quality casting of *Trelawny* (Sadler's Wells Theatre, 27 June 1973, transferred to Prince of Wales Theatre; 177) gave it a solidity that much of Slade's output lacked. His Bristol Old Vic musicals had always involved actors from the legitimate stage. On paper, the casting for *Trelawny* could hardly have been bettered, a perfect co-mixture of straight and musical actors. Ian Richardson's ripe Tom Wrench, Max Adrian (taking over from Bristol's Timothy West) as stick-in-the-mud Victorian Sir William Gower, and Joyce Carey as his sister Trafalgar (as

Adrian said it), headed the battalion of the Who's Who performers. Hayley Mills, cast as Rose Trelawny, was not a natural singer, joining the queue of similar Slade leading ladies. By the time *Trelawny* moved to London, Mills had been replaced by newcomer Gemma Craven. The other most significant cast alteration was having Sir William Gower recast with Adrian, when Adrian would have been better cast as the hammy James Telfer, clinging to the melodramatic, over-cooked acting style of the past. John Watts, unrewardingly cast as Rose's boyfriend, had an old-fashioned air of charm that subsequently helped him through the trauma of *Troubadour*. The Sadler's Wells contingent, the gypsies to whom Rose naturally moved, offered undemanding capering from Teddy Green and David Morton, and a vital Avonia Bunn in Elizabeth Power, delightfully describing her 'turn'.

How does *Trelawny* – a flop in the terms of this book, but to many Slade's finest work – rate among his work? It is superior to much of the rest. Gone is the open breeziness; there's not a hint of it here. That fresh wind blows through much of *Salad Days*, or at least did in the early 1950s, but the refreshing breeziness tended to blow out in subsequent revivals, and to many there has been a change in the barometer reading. How could *Free as Air* not fling the windows open, letting the light winds blow through Slade's work again? This is possibly the best of Slade, the most consistently tuneful, as cohesive as the score for *Trelawny*, if lacking its maturity. What distinguishes *Trelawny* is its fullness, its outpouring of sentiment that somehow avoids the cloying. For the last time they poured out of Slade, and for those with ears to listen they live on.

What makes Tom and Avonia's complaint about spending the rest of their careers forever 'Walking On' in small parts or in panto so touching?; what stirs at Rose's singing of 'The One Who Isn't There', one of the best, and simplest love songs Slade ever wrote? At last, too, we know it was Slade, not Reynolds, that wrote the lyric for *Free as Air*'s 'I'd Like To Be Like You' and, surely, the lyric for 'When You're Not There' in *Wildest Dreams*; Rose's dressing-room lament in *Trelawny* repeats the desolate feelings in the earlier pieces. The same melancholic strain invests the little exchange, 'Two Fools', between Sir William and Rose, an attempted bridging of generations. And nowhere else in Slade is there the glorious straightforwardness of 'Back To The Wells', and the splendid workings of the climactic 'Life'. These, despite some less effective moments such as 'Arthur's Letter', 'Rules' and 'On Approval', isolate *Trelawny* as one of the better British musicals of the past sixty years; a will and testament of what Slade was capable of.

Did it seem so to the critics of 1972, many of whom had turned up to gibe at many other Slade first nights? In the prevailing climate, it was as if a strange bird from an unmapped country had lost its way and landed in Shaftesbury Avenue. John Russell Taylor was for it, but 'don't go expecting miracles and a masterpiece; if you go hoping to be charmed and lightly amused you are much more likely to come away satisfied [...] it is never boring, never less than pleasant, never embarrassing. And that is quite an achievement for a new British musical these days.'[47]

At Bristol, *The Times* reported that 'although Mr Slade's lyrics induce frequent winces, he has written some fine old-style showbiz numbers, and others that genuinely advance the story [...] His style is as four-square as ever but on this occasion it fits.'[48] *Tatler* considered 'the music and a certain amount of the acting was a good deal thinner than the play demanded',[49] and Charles Lewsen heard 'colourless music and contrived lyrics – chortles being dragged in to rhyme with mortals and portals',[50] but *Trelawny* attracted many decent and enthusiastic notices. Moving from Bristol to Sadler's Wells and then on to the Prince of Wales probably wearied it. By the end of the run, the show wasn't what it had once been, and – so far as London was concerned – it was done with Slade.

The critic W. Stephen Gilbert spent a wasted evening at **Pull Both Ends** (Piccadilly Theatre, 18 July 1972; 36), a midsummer musical about Christmas crackers. What was so brilliant about this show that audiences couldn't be expected to wait until Christmas to see it? Absolutely nothing. As its title oh so wittily suggested, here was a musical that owed more than a little to Yuletide. *The Times* headlined its review 'Midsummer Panto'; after all, the heroine was called Cindy, perhaps reminding a few die-hard visitors to London musicals that shortly after its arrival in the West End the off-Broadway show *Cindy* had turned up its toes at the Fortune Theatre four years earlier. The Cinderella connotations were reinforced by the casting of cheery pop-singer Gerry Marsden as leading man, having previously taken over from Joe Brown in *Charlie Girl*, with Christine Holmes (the original 'Charlie Girl') as leading lady. If W. S. Gilbert (those initials surely striking terror into any producer) was to be believed, it wasn't worth the cast of *Pull Both Ends* hanging up their coats in the dressing-room. He reported 'a cloying anxiety to please everyone' and a 'feeble, leering script which hammers away at basic *double-entendres* and demands a plethora of bum-pinching so that Judy Bowen as Rita must be black and blue at the week's end. The crackers provide an excuse to rehearse endless jokes of the "elephant" school which the sparsely populated stalls had clearly heard dozens of times before.'[51] Of course they had: presumably they were chosen as suitable for those who considered mottoes in Christmas crackers the height of wit.

Brian Comport's book had three flat-sharing girls working at a cracker factory. One was the daughter of an American tycoon, and working as a spy, while some drama worked around a strike at the works. Promoted as 'John Schroeder's *Pull Both Ends*' (Schroeder had composed the songs with Anthony King), one of the main reasons for its existence was The Young Generation, a dance troupe of young, tightly packed and supposedly cool dancers styled by Douglas Squires for television fame, and now choreographed by Nigel Lythgoe. The Young Generation was surely the main draw, presumably attracting the millions that watched their gyrations on screen each week, but with swinging London showing early signs of arthritis, the transfer proved unsuccessful.

Milton Shulman explained that 'Charity prompts me to say little more about a show which will easily make my private list of the ten worst musicals of the decade',[52] while the *Sunday Telegraph* agreed that 'There is nothing to be said [...] that would not uselessly hurt or wound.'[53] Felix Barker for the *Evening News* was 'confronted with more clichés derived from past musicals, more old-fashioned boy-meets-girl sentiment, and more time-worn routines than I should have thought possible'.[54] A mystery remained: who was this show aimed at? Who would be lured to the Piccadilly by its cast, or the dreadful music, or the crass lyrics, as in Judy Bowen and Christine Holmes's description of themselves as 'Wallflowers'? It was generally agreed that *Pull Both Ends* plumbed depths of awfulness, despite its (very possibly unintentional) attempt to do a modern take on Lorenzo Da Ponte's 'Catalogue Aria' from *Don Giovanni*, as bright spark Marsden described some of the entries in his 'Little Leather Book' with puerile innuendo.

Hoping to repeat the commercial success of his *The Desert Song* revival of 1967, John Hanson was back starring in his own adaptation, music and lyrics, of **Smilin' Through** (Prince of Wales Theatre, 5 July 1972; 28), top price £2.00, and matinees at £1.25. Did Hanson know the musical version had already been done by no less than Vincent Youmans? Possibly, but it seems just as likely that he wouldn't have been bothered. Another addition to his list of flops, Youmans' *Through the Years* had played Broadway in 1932, lasting only 20 performances; at least Hanson's lasted eight more. Both works were essentially operetta, a form (at its most staid) that suited Hanson, although *Through the Years* had been passed off as 'a musical play', which anyway in 1932 was tantamount to admitting it was probably operetta. The *World Telegraph*'s critic Robert Garland marked Youmans' work as 'the kind of score Mr Sigmund Romberg assembles from memory almost any day between lunch and dinner'.[55] The brilliant Youmans was used to such treatment.

Allan Langdon Martin's patently melodramatic plot seemed made for operetta. John Carteret forbids the marriage of his niece and ward Kathleen Dungannon to Kenneth Wayne. Many years earlier, Carteret had been about to say 'I do' to Moonyeen when Kenneth's forebear Jeremiah Wayne killed her. Not surprisingly, the Waynes and the Carterets didn't get on with one another, but through the years Moonyeen's ghost returns to Carteret's side, finally getting him to agree to his niece's marriage. The dual role of Moonyeen/Kathleen had made a star of American actress Jane Cowl in the 1919 tear-jerker, which went on through three film versions, the last with Jeanette MacDonald. It helped that Allan Langdon Martin was Cowl's pen-name; she had co-written the piece with Jane Murfin. Now, Lauverne Gray, deserving a medal for good service in John Hanson tours, maintained the tradition of playing both roles. The fact that Hanson's leading ladies were frequently expected to leave the stage to make way for the male star probably made Gray's task less onerous. David Gardiner did his best as director-choreographer to bring Hanson's show to life, as did the skilful orchestrations of Ronald Hanmer.

The reviews were mixed. Philip Hope-Wallace likened the show to a poor man's *Bitter-Sweet*. 'All very innocent and tuneful, it will be thought pier-end concert party cod's wallop by the unfeeling.'[56] Felix Barker went further, for 'It works! All this preposterous stuff somehow fuses into more than acceptable entertainment [and Hanson] never mocks the sentiment or melodrama.'[57] George Baxt saw the show 'under an adverse circumstance. The curtain was up.' Many of the cast were 'so unbelievably wooden, one wonders at smoking being permitted in the auditorium. The sets could have been designed by Christopher Wren, and the costumes by Blind Pew [...] there are several ways at looking at this version of *Smilin' Through*, though I'm inclined to recommend closed eyes.'[58] Charles Lewsen could find 'not an ounce of romance in Hanson's performance [...] In acting terms the role demands that he move from Dr Soper to a mixture of Pickwick and the last act of *Cyrano de Bergerac* and be Romeo in the central flashback scene. All we get is a change of wigs.' Despite this, when it came to the songs, Lewsen 'liked what I heard', even though some of it reminded him of stuff he already knew.[59]

For Eric Johns, the 'corny' story 'slowly creaked its way through rousing male choruses of *The Student Prince* and *The Desert Song* vintage, and tear-jerking scenes played in a crude melodramatic style which suited the unimaginative book'. The show consigned itself to that tatty corner in which West End operetta revivals lurked, 'with its derivative music and banal lyrics proclaiming "Life's a song, when you're young", and costumes and scenery reminiscent of tasteless Number Two touring shows of long, long ago'.[60] Hanson and his faithful audience were easy targets for scoffing cosmopolitan critics, but of its type *Smilin' Through* was a plucky endeavour, much of its score recorded, with different players than in the London production, in 1972.

With the airs of a play with music rather than a full-blown musical, **Popkiss** (Globe Theatre, 22 August 1972; 60) rose from the ashes of Ben Travers' 1926 farce *Rookery Nook*. At Rookery Nook in 1929, Travers' characters are launched into a frenetic wedding night which Gerald Popkiss (Daniel Massey) is obliged to spend without his bride Clara (Patricia Hodge). Robertson Hare, a star of the original production of the play, watched the first night from the stalls. One set, no chorus and small orchestra suggested economy as David Heneker (co-composing with John Addison) moved into a chamber musical phase after the production luxuries of *Half a Sixpence*, *Charlie Girl* and *Jorrocks*. Anton Gill in *Plays and Players* saw 'a damp firework [...] you can't really have a farce *and* a musical [...] *Popkiss* emerges as an apology for *Rookery Nook*'.[61]

Perhaps realising that even so undistinguished a work as this ranked as a minor miracle for a British musical in the early 1970s, *Lady* stooped to praise a piece 'at once wistful and uncommonly amusing',[62] while Eric Shorter remembered 'a very jolly if flimsy evening of nostalgic period nonsense [...] sometimes comically tuneful and for the most part admirably staged'.[63] Philip Hope-Wallace consid-

**17** Never much of a musical? It was, as ever, a matter of taste. Daniel Massey as Popkiss in the musical of the same name, with Isla Blair still in her pyjamas

ered it 'funny and slick and I don't see why it shouldn't capture *The Boy Friend* audience, but there are risks all the same. Music tends to slow things, especially things farcical.'[64] The *Tablet*'s verdict was that 'the music evokes the era, but seems nervous of too positive a declaration. One is merely aware of a pleasant, but vague thread of melody. It does nothing and achieves little [...] A farce which is less than a triumph is an apology.'[65] Conversely, Eric Johns found 'an admirable transition to the musical stage [...] There was no question of vandalism.'[66] Perhaps not, but there remained the problem of having two composers, Addison having been brought in because Heneker was unsure of his ability to provide some of the more choreographic music needed for the play. There was also the fact that sound as the cast was, there was only one real singer.

*Popkiss* had its modest beginning at the Arts Theatre, Cambridge in May, directed by Richard Cottrell. Its credentials were solid, not least in the skilful libretto from Michael Ashton, whose *The Young Visiters* had briefly run in London four years earlier, but in its composers. Addison's theatrical music had included John Cranko's revue *Cranks* and the score for Cranko's only musical, *Keep Your Hair On* (20 troubled performances in 1958). Addison and Heneker had already collaborated on *The Amazons* for Nottingham Playhouse, a tasteful and vigorous treatment of Arthur Wing Pinero's play, but it hadn't reached London. *The Amazons* was a more expansive piece than *Popkiss*, and now the relative lack of musical strength in the cast emphasised the thinness of the evening, although Massey brought the natural warmth he had already exhibited in *Make Me an Offer* and *She Loves Me*. Most agreed that the highlight of the occasion was the late appearance of Mary Millar as the flag seller for lifeboats Poppy Dickey, enjoying a happier experience singing 'Doing My Bit' than in the title role of *Ann Veronica*. Excitement was hard to come by elsewhere, despite breezy numbers such as 'The Girl From Up the Road' and 'Tonight Was On the Way'. John Standing and the expertly battleaxe Joan Sanderson added to the fun, but diverting as it seemed, *Popkiss* suffered from being too small, and perhaps from being too tasteful. Its songs struck the incidental note.

Wolf Mankowitz and Monty Norman's **Stand and Deliver** (Roundhouse, 24 October 1972; 14) had its encouraging beginning at the Edinburgh Festival a month earlier. By now, the Mankowitz–Norman collaboration was running on low after the heady days of *Expresso Bongo* and *Make Me an Offer*. *Belle* had helped derail their praiseworthy attempts at establishing a distinctive school of British musical. Mankowitz's course had diverted into sheer commercialism in *Pickwick* with its easy-to-please Cyril Ornadel score and Harry Secombe belting out 'If I Ruled the World', and the supposedly libertarian *Passion Flower Hotel*, the middle-aged man's idea of what a 1960s 'hip', 'permissive' musical might be. Norman's musical theatre career had sidetracked into a series of provincial productions. *The Perils of Scobie Prilt* (1963), doomed from the start, embarked on a tour but gave up the ghost after the first week; intended for a Jewish audience, *Who's Pinkus, Where's Chelm?* couldn't find enough of one; *Quick, Quick, Slow*, inspired by the popularity of the TV series *Come Dancing*, sounded like a good idea but couldn't get a London transfer.

An account of the career of highwayman Jack Sheppard, Wendy Toye's direction of *Stand and Deliver* sounded echoes of *The Beggar's Opera*, of which *The Times* thought this 'a feeble imitation [...] Once again the pursuit of undiluted entertainment has yielded a show lacking in wit, sense or believable situations.' Nicky Henson (*Camelot, Passion Flower Hotel*) made for a convincing hero, although 'trying to glamourize the highwayman's trade is an uphill job'.[67] Michael Billington pronounced the book 'feeble' although 'Mr Norman's music and lyrics have a jaunty exuberance about them that just about sees the show through'. Anna Dawson drew attention with her anthem to adultery. Below the headline 'Even the Orgy Misfires',[68] Milton Shulman predicted 'a short life for this untidy venture'.[69] Felix Barker's claim that it was like 'a show by a suburban operatic society' recalled so many reviews of the previous decade, when the charge of amateurism had been flung at so many British musicals. After seeing *House of Cards*, *Plays and Players* had reported that several 'among the large cast would not have disgraced an amateur dramatic society'.[70] Booked into the Roundhouse for a two-week stay, *Stand and Deliver* went no further.

Operetta had once seemed the ideal milieu where royal romances might be musically celebrated, reaching a domestic apogee in Novello's Ruritanian *King's Rhapsody* in 1949, when King Nikki (rather a hell-raiser by all accounts) was reduced to respectability by an ice princess. Perhaps it was inevitable that somewhere along the line musical theatre would seize on British royalty, selecting a figure that had long since vanished. 1972 seemed an odd time to do it, and John Schlesinger one of the most unlikely of directors to bring it off. One gets the impression that he had little idea of Victoria's influence, or Albert's, and very little interest in either. There lurks the suspicion that Schlesinger's involvement began when he overheard Victoria mentioned at a smart cocktail party. Nevertheless, he steered *I and Albert* (Piccadilly Theatre, 6 November 1972; 120) into the West End with no pre-London opening, despite having no experience of directing in the theatre, and being sublimely ignorant of musicals.

Cast as his Victoria, Polly James, already applauded for her title role in the 1969 London *Anne of Green Gables*, recalled film-director Schlesinger begging her to 'take me to the cutting room' as *I and Albert* metamorphosed into an uncontrollable monstrosity, for which patrons were charged a top ticket price of £2.80. Five months ahead of opening night, the *Evening Standard* reported Schlesinger promising that 'It won't be anything like *Sixty Glorious Years*. That would be hopeless. It isn't a sort of sentimental show.' Sadly, it ultimately was, and extravagant (*grossly extravagant* if the stories about the costs of crowns, orbs, sceptres and male chorus member's kilts are to be believed) in all but ideas as it hopelessly tried to encompass the old queen's reign with sumptuous set pieces. In retrospect, it seems odd that Schlesinger should even have referred to Wilcox's 1938 movie about Queen Victoria, especially when Wilcox had already made an earlier version, *Victoria the Great*, in 1937, both with Anna Neagle, although the critic James Agate described its final Technicolor reel as like 'a present from Blackpool'. Odder still, there was something mystifyingly flat about much of Schlesinger's production that had shades of Wilcox's achingly straightforward approach to film-making.

Opening night was postponed for several days when the show's Albert, Sven-Bertil Taube, contracted influenza. 'An elaborate, worthy, hard-working, ambitious production', wrote Alan Brien; 'But for want of an all-embracing idea of where it is going, it begins and ends like a super-revue rather than a musical [...] stronger on incident than on plot, rich in attitudes but bankrupt of a viewpoint'.[71] Irving Wardle agreed that there was 'action but no plot'.[72] Michael Billington suggested that 'A vehemently tugged forelock is rapidly becoming the symbol of the West End theatre' but 'basically I was not amused'.[73] In the *Daily Telegraph*, John Barber endured 'much heavy trudging', for after two hours 'Nothing has surprised or involved us [...] the authors never pause to explore an emotional situation and neglect to exploit the domestic and political clashes.'[74]

There seems to have been much unreported dissension behind the scenes of *I and Albert*; Schlesinger didn't even like the title, wanting it renamed *Ma'am*. That, of course, would have presented the British public with an even more formidable problem; was it to rhyme with 'harm' or 'spam'? Essentially, the show was in the hands of its distinguished American writers, to whom London should have gone down on its knees in homage. Surely, if they knew anything about anything, they knew a good title when they heard it. Charles Strouse and Lee Adams were streets ahead of their British counterparts in quality, already having written a clutch of Broadway shows: *Bye Bye Birdie, All American, Golden Boy, It's a Bird... It's a Plane... It's Superman*, and *Applause*. An essential third party to *I and Albert* was the playwright Jay Presson Allen, for whom Victoria was a heroine. The writers combined to fashion a work that would coincide with Schlesinger's concept of what the musical should be. To be doubly sure that history was not misinterpreted, the historian Antonia Fraser was engaged as consultant. Such checks did not prevent a lack of focus, and a disappointing reception. Strouse looked to Schlesinger for its failure, citing the fact that the director was 'openly gay, and gays in London at this time were openly satirical about Queen Elizabeth and the Royal Family'.[75] This is curious. Was Strouse suggesting that only straight people refused to be satirical about the British monarchy? Oddly, this brilliant man of the theatre thought this gay slant might be the source of the show's failure, at the same time claiming *I and Albert* as one of the finest scores he and Lee had written. It wasn't, by a mile. It lags far behind their other works, having neither a strong book nor brilliant songs.

James faced the impossible challenge of playing Victoria from girlhood to old age with dignity, but the battle was lost. An insuperable structural problem was the early death of Prince Albert (bad drains or cancer), leaving her without a leading man for the second half of the show, and why did he die without ever even getting a solo? All sorts of ideas about Albertian England went unexplored, leaving Taube to do the best he could with a cardboard reconstruction. The focus was rather on the queen's Prime Ministers; Aubrey Wood's Melbourne and Lewis Fiander doing conjuring tricks (he was trained by Ali Bongo) as Disraeli singing 'When You Speak With a Lady'. Elsewhere, the score failed to come up with much, as if the writers *had* been British. How did two such skilful American writers think up a song title like 'I've 'eard the Bloody 'Indoos' 'as It Worse' (sung, according to the programme, by 'Street People'). Splendidly decorated with Alan Barrett's luxurious costumes, by Luciana Arrighi's nursery-toy sets, and by Gordon Langford's orchestrations, for too much of its time *I and Albert* was little more than a spectacle. Several years later, a recording of its songs with members of the original cast seemed to confirm the score's inadequacy.

# 1973–1976

**'A disgusting mixture of religiosity and sex'**
***Sunday Telegraph*** **on *Thomas and the King***

## 1973

*Kingdom Coming*
*The Card*
*The Water Babies*

Clocking in for its two-week season, *Kingdom Coming* (Roundhouse, 21 May 1973; 14) was little liked. Another car-crash that would never have withstood the West End, here was what everyone had been waiting for: the cryogenic musical about putting dead people in the freezer. A tiny audience witnessed its first night, some probably deafened by the appalling amplification system. The list of its creators, music Bill Snyder, lyrics Stanley Baum, with book and lyrics by David Climie and Ronnie (Ronald) Cass, represented an Anglo-American collaboration that was going nowhere. The evening involved characters being stuffed into refrigerators and (if they were lucky) being successfully defrosted. Richard Macdonald's sets claimed to be the first to be made entirely of fibreglass and polystyrene, but Charles Lewsen for *The Times* noted that *Kingdom Coming* was 'the first show in which both plot and dialogue are biodegradable'.[1] Climie and Cass's book was 'a cross-eyed wreck' in 'a show with something for everyone to dislike', for it was 'not every day you see a musical that ends with the refrigerated being carried out, like the rest of us, board-stiff'.[2]

What possible excuse was there for using Arnold Bennett's 1911 novel as the prop on which to hang *The Card* (Queen's Theatre, 24 July 1973; 130), with a score by popsters Tony Hatch and Jackie Trent? Hugely successful as they were in providing hit songs for popular singers or the theme music for the television soap *Crossroads*, could they extend their talents to writing a theatre score? Bennett had little regard for his story of Denry Machin, a lovable social climber, thinking his novel 'Stodgy, with no real distinction, but well invented and done to the knocker, technically, right through.'[3] Eric Ambler wrote the 1952 film screenplay for which William Alwyn wrote the score. Now, Keith Waterhouse and Willis Hall, whose work in musicals included *Joey Joey*, *Lost Empires*, *Budgie*, *Andy Capp* and *Billy*, adapted the book for the musical. With so much to their name, one would imagine that Waterhouse and Hall, with some claim to being the Alan Jay Lerner or the

Oscar Hammerstein II of Britain, would rank as prominent figures in the British musical, but their contribution to the genre has gone largely unrecognised. Their reputations were instead made on an appreciation of their novels and plays. The book writers of musicals, the librettists, the lyricists, win favour for their lyricism: consider Hammerstein and 'Oh What a Beautiful Morning'. Seek that lyricism in the work of Waterhouse and Hall. It may exist. I am not sure anyone has ever bothered to find out, for when it came to the British musical Waterhouse and Hall were, along with most of their colleagues, considered journeymen.

*The Card*'s best hand and only ace up its sleeve was its Denry, Jim Dale, a performer with a naturally friendly appeal who might have achieved far more in London had producers and writers had the wit to nurture him. Like Denry, he remained blameless for what was wrong with the production. Nine years before, he had brought a slack charm to the American Victoriana pastiche musical melodrama *The Wayward Way*. On the production side, things looked promising for *The Card*: an experienced director in Val May, choreographer Gillian Lynne and designer Malcolm Pride, but something was lacking. The show suffered from the 'too many leading ladies syndrome' (how on earth did they equably sort out the dressing rooms?), with Millicent Martin, Marti Webb, Eleanor Bron and, perhaps most out of her comfort zone, Joan Hickson, vying for attention. Helping to clear the field, Bron played the first night and then went home for good, complaining of having been downsized.

A sense of period, a sense that the spirit of Bennett imbued the evening, was missing, but at least Hatch and Trent's score was breezy and determinedly upbeat. There was, of course, no reason why writers of popular songs should not write popular musical theatre. Burt Bacharach wrote them, and came up with the glorious *Promises, Promises*, seen in London in 1969. Whether such a score would have worked when matched to a period piece is arguable, but the intrinsic quality of Bacharach's work is unquestionable. The difference between Bacharach and his lyricist Hal David, and Hatch and Trent, is that Bacharach and David dug deeper into their characters, insecurities, inadequacy. All that *The Card* did was keep readying itself for another number that sounded like something that had been done just as poorly in the previous decade. Its relentless jollity stripped it of any depth. How the heart sinks even at the song titles: 'Come Along and Join Us' or 'That's the Way the Money Grows' or 'Nothing Succeeds Like Success'. Weren't these songs the sort someone should have cut from *Charlie Girl* or *Phil the Fluter*? At best, the Hatch–Trent style came through with Martin's driving ballad 'Moving On', and Dale and Webb's chirpy duet 'Opposite Your Smile', but it was catchpenny stuff.

Despite its bright smile, *The Card* had a lukewarm welcome. Jack Tinker in the *Daily Mail* decided that 'the real spirit of Bennett's trail-blazing hero is missing from this glib adaptation'.[4] Milton Shulman witnessed 'a conventional English musical [whatever that might be. Did he mean conventional in its inadequateness?]. Most of these songs, lyrics and situations could have been just as relevant to a musical about a pop singer, a tax collector or a bullfighter as they are to a sharp card from the Five Towns.'[5] For Shulman, Dale saved the show from complete orthodoxy. The *Sunday Telegraph* dismissed it as 'signally devoid of flavour, originality, and sheer basic interest';[6] the *Daily Telegraph*, under the headline '*The Card* Has Little But Verve and Vitality', detected 'no tenderness in the treatment of the period'.[7] Michael Billington's notice sounded an understandably desperate note. 'What we don't have is even the slightest scintilla of Bennett's feeling for the Potteries or any suggestion that the story springs out of a definable community [...] When, O when, will the British musical gain contact with reality instead of the outmoded values of showbiz?' Billington saw only 'a collection of production numbers with no feeling for the pulse and sinew of its splendid source'.[8] Three years earlier, Trent had been an unlikely Nell of Old Drury in the touring musical *Nell!*, for which Hatch had been musical director, and in 1974 they scored David Wood's *Rock Nativity*.

Published in 1863, Charles Kingsley's 'fairy tale for a land baby', *The Water Babies*, followed the adventures of chimney-sweep boy Tom, who falls into the river and turns into a water baby. A musical version by Frederick Rosse, Alfred Cellier and Albert Fox played a London season of 100 performances in 1903, in which Madge Titheradge, a notable Peter Pan, made her West End debut as Second Water Baby. For the first London adaptation since 1903, producer-director Ross Taylor claimed to have held 2,000 auditions for the role of Tom, giving it to Richard Willis. Like the other 1,999, he had been required to sing 'Happy Birthday'. Given twice daily, at 11.15 am and 2.30 pm with a top ticket price of £2, *The Water Babies* (Royalty Theatre, 24 July 1973; 67) presented 'a mass turnout for the dancing tots of London's theatre academies, equally artificial as soot-daubed urchins or lamé-clad playmates in the magic pool'.[9]

Front of staff at the Royalty had to be on their toes. Every photograph of the Royalty's adult evening show, the nude revue *Oh! Calcutta!*, had to be hidden from public view before the kiddywinks arrived for the matinees. After seeing *The Water Babies* in a two-thirds empty theatre, Mrs A. Lewis of London wrote to the *Evening Standard* praising this 'splendid outing'. The songs were by John Taylor, previously of some *Charlie Girl* songs, some *Strike a Light!* songs, and all the songs of the much-maligned *Mr and Mrs*. Some curious theatregoers no doubt made the effort to witness the return (her last) to London of one of Britain's greatest musical stars Jessie Matthews, whom the Taylors had once considered for both *Charlie Girl* and *Strike a Light!* Playing Mrs Doasyouwouldbedoneby, topped with a pink top hat and swathed in amply upholstered gossamer, Matthews was pulled on stage at the end of a rope, but subsequently had little to do except sing a number called 'I Like To Cuddle Little Babies'. It was her final London appearance.

In 2014, the Leicester Curve presented a new adaptation with book and lyrics by Ed Curtis and Guy Jones, and music by Chris Egan. Advance publicity promised an innovative and startling take, but critics hurrying back to London had their reservations. The *Daily Telegraph*'s Dominic Cavendish admired its strongly vocal cast but their 'strong-lunged finesse only swells the dread tide of earnestness ... was I ever hooked, immersed? Not a teensy-weensy bit.'[10] *Whatsonstage*'s enthusiasm was dampened: 'Whilst the content and plot are somewhat basic, the musical is pleasant and enjoyable.'[11] *The Times* seemed to have at least taken note of Kingsley's tract: 'Mrs Doasyouwouldbedoneby keeps moralising about how we make life choices and can change track. Might I suggest beating a retreat from this show?'[12]

# 1974

*Bordello*

*Jack the Ripper*

It would be another 26 years before London got another musical about Toulouse-Lautrec. Now, it had to make do with *Bordello* (Queen's Theatre, 18 April 1974; 41), a mini-musical about the diminutive French artist, played here by Henry Woolf, surrounded by an all-female cast. Returning from a spell in an asylum and recovering from alcoholism, Lautrec wanders into a brothel where the Madame (Stella Moray) organises a flashback through his life. The book was by Julian More, collaborating as lyricist with Bernard Spiro. A prime participant in some of the most prominent British musicals of the 1950s, More had hit a jackpot with *Grab Me a Gondola*, written with composer James Gilbert following their first collaboration, *The World's the Limit*.[13] More's reputation grew as part of a triumvirate with David Heneker and Monty Norman through *Expresso Bongo* and the adapted from the French *Irma la Douce*. More and Gilbert's successor to *Grab Me a Gondola* – *The Golden Touch* – failed, as did an interesting revue *The Art of Living*, built around the writings of Art Buchwald. At Birmingham he reunited with Norman for *Quick, Quick, Slow* and with Gilbert for *Good Time Johnny*. After *Bordello*, More did some of his best work providing pastiche lyrics for Norman's *Songbook*, and the Broadway flop *Roza*. *Bordello* was popular song composer Al Frisch's only staged musical. The theatre programme announced that another collaboration with Spiro, a musical version of Synge's *The Playboy of the Western World*, would be opening in New York in 1975. It didn't.

With no star names above the marquee, *Bordello* struggled to attract visitors, despite the earthy talents of its in-all-but-name star Stella Moray, whose career went back to *Belinda Fair*. A brilliant takeover in *The Most Happy Fella*, a solid support in the London *Funny Girl*, an excellent Miss Hannigan in the London *Annie*, a much-respected stand-in for Elaine Stritch during the West End *Sail Away*, a bright presence in *House of Cards*, and as Wilson given one of the best songs of *Robert and Elizabeth*, 'The Girls That Boys Dream About', once again Moray side-stepped stardom. Neither she nor Woolf attracted notices in a show that was considered uninteresting.

The curtain rose on a tableau of one of Lautrec's paintings of Parisian whores, but *Plays and Players* thought 'The sad and dreadful thing about the show is that it tries to put a picture frame round titivation, and doesn't even know how to draw it.'[14] The *Sunday Telegraph* reminded readers that 'artists make bad copy for the dramatist – even when they are dwarfish'.[15]

*Bordello* tried to titillate. It was only natural that its working girls should be naked, and at some stage its writers or director John Cox must have seen nudity as one of the show's ace cards. In the event (and possibly neutered by the nudity of *Hair*) most of the critics looked the other way. Oddly in so supposedly French a work, British prudery pervaded. Irving Wardle complained at the lack of a story, and about the fantasy scenes 'being played out behind locked doors in a ritzy girl's boarding school'.[16] If only, wished the *Sunday Times*, 'it had different principals, better jokes, less banal dialogue, catchier music, and a more talented chorus, it might be endurable. But it hasn't, and it isn't.'[17] And very soon it wasn't.

The beaming features of producer Larry Parnes, relaxing at his desk with a Silk Cut, welcomed theatregoers when opening their programmes at *Jack the Ripper* (Ambassadors Theatre, 17 September 1974, transferred to Cambridge Theatre; 228). 'In this day and age,' Mr Parnes condescendingly informed them, 'you all have very varied tastes, but I always like to think that these tastes will include a charming musical like *Jack the Ripper*.' Had Mr Parnes been smoking something a little stronger than a cork-tipped? In a way, though, he encapsulated the principal problem that many had with this Players' Theatre-commissioned biomusical about the Victorian age's best-known serial killer. It was a question of concept, and the critics (no matter what Parnes's selected quotations from the newspapers might suggest) had their doubts, as the headlines made clear: 'How They Murdered Jack the Ripper'; 'When the Ripper Leaves You Cold'; 'Cardboard Ripper'. *Plays and Players* wondered who the musical was *for*. 'Intellectuals? Too jolly. Tired businessmen? Too tame. The family? Well, if your old gran likes nothing better than to watch prostitutes being knifed by a maniac, I can only suggest you take her to the nearest psychiatrist.' What was more, the songs were 'about as catchy as bars of soap fired from a howitzer'.[18]

Perhaps it was inevitable that the horrors of the 1888 Whitechapel murders would be wrapped up in the context of Victorian music hall, framed by a jocular chairman and choral ribaldry. This is what gave the show birth at the Players' Theatre, with the serious aspects of the crimes emerging from and around the musical knees-up, and observation of the long-cherished traditions of the 'Late Joys' music-hall recreations on which the Players' had made its name. Ron Pember and Denis de Marne's libretto sometimes struck the right note in those 'serious' moments, notably in three excellent numbers, 'Goodbye, Day', 'Half a Dozen Pints' and the show's eleven o'clock 'Step Across the River'. The 'musical reconstruction of incidents relating to the murders' faded in and out between real and

**18**   Cross-dressing in the Met. 'We've Gone and Got Dressed Up In Women's Clothes', a constabulary ruse based on the flimsy excuse of capturing the Whitechapel murderer. British musical veteran Charles West (right) leads the search in *Jack the Ripper*

theatrical. One minute the stage was a dim alley in Whitechapel, the next the stage of a penny gaff, from which a sort of reality now and again surfaced, broke free and dissipated. In a show with so much chorus work (subsequently making it a magnet for amateur societies that mistakenly thought this made it an ideal show for its non-principals), much of the evening demanded rhubarbing through countless ensemble numbers.

The problem was, how could audiences feel involved with the personal tragedies of the doomed women of Whitechapel, when the bitter cake had such thick icing? In a way, the central characters – the suspected candidate for the killer, Montague Druitt, and the one woman around whom the show revolved, Marie Kelly – had to fight against all those bright company routines, all that very forced jollity. Druitt remained nothing more than a cipher. The saving grace of the occasion was the Marie Kelly of Terese Stevens. A docker's daughter from Peckham, Stevens had played the title role in an American tour of *Gigi* with Katharine Hepburn, had attracted attention as one of the Rector of Stiffkey's girls in *The Stiffkey Scandals of*

*1932,* and as a 'rock' Carmen at the Roundhouse. At the time of *Jack the Ripper* the writer and director Patrick Garland was writing a one-woman show, *The Cockney,* for her. Many of the notices for *Jack the Ripper* failed to mention her, but some thought her dazzling. For John Barber in the *Daily Telegraph* she was 'limber and beguiling [...] We shall hear of this young artist again.'[19]

Six years later in London, *Sweeney Todd* had buckets of blood as the demon of Fleet Street's customers were despatched one by one, black humour, brilliant lyrics, superb orchestration, outstanding performances, total professionalism. *Jack the Ripper* had none of those advantages. Its beginnings at the Players' Theatre pointed its future with that theatre's particular style stamped throughout. Reginald Woolley not only designed the dowdy sets (expertly, especially remarkable in 'Step Across the River' when Stevens and Eleanor McCready seemed to vanish into eternity on the tiny Ambassadors' stage) but directed, with Doreen Hermitage's ceaseless choreography perfectly evoking period and milieu. Just as *Belle* tried to rework the Crippen murder into musical theatre, *Jack the Ripper* faced the same problem of a liaison between tragedy and musical theatre.

In 1960, Phyllis Tate's opera *The Lodger,* taking its inspiration from Marie Belloc Lowndes' novel, faced the Ripper murders head on with not a prostitute in sight. Tate's treatment is extraordinarily simple, focusing on a homely, God-fearing East End housewife who innocently takes in a stranger looking for rooms. She soon realises that her lodger is the murderer the police are searching for. At the close of the opera, he leaves, and she resumes her life, clinging to the Bible's belief in the greatness of charity. Only once, in a glorious breakout of drunken revelry, does Tate come anywhere near striking a note that might be recognised in *Jack the Ripper. Opera* magazine admired the way she had tried to 'bridge the all too wide gap between the opposed worlds of more advanced contemporary music and that of popular entertainment'.[20]

Tate manages to match those disparate worlds in a manner that *Jack the Ripper* signally refuses to contemplate. The differences between reality and theatricality in *Jack the Ripper* are never satisfactorily resolved. The Pember–de Marne approach to the material lacked ambition, shackled as it was to the specific demands of its commissioning theatre. The *Daily Telegraph* noticed how 'the moments of Grand Guignol hardly interrupt the relentless thump-thump of the four-square-tunes, or the hearty blatancy of the lyrics'.[21] *Over 21* decided 'All that's wrong is the concept [...] this polished West End version is vulgar in the colourless sense of the word'.[22] When Parnes moved his 'charming' musical across the road to the more cavernous Cambridge Theatre, he effectively killed it off. He must have known that this would be its fate. Stevens' career seemed to come to an end at the same time. When she returned to the West End, it was in a minor role in *Windy City.* London musical theatre had lost one of its most promising performers. She had been the beating heart of *Jack the Ripper.*

# 1975

*Jeeves*
*At the Sign of the Angel*
*Pilgrim*
*Thomas and the King*
*Glamorous Night*

It was, perhaps, a case of timing. Twenty-one years after *Salad Days* and/or *The Boy Friend* invested the British musical anew with an Englishness that none could deny, why shouldn't a musical based on the works of one of the country's most iconic comic writers, with music by the current (not only current but for the next at least forty years) wunderkind, do the same? Andrew Lloyd Webber and Tim Rice's very first musical, the 1965 *The Likes of Us*, written five years before *Jesus Christ Superstar*, would never get to London. Had it done so, would it have taken them in another direction? Possibly. In its way, *The Likes of Us* went on conventional lines to tell a story of Thomas Barnardo. In the context of 1965, it was remarkably assured for a first work from young collaborators. This was the year of *Passion Flower Hotel*, straining at the leash to be up-to-date-sexy. It was the time of Bart's fall from grace with *Twang!* The most potentially interesting of British shows may have been at Stratford East, where *Something Nasty In the Woodshed* made a musical out of Stella Gibbons' *Cold Comfort Farm*.[23] Up for a matinee in London, in 1965 you might also catch Millicent Martin and a few refugees from television in *Our Man Crichton*, or *Robert and Elizabeth*. At the New Theatre, several Fagins and Nancys and Artful Dodgers down the line, *Oliver!* was still pulling crowds. *Half a Sixpence* had recently closed up shop and moved, complete with Tommy Steele, to New York. If you needed convincing that the British musical was a hopeless case, you had only to go to the Piccadilly to sit through a Brian Rix-like knockabout, *Instant Marriage*,[24] with its leading lady from all those *Carry On* films, Joan Sims.

Against any of these, there was a fair chance that *The Likes of Us* might have succeeded. In the tradition of *The Sound of Music* (still going in 1965), *Oliver!* and *Tom Brown's Schooldays*, a bio-musical about the man who established Barnardo's Homes for destitute children offered heaven-sent opportunities to fill the stage with juvenile warblers who even got to sing the winsome title song. Rice showed himself an agile and capable lyricist. Lloyd Webber came up with a score that suggested he had learned something from Rodgers and Hammerstein and something from David Heneker, whose hit number 'Flash Bang Wallop' from *Half a Sixpence* surely inspired *The Likes of Us*'s eleven o'clock stonking 'Going Going Gone'. Besides, the show had strong ballads, quite as good as anything heard in London at the time or since, but *The Likes of Us* was put aside; its creators picked up their Bibles, and suddenly it was 1972; time for a second coming.

1972: *The Maid of the Mountains* revived on the cheap at the Palace; another *Oliver!* in *Tom Brown's Schooldays* (same director and leading lady); John Hanson in a series of mannerisms, just for a change mangling his own operetta rather then somebody else's; a ho-hum so-so American show about Queen Victoria that New York wasn't interested in; another Anthony Newley–Leslie Bricusse musical with

**19** The musical that Lloyd Webber forgot. David Hemmings and non-singing Michael Aldridge as Wooster and Jeeves, overlooked by a Drone in the unappreciated adaptation from P. G. Wodehouse, Palace Theatre, 1975

one of those long titles signifying nothing much at all, and Bart reduced to the off-West End for *The Londoners* and *Costa Packet*. The Lloyd Webber–Rice *Jesus Christ Superstar* and *Joseph and the Amazing Technicolor Dreamcoat* blew gusts of new airs through London musicals.

Expectation of what would follow inevitably built a head of steam. Rice and Lloyd Webber had considered a musical of Evelyn Waugh's *Brideshead Revisited* but settled on an adaptation from the novels of P. G. Wodehouse. When Rice withdrew, playwright Alan Ayckbourn was brought in as lyricist, although 'I think musicals are pretty damn boring, but I hope this is a bit different.'[25] Ultimately, one of the criticisms levelled at *Jeeves* (Her Majesty's Theatre, 22 April 1975; 38) was that it was merely 'a modest, well-written, unspectacular piece in the musical comedy tradition: everything stops when somebody gets a song'.[26]

When *Jeeves*' director, Eric Thompson, withdrew, Ayckbourn took over the reins. There was heightened interest when David Hemmings, long unused to theatre roles, and musically only known from long before as the original Miles in Britten's *The Turn of the Screw*, told the press he was terrified at the thought of returning to the West End as Bertie Wooster. In retrospect, he seems to have been the near-perfect choice, an actor linked to some 'New Wave' movies with an instinctive loucheness that fitted the moment. For some reason, his Jeeves was the much less starry Michael Aldridge, whose musical history took in *Salad Days*, *Free as Air*, the provincial *State of Emergency*[27] and (his third Slade) *Vanity Fair*. Oddly, but perhaps not so odd in the lop-sided *Jeeves*, Aldridge got nothing to sing here. Neither was *Jeeves* very woman-friendly. The excellent Madeleine Bassett of Gabrielle Drake got a few notes in here and there, but only Debbie Bowen had a number of her own, 'Female of the Species'. Originally billed alongside Aldridge, the revue veteran and star of *Keep Your Hair On* Betty Marsden was cast as Aunt Dahlia, but was dropped before London.[28]

When *Jeeves* first played at the Bristol Hippodrome, it was so inordinately long that audiences lost patience with it. It may not have been what they expected; but what *had* they expected? Here was the opposite of a stamping, blaring, extrovert, high-energy show; it didn't attempt to convey its period with high-stepping or mighty choral outbursts. This was a musical that behaved as if it were lying in a hammock on an unbearably hot English summer day; it almost watched itself go by, blinking at the sun. There had by now, however, been a weather change in British musicals, for which Lloyd Webber and Rice were in part responsible. The expectation for them to come up with something that justified the ballyhoo of their prominence in British musicals (a prominence hardly glimpsed by any of their predecessors, most of whom the public had anyway ignored or forgotten) may well have been clouded by the feeling that they might be riding for a fall.

A London critical elite, with a track record for vilifying the British musical, was as ready and willing as ever to oblige with a thumbs-down. It was a little late to wonder if Wodehouse, and Bertie Wooster and Jeeves, had been a good idea. A few days after the show opened, Vivian Ellis informed the *Daily Telegraph* that he had once been asked to compose the music for a proposed musical of the Jeeves books, done by Wodehouse and Guy Bolton. 'I was wild with enthusiasm at the project,' he wrote, 'but after reading the script felt that there are some things that are untranslatable into stage terms and that Jeeves was one.'[29] In this, perhaps, Ellis was wrong, because Lloyd Webber, unable to stomach a flop just as nature abhors a vacuum, was later to turn the show into a boiled-down version that ran successfully. To some, it seemed more sensible for him to have left well alone. In fact, did the original *Jeeves* need an apology?

The reviews for *Jeeves* seemed to agree with Ellis. Jack Tinker reported 'the all-British musical launched with the unsinkable formula of a Titanic [...] Yet it sinks like a stone with the band playing nothing likely to be remembered, fatally holed by an iceberg of immeasurable boredom.'[30] Of course, Her Majesty's was quite the wrong place for it, too yawning a space. *Jeeves* needed its audience close, to whisper in its ear, certainly at the start when Bertie was doing concert party stuff (a likely story) at the East London Club for Unmanageable Boys and, to cover a hitch in the proceedings by chatting to the audience, whiling away the time with anecdotes of some silly adventure or other. No wonder J. C. Trewin found the show 'self-conscious' and 'the whole framework of the show clumsy'.[31] Michael Billington's advice to those responsible for Jeeves was to see *A Little Night Music* '200 times before they lay hands on the unsuspecting musical form'; he had sat through 'a witless travesty [...] as close to the spirit of the original as Budleigh Salterton is to Timbuctoo'.[32]

There is, of course, no rule that obliges a musical to hug the spirit of its source; there is probably a book to be written (if anyone can be bothered) about this quandary. Whatever its fate in 1975, forty years on, Lloyd Webber's score squares up for reassessment. Is the spirit of Wodehouse here? What, anyway, is the Wodehouse spirit? It may be one thing to one, and something different to the next. Lightness in its comic touches, dexterous prose, inconsequentiality, charming eccentricity, shorthand silly ass. Is it possible that Ayckbourn and Lloyd Webber, shifting from, not closer to, those attributes, wrote a work of deeper meaning, of significance, of – surely not! – emotional depth, for which in Wodehouse – perhaps – one has to search more carefully between the lines? I suspect they may have. Set this against most of the scores of the last sixty years, and *Jeeves* sounds something, here and there, like a masterpiece, a jewelled vignette, a little canvas forced into the whopping great frame of a big London theatre, exposed to the public glare when all eyes and ears are lacking in sympathy.

Harold Hobson, that thoughtful theatregoer whose regular reviews in the *Sunday Times* had the reputation of going completely against the grain of his fellow critics, put *Jeeves* above *A Little Night Music*, claiming it as one of the best musicals of the past decade, but for Milton Shulman – almost predictably – the music came to life 'only during some jaunty jazz numbers of the 1920s [but surely these, if they existed, were the weakest of the lot?]. Otherwise, it remains remarkably uninspiring.'[33] One hates to think of those London critics wasting evening after evening sitting through British musicals of which they had very little understanding. Perhaps they were unnerved by the way the show veered away from silliness, for much here had a serious undertow of regret, clapped on to the skirts of an apparently old-fashioned musical play technique that bore no relationship to Lloyd Webber's other known work. Ayckbourn, after all, proved himself a good enough lyricist; the words stand up, resonate, catch a momentary sensation. Where else in musical theatre of the period are the equals of 'Travel Hopefully' (its melody taken from *The Likes of Us*), or the ballads 'Today' and 'Half a Moment'? Hemmings' opening number, 'Code of the Woosters', backed by the little all-male choir of the Drones Club, avoids the big curtain-raiser. Indeed, *Jeeves* dispenses with the chorus. Rather than lifting you out of your seat, those first moments of *Jeeves* tuck a cushion at your back. They are as unworried and unflappable as the imperturbable Jeeves himself and, ultimately, his monocled, lazy-voiced and delightfully contented master. 'S.P.O.D.E.' is one of the cleverest situation numbers of its type and – along with almost everything else – made suitably apt in the palm-court orchestrations by Keith Amos, David Cullen, Don Walker and Lloyd Webber. If in doubt, listen to the sublime 'Summer Song', a little work of art, infinitely touching.

The Players' Theatre policy of producing home-grown musicals was weakening by the mid 1970s, the management's coffers depleted by too many of their projects flopping after transfer to the West End. There can have been little hope of a transfer for *At the Sign of the Angel* (Players' Theatre, 24 September 1975; season). A stalwart Players' regular, Dudley Stevens, had turned to Shakespeare's *Henry IV* (Parts 1 and 2), distilling the Bard into one half of an evening completed by the theatre's more usual bill of fare, Victorian music-hall pastiche. The resulting little touch of Harry in the night had music by Geoffrey Brawn, who had succeeded Peter Greenwell as the Players' resident musical director; perhaps the management meant to promote him as a composer, as it had his predecessor.

The all-male cast brought together several Players' regulars including Robin Hunter as Falstaff and Clifton Todd as young Hal. The *Sunday Telegraph* reported that 'Good natured jostling around Falstaff to the *thé-dansant* tunes and hi-de-ho shuffles, switching to soldier acting from John Bailey's guilty king, keep the romp nicely confused both in text and spirit'.[34] Others were less keen. Milton Shulman prophesied that 'It will need all the loyalty of this theatre's members to make this Shakespearean hotch-potch a success',[35] while for *The Times* it 'rather resembles a forties prisoner of war camp concert [...] the vo-de-o-do rhythms of Geoffrey Brawn's music and the soft-shoe routines of Doreen Hermitage are more 1930s than 1630'.[36] Directed and designed by Reginald Woolley in the definitive style peculiar to the Players, there was never a risk of *At the Sign of the Angel* becoming popular.

*

A poor cousin trailing in the wake of *Jesus Christ Superstar* and associated biblical subjects, **Pilgrim** (Roundhouse, 15 October 1975; season) was shorthand for a free-handed adaptation of John Bunyan's *Pilgrim's Progress*, sent into London from the Edinburgh Festival. A Prospect Theatre production directed by Toby Robertson, *Pilgrim* had book and lyrics by Jane McCulloch and music by Carl Davis, a team that had already written a new version of *The Beggar's Opera* and a musicalisation of *Pericles* set in a Mytilene brothel. Another go at making a British rock opera, with a five-piece band and performers using hand-held microphones, the show had the pilgrim Christian (ideally cast in one of the cleanest-cut of young British actor-singers Paul Jones) wading through thirty musical numbers with titles that sounded as if they belonged to a Moral Re-Armament production ('Prepare Yourself For a Bloody War' and 'New Joy To Fill All Your Days'), with lyrics that often reworked Bunyan's original.

The *Daily Telegraph* was not impressed, deciding that Robertson's direction 'aspires to the dynamism of *Jesus Christ Superstar* and McCulloch's book to the ingenuousness of *Godspell*. Neither strikes home. [...] even at the Roundhouse this is a square show.'[37] Summoning the spirit of Bunyan's Mr Cynic, Disappointment, Purist, Intellectual Snob, High Standards and others to his side, Nicholas de Jongh imagined how they 'brought their review out, and scourged it with the knives of animosity and boredom [...] and so they pricked it with malice and they burned the show to death with the fires of scorn'.[38]

The broken body of the British musical could only incur more abuse with **Thomas and the King** (Her Majesty's Theatre, 16 October 1975; 20), an overblown pageant of mishandled historical absurdity that cost its producers H. M. Tennent and Sam Grossman (who assured the press that this was a 'landmark musical') £175,000. Its visual excesses were so tasteless that the *Daily Telegraph* thought it looked as if it were set 'in the Canterbury Hilton'.[39]

Michael Billington's *Guardian* review considered it 'about as relevant to our present needs as a pterodactyl. The basic problem is simple: the story of Becket's challenge to Henry's authority in matters spiritual and ecclesiastical is not one ideally suited to the quilted gaieties of the popular musical [...] The show falls between every available stool.'[40] According to the *Observer*, its two male stars 'wander on, thoughtless playboy and tight-lipped retainer, for all the world like Bertie and Jeeves in the latest musical shipwreck at Her Majesty's; this show is similarly maladroit and also (unlike *Jeeves*) plain stupid'.[41]

Indisputably glorious as Tim Goodchild's designs were, they dimmed beside the preposterousness of the attempt to sing the conflict between Henry II and Thomas à Becket. The book was by Edward Anhalt, who had won an Academy Award for his 1964 screenplay of Jean Anouilh's play *Becket*. There were lyrics by James Harbert, and music by film composer John Williams. The *Sunday Telegraph* checked out with 'This degraded travesty of Anouilh's *Becket* is sadistic, lewd and exceptionally boring; a disgusting mixture of religiosity and sex.'[42] Charles Lewsen's notice for *The Times* savaged Anhalt: 'This farrago, this omnifutile, pasteboard and plasti-coated bladder of blather is based on no work of art but on the barefaced assumption that, in the theatre, you can get away with any formless, illogical, unconsciable twaddle, provided you do it to music.'[43]

Of the actors obliged to deliver the twaddle, the Henry – James Smillie, a sort of lightweight Howard Keel – could sing; the Becket, Richard Johnson, could not. Johnson had no choice but to put over his numbers in what he imagined might be the Rex Harrison manner (not that Harrison would ever have agreed to twaddle). Hopeful hosannahs raised the curtain, with brazen girls luring their monarch to a pleasurable bed. Herbert Spencer's rich orchestration did its best to disguise what followed, with Becket forever having a chat with a remarkably unresponsive God, and demanding answers from the Almighty who, possibly understandably, regarded his questions as rhetorical. Something very strange indeed happened when king and priest got together for 'We Shall Do It': they changed into the twelfth-century Henry Higgins and Professor Pickering, as if the writers had slipped in the draft of an old Lerner and Loewe number that the brilliant pair subsequently thought would work better in *My Fair Lady* as 'You Did It'.

'Where is the answer?' asks Becket, rather too many times. 'Where, where, where?' Later, Becket is at it again, having another Higgins outburst as he demands of God 'Why did you make such a mess of Man?' Such indecisiveness from a man of such elevated station must have shaken the very roots of society. Most of *Thomas and the King*'s songs suggest that the characters are in urgent need of psychiatric help, not least the seriously unhinged Eleanor of Aquitaine (Dilys Hamlett), clearly off her head as she declares war in 'Power', and Becket in the First Act finale begging God (off-stage all night) to 'Batter me with love, Shatter me with love, Ravish me with love'. Either Henry or Becket (does it matter which?) eventually get round to wondering what we have all been wondering all night: 'Do I hear the tolling of a bell?' To this, at least, the answer is 'Very likely'. Drawing the short straw, the agreeable Smillie would collide with another fiasco, *Barnardo*, four years later.

As winter arrived, so did John Hanson for a prescribed eight performances of **Glamorous Night** (New London Theatre, 17 November 1975; 8), produced by impresario Alexander Bridge. Only the presence of Novello, hardly replicated by Hanson now playing young inventor Anthony Allen, could have alleviated the absurdities of its plot, made even less appealing because Bridge's cut-price production couldn't hope to match the glory of Drury Lane's management of the shipwreck in the original 1935 production. Had anyone ever explained to Hanson that the wily Novello never sang in his shows, despite a short-lived exception during *Careless Rapture*? Hanson's policy was to steal as many of a show's songs from the other characters as he could. He was lucky to have the experienced ex-D'Oyly Carte soprano Pamela Field as Militza Hajos, originally played by Mary Ellis. Hanson was about to embark on a farewell tour of *The Desert Song*. The tour must have been successful. Field was still playing Margot Bonvalet to Hanson's Red Shadow in 1979.

# 1976

*The Lady or the Tiger*
*Mardi Gras*
*Ride! Ride!*
*Liza of Lambeth*

Based on Frank Stockton's Victorian story about a disagreeable king who asks prisoners to decide their fate by choosing between two doors, one concealing a lady, the other a tiger, the understandably titled *The Lady or the Tiger* (Fortune Theatre, 3 February 1976; 52) was satisfactorily transferred from its season's run at the Orange

Tree, Richmond. According to Sheridan Morley, here was 'a musical of unique charm and elegance',[44] and the best thing to happen at the Fortune since the groundbreaking revue *Beyond the Fringe*. An almost casual entertainment ornamented by some tinsel, a few costumes picked up in the Portobello Road and musicians who hadn't bothered to dress up in more than bowler hats and jeans, the show's main characteristic was its lack of pretension (otherwise known as cheapness).

'Perhaps it is a little lacking in edge,' wrote Felix Barker, 'but it delights, and to bring so ingenuous a piece into cynical and permissive London is an act of faith.'[45] The *Daily Telegraph* agreed: 'The audience welcomed this slightly soporific concoction as if surprised by joy. *Salad Days* are here again.'[46] Others were less taken with Michael Richmond and Jeremy Paul's folk-hearted whimsy, the source of which had already been put to more substantial use as part of the Broadway musical *The Apple Tree*. Some were impressed with Kate Crutchley's princess, the *Evening News* reporting her 'triumphant West End debut'.[47] Richmond's other musicals, *She'd Rather Kiss Than Spin* and *Wild, Wild Women*, his only other West End musical, seen at the Astoria in 1982, never achieved wide recognition.

A reasonable run, a sturdy cast, some excellent notices (Harold Hobson, barking up his Sunday tree, went overboard by hailing 'a brilliant victory [...] the most exciting musical London has seen for a long, long time'[48]) and recognisable names among its creators indicated a brave effort, but in the coldness of day it's hard to retain much enthusiasm for *Mardi Gras* (Prince of Wales Theatre, 18 March 1976; 212). In a busy life, one would have thought Melvyn Bragg had enough to cope with without bothering to provide the book for a musical; he'd write another for *The Hired Man* eight years later. Now, *Mardi Gras* followed the story of aspiring jazz musician Lorne, played by the always welcome Nicky Henson, survivor from the British *Camelot*, *Passion Flower Hotel*, *Canterbury Tales* and *Stand and Deliver*. In New Orleans for the 1917 Mardi Gras, Lorne falls for the prostitute

Celandine, played by Dana Gillespie in a sequence of events that here and there recalled the goings-on of *Carmen*. Director Clifford Williams (*Our Man Crichton*) had assembled a first-rate company, among them Gaye Brown (*Man of Magic*) as Concepcion, Lon Satton, and Aubrey Woods (*Valmouth*, a Fagin takeover in *Oliver!*, *The Four Musketeers*, *I and Albert*).

The problem, perhaps, was with the piece itself, always pretending to be something it wasn't, particularly depressing because it was a British musical pretending to sound American. Against this, the general competence of the piece was not especially appealing. J. C. Trewin put his finger on it: 'One cannot help feeling that [the authors] met with an atlas and asked earnestly what part of the world, not recently used, would be suitably decorative.'[49] British musicals had rarely ever been at their best when forced into American accents, which helps explain why some British versions of American musicals fail to catch fire.

Audiences can still recognise a truth. Its very location started *Mardi Gras* off on the wrong, Dixieland-flavoured, feet, and the music and lyrics of Ken Howard and Alan Blaikley (who had both been at Oxford with Bragg) couldn't right it. Having no distinct voice of its own, the show lapsed into something that sat tight at the Prince of Wales, doing steady business, until Bernard Delfont decided its time had come. Others beside Trewin pointed a finger at Bragg. The *Sunday Telegraph* thought he had 'supplied a story that avoided parody by a mere hair's breadth';[50] for the *Observer*, 'he has not been able to deliver a story of more than conventional melodrama'.[51] Milton Shulman agreed, noting how 'an uncertain air of contrivance sits heavily' and 'in spite of the tunes and the prose style, one never feels closer to New Orleans than a short taxi ride from the Palladium'.[52] Herbert Kretzmer, possibly better disposed towards director Williams, who had staged Kretzmer's *Our Man Crichton* in the 1960s, endorsed 'Enough driving, strutting Dixieland numbers, high-spirited gospel songs and Voodoo drums to keep the theatre warm for months to come.'[53] That certainly was true, but it didn't make *Mardi Gras* something you'd enthuse about.

**Ride! Ride!** (Westminster Theatre, 20 May 1976; 76) was probably lucky to live out its few weeks in London, but this was one of the more captivating scores of the 1970s, music by Penelope Thwaites, lyrics by Alan Thornhill. Incidentally bridging a gap between classical and popular, its musicianly airs were not merely academic. The pity is that Thwaites didn't feel encouraged to write another musical. Its ongoing 'Riding Song', beginning and (never-) ending acknowledgement of John Wesley's tireless journeying through England to spread the message of Methodism, perfectly framed this work, through the first we learn of the preacher ('He's Just a Little Man', gently affecting), through tough Mrs Whitehead's fierce description of her upbringing ('Deep In the Blackness'), through Martha Thompson's dazed reaction on seeing London for the first time ('Strange City'), to Wesley's declaration of intent, 'The Whole Wide World Is My Parish'. Thwaites responds with style, even making room for two comic trios, 'Enthusiasm' and the gossamer-light 'A Nice Little Change of Air' that put to shame the frequently embarrassing comic cuts stuffed into so many other British shows. *Ride! Ride!* also had the advantage of experienced hand Peter Coe (*Lock Up Your Daughters, Oliver!, Tom Brown's Schooldays*) as director.

Here was a show where the words mattered. Its librettist Alan Thornhill had long been associated with the Moral Re-Armament movement. His drama about the human element in industrial conflict, *The Forgotten Factor*, although unseen in London, played sixteen countries. His other musicals included two Moral Re-Armament productions, *Annie* and the 1969 *High Diplomacy*. Perhaps it was Thwaites' influence that inspired his most assured work, for here it's an easy, unforced sort of poetry that in the earlier shows had reeked more obviously of the pulpit. Religiosity breaks out everywhere, naturally, just as it did in *Annie* with its central plea to 'Open Your Heart', but now it's Thornhill's use of language that marks out *Ride! Ride!* as it tells the story of Martha Thompson (Caroline Villiers), hoping to escape the misery of her upbringing by travelling to London, where she falls under the influence of Wesley (Richard Owens), before being thrown into Bedlam by his enemies.

Thornhill's feeling for this invests everything, even in the *mélange* of street cries ('I'm a crimp/ I'm a crimp/ Get y'coal from the crimp/ Straight from the hag-ship/ Up from the bag-ship/ Get y'coal from the crimp'), with Thwaites' musical response almost as classy as Gershwin's street-cries in *Porgy and Bess*, and no less effective than Bart's street-cries in *Oliver!*'s 'Who Will Buy?' Thwaites' restraint when Wesley delivers his underplayed hymn, matched again by Thornhill's clear involvement with the passion of it all, as the old man sings 'It's for every man that I burn', begs the question 'How many other British musicals come near this sort of quality?'

Reaching the West End on a budget of £100,000, 'London's Own Musical' *Liza of Lambeth* (Shaftesbury Theatre, 8 June 1976; 110) had a top ticket price of £3.50, with balcony seats at 75p. Renting the Shaftesbury at £2,000 a week, the need for success was obvious, but critical encouragement was not forthcoming. The source material was William Somerset Maugham's first novel, published in 1897, written when he was an obstetric clerk, helping deliver babies in the slums of South London. After an affair with a married man, Liza has a miscarriage and dies. In 1944, Maugham's short story *Rain* became the Broadway musical *Sadie Thompson*,[54] and in 1957 his novel *The Moon and Sixpence* was turned into an opera[55] at Sadler's Wells. Perhaps surprisingly, none of Maugham's catalogue of short stories has been plundered for musical theatre; but *Liza of Lambeth* shared tragic elements that thread through both *Rain* and *The Moon and Sixpence*. It needed subtle hands if it was to work as musical theatre. On this occasion, none were available.

Michael Billington reported ironic hisses, booing and jeers at the first night of

'That perennially ailing patient, the British musical', which 'last night suffered a severe relapse [...] although at the end the hospital orchestra gallantly attempted artificial respiration, it was clear as one quit the scene of the death that the malady lingers on'.[56] *Punch* thought the songs 'worth their weight in gold',[57] and *Where To Go* was quoted on the flyers as having found it 'extraordinarily well acted – in fact, I can recall no British musical with better acting performances' (perhaps the *Where To Go*'s dramatic critic didn't get out much), but the more hardened critics damned it. Milton Shulman detected in the songs 'that familiar catchy quality that one associates with toothpaste and detergents', clearly a reference to its composer Berny Stringle (co-librettist with the slumming satirist William Rushton, as well as the show's director), the winner of eighty awards for producing and penning jingles for television commercials. For Shulman, it was 'a remarkable feat of misguided judgement that so fragile a literary plant could be converted into such an ungainly aspidistra'.[58] The *Sunday Telegraph* held back, telling its readers that 'the truth about this drab, dull, drowsy, dreadful, dreary boozily drunken musical of late nineteenth century Lambeth is too brutal to be told in detail'.[59]

John Barber pinpointed one of the central faults of *Liza of Lambeth*: 'For years the idea has persisted that a great public awaits a Cockney musical to bring back the vigour of Victorian music-halls' of which this was 'yet another attempt'.[60] Knee-jerking japes, fingers hooked in the waistcoat for a celebration of the Old Kent Road, a forced jollity never encountered in anything like real life, had underpinned too many British musicals for too long; it was absurd that such stuff should still reach the stage and expect to draw a public as late as the mid 1970s. Godammit, those chorus boys are still thumbing their waistcoats in 2016!

Never mind: the hugely successful 1985 revival of Noel Gay's 1937 *Me and My Girl* showed that, a decade later, the public's enthusiasm for a sing-song had not abated. British musicals of the 1950s had disdained such antics; there is barely a trace of it in the works of Slade and Reynolds, or Sandy Wilson, and although Bart injected a fair amount of East End optimism into *Oliver!* ('Consider Yourself' and 'Oom Pah Pah' might stand as twentieth-century cockney originals), they avoid becoming the gross caricatures offered by several of his contemporaries such as Leslie Bricusse, Anthony Newley, John Taylor and David Heneker. *Half a Sixpence*'s hero, Tommy Steele, had a natural inclination to toothy cheerfulness that gave natural birth to 'Flash, Bang, Wallop!', and Taylor repeated the trick for Joe Brown's 'Fish 'n' Chips' in *Charlie Girl*. Shades of 'Flash, Bang, Wallop!' undermined many of Heneker's later works, meant to brighten up *Phil the Fluter* (1969) and *Peg*. The habit was infectious but unhelpful. Taylor's *Mr and Mrs* (1968) and *Strike a Light!* (1966) were at times almost defined by nothing *but* the cockney larking about, as was Bill Owen and Tony Russell's skirt-twirling score for the supposedly documentary *The Match Girls* (1966). The fact is, when cockney celebration broke out, subtlety and refinement mostly flew out the window.

Various valiant efforts to overcome this boisterous trend went largely

**15**  Is Angela Richards attempting to strangle Patricia Hayes after hearing her sing 'Red Jollop' in *Liza of Lambeth*?

unappreciated. The dance-heavy *On the Level* (1966) kicked up its heels with not a trace of cockney from its creators Ronald Millar and Ron Grainer, whose previous operetta *Robert and Elizabeth* (1964) had shown not much willingness to embrace it. The misfire biomusical of Marie Lloyd, *Sing a Rude Song*, had been unable to avoid it. The fallacy of cockney cheer reached its apogee in the works of Leslie Bricusse, scarring the awful *Sherlock Holmes* and the fabric of his film score for *Scrooge*. Meanwhile, Stringle and his collaborators gave credence to *Liza of Lambeth*'s flyer boast by the *News of the World* that 'It's knees up time in this new musical'. As long as there were waistcoats and thumbs, all was well.

If Liza's story had to be told, it could scarcely have been better cast, even if Maugham's name was the only one above the title, when the appealing Liza, Angela Richards, should have been there. Richards (*Robert and Elizabeth, Annie*) had the best of the songs, among them 'Is This All?' (perhaps a lament against the unending cockney goings-on) and 'Beautiful Colours'. There was a strongly masculine line-up, with Bryan Marshall and the doe-eyed Christopher Neil as the two men in Liza's life. The lethal dose of cockney was injected by Michael Robbins and his cohorts, and by veteran Patricia Hayes making her first appearance in a musical and lumbered with one of the very worst songs of the night, 'Red Jollop', plumbing unexplored depths of awfulness. She exhumed it the same year for an edition of the BBC's *The Good Old Days*, with the Players' Theatre supporting her. At one point, they must have had their thumbs in their waistcoats.

# 1977–1979

'The show gives the impression of having been assembled overnight'

*Plays and Players* on *Kings and Clowns*

## 1977

*Lionel*
*Fire Angel*
*Dean*
*Maggie*
*Drake's Dream*

'It's not my show. It may be garbage. It may be an obituary,' Lionel Bart told the press before the opening night of *Lionel* (New London Theatre, 16 May 1977; 40) This 'musical created from the works of Lionel Bart, Composer N.E.1' was an indignity that beggared belief, visited on the man who, seventeen years earlier, had been the saviour of the London, if not the British, musical. Society photographer Alan Warren, modestly describing himself in the theatre programme as a 'multi-talented personality', conceived and produced this disastrous tribute, hiring John Wells to write a script that had a very young Bart centrestage, flashing forward in time via a plotline that managed to grind its troubled subject's face deeper into the dirt. Inhabiting a sort of pastoral Stratford East, 'Li', played by adolescent Todd Carty, has dreams that take him off to wherever provided an excuse for one of Bart's old songs. Thus, Li's nightmare about war throws up 'Who's This Geezer Hitler?' from *Blitz!*, and so on through thirty numbers. Two practised performers of Bartiana, Avis Bunnage and Aubrey Woods (a Fagin take-over in the original *Oliver!*), had the style necessary for this stuff, but *Lionel*, mercilessly recalling Bart's recent years of failure, bankruptcy and professional isolation, must have been a difficult thing for its off-stage hero to stomach.

Bart had been banned from rehearsals, but did see the show, accompanied by his teddy-bear. The critics, for once, were united with him in not taking it seriously. Michael Billington lamented 'a plot-line that is fatuous to the point of incomprehensibility',[1] while the *Sunday Telegraph* looked on as 'dreams turn to nightmares, and nobody pays his bills' in a show that 'carries foolhardiness into the area of masochism'.[2] It surely deserved B. A. Young's description of a 'save-trouble musical', cobbled together by choreographer Gillian Gregory, unable to disguise the fact that 'Revisiting these songs now reveals them as ephemeral. They offer little beyond happy memories of the dawn of pop.'[3] That Bart's achievements should have been so lowly valued was itself an indictment against Warren's misjudged enterprise. It is little wonder that among the production credits his psychiatrist was listed. His involvement did not prevent Warren suffering a nervous break-down during the production.

Somebody should write a book about Shakespeare and musicals, the most inter-esting fact about this being that Avon's Bard had never heard of such things. As it turns out, he has fared better in American hands than in those of his country-men armed with ready-to-be-stuffed-in songs. There are natural contenders for top prizes: *West Side Story* from *Romeo and Juliet*;[4] Rodgers and Hart's *The Boys from Syracuse* from *The Comedy of Errors*.[5] What place for Galt MacDermot's *Two Gentlemen of Verona* or the jazzed-up *Midsummer Night's Dream* of the revue-like Broadway *Swingin' the Dream*?[6] Pop influences transformed Jack Good's take on *Othello* into *Catch My Soul*,[7] and an off-Broadway *Twelfth Night* into *Your Own Thing*.[8] The British contributions were more restrained, the most operetta-like being *The Three Caskets* with its Peter Greenwell score.

Ronnie Barker was Falstaff for Birmingham's *Good Time Johnny*, Julian More and James Gilbert's rearrangement of *The Merry Wives of Windsor* in 1971;[9] the Players' Theatre had another go with *At the Sign of the Angel*. Gyles Brandreth's attempted musicalisation of *Twelfth Night* by adding '100 of the greatest tunes of all time', with Brandreth as Malvolio, promised an Enid Blytonesque entertain-ment, but *Five Go To Illyria*[10] was dull stuff. On the sidelines, an Arthur Askey vehicle, *The Kid from Stratford*,[11] had the little busy-bee concert-party comic deep in Shakespearean trouble, and Shakespeare himself turned up as a character in *No Bed for Bacon*, a Ned Sherrin–Caryl Brahms show that never got further than Golders Green.[12]

It was only a matter of time before Shakespeare rocked. **Fire Angel** (Her Maj-esty's Theatre, 24 March 1977; 42), originally announced as *Sun Man*, turned, as had *The Three Caskets*, to *The Merchant of Venice*, with less melodic and decid-edly less prettified results. First seen as *Shylock* at the Edinburgh Festival in 1974, Ray Cooney's production came at the end of two years' work, into which he sank £60,000 of his own money. Director Braham Murray took up the show after listen-ing to the songs performed by lyricist Paul Bentley and Roger Haines, on which occasion he heard 'half a remarkable show and half a dud'. In this, at least, *Fire Angel* was not unique. For Murray, the songs 'achieved the power of a genuine opera and were absolutely true to the material'.[13]

The change of gear from play to musical shifted the action to New York's Little Italy, infiltrating Shakespeare's play with the Mafia. Cooney further distanced the original by altering the character's names, so that Shylock became Barach. Musical director Anthony Bowles was convinced that *Fire Angel* would have a profound effect on the future of the domestic musical, but the pre-London opening at Wim-bledon was disastrous. Cooney removed Murray, but insisted that he return when the show reached the West End. By now, the score was pumped out by a six-piece

**21**   A musical merchant of Venice: Derek Smith and dancers working out
in *Fire Angel*

rock group, an eight-piece orchestra and the London Saxophone Quartet, above which the appallingly amplified cast was mostly inaudible. Cooney's solution was to give the entire chorus hand-mikes. Murray departed for good.

The reviews were dismal. The *Sunday Telegraph* looked on as 'yet another doomed attempt at a British musical galumphs on to the stage, topples slowly over, and lies in a heap breathing stertorously', performed by 'the largely terrible cast'.[14] Wishing that British musicals would not ape those from Broadway, *Punch* could not see 'how the West End can go on attempting the ludicrously impossible with such blithe indifference to the laws of theatrical reality'.[15] For another critic, here was 'an excuse for singers to shriek almost totally incoherent lyrics into hand-held microphones'. With poor attendance, and a weekly running cost of £16,000, Cooney's intended successor to *Jesus Christ Superstar* could not succeed.

*

Building musicals around the lives of iconic cinema idols has not always proved lucrative. *Dean* (Casino, 30 August 1977; 35) flared a path for the years that followed in its treatment of the legendarily rebellious James Dean. The librettist was a Dean biographer, John Howlett, and the music by the 22-year-old composer Robert Campbell. It was as if a conscious effort was being made to let a youthful team loose on a project that would appeal to a younger audience, exploiting the potential opened by Lloyd Webber. As it happened, subsequent shows about cinema idols focused on stars in which more youthful audiences probably had little or no interest. *The Biograph Girl* (1980), like all David Heneker's work, was clearly aimed at the middle-class, middle-of-the-musical-road, middle-aged-or-above patron, who might just have heard of Mack Sennett, Lillian Gish and David Griffith, while *Blockheads* (1984) looked back to Laurel and Hardy. So far as audiences were concerned, these were black and white musicals, as was the much superior *Mack and Mabel*, bringing Jerry Herman's memorable score to London in 1995, erasing all memories of *The Biograph Girl*, which had tentatively and less ambitiously covered some of the same ground. The 1983 *Marilyn!* was much more in the *Dean* mood, but none of these shows was particularly successful. Ironically, the most successful musical to centre on an iconic movie star was *Sunset Boulevard*, but here the star – Norma Desmond – was a fiction.

As Dean, producer Steven Bentinck cast a 24-year-old lookalike Californian, Terrance Robay, in a blaze of publicity that petered out when Robay was paid off during rehearsals with a settlement of £15,000, to be replaced with British actor Glenn Conway. The original director, Robin Hawdon, was jettisoned and succeeded by Robert H. Livingston. Derek Godfrey, cast as Elia Kazan, quit, citing cuts to his role; musical director Richard Leonard departed. There were doubts about the score when Bentinck explained that 'Robert Campbell is not able to write music and Dick [Leonard] has been writing down the notes Robert plays on the guitar.' Disagreements with the choreographer Noel Tovey compounded the problems. With the show unready, the Wimbledon try-out was cancelled, and *Dean* opened cold in London with production costs of around £220,000, and a top ticket price of £4.50.

The reviews were not as dismissive as the pre-opening accumulation of difficulties might have suggested, although *Punch* thought that 'the overall result is not unlike a mortician's benefit night'.[16] John Barber criticised it for being 'too much in love with the brash superficialities of show biz to make a worthy job of a romantic biography', but 'with an author, a director and a composer who have not worked before on a major West End musical, the result is surprisingly competent. I can put it no higher.'[17] No matter: for a British musical in the 1970s, this passed for a ringing endorsement. Campbell's music was praised, with Milton Shulman recalling 'some vibrant songs that range from the tender to the punchy' in a show that was 'better than just the routine backstage musical'.[18] Contrarily, John Peter in the *Sunday Times* wished it 'could at least have tried to be early hard rock [...] but no, it turns out to be the sort of rhythmic mish-mash they play on aeroplanes during take-off to dispel your sense of impending disaster'.[19]

The cinematic idol musical had the same problem as every other biomusical: how to play out its subject's life and career in anything other than linear form, in a frame that mixed truth with theatrical licence. *Dean* used the conceit of playing out its drama in the context of a Hollywood studio, with the action taking place in New York, Los Angeles and the mind of James Dean. *Marilyn!* would go that bit further, making 'Camera' the show's leading man, probably an easier and less confusing option when faced with the logistics of having to include so many Mr Monroes.

At the end of *Dean* the on-stage oil-well, emblematically introduced from the movie *Giant*, exploded in a phallic climax of golden sparks that must have stirred the stalls, but the show had hardly opened before business dropped to 40% capacity, and *Dean*'s travails were over. On leaving the theatre, the critic J. C. Trewin overheard one of the audience say 'It's not much like *Show Boat*, is it?', suggesting that not all customers of this period sitting through British musicals were good at coping with change. From the performer's point of view, playing these cinematic idols proved something of a poisoned chalice. One of the lines in *Dean* had warned as much: 'You gotta be dead to be immortal.'

An antidote to the sort of brazen modernity evident in *Dean* was not long in coming. Despite having written over 40 musicals, including adaptations of *Ballet Shoes*, *The Loves of Joanna Godden*, *Little Lord Fauntleroy* and (Frances Hodgson Burnett again) *A Little Princess*, and *The Importance of Being Earnest*, as well as biographical musicals about Lilian Baylis, Henry VIII, Pinnochio, Sarah Bernhardt and Josephine Baker, the only one of Michael Wild's works to reach the West End was *Maggie* (Shaftesbury Theatre, 12 October 1977; 42), with a top price of £4. It was not, as some might have hoped, a tuneful romp through Margaret Thatcher's life, but based on J. M. Barrie's *What Every Woman Knows*. In as close to a feminist statement as any of Barrie's plays ever came, the apparently charmless Scots spinster Maggie Wylie is persuaded to agree to an arranged marriage with the ambitious, unsmiling student John Shand, of whom one of Maggie's unimaginative brothers asks 'Are you serious minded?'; Shand assures him 'I never laughed in my life'. Marrying without love, Maggie sculpts Shand's future as a successful politician, quietly proving that every woman is a power behind the husband's throne, with never a thought of usurping him. Barrie's stage direction at the close of the play describes the moment when, at last, Shand laughs for the first time in his life:

A terrible struggle is taking place within him. He creaks. Something that may be mirth forces a passage, at first painfully, no more joy in it than in the discoloured water from a spring that has long been dry.

Barrie's stage direction might as well sum up the critical reaction to Wild's adaptation, an import from the Forum Theatre, Billingham, whose short London run was not necessarily explained by its star's suggestion that 'The uncertainty of the blackouts [at a time of prolonged energy supply disruptions in Britain] kept the public away'.[20] That star was Anna Neagle, the much-loved actress whose glamorous and sometimes brave impersonations on stage and screen had singled her out for public adoration. The role of the Comtesse de la Brière in *Maggie* had been intended for the less well-known Lally Bowers (*Call It Love?*, *The Dancing Heiress*), but Neagle's success in *Charlie Girl* and in a critically maligned revival of *No, No, Nanette* at Drury Lane was a late-life gift-horse, and ensured that she continued to be treated as theatrical monarchy. Neagle was treated as a performer 'for whose gracious appearances the lights, groupings, and manners of Tom Hawkes' company are instantly adapted as if for royalty alighting at a provincial railway station'.[21] The

**22**  Dame Anna Neagle and Barry Sinclair gingerly stepping out at a rehearsal of Michael Wild's *Maggie*, a genteel musicalisation of J. M. Barrie's *What Every Woman Knows* at the doom-laden Shaftesbury Theatre

respect was deserved; the woman who for years had been one of Britain's most popular stage and film stars was nothing but an asset to a piece of so little pretension, lending the Comtesse a French accent that had to be heard to be believed. The *Evening News* celebrated 'a star in total command of her part and our affection'.[22]

Anna Sharkey had done good work for British musicals, mostly soubrettish roles in flops such as *The World of Paul Slickey*, *Joie de Vivre*, *Divorce Me, Darling!* and *The Young Visiters*, before being cast in the title role of *Maggie* opposite Peter Gale (one of Neagle's co-players in *No, No, Nanette*) as Shand. Another attempt to add gravitas was the casting of Barry Sinclair (as a regular understudy to Ivor Novello, he had been pulled out of the RAF to cover the imprisoned star during the run of *The Dancing Years*). When Sinclair left *Maggie*, he was replaced by Charles Stapley, who had succeeded Rex Harrison in the London *My Fair Lady*.

No one quite seemed to understand how *Maggie* had found its way into London, but the critics dutifully turned out. The *Observer* reported that 'this archaic stuff [Barrie's play] has now been knitted, purled and purloined into a musical [which] can only exemplify the grossly suicidal turn the British musical has taken. Michael Wild's adaptation slits its wrists on seventeen ditties, forgettable for their music and unforgivable for their words ... and breaks its back in its blind impatience to hurry through the plot and be done.'[23] *Punch* discovered 'a wan and pale affair. [Wild] seems to be trying to recall the better moments of *Gigi* ... no matter that neither Novello nor Coward nor yet Julian Slade would have been seen dead near a score like this.'[24] The *Gigi* comparison was exampled by Neagle's duet with her old flame, Mr Venables, 'Do You Remember?' ('All those nights on the Bosphorus / When the sea was like phosphorus'), recalling Lerner and Loewe's 'I Remember It Well'. 'Why plough up the dramatic line with insipid songs?' asked Irving Wardle, describing 'another burnt offering on the primitive altar of the British musical'.[25]

Neagle regarded the show as 'in the same category of *Robert and Elizabeth*' (presumably only as a costume piece), defining it as 'a play with music', a description that accurately fixes Wild's generally small, quickly-done-with numbers, too few of which were fully developed. Sharkey made the most of the Jerry Herman-like title song and the central anthem 'Till the End of Time', but Wild's lyrics lagged behind even the most beguiling of his melodies. Serious undermining was achieved by such cuttable items as the 'London Waltz' and the huffing and puffing of Maggie's brothers celebrating 'Dougal Drummond's Railway'.

The *Sunday Times* assured readers that *Maggie* was 'guaranteed to age you fifteen years in a short evening. Book music and lyrics are all by Michael Wild, and appear to have been strained through cheesecloth.'[26] There was probably an audience for *Maggie*, and deservedly an audience still for appreciating the talents of Neagle and Sharkey, but it was ageing, as were the styles to which Wild's adaptation and score, despite its many moments of light charm, clung. Sadly, Wild was not invited to the first-night party.

*

Was *Drake's Dream* (Shaftesbury Theatre, 7 December 1977; 82) Freudian or Jungian?; it was certainly a little confusing. Promoted as family entertainment ('fun-tastical' according to its publicity), it seemed uncertain of its audience, with its randy sailors pillaging Plymouth in search of the city's whores and cracking jokes about tattooed backsides. As if this wasn't muddling enough, the production advertised itself as 'the New 16th Century Rock Musical'. Setting sail in Plymouth, the show galloped through Francis's three-year exploration of the globe, interspersed with commercials for washing machines from Tudor television. *Drake's Dream* was the sort of show in which the ruler of the Spice Islands was a 1960s' hipster, and by the finale Drake had abandoned ship and become a pop star. Paul Jones, of obviously exemplary character, made an appealingly heroic Drake; how could anything remotely tasteless happen on his watch?

Irving Wardle recognised a product aimed at the Christmas market in 'a jovial narrative [...] With this one out of the way I feel I have nothing to fear from the other Christmas shows',[27] while the *Illustrated London News* found it 'a bewildering affair, now primed with comic anachronisms, now developing into cloak-and-sword, and never sure of itself in either vein'.[28] In a bid for press coverage, 61 'Drakes' and a contingent from HMS *Drake* in Plymouth were given free seats. With no continued hope of filling the Shaftesbury after the Christmas festivities had paled, *Drake's Dream* removed in a revised and reduced version by Ken Hill, to the smaller Westminster Theatre, where it ran out a further four weeks.

# 1978

*Kings and Clowns*
*Big Sin City*
*Bar Mitzvah Boy*
*Troubadour*

Somewhere, someone in 1978 must have wondered 'What happened to Leslie Bricusse?' Of course, everyone *knew* what had happened to Leslie Bricusse; after his early successes co-writing with Anthony Newley he had gone on writing musicals, but what *had* happened to Leslie Bricusse? His first effort, *Lady at the Wheel*, had got no further than Hammersmith. J. W. Lambert had shrugged it off: 'A little piece built around motoring, even the name of which I forget, made plenty of noise but never fired on more than two cylinders.'[29] From 1961 there was consistent commercial success with *Stop the World – I Want To Get Off*[30] through *The Roar of the Greasepaint – The Smell of the Crowd*[31] (not seen in London) and *The Good Old Bad Old Days*,[32] although the effectiveness of these works, directly descended from *Stop the World*, had a downward trajectory. Released from his commitment to Newley, Bricusse certainly established his own style, already evident in his lyrics for *Pickwick*. The Bricusse chirpiness, the Cockney jape, was already there in the song titles. 'You Never Met a Fella Like Me' and 'That's What I'd Like For Christmas' are templates for similar numbers in later Bricusse. *Goodbye Mr Chips*, his adaptation of James Hilton's novel about a fuddy-duddy schoolmaster (John Mills) now reduced to

**23** Don't ask about Number Six ... Five of Henry's wives hoping for the best of the dressing-rooms in Leslie Bricusse's *Kings and Clowns* at the Phoenix in 1978

gloopy sentimentality, didn't transfer to London following its Chichester run in 1982.[33]

*Kings and Clowns* (Phoenix Theatre, 1 March 1978; 34) was jolly and silly and jolly silly, labelled 'another ghastly British musical' by *The Times*.[34] A musical about Henry VIII? Sandy Wilson had written one, never seen. Michael Wild of *Maggie* had written one, ditto. Two years before Bricusse's version, even Richard Rodgers had written one. That had the advantage of a top-notch book-writer Sherman Yellen, and lyrics by the distinguished Sheldon Harnick, but even coupled with Rodgers' music they couldn't make *Rex*[35] a hit. It so affected its grumpy British leading man, Nicol Williamson (neither an Edmund Hockridge nor John Hanson, and one of the most unlikely candidates for romantic lead in a musical) that one night during curtain calls he thumped one of the chorus boys. At least Harnick's lyrics for Henry Tudor didn't go on a Bricusse-type rhyming bender: shrewder, lewder, wooed her, viewed her, nuder, pursued her, chewed her, ruder, cruder, shooed her, booed her, poo-pooed her (etc, etc).

Bricusse's Henry was Frank Finlay, residing at a court where the jester (Ray C. Davis in another of his several thank-goodness-he-got-a-part-in-it-to-liven-it-up-a-bit parts) skateboarded, and the jokes were of the 'A funny thing happened to me on the way to the Reformation' variety. According to Finlay, the first draft of the show had been written by John Mortimer, but by the time it reached the Phoenix, 'There is no need to send to know for whom the bell tolls for this disaster: it tolls for Leslie Bricusse.'[36] Along with *Bordello* and *The Mitford Girls*, *Kings and Clowns* also suffered from Too Many Leading Ladies syndrome. Perhaps on this occasion dressing-rooms were allocated to them in order of divorce or execution.

'The only excuse for a feeble musical like this', wrote Milton Shulman, 'is that it shelters under the word "entertainment". It is a facetious look at the sex life of Britain's most married monarch as seen from the viewpoint of a gag writer under the Royal bed.'[37] There is probably a decent musical to be written about a man who sends his wives to the scaffold. Italian opera throbs with 'entertainments' that exult in the most bloody and terrible acts. Donizetti sends Anne Boleyn to her death with choral relish, but Bricusse under any circumstances is incapable of making a profound point, textually or musically. It may simply be that he believes profundity has no place in the musical, a belief he has successfully upheld. He is very possibly correct.

Condemning *Kings and Clowns* for the rubbish it undoubtedly was, Steve Grant in *Plays and Players* suggested that British musicals failed because

> we do not take them seriously enough. Could it be that a culture that is founded on Shakespeare and Shaw cannot believe that a musical can be anything but small beer? In the case of the now-extinct *Kings and Clowns* this would seem to be the case. From the dreadful concept through the unbearable computerised melodies and lyrics to the xenophobic, sexist and hoary gags, the show gives the impression of having been assembled overnight.[38]

Another here today/gone tomorrow attempt to strike an up-to-the-minute note, *Big Sin City* (Roundhouse, 30 May 1978; 6) billed itself as 'the spoof to end all spoofs'. Written by brothers Neil, Lea and John Heather, and produced and directed by Bill Kenwright, here was a send-up of the music business that seemed almost tailor-made for a teeny-bopper audience, following the exploits of an ordinary country lad Al (Michael Price) who comes to London with girlfriend Dolores and, helped by his road manager (Jack Wild), becomes a pop singer. Populated as it was by two rival gangs, *Big Sin City* suggested vague echoes of *West Side Story*. There is no reason why creators of musicals should have any prior knowledge of musical theatre, or what has gone before them, but what was the point of having a number called 'Kids', when anyone who knew anything about musicals knew that Charles Strouse and Lee Adams had already given that title to one of the hit songs in *Bye Bye Birdie*? For the *Sunday Telegraph*, *Big Sin City* was merely 'the latest British musical to fall flat on its face'. Recalling that 'Mr Wild squeaks away like an upstart Archie Andrews', Michael Coveney thought the show 'While it does not quite make *Fire Angel* look like *Oklahoma!* it is not far off doing so.'[39]

*

*Bar Mitzvah Boy* (Her Majesty's Theatre, 31 October 1978; 78) had good things about it. How couldn't it? – the music was by Jule Styne. The piece had a promising start in Jack Rosenthal's television play about the 13-year-old Jewish boy Eliot Green going slightly off the emotional rails as his bar mitzvah and manhood approaches, and Rosenthal was there to turn it into the musical's book, even if Styne said 'To some extent, we have had to de-Jew it, if that is the right phrase.' Styne wanted to change the title, too, but Betty Comden and Adolph Green, two of his most prominent collaborators, once said that many of Styne's ideas came from Mars. If the musical version had a besetting fault, it was its physical drabness. The dullness was only glimpsed now and again in the score (with Don Black's lyrics), a good deal better than some of Styne's later works like *Sugar*[40] or *Look To the Lilies*,[41] but nowhere near *Gypsy* or *Funny Girl*. Somehow, by the time it reached London, *Bar Mitzvah Boy* ran out of chutzpah. After the Manchester try-out, eight of designer Michael Annals' sets were torn apart and remade, Annals' name removed from the bills, and the first-night credits had no named designer.

Director Martin Charnin wanted major alterations before London, but Charnin seems to have set his heart on turning the show into another *Annie*, for which he'd been lyricist and Broadway director. *Bar Mitzvah Boy* may have been another show about a not grown-up person, but it was a totally different cup of tea to Little Orphan Annie's. Rosenthal wasn't happy with Charnin. Third-billed Vivienne Martin's comedy role of a hairdresser was pruned back and her number 'Maurice Caplan of Hampstead Gardens' scratched after Manchester. For television, Rosenthal had the ideal Jewish harassed mother for Eliot Green in Maria Charles. Charles had enjoyed success in *The Boy Friend* and *Divorce Me, Darling!*, but director Charnin rejected her, casting Joyce Blair as leading lady. Backgrounding in revue, Blair had taken over from Joan Heal in *Grab Me a Gondola* and originated roles in the British productions of *Little Mary Sunshine*, *Dames at Sea* and *Romance!*, without establishing herself as a star. *Bar Mitzvah Boy* might have turned the corner for her, but compared to the sort of material Styne had written for his leading ladies in the past, Blair's material was too feeble for her to overcome. It was bad luck for Blair that her one big number, 'Rita's Request' was one of the weakest of the night, but even on a good day Blair was not known for her comedy. One of her obituaries noted that in the Styne–Black numbers 'she showed what a powerful, Ethel Mermanish voice she had developed'.[42] But as the star of a Jule Styne musical she was competing with Judy Holliday (*Bells Are Ringing*), Ethel Merman and Angela Lansbury (*Gypsy*), Barbra Sreisand (*Funny Girl*), Patricia Routledge (*Darling of the Day*) and Shirley Booth (*Look To the Lilies*). No pressure there, then.

As her cabbie husband, Harry Towb made for a solid leading man, although one wonders if Rosenthal would have preferred, as with Charles, to keep his original actor from the TV play, Bernard Spear. A tiny titan of London musicals, Spear deserves to be better remembered for his untiring work in major roles of American musicals in the West End. It's a staggering roll call that includes *Wonderful Town* (1955), *Plain and Fancy* (1956), singing 'Shipoopi' in *The Music Man* opposite Van Johnson in 1961, *How To Succeed In Business Without Really Trying* (1963), *Little Me* (1964), playing Horace Vandergelder opposite Dora Bryan in *Hello, Dolly!* (1966), Sancho Panza opposite Keith Michell in *Man of La Mancha* (1968), and *Promises, Promises* (1969) – an extraordinary career of long runs. The word flop does not seem to have been in Spear's vocabulary. The comedy of *Bar Mitzvah Boy* would surely have been in surer hands with Spear, whose other characteristics as listed in his *Guardian* obituary, 'modest, humble, sincere and gentle',[43] mark him out as someone quite rare among leading men. In retrospect, both Blair and Towb may have been miscast.

The ballads won the prize, the most memorable sung by Leonie Cosman, 'Where Is the Music Coming From?' and 'It Wouldn't Be You'. *Bar Mitzvah Boy* was only partly by default a British musical, but to hear music of this quality coming from a London musical in 1978 was close to a miracle. Ray C. Davis resurfaced from the idiocy of *Kings and Clowns* to take his place in 'The Harolds of This World'. Many of the numbers worked well in context: the Green family's determination that 'This Time Tomorrow' everything would be alright; the simple domestic hymn of suburban contentment 'We've Done All Right'; 'Thou Shalt Not', and the company-embracing 'The Sun Shines Out of Your Eyes'. Following the Manchester try-out, other numbers – 'Why Can't He Be Like Me?', 'The Cohens Are Coming' and a duet for Victor and Rita, 'Kill Me' – were excised. The new numbers listed in the London programme were 'The Bar Mitzvah of Eliot Green', 'This Time Tomorrow' and 'Where Is the Music Coming From?' The writers had apparently been unable to come up with a replacement for the weak 'Rita's Request'.

Nevertheless, B. A. Young in the *Financial Times* cheered. 'What makes *Bar Mitzvah Boy* almost uniquely enjoyable among recent musicals is the intelligent, witty, sympathetic book by Jack Rosenthal, and the music is by Jule Styne, in his best form.'[44] Robert Cushman praised Rosenthal for turning out 'a thoroughly professional musical (it doesn't look like an accident, which, since it is a predominantly British show, makes a pleasant change), but it is difficult to watch it without feeling a bit torn: half willing the author to be ruthless, half regretting the changes he actually has made'.[45] For some, the score was the problem. 'Songs interrupt the story instead of opening it up,' wrote John Barber. 'Wisecracks and unmannerly bustle displace the humorous exactitude of the original. And the show is disastrously static.'[46]

*Bar Mitzvah Boy* didn't get to Broadway, although an American version surfaced in 1987. Stewart Nicholls' 2016 Upstairs at the Gatehouse revival used a script reworked by David Thompson that had received a workshop reading in 2007. New songs were introduced, with Black providing lyrics for some Styne trunk numbers, alongside much of the original score, although 'Thou Shalt Not' and 'Where Is the Music Coming From?' were cut, finding no place in Thompson's reduced version, which focused more securely on the Green family, cutting out what in the 1978 production had seemed extraneous. Considered by some to be Styne's most sophisticated score, the 1968 Broadway *Darling of the Day* was Styne's only other musical set in Britain, this time in Edwardian London. Never produced in the West End, this autumnal work was revived at the Union Theatre in 2013, on which occasion one critic suggested that the management would have been better off reviving *The Card*. That any critic should have promulgated such an idea gives grave cause for concern.

Self-indulgent follies were seldom as folly-filled as *Troubadour* (Cambridge Theatre, 19 December 1978; 76). What had anyone done to deserve a musical about the Third Crusade, centuries later generating a crusade of its own? Its author, lyricist and producer Michael Lombardi had already written a thesis on 'Plauton and Terentian Elements in Machiavelli's Comedies'. The programme for this 'musical to fall in love with' introduced Lombardi as 'a business man of extraordinary achievement', President of the Japanese Motivation Institute, who 'considers himself primarily to be a creative writer'. Few visitors to *Troubadour* agreed. Opulence – visual in Tim Goodchild's designs, and musical in Ken Thorne's extravagant orchestration – was the only saving grace of this tale of the twelfth-century male chauvinist and cheery wife-beater (he sets out his stall in 'The Wife-Beating Song') Lupus, who aspires to become a troubadour at the French court of Viscountess Ermengarde. For an actor to play Lupus, Lombardi wanted a cross between Oliver Reed and Howard Keel.

The dialogue did little to inspire confidence. John Barber in the *Daily Telegraph* complained that 'everyone talks in the pretentious language of the Hollywood costume drama, and they often break into Christmas cracker verse'.[47] At one moment Sandra Berkin (unluckily wedded to wife-beater Lupus) announced 'You have betrayed me. I am going to become a nun.' Poor Lupus was soundly criticised: 'You call yourself a man with your puerile ejaculations.'

Lombardi's skills as a lyricist were just as dubious. Artfully, he attempted authenticity by writing lyrics in the archaic Langue D'Oc. Kim Braden, haplessly cast as the Viscountess, had an absurd aria, 'The Loneliness of Power', which would probably have *benefited* by being in the Langue D'Oc, during which she sang the immortal line 'I pick up my needlework and stew'.

Composer Ray Holder had laboured long and hard in musical theatre, his work including dance arrangements for *Evita* and *Bar Mitzvah Boy*, but too often the setting of Lombardi's arthritic rhymes proved a hopeless challenge: 'Though of the weaker sex / Women should be listened to more than the world expects'. Nevertheless, Holder did better than his collaborator could have expected. Lombardi announced at the after-show party at the Café Royal that 'This musical is unique, and the critics will be nonplussed.' His confidence is all the more surprising because he had another day job as dramatic critic of the *Mainichi Daily*

*News*. Uncharitably, his fellow critics showed little mercy to *Troubadour*. Milton Shulman's review, headed 'Oh! Jerusalem!', noticed that 'John Watts, as Lupus, has the justifiably worried look of a troubadour who may soon find himself out of a job'.[48] B. A. Young thought the plot 'monumentally silly' and Holder's music 'enervescent'.[49]

Further chilliness descended when Larry Parnes, owner of the Cambridge Theatre, turned off the heating in an effort to deter both cast and audiences from attending; the critic Nicholas de Jongh complained of the freezing cold auditorium. On 31 December, days after the show had opened, Watts sent Lombardi a triumphant telegram: '*Troubadour* ... Now in its second year!' It is doubtful that Mr Lombardi appreciated the joke. *Troubadour* closed with losses of over £500,000.

# 1979

*A Day In Hollywood, A Night In the Ukraine*
*Songbook*

*A Day In Hollywood, A Night In the Ukraine* (May Fair Theatre, 28 March 1979; 168) negated its claim to be an original British musical. Nifty as was Dick Vosburgh's witty satire on Hollywood musicals, it sometimes took the easy path by pulling in numbers by George Gershwin, Frank Loesser, Hoagy Carmichael and the like, somewhat marginalising the original music of Frank Lazarus.[50] The format of two one-act musicals making up the evening wasn't one likely to appeal to most West End theatregoers, as the American import *Romance, Romance* discovered when it flopped in 1997.[51]

The first one-acter of the night, *A Day In Hollywood*, had the theatre ushers in a celebration of Tinsel Town's Golden Age movies; second came *A Night In the Ukraine*, 'a New Old Marx Brothers' Musical loosely based on Chekhov's *The Bear*', in which Sheila Steafel made a particular hit as Harpo. Originally staged at Hampstead's New End Theatre, the London transfer once again emphasised the lack of a significant 'off-Broadway' arrangement in the West End. Although in the diminutive line of *Dames at Sea* and *The Great American Backstage Musical*,[52] Vosburgh's entertainment was quirkier, in some way more original, and leaned to revue. The *Guardian* decided that *A Night In the Ukraine* 'is more ingenious than the banal, threadbare assortment that precedes'.[53] An unlikely candidate for such success, the much-revised show was produced on Broadway in May 1980, when it was enhanced by some new numbers by Jerry Herman, including a spoof on the highest paid in the world suet-pudding of a singer, Nelson Eddy. At 588 performances, the New York showing far outstripped that of London.

*

**24** Terry Jones and Frank Lazarus erupting for *A Day in Hollywood, A Night in the Ukraine* at New End Theatre, 1979. The show became an unlikely and rare Broadway success

The next of the year's flops – something it had in common with Vosburgh's show – was never quite a musical. It presented itself as 'a tribute to Moony Shapiro', of whom the public had never heard because he didn't exist. That's a clue to the show's trickiness, its wry wrangling with stuff that hadn't happened. There must have been *something* going on with *Songbook* (Globe Theatre, 25 July 1979; 208); even Stephen Sondheim and Harold Prince gave it a moment's thought, because it somehow avoided being mistaken for a British musical. One of the best-devised shows of the decade, it was a near-perfect matching of Julian More and Monty Norman, whose working partnership went back to the 1950s. How come that such an interesting piece had to make its first appearance well out of town, almost off the map, at the University of Warwick Arts Centre? What did this say about the extent to which innovative work was sidelined by mainstream musical theatre? Taken up by the Cambridge Theatre Company, the casting was superb, better than when the production reached London, when David Healey stepped into Bob Hoskins's shoes as Moony, the songwriter who seemed to have been around through every changing taste in popular music. At the Globe, Jonathan Lynn's production retained the other original company members, Diane Langton, Gemma Craven, Anton Rodgers and Andrew C. Wadsworth.

*Songbook* was caviare to the general, relying on its textual and musical dexterity to get it through the retelling of the up-and-down-here-we-go-around the-merry-go-round career of popular songsmith Moony Shapiro as he bends his style to each passing phase, turning out what fashion and, now and again, his personal feelings, demand – a sort of musicalised *This Is Your Life*. Norman's score is a near masterwork of parody, at which he had already shown himself a master in *Belle*, and for which quality he was no doubt hired for *Poppy*. The lack of general appreciation for Norman's work is testament to the lack of appreciation of stylistic invention when it comes to the British musical, as for almost every other British art form. *Songbook* turns the pages from the 1920s through to the late 1970s as hard-working Moony churns out songs that just might take the public fancy: an East River Rhapsody for a drowsy movie; war songs (surely Cicely Courtneidge would have romped home with the ghastly 'Bumpity Bump'); songs for soon-to-be-forgotten Hollywood flicks; a Broadway flop musical happening a long way from *Oklahoma!*; meaningful social message songs written with heart on the sleeve sentimentalising about useless wars, and eventually caving in to the influence of the Beatles. One of the more intelligent musicals of the period, *Songbook* knew its limitations and stayed true to its reason for being. Nothing much followed in its path. There was a sort of appropriateness to the fact that when it transferred to Broadway it was a complete flop, just as poor Moony's one big musical, *Happy Hickory*, had flopped. *Songbook*'s opening night on Broadway coincided with its closing night.

# 1980–1983

'One more show off the camp necrophiliac assembly line'
*Financial Times* on *The Mitford Girls*

## 1980

*Barnardo*
*Colette*
*The Biograph Girl*

Teeming with chirpy (but sometimes starving or dying) children, telling 'A Legend Set to Music', with its hero's name known to every charity-conscious theatregoer in the land, and with a percentage of each ticket sold going to Barnardo's Homes (it had worked for *Peter Pan* and Great Ormond Street Hospital), how could *Barnardo* (Royalty Theatre, 22 May 1980; 43) fail? The pre-performance ballyhoo promised a sentimental and plucky experience: 'It will make you laugh, cry and will capture your imagination from the rise of the curtain to the end of the show. You'll love the children – Ginger, Monty Something-stein, Jim Jarvis, Tosh and many other cockney characters.'

Punters couldn't say they hadn't been warned. At the Royalty, safely away from the West End on Kingsway, the George Mitchell Singers, or a section of them temporarily relieved of their duties in *The Black and White Minstrel Show*, were ready with songs that had sentimental, plucky titles, 'Snuggle Up' and 'Lovely 'ot Pies' (why never 'Hot' in such cases?). Book, music and lyrics were the work of its director Ernest Maxin, best known as a television producer of popular entertainment. On this evidence, his knowledge of modern musicals was negligible. As it happened, he could hardly have chosen a more serious subject, although it's likely that any attempt to dramatise it would have unleashed just as much cockney capering.

One of the great humanists of his age, Thomas Barnardo roamed the poverty-stricken hell-holes of Victorian London, rescuing boys who had fallen into starvation, destitution and were prey to all manner of abuse. From such beginnings grew the estimable organisation that would bear his name. Maxin's seemingly irreconcilable dilemma was how to paint the tragic picture, including the various personal tragedies that fall into any life, but keep audiences believing they'd come in out of the cold to see another *Oliver!* There was an attempt to present an authentic picture: Ivan Henry, who conceived the idea of musicalising the story and in 1972 persuaded Maxin to take it on, was credited in the programme with

'Research'. The job of finding young sprites to play the waifs of the Empress of India's back alleys apparently involved the auditioning of some 2,000 children (always a good ruse for getting press coverage).

Likeable James Smillie, a sort of Australian Howard Keel with a pronouncedly 1980s mullet, was an appealing hero, singing while holding a dead son in his arms, with Fiona Fullerton as his long-suffering wife Syrie. She wanted twenty minutes cut from the show; the critics agreed it was much too long. Barry Westcott, musical director, thought it needed more music. What it probably didn't need was the George Mitchell Singers, complete with a side serving of 'George Mitchell's East End Kids' stomping about the stage to pre-recorded music. Not only was this filtered through a sound system with permanent interference; it was an experience that mystified the rest of the cast, who were obliged to make do with a live orchestra.

Rather more worryingly, Westcott thought *Barnardo* needed more production numbers for Ginger, Monty Something-stein and crew. Westcott told the press that when it came to the second half 'it was just sit back and coast along to the finish'. As this had been the case in dozens of other British musicals, it didn't seem of major concern. Adding more production numbers would anyway have prolonged the agony for the cast faced with minuscule audiences in 'a mawkish excursion into mediocrity which I found both interminable and embarrassing'.[1] When a principal backer withdrew £65,000, the production company Gold Star sued him. Despite all, Smillie was on stage every night singing 'I'm the winner, like the man who came to dinner'.

'The night, alas,' wrote J. C. Trewin, 'has to be tinged with embarrassment; so much effort and loyalty, and in the end so little to show.'[2] For *Punch* it was 'an endlessly uneventful evening [...] the latest in the long line of catastrophic British stage musicals'.[3] B. A. Young in the *Financial Times* heard 'music descended from the palm court school, with lyrics free of harmful sophistication; choreography in which energy replaces imagination'.[4] The *Gazette* wondered that 'Characters who sing and dance their way through a world of hot pies, cosy orphanage beds and fairy-tale weddings have a credibility that is lost when they start having their children die and their wives leave them.'[5]

The lyric delivered by the good doctor towards the end of the show, 'Am I running out of time?', struck a rhetorical note. With the closing notice posted, the show's managing accountant Alan Bobroff complained that 'The critics were unnecessarily brutal in their reviews and it is obvious from the reaction of the audiences that have seen the show they did not share these views.' Mr Bobroff probably forgot that British audiences usually only express their true reactions to what they have seen on the homeward bus. Another attempt at musicalising Henry Mayhew's downtrodden Victorians, in the trail of such as *The Match Girls* and *Strike a Light!*, had bitten the dust. Fifteen years earlier, Andrew Lloyd Webber and Tim Rice had completed their very first collaboration, *The Likes of Us*. It used the Barnardo story much more skilfully, but remains unperformed in London. Good intentions have never been enough to save a British musical.

Musicals built around famous writers are difficult to bring off. Few writers lead particularly interesting lives or are especially nice to know; paying money for a ticket to watch one singing and (at a stretch) dancing all night is a price too heavy to pay. Among the few foisted on the London public were *Beautiful and Damned* about the eminently unlovable Scott Fitzgeralds, Mike Read's derided *Oscar Wilde*, an account of the last days of Ernest Hemingway (*Too Close To the Sun*), Julian Slade and Gyles Brandreth's A. A. Milne musical *Now We Are Sixty*[6] (half Slade's music and half H. Fraser-Simson's, and neither fish nor fowl), and the 2016 adaptation of L. P. Hartley's *The Go-Between*.

Some of those names seem odd choices for so tricky a medium as musical theatre. Surely there were better candidates? Where, for instance, is the musical about Marie Corelli, that monstrous authoress beloved of every Victorian parlourmaid and secretive sensation seeker? Soaked in mawkish religiosity, absurdly purple philosophising and providing oodles of unintentional hilarity, Miss Corelli, the simpering but poisonous scourge of Stratford Upon Avon, would make an admirable heroine, ever-ready to burst into chirruping song. Those considering a musical of this compelling woman would also have to cope with the personal tragedy of her last years – an epic British musical waiting to be written.

One of the problems of *Colette* (Comedy Theatre, 24 September 1980; 47) was that its subject was French, a fact unlikely to appeal to patriotic British theatre-goers, who didn't bother to turn out for *Lautrec* or *The Umbrellas of Cherbourg* (two failed productions in London) either. Who, casual passers-by asked as they gazed at the marquee, or indeed *what*, was Colette? If and when they discovered she was a writer they wondered why that made her interesting, or pertinent, or want to break into song for two and a half hours? Colette lived to be an old woman. If you wanted a musical about an old woman who wrote, wouldn't it have been more interesting to have made a musical about a different old woman that wrote books? Jean Rhys? More of the public had probably read *Wide Sargasso Sea* than *Gigi*, and Rhys as the subject would bring the exoticism of the tropics, the shabbiness of dull old England in Rhys's touring days as a chorus girl in tatty musical comedies, shades of her other much less appreciated but brilliant novels such as *Voyage In the Dark*. Rhys's story might have withstood a singing (and dancing in pastiches of those knocked-up old shows), even if Paris played its part in Rhys's story too. Colette's life seemed a less promising bet.

John Dankworth's 'story with music' traced Colette's career through two World Wars and three marriages, from childhood to the age of 80. The reason for the show was Dankworth's wife, the distinctive Cleo Laine. Her earlier London appearances included taking over from Bertice Reading as the black masseuse in *Valmouth*, playing in the four-hander all-black Christmas semi-revue entertainment

**25**   Johnny Dankworth's *Colette*, with Cleo Laine and Kenneth Nelson,
Comedy Theatre, 1980

*Cindy-Ella*, and playing Julie in Harold Fielding's much-trumpeted 1971 revival of
*Show Boat. Colette* left her exposed on stage at the Comedy as the only woman in a
three-hander, with John Moffatt linking and Kenneth Nelson playing all the other
characters. First seen at the Stables Theatre, Wavendon, *Colette* never settled
happily into its London home. 'You'll see Puccini and Zola, Toulouse-Lautrec
in his bowler' trilled Laine, but, squint as they might, audiences could see only
Laine, Nelson in a selection of hats, and Moffatt in a bright red jacket. In fact, the
*Observer* remembered that 'Occasionally the lighting goes the same colour [as Mr
Moffatt's jacket] and Tim Goodchild's elegant set takes on the complexion of a
tandoori chicken. Or, perhaps more appropriately, a tandoori turkey.'[7]

A septet accompanied the songs, many with the dispiriting titles that seemed
to stalk British musicals; 'Paree!' and 'You've Got To Do (What You've Got To Do)'
that sounded perfect for a Moral Re-Armament musical. Wendy Toye's direction
could not stave off poor reviews. For *Punch* it was all 'fairly terrible'; 'a singer and
some songs in search of a show'.[8] There was no denying the talents of its star, but

'Even Miss Laine strains one's fidelity when, under an ugly wig, she cavorts around as an octogenarian, or an outsize and bosomy schoolgirl.'[9] Budgeted at £125,000, *Colette* played to poor houses and closed with a loss of £100,000. H. M. Tennent's producer Nick Salmon blamed the notices, which had been 'very vitriolic', for its collapse. The *Sunday Times*' explanation may have been nearer the truth: 'The essential flaw of *Colette* is that it displays in the least manageable way the great talents of both the Dankworths.'[10]

Long associated with the musicals of David Heneker via *Half a Sixpence, Charlie Girl* and *Phil the Fluter*, the kindly but (when it came to paying his cast) penny-pinching Harold Fielding continued to support Heneker as his career shifted from major stagings to more modest product. Despite its smallness, there was nothing shy about the ambitions of *The Biograph Girl* (Phoenix Theatre, 19 November 1980; 57), a bright-eyed biomusical about America's pioneering stars of the silent film. Broadway had done it better and more expansively eight years earlier with *Mack and Mabel*.[11] Herman's account of Hollywood's silent movie industry was patently American; in London, book-writer Warner Brown and 74-year-old Heneker's take was essentially British. If the West End wanted a musical about silent film stars (silent no longer as now they burst not only into speech but song), why didn't Brown and Heneker more adventurously write one about the *British* film industry? That at least would have been an untold story. Electing to turn to America for his material, they landed *The Biograph Girl* with an artificiality that couldn't be disguised. There was just as interesting, certainly more rarely told, story to be told of the British pioneers, but *The Biograph Girl* opened the door to an evening of bogus accents. By trespassing on foreign material, the show sacrificed much of its integrity. Herman, on the other hand, was at ease with the tone of his material. At their best, the most heartfelt of his songs – 'I Won't Send Roses', 'Time Heals Everything' – have a direct emotional appeal that Heneker's numbers simply can't match. Never less than professional and crafted, Heneker's songs work well enough in the theatre, but outside of that proscenium arch the stuff fades, so that the affecting 'Put It In the Tissue Paper' loses what efficacy it had on stage.

*Mack and Mabel* – the title told it all – concentrated on its two stars, Mack Sennett and Mabel Normand, but *The Biograph Girl* (aka Mary Pickford) spread itself a little more liberally, offering a major role for D. W. Griffith. As a male lead, Australian Bruce Barry's perfectly assured performance was never going to challenge the starriness of Robert Preston's in *Mack and Mabel*. The one indisputable hit of the evening was Sheila White, who had allegedly already become a musical theatre star overnight by singing 'Bleep-Bleep' in *On the Level* fourteen years earlier, after which the producers of British musicals, true to form, hadn't a clue what to do with her. When she stepped up as Pickford, the critics were in no doubt: she was 'a star who shines brightly against a murky sky'; 'wickedly clever'; 'quite superb'; 'a joy'; 'a revelation'; 'simply adorable'. After *The Biograph*

*Girl*, those producers of British musicals just carried on ignoring her. Strangely, one critic asked 'Do I see Miss White as the Anna Neagle of the eighties?'[12]

It was generally agreed that Heneker did better than Brown, who hadn't bothered with much of a plot. Victor Spinetti's direction exercised the small company's vitality, inspired by his Joan Littlewood training at Stratford East. Getting the best out of the company by getting them to stand on stage and swear as loudly as possible while he watched from the gods had worked for Littlewood. Ultimately, *The Biograph Girl* came over as a neat ensemble piece, performed with a brisk professionalism that should have been much more welcome in 1980, when such qualities were in short supply. The little supporting company constantly stepped up, as if confessing 'We're only a tiny show but look how lively we can be! We're exhausted by the time the curtain comes down.'

White had the signature number 'Working in Flickers', but Heneker had written solid stuff for Griffith, 'The Moment I Close My Eyes', 'Beyond Babel', 'Gentle Fade' and 'One of the Pioneers'. The weaker items fell to the colourless characterisation of Lillian Gish, played by newcomer Kate Revill, lumbered with two submissively anti-feminist numbers, 'Every Lady Needs a Master' and 'More Than a Man', inevitably overshadowed by the spark of Pickford's items. The saddest reflection on the passing of the silent film world, 'Put It In the Tissue Paper' made for some effective final moments. After seeing herself played on stage by Revill on the first night, the 84-year-old Gish, who had flown into London for the occasion, told the press 'It was the most thrilling evening of my life.' Jane Hardy, playing Wally, received a letter from the Ritz Hotel dated 19 November.

> My dear Jane Hardy
> 　'Wally' I feel is a combination of all my dear friends from the film industry. May playing her bring you the happiness, joy and success they have brought so many.
> 　　Ever fondly
> 　　Lillian Gish

Harold Hobson's ecstatic notice implored Londoners to flock to the Phoenix. Wendy Trewin in the *Lady* reported 'There is much to delight in *The Biograph Girl* but not enough to make it an entirely satisfactory musical. Somewhere in the middle, Brown seemed to lose his way. The result: a certain limpness, and not even the energy of twenties dance routines [...] can rescue it from flagging.'[13] Michael Billington for the *Guardian* thought the show was 'amiable, slender and trite [but has] a series of skilful numbers put across by a young cast with some style [...] the one unqualified hit of the evening is Sheila White [...] she seems to occupy the stage by right rather than default'.[14] Milton Shulman could raise little enthusiasm for 'All in all, a minor musical with some pleasing moments that misses more opportunities than it takes.'[15] Despite the skills on show, *The Biograph Girl* was left with a bundle of decent notices and a few weeks to eke out its existence.

*

# 1981

*Eastward Ho!*
*One Night Stand*
*The Mitford Girls*
*Restoration*

Bernard Miles's control of the Mermaid Theatre gave it a style and flavour all its own. Like many of the plays and writers that enthralled him, Miles wanted to hold up a mirror to London's past. Ben Jonson's play *Eastward Ho!* had originally played at the Black-friars Theatre in 1605. References to King James I and the Scots resulted in Jonson, along with George Chapman and John Marston, being thrown into prison. The play was a favourite of Miles, and one that stayed with him for years. Things had begun splendidly for his theatre at Puddle Dock with his adaptation of Henry Fielding's *Rape Upon Rape*, music by Laurie Johnson, lyrics by Bart, in 1959. *Lock Up Your Daughters*, a raffish enterprise for its time, was to be the Mermaid's biggest winner, lasting 328 performances in its first run, and twice as long at the 1962 revival. A Brechtian–Weill-ish satire, *Mr Burke M.P.*, had not scored in 1963. Miles would even then have preferred to musicalise Jonson's play. Some saw the 1963 *Virtue in Danger* as an obvious follow up to the Fielding adaptation, but despite a better score than its predecessor its West End run was brief.

As early as 1962, Miles was in discussion with the composer-lyricist Raymond Dutch about the possibility of a musical version of Jonson's play, but after taking advice decided it was unsuitable for musical treatment, and instead went ahead with a straight revival with incidental music by Bridget Fry and Fritz Spiegl. Miles had already presented the play at the Royal Exchange as part of the Corona-tion's festivities, but he at last achieved his ambition to produce it as a full-blown musical. For *Eastward Ho!* (Mermaid Theatre, 7 July 1981; 45) Miles hired director Robert Chetwyn, lyricist Howard Schuman, creator of Thames TV's *Rock Follies*, and composer Nick Bicât. 'Now, London, look about,' warned Jonson in the play's final moments, 'And in this moral see they glass run out,' but Jonson's original underwent radical surgery from the team of writers in its three-month prepa-ration. There were disagreements between Miles and Chetwyn, Miles basically wanting a revival of the play with songs and Chetwyn intent on turning it into a revisionist musical.

Francis King regretted that 'the serviceable old comedy has been hacked about, with Howard Schuman's lyrics full of clumsy anachronisms and Nick Bicât's music never extending its fluent eclecticism beyond our own times. In general, the acting is enthusiastically amateurish.'[16] *Country Life* didn't care for the 'unarresting lyrics' ('Lancelot' rhymed with 'rancid lot'), or the music which 'settles for a creamy, occasionally thumping, banality' in a rethink of Jonson 'seriously compromised as to both musical and dramatic form, veering off at its extremes in the direction of pantomime and rock opera'.[17] *Eastward Ho!* became just another British musical to be waived aside: 'quite lamentable [...] an example of the British musical at its most inept'.[18] Tempted into trying their hand at yet another musical intended for commercial success in the current climate, the writers had provided Miles with a dud. Sheridan Morley realised that 'What kills *Eastward Ho!* is a deep inability to decide what kind of musical it wishes to be. The score desperately lacks the confident jollity of *Lock Up Your Daughters*, while Schuman's lyrics strain after Sondheim and end some way short of Lionel Bart.'[19]

Admirers of the entertainer Mike Harding flocked to his 'comedy-musical' *One Night Stand* (Apollo Theatre, 21 July 1981; 47) when it originally played the Oldham Coliseum. This 'Shocking ... Rocking ... New Comedy' reached Shaftesbury Avenue with the full Oldham cast, with a top ticket price of £6.80. During the 1960s Harding had played in a pop group, The Stylos, from which experience he no doubt fashioned much of the new work, charting the rise and fall of a boys' band of that period, formed at a Catholic school, climbing from obscurity to the dizzy heights of the London Palladium, and back to rock bottom. It seemed perfectly formed at Oldham, where Harding's earthy material had a genuine local appeal, but changes inflicted on the production to make it 'suitable' for the West End plush of the Apollo did it no favours, and the portrait of Rocky Young and the Teenbeats, heading for fame in 1962, didn't take so well.

Critical response was mixed. The *Daily Mail* welcomed a dose of 'genuine sixties nostalgia',[20] the *Evening Chronicle* an evening 'witty, entertaining, rumbustious, colourful, vulgar and rude – it's quite incredible'.[21] Defining Harding's songs as 'bland parodies of famous originals', the *Guardian* lamented 'an awful musical and one that proves yet again that rock and roll and show business don't go together',[22] a judgement eventually blown out of the water by the many subsequent West End 'jukebox' musicals that would run and run. Nevertheless, *One Night Stand* entertainingly recalled a showbiz time when fame was counted by appearing at Great Yarmouth on the same bill as Donald Peers and Sooty, or signing up for a tour with Frank Ifield and Mr Pastry. Ultimately, cheekily home-spun as his northern slant on life might be, Harding's show fell foul to the sort of snobbery that stalked the West End, where *One Night Stand* was something foreign from up North. The *Lady* condescendingly acknowledged that Harding was 'determined to be funny, and in a manner that does seem to me to be embarrassing on a Shaftesbury Avenue stage'.[23]

The only reason for seeing *The Mitford Girls* (Globe Theatre, 8 October 1981; 105) was the British musical actresses it gathered together in one place. Pilfered from the works and utterances of Nancy, Jessica, Diana, Pamela, Unity and Deborah, the show barely deserved its place in London, although it had been lapped up at Chichester. Even the set looked as if it wasn't supposed to hang together for long. The very idea of spending three hours in the company of even *one* of those Mitfords was depressing enough, but to withstand six was overdosing. Denied a proper libretto or imaginative concept, the show suggested that the gilded siblings enjoyed nothing more than singing some very old songs such as Vivian Ellis's 'I'm On a See-Saw' and 'Other People's Babies'. These were certainly a good deal better than the scattering of numbers by Peter Greenwell, too many of which went on and on about falling in love (very searchingly, along the lines of 'is it a good idea or is it not?'). After the attempts at moving the British musical forward with *The Crooked Mile* and less successfully (indeed, pedalling backwards) with *House of Cards*, his score for *The Mitford Girls* was of minimal interest. It might have been better if Caryl Brahms and Ned Sherrin had come up with a better structure; there just didn't seem a good enough reason for the show having happened.

Michael Coveney in the *Financial Times* disliked 'this entirely trivial cocktail concoction [...] just one more show off the camp necrophiliac assembly line. It exists primarily as a home for old-fashioned talent.'[24] *The Times* liked it no better, reporting 'the most trivial sentiment imaginable, compacting the allure of Britain's lost empire and the history of the Mitford family, with all its socialite, socialist, communist and fascist leanings, into a tuneful chunk of mindless, nostalgic entertainment'.[25] Unsurprisingly, the *Lady*'s critic, in the tone of a respectful courtier, acknowledged the only British musical to concentrate solely on one highly privileged upper-class family, insisting that 'We have seldom so bountiful a libretto as this one,' praising Brahms and Sherrin for 'their natural springing wit mingled with the wit recorded by the Mitfords themselves'.[26]

If one definition of a musical is the sort of show that will eventually wind up being done by your amateur operatic society, *Restoration* (Royal Court Theatre, 21 July 1981; 62) isn't one. Or is it? It's one of those musicals that doesn't want to own up to being one, and wouldn't get many votes if it did. Just as John Osborne's *The Entertainer* never becomes the ground-breaking musical it might more happily have been instead of a severely dislocated and lopsided play, just as the book and film of *Trottie True* never stop convincing you that they would have been much more at home as a musical, so does *Restoration* sit on a fence. There is, of course, the giveaway that no songs were listed in the theatre programme. Can you imagine having no list of musical numbers when you open the programme for *Oklahoma!*? It's unthinkable. Rodgers and Hammerstein *want, need* you to remember those titles. On the homeward bus, we want to be reminded of the delightful turns of 'Out of My Dreams', be jolted back by the title 'People Will Say We're In Love'. But some shows never learn. As late as 2016, the programme for *The Go-Between* listed no musical numbers (with some justification, as on that occasion they were scarcely discernible).

*Restoration*, the first project for which the Royal Court accepted commercial sponsorship, was described by its author Edward Bond as a 'pastoral', a 'Festive comedy set in 18th Century England', concerning the marriage of the penniless fop Lord Acre to the coal-miner's daughter that he murders. Obviously a pastiche of Restoration comedy, the message was 'driven home by Nick Bicât's sparkling, but insistently percussive, music'.[27] For *Punch* it was 'an extraordinarily if not loonily brave attempt by a contemporary writer to come up with a completely new restoration comedy and then add to it a series of equally original semi-Brechtian songs'.[28] As for those songs, 'Bond's lyrics are almost literally unspeakable and Nick Bicât's music is, as ever, grindingly inelegant'.[29] Bond's intention was to point up the social inequalities of the period, with the numbers mainly performed by the lower orders acting as a Greek chorus of discontent.

Simon Callow headed the company, enlivened by the glorious grande dame, 80-year-old Irene Handl. In rehearsal, Bond had agreed that Handl, who left the press in no doubt of her distaste for the theatre, could nurse her pet chihuahua Beulah on stage, but had second thoughts and banned it. His disenchanted elderly star threatened to withdraw, but didn't.

# 1982

*Wild, Wild Women*
*Windy City*
*Andy Capp*

London's first specifically designed theatre-restaurant opened with Michael Richmond and Nola York's 'fun musical' (no doubt the definition of its producer Ray Cooney rather than its authors) *Wild, Wild Women* (Astoria Theatre, 15 June 1982; 29). Luck was on its side when its only London competitor, The Talk of the Town, shut up shop the same week, but the 750-seater revamped Astoria got off to a shaky start, the first-night critics moaning about having to queue for the carvery (in the manner of carveries, lukewarm by the time you got it back to your table), depressing starters, tepid white wine and diners packed too closely together. If all that wasn't bad enough, the desserts cost extra. In the circumstances, it's a wonder anyone noticed the show, for which there was a fair amount of praise. Previously seen at the Orange Tree, Richmond, *Wild, Wild Women* charted the adventures of a Wild West Lysistrata (Susannah Fellows) who organises a sex strike in an effort to curb the out-of-hand gun wars in a one-horse 1880s mining town.

The evening was too long (blame the pudding interval) but the *Financial Times* found it 'a cheerful enough romp [that] looks like an end of season release of spirits by a rep company that has been overdoing it on the Agatha Christies [...] an oddly flavoured but not unpleasant evening'.[30] Praising Fellows, and Lesley Joseph as the local 'madam', the *Sunday Telegraph* reported 'Some of the other members of the cast display all the strenuous eagerness of hopefuls doomed to disappointment at an audition' in a theatre that would probably appeal to the 'less sophisticated' theatre-lover.[31] *Punch* summed it up: 'the show has to be at least as good as the food'.[32] The rootin' shootin' entertainment, directed by Richmond and featuring a five-piece band, had echoes of another, much more reviled, musical of the wild west, *Belle Starr*, a London catastrophe despite the presence of Hollywood super-star Betty Grable. The strain of Aristophanes to be found deep somewhere within *Wild, Wild Women* had already found its way into the Soho-set *The Crooked Mile* thirty years earlier.

**26**  As much as you can eat at the roistering *Wild, Wild Women*

There was much to be grateful for in *Windy City* (Victoria Palace, 20 July 1982; 250), overlooking the overriding difficulty that it was another British musical trying to imitate the American. Its intentions were good, its credentials impressive, as any trifling with Ben Hecht and Charles MacArthur's play *The Front Page* needed to be. Any home-grown product aspiring to be as gritty and pithy with music needed to be. It's Chicago (the windy city), 1929, and the young anarchist Earl Williams (Robert Longden) awaits execution. In the pressroom of the Criminal Courts Building, reporters sit awaiting the final news. Enter the *Herald Examiner*'s Hildy Johnson (Dennis Waterman), scourge of the paper's boss Walter Burns (Anton

27   The perils of adapting a Hollywood classic. As American as could be:
*Windy City*, with Anton Rodgers, Amanda Redman and Dennis Waterman

Rodgers). So much about *Windy City* had quality, staged at an estimated cost of
£600,000. If it had to be done in London, there was the right team for it in librettist
Dick Vosburgh and composer Tony Macaulay, with a line-up of top practitioners,
musical director Anthony Bowles, a brilliant all-encompassing and movable set
by Carl Toms, orchestration by Ian Macpherson and direction from the distinguished Peter Wood in a rare association with musical theatre. Wood was hired
when the original director Burt Shevelove, who had ended up directing *Twang!*,
died shortly before rehearsals began.

Vosburgh had written for revue and had won favourable reaction to *A Day in
Hollywood, A Night in the Ukraine*. A show about Al Capone collapsed when its
intended producer dropped dead in the street. After considering an adaptation of
Lewis Carroll's *The Hunting of the Snark*, Vosburgh moved on to *The Front Page*,
writing forty lyrics before writing a script that he claimed was modelled on Yip
Harburg and Johnny Mercer. Macaulay had composed several popular songs, with
38 'top twenty hits' in the British charts, writing Elvis Presley numbers as well as
scores for two Ken Hill shows at Stratford East, *Is Your Doctor Really Necessary?*[33]
and *Gentlemen Prefer Anything*.[34]

*Windy City* was never embarrassing, but how authentic could it be? Part of the problem was in its leads. Waterman had made an early start in musicals with London's *The Music Man* in 1961, but had made his name elsewhere; now, his growly vocalisations gave a passable impression of Hildy. Rodgers had cropped up in a number of musicals, among them *The Crooked Mile*, *Pickwick* and *Songbook*. He and Waterman, both well known from British television series, must have been reckoned a draw. Casting continued strong further down the running order, with Victor Spinetti, somewhat underdone as Bensinger, saddled with a weak number; Diane Langton as prostitute Mollie Malloy getting one of the worst songs of the night, 'Waltz for Mollie' as well as the best, 'I Can Talk To You', and a full-throated Amanda Redman sturdy in two solos. Finest of all was Longden, compellingly truthful as the tragic Williams. Tucked away in a bit part was Terese Stevens, not so long since considered one of the hopes of the British musical.

After the cast vanished behind the first night's six curtain calls, Sheridan Morley enthused. Here was the third new musical, in the train of *Evita* and *Cats*, to send to Broadway! Here, apparently, was 'a smashing, lilting, big-brass, senti-mental, singalong succession of fifteen numbers', 'although listening to the score there is little trace of lilt or singalong'.[35] For the *Daily Telegraph*, Macaulay's music was 'tearaway, slick and accessible',[36] in what the *Daily Express* called ' a memora-ble blend of catchy tunes'.[37] Not all agreed. Michael Billington decided 'I can't help feeling [the play] needs music like the Sahara needs sand.'[38] The *New Statesman* categorised the show as of 'a kind whose songs aren't a lot more than a sort of decorative Polyfilla, gratuitously plugged into the holes that have been pointlessly blown in the body of the original [...] But, oh, wouldn't we far, far rather have seen *The Front Page* itself?'[39] But then, as *Country Life* pointed out, *Pygmalion* hadn't needed music either.

Fashioning musicals from cartoon characters is a peculiarly American habit. Con-sider *L'il Abner* courtesy of Al Capp; Charles Strouse and Lee Adams's *It's a Bird ... It's a Plane ... It's Superman* and one of the most expensive musicals to be staged on Broadway, *Spider-Man: Turn Off the Dark*. Off-Broadway exported *Snoopy!!!* and *You're a Good Man, Charlie Brown* to London. *Bat Boy* landed in the West End in 2004. Most globally successful was Little Orphan Annie's transfiguration into *Annie*, although her next outing as *Annie 2* was disastrous enough to close before reaching Broadway.

British cartoonists have proved less appealing to musicalisation. No one has chanced a musical based on regular favourites of the boys' comic *Eagle*, although bringing together P.C. 49, Dan Dare and Harris Tweed would have provided a nostalgic treat. The *Daily Mirror*'s strip (in more senses than one) cartoon Jane, a blonde accompanied by her dachshund Fritz, has also escaped adaptation. Jane specialised in getting her skirts caught in doors, leaving her exposed but unwor-ried in knickers. Christabel Leighton Porter played Jane in the 1940's strip revue

*Hi-Diddle-Diddle*, and in a magnificently crude British movie *The Adventures of Jane*. One wonders if Jane's escapades might have made a better peg on which to model such a piece as *Mrs Henderson Presents*.

Written for Manchester's Royal Exchange Theatre, the musicalisation of Reg Smythe's layabout anti-hero Andy Capp was the idea of singer-composer Alan Price, teamed with director Braham Murray and librettist Trevor Peacock. Peacock had long been a field worker in British musicals, although little had registered with the public: *Passion Flower Hotel* had little lasting success, *'Erb* was a quick failure, and *Leaping Ginger* got no further than Manchester. Peacock and Price seemed the ideal team for a belt-and-braces celebration of the boozy, flat-capped Capp, but several critics thought the elements failed to gell. In his only musical, Tom Courtenay was stellar casting, but was dubious about transferring to London. Patsy Rowlands, originally cast as Capp's long-suffering wife Flo, was replaced by Val McLane. It seemed organically correct that Price's regular musicians should provide the musical accompaniment, but they were dispensed with for London, although Price remained at the piano, an essential and truthful component of the show.

Revised and possibly reinvigorated, *Andy Capp* (Aldwych Theatre, 28 September 1982; 99) enjoyed some glowing, some damning reviews. Michael Coveney's insistence that 'There has not been a better British musical all year,'[40] balanced Milton Shulman's observation that 'we can see how far the British musical has lowered its social sights since the days of Ivor Novello'.[41] The *Daily Telegraph* prophesied that 'Its success would put back the English musical for years [...] A simple, unpretentious musical as plain as plum duff [it] is aimed at theatregoers who rate energy above style and ask no more than a jolly chorus to a rum-ti-tum tune.'[42] *Punch* gave the thumbs-down: 'if ever a strip cartoon defied musicalisation, this one is it. [The writers] have been unable to cobble together more than the barest outline of a plot.'[43] For *The Times*, Irving Wardle noted the difficulty of matching the cartoon world to the real: 'Mr. Price's score sticks mainly to the same track of the music-hall musical, but there are two numbers that halt the show in its tracks, the first a rhythmically witty catalogue of Andy's old girl friends (after whom he names his pigeons) and a martially wounded solo for Flo that moves from the strip cartoon world to that of direct human experience.'[44]

Audience attendance was disappointing. The fact that neither Courtenay or Price could pull in customers suggested once again that the British public wasn't particularly keen to sit through musicals involving the working classes (*The Match Girls*, *Strike a Light!*, *Love On the Dole*, *The Hired Man*). As he had no intention of ever joining the working class, Andy Capp was an exception to the rule. Bereft of sentimentality, Price and Peacock's score now seems very much more skilful than its critics suggested. These are indeed, as Price memorably sang in his Greek-chorus-like persona, 'Frozen Moments'. Audiences seemed happier with the tooth-aching syrup of Leslie Bricusse's *Goodbye Mr Chips*, then playing at Chichester. *Andy Capp* came without graces or ornamentation, 'an ignoramus who's so thick it made him famous'. As a biomuiscal, this is a show that outdoes biomusicals based on real people. The songs have a genuine bite, an aftertaste of bitterness and disappointment, as in Andy and Flo's duet 'Don't Tell Me That Again', ending in Andy's devastating riposte to Flo: 'You're as ugly as a crow.'

# 1983

*Marilyn!*
*Bashville*
*Dear Anyone*
*Jean Seberg*
*Poppy*
*Swan Esther*

The temptation to believe that translating a famous real life into musical theatre will draw crowds of eager playgoers is one that over the years many managements have been unable to resist. There are of course lives that have responded well to having song and dance utilised in the telling of their (very often highly fictionalised) stories; think Fanny Brice in *Funny Girl* or Gypsy Rose Lee (although she isn't in fact the heart of the Styne–Sondheim musical *Gypsy*). It is easier to come up with a list of less successful efforts, even when the names have been mega. Anthony Newley's *Chaplin* closed on the road en route to Broadway. Libi Staiger's impersonation of Sophie Tucker, *Sophie*, had a mercy killing after 8 performances in New York. British musicals have persisted in thinking that biomusicals might lay a golden egg, but experience suggests they come with a health warning. Think of the British subjects that all too quickly found their way into theatrical obituaries: Winston Churchill (*Winnie*), Mrs Simpson and Edward VIII (*Always*), Joseph Grimaldi (*Joey Joey*), Martin Luther King (*King*), Harry Houdini (*Man of Magic*), C. B. Cochran (the revue *Cockie!*), Henry VIII (*Kings and Clowns*), Dr Barnardo (*Barnardo*), Albert and Victoria (*I and Albert*), the Mitford sisters (*The Mitford Girls*), an Indian princess (*Pocahontas*), Marie Lloyd (*Sing a Rude Song*), the Reverend Harold Davidson (*The Stiffkey Scandals of 1932*), Thomas Becket (*Thomas and the King*), the cast of the Profumo scandal of 1963 (*Stephen Ward*), et al.

*Marilyn!* (Adelphi Theatre, 17 March 1983; 156) was a rarity among British musicals of its period in that its subject was American, the cinematic icon Marilyn Monroe. Despite having worked extensively in the business, neither composer Mort Garson nor librettist Jacques Wilson had written for musical theatre when they decided to musicalise her life. One of the reasons for premiering the show in London may have been because Broadway would have meant a heftier bill, but *Marilyn!* still cost around £2 million. Another good reason for doing the piece in London was Stephanie Lawrence, who left her role as *Evita* to star, and was voted 'Best Actress of the Year' in a musical, as well as being nominated for an Olivier Award. Appointing Larry Fuller as director and choreographer was one of the production's assets, with Fuller instilling some Broadway beefiness into the all-British company. Fuller had also brought in Bill Byers as orchestrator (there was nothing wrong with the brilliant sounds coming from the pit), they having worked together on the recent Henrik Ibsen disaster musical *A Doll's Life*.[45]

Technically and visually, *Marilyn!* was never less than interesting, with its Australian leading man John Christie swinging into place as 'Camera'. This was one of the show's best conceits, emphasising Monroe's relationship with the paraphernalia of photography and silver screen rather than her less happy relationships with the opposite sex. After an electrifying opening, with Judith Bruce as Monroe's deranged mother demanding of the audience 'Did you know Marilyn Monroe? Did you know her? Did you know her? Marilyn Monroe!' the show never quite realised its promise, as the linear, episodic progress of the star's life played out to its inevitable end. Lawrence was not best served by some of the numbers; her opening 'Somebody Will Love Me' made no impact; 'The Most Beautiful Girl of Them All' was the nearest Garson and Wilson got to an effortful hit.

Overlong dance sequences added nothing to a show that dissipated its energy through a total of almost thirty forgettable numbers. Ned Sherrin wrote that 'several excellent performances are submerged, but, to their credit, not humiliated, by the nonsense words and lugubrious music'. Moreover, 'The key to this sort of witless evening is, of course, to keep the stage so busy that no one has time to wince at the words. Hal Prince is the headmaster of this school of production and Larry Fuller has yet to reach the First grade.'[46]

The greatest injustice was suffered by Lawrence at the end of the show, when a brilliant sequence of film clips of the real Monroe, including some of her most famous moments, dominated the stage, scuppering everything the hard-working Lawrence had achieved. Despite unflattering reviews, *Marilyn!* built a cult following and had a sensational last night, the American backers having kept the production afloat despite poor audience numbers. At the end of the year, only months after the Adelphi had moved on from *Marilyn!*, Broadway staged its own 'American fable' biomusical, *Marilyn*. It took six writers to concoct and lasted 16 performances.

The first genuinely British entry of the year was the first musicalisation of a George Bernard Shaw play since *My Fair Lady*. In no way was this show a flop. Fresh airs arrived in healthy gusts with **Bashville** (Open Air Theatre, Regent's Park, 2 August 1983; season). Ten minutes into the first half on opening night a thunderous downpour sent the audience temporarily fleeing for shelter, before the show resumed and 'clearly enchanted a very damp audience'.[47] Shaw had written his novel about prizefighting, *Cashel Byron's Profession*, in 1882, but was unable to find a publisher. Nineteen years later, he turned the book into a one-act play in order to protect his American copyright.

Redressed as *The Admirable Bashville* and written in iambic pentameter, it was Shaw at his most playful in a sylvan romance that matched his illegal prizefighting hero Cashel Byron with the wealthy, sophisticated heiress Lydia Carew. David

William and Benny Green's adaptation rescued the play from almost total oblivion, perhaps learning from Lerner and Loewe that as much as possible of Shaw should be left intact, with room enough for the songs to breathe. At Regent's Park, the hero was first glimpsed in white singlet and breeches emerging from trees in the glade of Wiltstoken Park and falling in love with Lydia. Cursing his bad luck at being so taken with a high-born woman ('I took you for / The daughter of some farmer./ Well, your pardon./ I came too close: I looked too deep. Farewell), Cashel sees no future, but Lydia is impressed ('He's literate: Shakespeare he quotes unconsciously.').

What was happening here? With this sort of material, there was the possibility that decent writers and a half-decent composer might fall in line with Shaw's absurdity. What chance of that in a British musical? In the 1960s, *The Young Visiters* was a thoughtful attempt to bring Daisy Ashford's juvenilia to the stage, but a one-man play in blank verse? The bookies can't have offered good odds. In fact, *Bashville* had an organic rightness about it. Green was as fanatical about Shaw as he was about every one of his passions. He had already collaborated with John Dankworth on the Shaw biomusical *Boots with Strawberry Jam*, written for John Neville and Cleo Laine and directed at Nottingham Playhouse by Wendy Toye in 1968. Green's passion for GBS seeps into these lyrics. Listen to Cashel's lyrical realisation that he's in love with 'Lydia'. Green had the advantage of Peter Woodward not only playing the prizefighter but arranging the fighting sequences, in one of the finest male performances in a musical of the period.

Green doesn't write a lyric, he writes an outpouring that goes straight to the heart, with none of the portentous ersatz emotion that mucks up so many British musicals. The moment that Cashel realises there are not *two* syllables in 'Lydia' but *three* is pure joy. You can almost sense with what delight composer Denis King snatches at Green's lyric. The same happens when Bashville, Lydia's factotum, declares *his* feelings for Lydia in 'Because I Love Her' ('I shine her spoons wherein I see me / Perhaps it's moonshine, a touch too dreamy'). King has a natural sympathy with this stuff, and arranges it for the twelve-piece orchestra with taste and skill.

Not that his achievement ends there. Catching any of *Bashville*'s numbers you might justifiably think that's a David Heneker number, or something we've completely forgotten about in *Hooray for Daisy!* (how about 'Take the Road To the Ring'?), or a Leslie Bricusse horror (take the cake-walky lower orders below-stairs complaining about having only 'One Pair of Hands'), or does 'One Pair of Hands' sound like something the servants in *Peg* kicked up their skirts to, or a jolly non-sensity Julian Slade dreamed up one summery afternoon? Then, there's a stomping title song to send everyone home happy that Jerry Herman must once have invented and discarded for *Hello, Dolly!* or *Mame*. Perhaps it's a sort of cockeyed nod to *A Chorus Line*? King's music is all smoke and mirrors, its corn as high as the eye of that Oklahoma elephant. The pastiche is brilliant. In the circumstances, in the context of Shaw's fragile, supremely silly Tennysonian extravaganza, it's a little

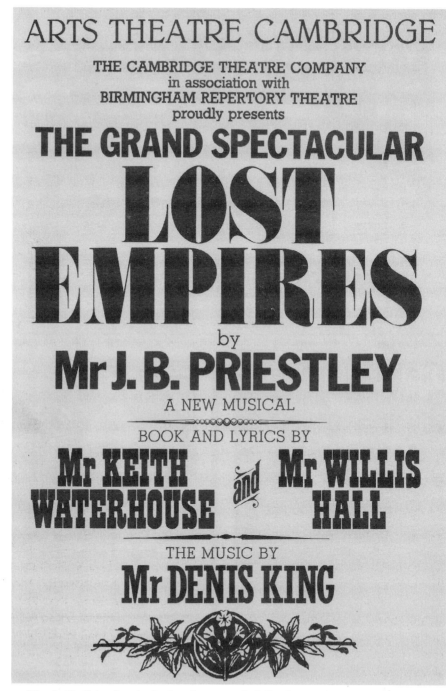

ARTS THEATRE CAMBRIDGE

THE CAMBRIDGE THEATRE COMPANY
in association with
BIRMINGHAM REPERTORY THEATRE
proudly presents

THE GRAND SPECTACULAR

# LOST EMPIRES

by

## Mr J. B. PRIESTLEY

A NEW MUSICAL

BOOK AND LYRICS BY

**Mr KEITH WATERHOUSE** and **Mr WILLIS HALL**

THE MUSIC BY

## Mr DENIS KING

**28** J. B. Priestley had already proved difficult to musicalise in André Previn's score for *The Good Companions*. The very dull *Lost Empires* never got to London

gem. The fact that King can bring off the marvel of making 'Lydia' touching amid all this chicanery is an achievement to relish.

Saluting a 'Shavian Tuneful Parody', the *Daily Telegraph* thought it was staged with 'just the right degree of tongue-in-the-cheek solemnity and acted at a level of burlesque seldom encountered beyond the Players' Theatre [and] performed with polish'.[48] The *Guardian* declared it 'great fun [...] Benny Green's skilful adaptation of the blank verse original allows George Bernard Shaw to laugh at himself as he would have wished'. There was praise for King's music, 'at its best in the rum-ti-tum vein'.[49] *Punch* hit home, insisting that 'Green's lyrics are impeccable. As for the music, Kenneth Tynan once called Jule Styne the most persistently underrated of popular composers. Denis King now holds that title in this country.'[50] Much admired, *Bashville* returned the following year to Regent's Park, but never got its deserved West End transfer.

Originally staged by Birmingham Repertory, and about as British as could be, *Dear Anyone* (Cambridge Theatre, 8 November 1983; 65) was a quasi-American musical. It was set in New York, where 'Pandora', in real life plain little Lillian Sherman, is the unhappy Miss Lonelyhearts of a Big Apple newspaper. The publicity absurdly promised 'The Musical for Everyone!', an experience that would be 'off-beat, funny, sad and moving as well as witty and wise, entertaining and hilarious'. The collaboration involved Jack Rosenthal (late of *Bar Mitzvah Boy*) as book writer (not mentioned when the 'concept album' was released in 1978; Willis Hall did the sleeve note), Don Black's lyrics, and music by Geoff Stephens, best known for such pop hits as 'Winchester Cathedral' and Ken Dodd's 'Tears Won't Wash Away These Heartaches'.

It was an interesting mix, but *Dear Anyone* comes back out of the mist as one of those musicals that nobody was ever much interested in. Its conception was not without difficulty. Only a handful of the song titles recorded for the 1978 album made it into the Cambridge Theatre programme. Michael Coveney for the *Financial Times* certainly thought this 'competent mini-opera' wasn't a winner: 'The idea that the personal life of an agony aunt is (a) interesting or (b) important seems to me spurious at the best of times.'[51] Under the headline 'All Too Knowing an Imitation of America', Irving Wardle warned that 'the show is badly dislocated, and comes over as a knowing imitation of America rather than America itself'.[52] Expressing doubts, Francis King suggested that Rosenthal's script, 'though it contains some cracking one-liners, is clumsily ill-paced [...] if this had been an American musical, there would have been some drastic revisions on tour'.[53] A thumbs-down from the *Sunday Times* described the material as 'mostly flimsy'.[54]

There was nothing unprofessional about Jane Lapotaire's performance. Peter Blake, as Pandora's boyfriend, would go on to endure another British musical flop, *Hard Times*, and collide with two of the very worst, *Money To Burn* and *Oscar*

*Wilde*. A genuine dash of Americana came with the casting of Stubby Kaye, last spotted in London in *Man of Magic*. Coveney recognised Kaye's big number in *Dear Anyone*, 'Ain't Coming Down', as a shameless echo of the much cleverer Frank Loesser's 'Sit Down, You're Rocking the Boat' (which had made Kaye's name) from *Guys and Dolls*. He told his readers that 'we are left with a soft-soap, a trashy hymn to the life and times of a mixed-up self-appointed newspaper physician'.[55] Even with a top ticket price of £11.50, with senior citizens let in out of the cold for £5, *Dear Anyone* failed to excite much interest. Something about it still evokes the dull, plasticated atmosphere of several British musicals of the 1980s.

*Jean Seberg* (National Theatre, 15 November 1983; season) patently American in origin, had the unforeseen (at least by director Peter Hall and the management of the National) disadvantage of accentuating the ineptness that too often took over when the British got their hands on a musical. Two actresses, Kelly Hunter and Elizabeth Counsell, played the younger and more mature film star respectively; both, according to the *Sunday Telegraph*, shrill. There was little enthusiasm for a work that the British tax-payer was helping to fund, against the National Theatre's hope that once the show was posted back to Broadway, the money would roll in, highlighting the questionable practice of the National being so involved with what was so clearly a commercial venture (a trick subsequently played by the English National Opera). Only a few months earlier, *Marilyn!* had at least dealt with a name that everyone knew; Jean Seberg's name was one for cineastes. Better constructed and better cast, *Marilyn!* was the stronger musical. While Seberg's career faltered after Otto Preminger had cast her as St Joan, Monroe had gone into legend.

The notices were mostly poor: 'irredeemably banal';[56] 'ruthlessly manipulative junk'.[57] In an article, 'The Iceberg That Snowballed', Bernard Levin attacked Christopher Adler's lyrics and Julian Barry's book as 'not just appalling – trite, witless, tired, without punch or bite – they were suffused from end to end with the fatal quality of the British musical – amateurishness'.[58] For Levin at least, despite its American provenance, here was a British musical. No wonder audiences, if bothered, were confused. Along the way, artistic differences between Hall and the American team started rumours that all was not well. Choreographer Stuart Hopps was replaced by Irving Davies. Response at the previews was tepid. 'The last part of the show is hysterical,' the 19-year-old Hunter told the press. 'I have a miscarriage. I go to a funeral. I have a nervous breakdown and get burnt at the stake. It's hilarious.'[59]

Dilys Powell, who knew a thing or two about Seberg, thought that 'what is missing is the exhilaration which the American musical has led us to count on, especially in the dancing. Here the dancers can dance, but one feels they don't *have* to.'[60] To those who had looked forward to it, *Jean Seberg* was a major disappointment after Marvin Hamlisch's successes with *A Chorus Line* and *They're*

*Playing Our Song.* After six months of often ill-attended performances in repertoire, the National withdrew it. Three years later, Hamlisch's *Smile* enjoyed a brief
run on Broadway.

Alan Melville's 1944 intimate revue *Sweeter and Lower* had a sketch in which
Henry Kendall, dressed as a Duchess, was sitting in a box at the theatre with a
young American GI, Bonar Colleano. They were watching a British pantomime.
A mystified Colleano watched as his gracious hostess attempted to explain what
was going on. 'Say, who's the dame?' asked Colleano. 'That's not the Dame,' replied
the Duchess, 'that's the Principal Boy.' It must have got even more perplexing after
that. Anyone who had never been to the panto would have been totally mystified
by *Poppy* (Barbican, 25 September 1982 [season]; Adelphi Theatre, 14 November 1983; 97). A feather in the cap of the British musical, it was well received at
the Barbican when it was first presented by the Royal Shakespeare Company, and
somewhat less enthusiastically received when it reappeared in new guise at the
Adelphi in 1973, on both occasions directed by Terry Hands. If the British musical
was to have any meaning beyond entertainment for that fabled but little-glimpsed
figure, The Tired Business Man, it needed works like *Poppy*.

The collaboration seemed perfect: book and lyrics by Peter Nichols, music by
Monty Norman. Nichols' reputation as a playwright with a number of critically
and commercially successful works behind him, among them *A Day In the Death
of Joe Egg* (about parents of a child with cerebral palsy), *Forget-Me-Not-Lane* (a
beguiling play about the meaning of nostalgia), *The National Health*, a satire on
the National Health Service that bared Nichols' satiric teeth, and the semi-musical
*Privates On Parade*.

For Norman, *Poppy* was a natural stepping-stone along his musical theatre
career. Since the heydays of his early works, *Expresso Bongo*, *Irma la Douce* and
*Make Me an Offer*, Norman committed to musicals that might be said to have
at least some sort of social significance, as in his collaboration with Wolf Mankowitz for *Belle* in 1961. In this, as in *Songbook*, Norman showed his aptitude
for musical pastiche. For *Belle*, the Edwardian pit-band at the Strand Theatre had
been blatantly second-rate, just as it would have been on those evenings when
Walter Sickert went to the Bedford to see Little Dot Hetherington. Then, for the
little dentist and his lover Ethel Le Neve, Norman's music suddenly turned into
something absurdly operatic, turning them into Hilldrop Crescent's Tristan and
Isolde. Norman knew how to do pastiche, and *Poppy* cried out for it.

The show had a political relevance that lay heavily across the work, and Nichols'
intent was to point it by using the conventions of pantomime. Its theme was the
Opium wars. In 1840 Queen Victoria, only 21 years old, rules supreme, a dain-
tily ruthless barbarian. After a jolly opening chorus around the village pump
of Dunroamin-on-the-Down, Nichols' characters make their entrances: Dick
Whittington (female principal boy), and his mother Lady Dodo, dowager Lady

Whittington (Dame). Randy the horse stands in for Whittington's cat, with a love interest for Dick in the schoolmistress Sally Forth (principal girl). They are persuaded to journey to the poppy fields of India and so on to China, whose Emperor insists that Victoria must cease the British poppy trade. Her Majesty rises to the challenge, explaining the need for 'The Blessed Trinity'. Here, Norman draws a direct comparison with *Belle*'s 'Dit Dit Song' when Marconi's telegraph traps Crippen and Le Neve on board the SS *Montrose*. China is finally conquered and pillaged by the British (and, to be fair, the French). As Nichols explained, 'Most of the British live happily ever after and the Chinese learn to kowtow.'

The revamped *Poppy* may have lost something in its rebirth. Jack Tinker thought the 'brash new slickness it has acquired actually acted against its raw initial impact'.[61] For Michael Coveney, Norman's score was 'rather disappointing. It was pastiche – of Gilbert and Sullivan, of *Hair*, of Ravi Shankar in a gorgeous Indian interlude, of rabid hot-gospelling in a hymn to the Holy Trinity [...] but it has no clinching signature (tune) of its own.' But wasn't Victoria's manic endorsement of the Holy Trinity its centrepiece, a signature if there had to be one? The *Daily Telegraph* had difficulty with 'this dish of sweet-and-sour. Its steely wit remains at odds with campy theatrical routines'.[62] Much the same problem had affected *Belle*, although there's no pretending that Wolf Mankowitz's manner of telling Crippen's story was much less skilful than Nichols's in *Poppy*.

*Another* biblical musical? ***Swan Esther*** (Young Vic Theatre, 17 December 1983; 26) added little to the catalogue in its efforts to update the Old Testament to disco and aerobics. Nicholas D. Munns' music and the lyrics of J. Edward Oliver had first been heard on a 1983 concept album, with Stephanie Lawrence as Esther singing 'My Love Is Like a Dream'. Producer David Land, with *Jesus Christ Superstar* and *Joseph and the Amazing Technicolor Dreamcoat* behind him, saw *Swan Esther* as their successor. Following the London run, producer Bill Kenwright toured the show as *Swan Esther and the King*. The reviews of the Old Vic production were not unkindly. Martin Hoyle wrote 'If it lacks a sure-fire all-stops-out hit [...] it has none of the inflated padding of more famous shows';[63] for Michael Billington, it showed promise as a first musical. In his final production for the Young Vic, Frank Dunlop superintended the adventures of Esther (Amanda Redman) who wins a beauty contest and gets to marry the King of Persia as first prize. Peppered with Gilbert and Sullivan-like pastiches, and a sort of tribute to *A Chorus Line* at the close of Act One, *Swan Esther* was agreeable entertainment, without ever threatening the popularity of its predecessors.

# 1984–1989

## 1984

*Blockheads*
*Peg*
*The Importance*
*The Hired Man*

None of the 1984 British musical flops roused the enthusiasm of audiences. *Blockheads* (Mermaid Theatre, 17 October 1984; season) had a decent provenance, and decent enough actors to play Laurel (Mark Hadfield) and Hardy (Kenneth H. Waller). Mounted for £300,000, and encouraged by the success of the London production of *Snoopy!!!* for both of which shows the American Hal Hackady wrote the lyrics, the show was intended for Broadway, but never made it. Hackady had a busy career as lyricist, without much commercial success, having contributed to Broadway revues and musicals including *Minnie's Boys* and *Ambassador*, panned on both sides of the Atlantic. For some reason, the music for *Blockheads* was by the Russian pianist and classical music and motion picture composer Alexander Peskanov. For the *Financial Times* 'This patchy, likeable work has its moments, but lacks dramatic tension',[1] while the *Sunday Times* criticised 'a plodding storyline [...] a slow, myopic stage biopic earnestly indexed with dates', and music that was 'undistinguished'.[2] The *Standard* agreed that 'The tunes [...] are jaunty but predictable' and the lyrics 'pedestrian enough to be accused of loitering'.[3] Hadfield and Waller's impersonations of the famous duo were appreciated, but *Blockheads* failed to generate enough interest to take it beyond its Mermaid season.

In the West End, David Heneker's run of luck with splendidly mounted British musicals (*Half a Sixpence, Charlie Girl, Jorrocks, Phil the Fluter*) was running dry by the mid 1980s, by which time his idea of what a British musical might be seemed out of step. *Peg* (Phoenix Theatre, 12 April 1984; 146) aged itself by presenting as 'A Romantic New Musical'. At least here was a show born of Anglo-American co-operation, courtesy of its American producer Louis Busch Hager, who travelled to England 'because of my desire to work with David Heneker'. The hope was that after its London opening following a spell at the Yvonne Arnaud Theatre in Guildford, the show would get to Broadway; a hope doomed to be forlorn. The idea of adapting J. Hartley Manners' 1912 play, written for Laurette Taylor, was suggested to Heneker by Roy Sone, an actor noted for thanklessly taking over the leading male roles in *Half a Sixpence* and *Charlie Girl* when the stars were off sick or moved on. How many times were such unfortunates waiting for the curtain to rise as they heard the concerted groan of disappointment from the audience?

Ian Judge's production of *Peg* reached London with no book credit, suggesting that Heneker had simply popped the songs into an acting edition of Manners' script. The ten-strong cast did its best to fill the stage, but against a background of Peter Rice's skeletal sets, the atmosphere was constrained, although Larry Wilcox's overture promised a much bigger show than the shrivelled relic revealed when the curtain went up. Wilcox's subsequent orchestration did its best to keep spirits up. Siân Phillips headed the company as Mrs Chichester, but the best Heneker could do for her was an underpowered comedy number 'The Fishing Fleet'. *Peg* failed to come up with a dynamic plot, making do with stock characters including handsome but bespectacled hero (Martin Smith in some wincingly coy numbers), lively and loud maid (the no-microphone-necessary Julia Sutton), young Bertie Wooster-type silly ass (Edward Duke), and wide-eyed American girl on the brink of womanhood (Ann Morrison).

How Morrison's Peg would have fared in a straight performance of Manners' play is unknown, but Heneker had written some appealing numbers for her, not least 'The Steamers Go By' and 'Pretty Dresses'. Although Morrison failed to set London alight as Laurette Taylor had set Broadway aflame in the same role seventy years earlier, she brought charm to the title role and took the night with the roaring 'Manhattan Hometown'. Sutton's 'How Would You Like Me?' had already been heard in *Phil the Fluter* (now more effective, and – with Sutton – louder), and other moments recalled Heneker's earlier work. Older audience members would have known the central number, 'Peg o' My Heart', before entering the theatre; Alfred Bryan and Fred Fisher's song had first aired in 1912, but its inclusion dislocated the show. Martin Hoyle regretted the waste of Patricia Michael as Ethel, for her 'style and vivacity deserve better. First, *The Mitford Girls*, now this. She needs a break.'[4] The break was forthcoming, for *Peg* was Michael's last West End appearance before – perhaps an unnecessarily dramatic reaction to having been in so many London musicals – she left the profession and emigrated to America.

Hopefully, Hager's belief that 'There is a definite sense of gentleness left in England's dramatic world'[5] survived the unenthusiastic reviews. The *Evening Standard* recorded 'an evening of generally insipid entertainment',[6] while the *Financial Times* thought Heneker's work 'not too unworthy, merely here rather dull', with its opening chorus pinned 'to the chuggingly unmemorable rum-ti-tum that has innocuously served most British musicals since the 1940s'.[7] The *Sunday Telegraph* declared *Peg* 'for antediluvian tastes: it's composed as if nothing much had happened in musicals since the 1950s. It's set in Sussex in 1913, and will appeal to people who like to think that the world is still like Sussex in 1913.'[8] For anyone longing for a return to a gentler age of British musicals, there was neverthe-less much to enjoy in Heneker's sometimes more than workmanlike score in its brighter moments such as Duke's salute to Peg as 'A Genuine Hall-Marked Alpha-Plus Little Brick'. *Peg* clung on for four months.

*The Importance of Being Earnest* had been neglected by those looking for a suita-ble case for musical treatment for almost thirty years, after a concentrated attack on it in the 1950s. Allon Bacon's adaptation of Wilde's play, retitled *Found in a Handbag*, got no further than Margate in 1957, a year after Bacon's only West End musical, *She Smiled at Me*, closed after 4 performances.[9] Most promisingly, Vivian Ellis's attempt, *Half In Earnest*, had premiered in Pennsylvania in 1957, before opening the Belgrade Theatre, Coventry the following year, where the redoubta-ble Marie Löhr was Lady Bracknell, but Ellis's sprightly score was never heard in London.[10] *Earnest in Tune* played Canterbury in 1958, and Malcolm Sircom's score for yet another attempt, *Ernest*, was produced the following year at Farnham. The most successful was the off-Broadway *Ernest in Love* (1959) with pert songs by Anne Croswell and Lee Pockriss, but there was no transatlantic crossing. London had to wait for *The Importance* (Ambassadors Theatre, 22 May 1984; 29).

The first musical to be presented by Ray Cooney's Theatre of Comedy was decently cast, with strong male leads in Patrick Ryecart and David Firth, a twitchy Miss Prism in Sheila Bernette, and Judy Campbell a somewhat undercooked Lady Bracknell. The adaptation by Sean O'Mahoney, here masquerading as John Hugh Dean, was unappreciated. Suggesting that *The Importance* may have been an unfortunate title for so forgettable a piece, the *Financial Times'* headline cut to the chase: 'Of No Importance'. Michael Coveney went on: 'It opened on Thurs-day night and should, if there were any justice in this world, have closed by this morning. It is coarse, incompetent, joyless, simpering and, not to mince words, dreadful.'[11] Announcing 'A Musical of No Importance', Anthony Masters for *The Times* asked 'Did nobody in the West End wonder why people were strolling about in green carnations halfway through the evening? They had escaped with the man-agement's complimentary button-holes, a painful reminder of Wilde's epigrams thudding to the floor, and doubtless a blessed sense of release. With luck, recall of the first act's musical numbers had been erased.'[12]

Wilde's work had already showed resistance to musical adaptation with Cow-ard's *After the Ball*, his sedate take on *Lady Windermere's Fan*, on which critics had poured scorn in 1954. 'Why,' wondered Cecil Wilson, 'could Mr. Coward not have let sleeping dogs lie and created something entirely his own, instead of staging a contest that left Oscar Wilde panting foolishly at the ropes?'[13] Booked into the Ambassadors for a longer season, *The Importance* cut its losses after 29 perfor-mances.

*

Respect is due to Howard Goodall, a composer who has turned now and again to musical theatre. There could be no doubt about the origins of *The Hired Man* (Astoria Theatre, 31 October 1984; 164) with its emblazoned legend 'Great British Musical'. If this gives the show the feel of a product, it sometimes gave the impression of being one. Promoting the show as 'Melvyn Bragg's Second Musical!' would have been an alternative, but possibly not much of a recommendation to those who'd sat through his *Mardi Gras*. *The Hired Man* might have quietly clocked in and clocked off at Southampton where it was first seen, had Lloyd Webber not realised its unquestionable dignity and quality and helped to finance its move to London. Bragg's story of working folk bestrode the 1890s through to the aftermath of the Great War, highlighting the life of John Tallentire, obsessed with work, 'work whose nature so bound men that they could not survive in nay [sic] way without it'. Variously hailed as a Cumbrian version of *Gone With the Wind* and popular oratorio, *The Hired Man* had a cast accompanied by a pit band of five musicians (piano, harpsichord, trumpet, harp and brass). It also held auditions for whippets.

Some of the critical flak was laid at Bragg's door in a show that came 'seriously unstuck the minute the music stops'. Moreover, the lyrics were 'awful' and the 'operatic representation of Tallentire, Emily and the neighbourly lover is slightly embarrassing'.[14] *The Times* complained that Bragg's dialogue was 'seldom inspired and his lyrics dogged by false rhymes', resulting in 'a hole at the centre where a plot should be, leaving the show, rather unfairly one feels, earnest but unsatisfying'.[15] There was a critical overview that perhaps the show was worthy, with much talent having gone into its making. John Barber in the *Daily Telegraph* warned readers that 'The frivolous will find the story plodding, the people unengaging and the absence of humour a pity.'[16]

Bragg acknowledged Goodall's music as being 'out of that ancient English choral tradition', but the score pitches itself somewhere between olde English folk song and Broadway. It's a substantial score, restrained by the workmanlike lyrics, by which the audience was blasted for long periods via community singing. If the show is intended as a polemic for the working man, it can hardly avoid its obvious artificiality as it tries to musicalise an underclass. The plea for dignity never lacks integrity, but the songs, the heartbeat of any musical, sound hollow out of context, suggesting that something about *The Hired Man* misses the mark. The generous shift of Goodall's score to the choral tradition lends it profundity but cannot always avoid tedium.

# 1986

## *The Gambler*

*The Gambler* (Comedy Theatre, 2 July 1986; 45) was a minnow among sharks. This ill-doomed attempt at a 'comedy musical' about the patently unfunny world of gambling, charting twenty-four hours in the lives of an amateur (Bob Goody) and professional (Mel Smith) addict, with a five-strong all-male cast, had them playing all the parts, from bookies to barmaids. Premiered at Hampstead, the West End transfer was 'All in all great fun' according to the *Financial Times*,[17] and 'a winner all the way' according to the *Daily Mail*.[18] Smith was famous enough as a comic to be expected to draw a crowd, but few turned up, perhaps put off by the title, or the idea of finding Smith in unusual surroundings. Its investors lost £120,000. The closure was regretted by Miles Kington, who hadn't sat through a musical for years. In the 1950s he'd seen *Salad Days*, and a decade later *Hair*, at which point he decided he preferred Slade to MacDermot. In the 1970s he found Sondheim unexciting, but faced up to *Starlight Express* in the 1980s, an experience that finally convinced him the musical had touched rock bottom. Kington was now 'enraged to see such a fine musical as *The Gambler* come off at the end of this week, and *Starlight Express* go on until the next century'.[19] For Kington, musicals were not doing what they ought. Sadly, in coming back into the musical loop after so long away, he was coinciding with one of the most arid, drab, hopeless periods in the history of the British musical. For a man who clung no matter how inexplicably to the delights of *Salad Days*, these were grim times.

# 1987

## *The Secret Garden*
## *Spin of the Wheel*
## *Girlfriends*

Diana Morgan, the prolific dramatist, contributor to British revues, and screenwriter (her credits included co-writing *Went the Day Well?*, Alberto Cavalcanti's unparalleled fantasy about the Nazis invading an idyllic British village), made a late return to London theatre with her book and lyrics for *The Secret Garden* (King's Head Theatre Club, 12 January 1987; season). Cardiff-born Morgan relocated Frances Hodgson Burnett's Yorkshire novel to Wales, explaining that she was happier working in her native idiom. Joan Kemp-Welch was a sympathetic director for this modest piece, with choreographer David Toguri managing on the King's Head's postage stamp stage, designer Tim Goodchild scaling down from such mammoth undertakings as the Drury Lane *Gone With the Wind*, and Ray Holder's orchestrations for cello, clarinet and flute. Praising 'a small but perfectly formed success, full of charm', the *Evening Standard* acknowledged 'an exceptionally good cast', and the music of Steven Markwick with its 'many memorable moments'.[20] The *Guardian* was less complimentary, accusing Morgan of bathing 'the piece in honey, glycerine, Ivor Novello and a dollop of 1920s innocence' with lyrics of 'an ancient naivety' in a production that was 'as arch and as marble as the central London location'.[21] Few remarked how extraordinary it was that a

London theatre, no matter how small, should produce so modest and patently old-fashioned a British musical in the unfriendly theatrical milieu of the late 1980s. The King's Head didn't give up after *The Secret Garden*, subsequently wandering – as it were – down the same neglected path for its revival of Vivian Ellis's *Listen To the Wind*.[22] Was the *Independent* on to something when it described Morgan and Markwick's work as 'A night out for the young in heart and the old in mind'?[23]

Musical actors moving into the little theatre at a bend of Panton Street must often have wondered if it was worth unpacking the suitcase; along with the Shaftesbury and Piccadilly, the Comedy Theatre had a reputation for quickly spitting out its musicals, among them *Colette* and *Little Mary Sunshine*. **Spin of the Wheel** (Comedy Theatre, 7 April 1987; 36), moved up from Watford, was no exception. 'Tonight', promised the programme, 'you'll be participating as the studio audience to a typical game show [...] and taken behind the scenes.' An objectionable American Hughie Green-type compere Danny Lemon (Neil McCaul), 'disgustingly sleazy' according to the programme, fixes the show's fortunes on dumb blonde Janie Jones (Maria Friedman, getting the best of the notices) who becomes the viewing public's favourite, misleading the sponsors into making sure she keeps on winning, until popularity wanes and suburbia starts switching the thing off. Written and directed by Timothy Prager, the show had songs by Geoff Morrow, but *The Times* advised that 'Lovers of musicals will not find much pleasure here'.[24] For Martin Hoyle in the *Financial Times* it was 'instantly forgettable [...] the mid-Atlantic show *par excellence*' with 'the synthetic quality peculiar to ersatz Americana produced by Englishmen'.[25] The mock-American show was withdrawn on 2 May.

Celebrations around the arrival of **Girlfriends** (Playhouse Theatre, 16 October 1987; 43) centred as much on the reopening of the old theatre, closed since 1950, on the Embankment. *Girlfriends* had already played to appreciative audiences at Oldham Coliseum in 1986, where director John Retallack co-wrote the book with Richard Curtis. London wasn't so appreciative. Having written the music for the male-dominated *The Hired Man*, Howard Goodall wanted to tip the scales with this hymn to group feminism, set in an age when feminism was an unknown word: World War II. In their ways, both *The Match Girls* and *Strike a Light!* had been trailblazers in the mid 1960s; here, Goodall was inspired by reading Mary Lee Settle's autobiography *All the Brave Promises*, detailing her experiences in the WAAF (Women's Auxiliary Air Force), to write a piece focused on the personal and moral dilemmas that women faced when they subscribed to that commitment. Rooted in the choral tradition, Goodall's commitment to his subject was obvious enough. Beyond any commercial consideration, *Girlfriends* was carried through with integrity, a component never in short supply in *The Hired Man*. If the modern British musical was to reflect real life, why not by this acknowledgement of the selflessness of these women? The vulgarity that had infested British musical theatre from its beginning had little place here. Its appeal, as Goodall must have realised, would be largely to those who had no real longing to sit through what West End managers had long considered made a musical. Anyway, if a musical had to be labelled feminist, in this case it wasn't the feminism that pervaded *Prisoner Cell Block H, Bad Girls* or *Made in Dagenham*. None of those depicted nobility.

Oldham responded to Goodall's straight-down-the-line sentimentality, the heart-warming atmosphere. In fine, expected fashion, the London critics used the show as just another blunt instrument with which to belittle the genre. The headlines were enough to discourage excitement: the *Evening Standard*'s 'The Battle of Britain Girls Lose a Battle';[26] the *Independent*'s 'A Display of Formation Singing'.[27] The *Financial Times* criticised it for being 'little more than a *je june* musical doodle devoted, for no apparent reason, to the Women's Auxiliary Airforce in the last war' with music that was 'a curious hybrid of anthem, chant and ballad that, unlike the bombers, goes precisely nowhere all evening'.[28] For Jack Tinker, the show was 'the most mind-numbingly musical imaginable', and it had been unwise to have a song titled 'Wake Me, O Wake Me' in Act II, during 'an evening calculated to bore one to death and back'.[29]

Many agreed that the evening didn't work. The programme had set the scene for the audience: 'Jane enters through a hole in the fence of a derelict Bomber Command Station.' As she day-dreams, 'the ghostly aerodrome comes to life, exactly as it might have done one day some 45 years before in November 1941'. On the first night, however, a note slipped into the programme informed patrons that the whole of the action of the play took place in 1941, suggesting that this might not have been the only last-minute adjustment to the proceedings. With its modest requirements – twelve women, two men and minimal musical accompaniment – and the reputation of its composer, *Girlfriends* has thrived rather better outside the West End than in. When it resurfaced in a reduced version at the Union Theatre in 2014, the *Stage* hailed the work as 'a flawed wonder'. Making no attempt to glamourise its subject matter, and with Goodall's airs blowing in the opposite direction to so many of those filling London theatres every night, *Girlfriends* was denied popular appeal.

# 1988

*Nite Club International*
*Winnie*
*Budgie*

Not so much a musical, more a musical pastiche, perhaps a prolonged night (or nite) club cabaret, possibly a collection of well-known popular songs (see also *The Mitford Girls* and *Winnie* for other unsuccessful attempts to do the same sort of thing) interrupted by a collection of new songs that would never be popular; what was the public to make of *Nite Club International* (Playhouse Theatre, 9 March 1988; 29)? Why confuse things even more by billing it as 'The "New" Fifties Musical Comedy'?

Anyone learning that its main writer/director/choreographer/composer and lyricist Dennis Deal was already at work on his new project, 'The Destruction and Musical Embellishment of Aristophanes' *Lysistrata*' was entitled to do some serious head-scratching. Let Deal's programme note clarify: 'To regard *Nite Club International* as merely a parody or spoof is to overlook much of what makes this show work and play successfully, and which gives it its particular flavour and identity. [It] should not necessarily be categorised with such shows as *The Boy Friend*, *Dames at Sea* and *Little Mary Sunshine*.' Conceived by Deal, Albert Evans and Jamie Rocco, Deal and Evans's new songs never overshadowed the standards that sparked recognition. The audience had been invited to a pastiche of 1950s Hollywood movies, the curtain rising on a corpse, courtesy of a murderous, ageing cabaret star (Ruth Madoc), in a show that 'In spite of some inventive parody and some melodic music [...] remains a small joke that unfortunately has pushed its luck too far'.[30] The *Daily Telegraph*'s headline 'Out of Tune With Today' didn't sound too happy,[31] but the *Observer* found it 'Great fun, could catch on'.[32] Mark Steyn knew that the show 'will not run because, in the words of the legendary Max Dreyfus of Chappell's, the public know they don't mean it. After the buffs have spotted the Fifties film and pop references, what else is left?'[33] *Nite Club International* would have sat better (but not any longer) at the Lyric, Hammersmith, thirty years earlier; for London in the late 1980s, it seemed a reckless endeavour.

How much better or worse might *Winnie* (Victoria Palace, 20 July 1988; 63) have been had it truly been a musical, but it wasn't; it was a concoction, and like *Nite Club International*, it hedged its bets by clawing in a wealth of old numbers, ending up a thing of shreds and patches, defiantly extolling the glories of the London Blitz. This disastrously conceived tribute to Britain's bulldog Prime Minister of World War II, as directed by American Albert Marre, proved not for the first time that patriotism is not enough.

From the beginning, nothing went well. The original idea was that Robin Hardy's script would be peppered with well-known songs from the period, with some new material from composer Cyril Ornadel and lyricist Norman Newell, orchestrated by Alan Braden who specialised in recreating the sounds of the 1940s. Marre disliked Newell's work. Others, among them Braden, Tony Hatch and Mike d'Abo, submitted songs for inclusion. With Newell no longer involved, Ornadel turned for collaboration to Hal Shaper, his writing partner for Mermaid Theatre's *Treasure Island* and an adaptation of *Great Expectations*. Shaper had hardly materialised when he was thrown over following disagreements with Marre. Choreographer Molly Malloy barely had time for an entrechat before she was removed and replaced with Sheila O'Neill.

Lionel Bart, who hadn't had a West End show since *Twang!* twenty-three years before, was appointed the show's official composer, demoting Ornadel to musical director. Meanwhile, composer Hubert Gregg gave his World War II hit 'I'm Going To Get Lit Up When the Lights Go On In London' a facelift with new lyrics that rhymed 'factotum' with 'grab Hitler by the scrotum'. Along the way, Robin Hardy's script was reworked by Richard Sparks.

One of the more interesting participants in the gathering fiasco was American veteran Arnold Sundgaard, now brought in as lyricist. Sundgaard had debuted on Broadway with his libretto for *Everywhere I Roam* in 1938, and was co-librettist for the 1944 operetta *Rhapsody*. He collaborated with Kurt Weill on the opera *Down In the Valley*, and wrote book and lyrics for the 1961 off-Broadway *Kittiwake Island*, a light-as-feather whimsy with a natty Alec Wilder score. Each of these had flopped, fully qualifying Sundgaard for service in *Winnie*, although collaborating with Ornadel after having worked with Weill may not have seemed like promotion.

No sooner had rehearsals begun than three principals departed: Victor Spinetti, John Bardon and Susannah Fellows, each complaining their roles had been whittled away. Those that remained made up a respectable company headed by Robert Hardy as Winston Churchill and Virginia McKenna, previously a notable Anna to Yul Brynner's monarch in *The King and I*, as Clementine. In a straight play, they might even have been ideal casting. As it was, Francis King considered that Robert Hardy 'possesses about as much talent for singing as I do', although he brought 'remarkable artistry' to his speaking of the great man's speeches.[34] There was a wealth of experience in the supporting players, among them Toni Palmer (*Fings Ain't Wot They Used T'Be, Blitz!*), Frank Thornton (*The Young Visiters*), John Larsen (*The Crooked Mile*), Charles West (*Ann Veronica, Strike a Light!, Jack the Ripper*) and Larry Drew (the original *The Boy Friend*'s boy friend).

Among the ongoing chaos, the first previews were cancelled. The Manchester opening was shaky, with Bart named as composer on the posters, much to Ornadel's annoyance because Bart had never written a note for the show and had long since vanished. Ornadel was even more displeased to be named as lyricist. By now, Robert Hardy and Marre were not speaking but communicating through a third party. During the Manchester try-out the money drained away. Essex Music injected £80,000 to keep the show afloat, but from here on financial anxiety plagued the production, which had been made possible via German, Canadian, Italian and Japanese funds. As the Manchester season came to an end,

**29**   All smiles for *Winnie*'s pre-opening photo call are Toni Palmer, Virginia McKenna, Robert Hardy, Lesley Duff and Frank Thornton. The smiles were short-lived

Robin Hardy insisted on significant changes to the production before the London opening. Robert Hardy and McKenna were furious, feeling that the Manchester try-out had been a complete waste of time. At the Victoria Palace, the curtain rose on a bombed-out theatre in Berlin on the late afternoon of 26 July 1945. The conceit of the show was that Robert Hardy played an ENSA impresario who transmogrified into none other than Churchill. This spectacle was available for the top ticket price of £18.50.

Francis King for the *Sunday Telegraph* suggested 'If Robin Hardy had chosen Winnie-the-Pooh or even Godfrey Winn [...] as the subject for his musical, the undertaking might have been less surprising.'[35] Someone else suggested Winnie Mandela as the Winnie of choice. The *Financial Times*' verdict was 'nostalgic and respectful', enumerating 'Amazing quick changes; loud bangs [a bomb going off on stage shook the public house next door to the theatre]; revolves; a tank; and an apathetic bulldog.'[36] For the *Independent*, Mark Steyn encountered 'all the wearisome jollity of an ENSA concert party, without the mitigating circumstance of a World War [...] One of the worst structured pieces of drama I've ever seen, *Winnie* has nothing to offer but its title and a clutch of fondly remembered songs, plumbing new depths in the parasitic exploitation of nostalgia.'[37]

One of the most respectful reviews came from the journalist W. F. Deedes, noting that the show 'mixes most judiciously patriotism and fun. *Winnie* is a musical never in danger of taking itself or its subject too seriously.'[38] But why shouldn't it, why *didn't* it, take its subject too seriously? Deedes was clearly someone not particularly involved with or passionate about the British musical as an art form. He did, however, sum up some of the artistic predicament of *Winnie* by highlighting its capacity for 'patriotism and fun'. How much lower could the genre set its standards? *Winnie* was not so much a tribute as an insult, an insult to the man it traded on to attract its audience, and an insult to the intelligence of its audience. The evidence is clear enough in its rag-bag score. Was Ornadel really the best composer to make Churchill and Clementine sing? Possibly, in different company, Sundgaard was an appropriate lyricist. Ultimately, the decision to flesh out the feeble bones of the show with sing-a-long numbers from the dark years of London's Blitz was slap-happy. The selection itself showed how ill-informed, how disinterested in giving audiences anything of interest, was the management and production team. *Winnie* was messed by a string of old favourites that at any other time in British history just might have been rejected as a load of old rubbish. Its insistence that Britain was great gave *Winnie* its excuse to string out the chestnuts, 'We'll Meet Again', 'London Pride', 'A Nightingale Sang in Berkeley Square'. On and on the list of chestnuts depressingly proceeds. Deedes' praise of all this 'patriotism and fun' cuts at the throat of treating the British musical as an enterprise of any worth.

Rumours of the show's closure swirled around it. The *Independent* reported that it *was* closing on 25 June; Robin Hardy assured the company it was not. Everyone was asked to take a 25% cut in salary. Equity politely declined to agree to this arrangement. *Winnie* closed on 9 July (the notice posted the day before) amid widespread acrimony, with a loss of around £1.5 million. Ornadel, for one, was never paid. *Winnie* might have won a little more respect had he and Sundgaard been given the chance to write a proper score, throwing those interminably popular period numbers out the door. It might then have held its head up as a respectable flop. The suspicion remains that it was conceived merely as a moneymaker. This will never be reason enough.

So many musicals come and go without ever having been wanted, needed or regretted in their passing. They may not be spectacularly bad or particularly good. Their credentials may be solid: experienced writers, recognisable stars, some sort of ready-made recognition already in the public consciousness, in this case a highly

**30**    Adam Faith and Anita Dobson, with composer Mort Shuman, pose for
the press at the approach of *Budgie*

successful television series, with its original lead performer on stage for ***Budgie***
(Cambridge Theatre, 18 October 1988; 110). There wasn't a whiff of amateurism
about Keith Waterhouse and Willis Hall's book; having written the TV version,
they knew what they were about. Don Black, who a decade earlier had done the
same for another musical taken from television, *Bar Mitzvah Boy*, was lyricist.
Composer Mort Shuman had an impressive track record in popular music, including 'Why Must I Be a Teenager In Love?' and 'Can't Get Used To Losing You', and
had been lyricist for the revue *Jacques Brel Is Alive and Well and Living In Paris*.

Thirty years after the 'kitchen-sink' musicals of the 1950s had challenged the
cosy complacency of the British musical, Soho was once again centrestage, but
lacking the potency, the sense of daring, of *Fings Ain't Wot They Used T'Be* and *The*

*Crooked Mile.* Ex-pop singer Adam Faith, one of the few such to break through into mainstream theatre (Tommy Steele, Mark Wynter, Paul Jones and, momentarily in *Bye Bye Birdie*, Marty Wilde, were some of the others), played the charming but luckless Budgie, living on his wits on the streets of Soho. Faith had a quality that separated him from many in the pop stable, a natural sense of well-being and intelligence that got him interviewed by John Freeman on the controversial *Face To Face* television series. But the television version of *Budgie* had aired seventeen years before the musical appeared. Could what had made Faith an icon of the small screen be recreated so many years later?

There was no lack of respect for Faith's performance. Michael Coveney found him 'a likeable, unassertive stage personality with a merely adequate voice that he uses to effective, tear-stained effect at the end'.[39] Mark Steyn was enthusiastic for the show's willingness to 'embrace its environment [...] here, at last, is a British musical that's really British – and all the more remarkable for not being cobbled together from some venerable old buffer like Dickens'.[40] Michael Billington saw the show as another 'Soho pastoral', noting that it was technically proficient, but 'what it lacks is any real character. What it also lacks is much in the way of a plot' in what was a 'curiously charmless and morally vacuous musical'.[41]

For anyone bothered with the musical's past, *Budgie* couldn't escape comparison with those kitchen-sink shows that had seized London by the throat before *Oliver!* blanked them. The *Evening Standard* couldn't resist its headline, 'Fings Lose Their Charm'. Charm, anyway, was a lost commodity by 1988, and neither the assemblage of good writers, Anita Dobson as Budgie's girlfriend, the excellent Faith, or the direction of Jonathan Lynn, managed to regenerate it. It may be that it was simply too close to the late 1960s to make it work as a period piece; too close to the period from which it sprang. Thirty years on, we might see *Budgie* in a new light.

# 1989

*Metropolis*
*Sherlock Holmes*

'The Machines Are Marvellous' ran one of the song titles in *Metropolis* (Piccadilly Theatre, 8 March 1989; 214), and in Ralph Koltai's magnificent settings, they most emphatically were. Even so, the men moving the show into the Piccadilly probably wondered how long it would be before they would be moving it out again; those who had already shunted other musicals into the Piccadilly probably thought it wasn't worth reparking the van. Fritz Lang's 1926 film was claimed by its creator as the 'costliest and most ambitious picture ever made in Europe'; it was imperative that audiences in the theatre should be left gasping at spectacle. The musical was naturally based not only on Thea von Harbou's screenplay for Lang's movie (she worked it up from her novel), but also on the public perception of the film itself, its extraordinary images etched on the retina. The musical might be said to have concentrated too much on the filmic aspects of the transformation, rather than on von Harbou's narrative. No matter how splendid the production, the Piccadilly was too small a space to make it financially viable. Largely made possible by Japanese and American backers, *Metropolis* also had to contend with rail strikes and hot weather and running costs of around £80,000 a week. Its early closure left a loss of £2.5 million.

With book and lyrics by British playwright Dusty Hughes and music by American composer Joe (Joseph) Brooks, supplemented with additional material by David Freeman, Jerome Savary directed a cast of this 'Passionate Love Story' headed by Graham Bickley, Judy Kuhn – a girl with 'all the passion and pathos of a young Judy Garland'[42] – and Brian Blessed. In a penetrating analysis, Peter Holland wrote that 'in its transformation of the ending, the musical's refusal to contemplate reconciliation manages, with all its spectacular effects, to mock itself, appearing to celebrate, patronisingly, simple virtues to which it cannot itself aspire'. So there should be no doubt, Holland went on to state that 'Its characteristics can be quickly summarized: the music is adequate, the acting appalling and the sets magnificent'. He pointed to the 'impossible rubbish the performers are forced to sing'.[43] For *Time*, this was 'a rousing, even spell-binding addition to the West End's current offerings'.[44] Distanced from the German expressionism of Lang's original, the visual delights of the musical *Metropolis* were the crucial component, but even the promise of scenic opulence kept audiences at home. No doubt someone was suggesting that people weren't turning up at the Piccadilly because the title meant nothing to the man in the street. But how many of the trillions of patrons turning up for *Cats* had ever read T. S. Eliot? Ultimately, there was the feeling that it was the sets, the physically giant impression demanded of its designer, that dictated the reason for making a musical of something so stupendous, so extraordinary, so unrepeatable, as von Harbou and Lang's visionary warning, a masterpiece that would exist, unlike the musical, for ever.

Broadway had already pressed a doubtless protesting Sherlock Holmes to its bosom in the 1965 *Baker Street*, headlined by Fritz Weaver as Conan Doyle's self-assured private detective, and Inga Swenson as 'that woman' Irene Adler, with British players Peter Sallis as Dr Watson and Teddy Green as the prancing Wiggins of the Baker Street Irregulars. Marian Grudeff and Raymond Jessel's score was no masterwork, but sounded like one when compared to the British Sherlock Holmes musical imaginatively titled *Sherlock Holmes*. 'Book, music and lyrics by Leslie Bricusse' had an ominous ring. After all, Bricusse's most recent shows had included the oleaginous *Goodbye Mr Chips* based on James Hilton's sentimental novel and seen only at Chichester; *Scrooge*; his third collaboration with Anthony Newley *The Good Old Bad Old Days*, and the ludicrous *Kings and Clowns*. The list must have struck terror into the hearts of Conan Doyle purists. While *Baker Street* modestly set about its task with taste and a sense of period,

*Sherlock Holmes* (Cambridge Theatre, 24 April 1989; 97) proved to be rather more than a three-pipe problem.

Although creating Fagin in *Oliver!* put Ron Moody at the top of his class in British musical theatre, his subsequent efforts were less happy, punctuated by *Joey Joey* in which Moody retold the life of Joseph Grimaldi. The idea of playing Holmes probably appealed to Moody's self-avowed intellectualism, but the result was embarrassing. Moody was no one's idea of a romantic lead (neither was Holmes, come to that), but was now expected to gaze longingly at leading lady Liz Robertson playing Bella, the daughter of his old adversary Moriarty, as they duetted 'The Best of You, The Best of Me'. The very idea that Holmes would come out with such piffle showed the desperateness of the lyrics.

Even Holmes's right-hand man fell into reverie of the opposite sex with a squelchingly embarrassing hymn to womanhood in 'Her Face', tactfully conveyed by Derek Waring's inoffensive Dr Watson. Otherwise, 221B Baker Street was dominated by the long-suffering Mrs Hudson, with the veteran Julia Sutton raising the roof in her ear-splitting description of 'A Lousy Life'. A rare inventive moment arrived with 'Vendetta', a striking duet for Bella and her mother, but the limpness of the rest of the score was all too apparent, reaching at least one of its nadirs (there was a choice) in a Cockney knees-up, 'Down the Apples 'n' Pears', that sounded like something rescued from David Heneker's wastepaper basket. A further sign of desperation was incorporating the irritatingly parochial 'London Is London' already heard in the movie of *Goodbye Mr Chips*.

Tensions between the company blighted the shakily funded production from the start, with director George Roman undermined at every turn. Cyril Ornadel, brought in as musical director, clashed with Ian Fraser who had been musical director for the Exeter opening. Ornadel was at odds with the choreographer and company manager. Adjustments he made to the music were reversed by Fraser. Robertson would do nothing without Fraser's consent, and did not get on with Moody. Ornadel realised that Moody was 'a star performer, and expected to be treated as such. The problem in Exeter had been that no-one had treated him with the respect due to his status.' Moody's wish to react flexibly with the music met with Fraser's strict refusal, turning Moody into what Ornadel called 'a caged tiger' in a company that was 'at war with itself, which was no basis for a hit show [...] it developed into a quasi-amateur theatrical society production, except they weren't amateurs, they were professionals hitting out in all directions in an uncontrolled panic ...'[45]

The review headlines said it all: 'The Musical That Time Forgot';[46] 'Clueless in Baker Street';[47] 'This Singing Detective Just Hasn't a Clue';[48] 'Crime Against Sherlock Holmes'.[49] Milton Shulman longed for another Reichenbach Falls from which *Sherlock Holmes* might be plunged into a bottomless abyss. As for Moody, Charles Spencer thought him 'an unendearing Holmes, a jovial vulgarian much given to bad jokes and actorish rant'. Derek Waring's Dr Watson was 'equally charmless', and Robertson 'suffers from the Julie Andrews syndrome'.[50] For the *Financial Times*, Moody 'plays Holmes with a hint that his mind is elsewhere. The supporting cast struggles with material so characterless as to be scarcely existent' in a piece that was 'faded, unimaginative and sadly out of time and place'.[51] For Mark Steyn, this was 'not a musical; it's a play interrupted by knees-up'.[52]

Business wasn't helped by roadworks around the theatre and a strike on London Underground, of which Moody made use on stage (he had come completely out of character in *Joey Joey* too, effectively killing its period authenticity; this was probably his old revue training breaking through). A revival of Bricusse's show with Robert Powell as the great detective toured in 1993, but failed to overcome its shortcomings. It was subsequently released for amateur performance as *The Revenge of Sherlock Holmes*. Whatever it was called, it was a show that marked a thoroughly depressing finale to the British musical flops of the 1980s. Recovery, of which there seemed little hope, was a long way off.

# 1990–1999

## 1990

*Someone Like You*
*King*
*Bernadette*

'Blood and No Guts'[1] and 'Dixieland Blues'[2] were two of the discouraging headlines after the first night of yet one more 'musical love story', *Someone Like You* (Strand Theatre, 22 March 1990; 44). It would have stood very little chance of reaching the stage without the involvement of Petula Clark as both star and writer. Clark was inspired to write it after visiting the Civil War battlefields around West Virginia; co-inspired, in fact, as she credited Ferdie Pacheco with sharing the original idea. Some of the music had already been composed by the time she teamed up with lyricist Dee Shipman, but by the time the show premiered in October 1989 at Cambridge Arts Theatre it had been through a pretty rough war of its own. Its ace card was Clark in the lead role of English nurse Abigail, searching for her missing husband and falling in love with 'The Major' (the show's other main asset, Dave Willetts). With a cast of twelve and one static (and, for him, quite dull) set by Tim Goodchild, and an eight-piece band, *Someone Like You* was taken up for London by producer Bill Kenwright. Novelist Fay Weldon was brought in on the book to create a female triumvirate of writers, altering the tone of the show by turning it into some sort of allegory of Greek tragedy. Once in rehearsal at Cambridge, director Robin Midgley rewrote it with (and without) Weldon. Midgley's apparently autocratic manner towards Clark and the company was an unsettling influence. As the show headed for London, the project was taken over by Harold Fielding, about to be brought down by his own financial problems.

Willetts thought that the show might have suffered from so strong a feminine basis. Argumentative rehearsals did not help. Along the way, it slipped away from the piece it had started out as, something supposedly life-enhancing about how the human spirit overcomes devastation. *Someone Like You* got stuck with being worthy and took a turn for the worse by being dreary, and nothing – its songs, its set, its stars – could pull it back. It was 'ponderous entertainment';[3] it had 'an execrable script and tuneless songs'[4]. Michael Billington regretted 'the sheer dogged triteness of the evening', proving that 'history appears the first time

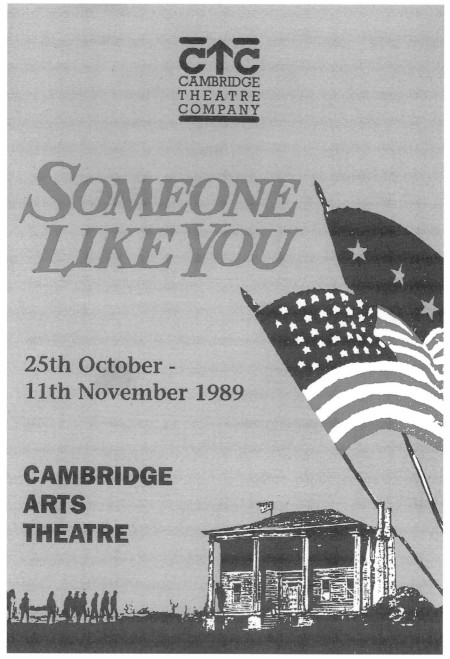

**31**   Petula Clark's very own American Civil War musical had battles of its own

around as tragedy and the second time as musical comedy.'[5] None of the reviews, or photographs of the production, went up outside the Strand, a sure sign that the show was in serious trouble. On arriving at the stage door for a mid-week evening performance, the company found themselves locked out. They were given three hours to clear their dressing-rooms. Fielding's business empire had collapsed, and *Someone Like You*, one of its final whimpers, went down with it.

The British musical's natural inclination to disaster continued through the year. 'In the end,' wrote Rodney Milnes in the *Daily Telegraph*, 'there have been too many writers, too many directors, too many compromises. If only good intentions were enough.'[6] British composer Richard Blackford, already with four operas under his belt, originally conceived *King* (Piccadilly Theatre, 7 April 1990; 58) as a folk opera. The intention was that the biomusical of Martin Luther King would be produced on Broadway to coincide with the anniversary of his death, but the project switched to London. It was eight years in the making, and they were troubled times. Coretta King wanted to combine elements of the opera and musical theatre to create a 'very powerful musical drama depicting a very powerful theme',[7] but eventually King's widow's enthusiasm dwindled, unhappy that her husband was being depicted as a womaniser. The original director, Gotz Friedrich, departed, to be replaced by Graham Vick. Vick was in turn replaced by Clarke Peters until, perhaps in desperation, the Royal Shakespeare Company sent help in the form of Terry Hands and John Caird. The novelist Maya Angelou withdrew her lyrics, citing irreconcilable differences. The original book writer, Richard Nelson, withdrew. The final product credited Alistair Beaton as lyricist and Lonne Elder III as book writer. Opening night was postponed three times. Despite all, its committed star Simon Estes kept his passionate belief that 'this musical can go throughout the world and touch people's lives'.[8]

The critics were less sure of its potency. King himself had said he was no Messiah, but the musical made out a case for it, having him descend from Heaven on a gantry. Pitiful attendance followed on poor reviews, and being at the Piccadilly was unhelpful. 'The cross we have to bear,' wrote Jack Tinker, 'is lyrics which dilute fire and brimstone rhetoric to tepid milk and water cliché and tunes which are the musical equivalent of warm treacle. To drown King's "I Had a Dream" speech in the syrup of such banality is in itself a crime against humanity.'[9] With a top ticket price of £25, *King* played to poor houses, closing on 2 June with an estimated loss of £3 million.

With the blessing of the Pope, the support of the *Daily Mirror* and the sort of advance publicity that many British musicals would have given their eye teeth for, *Bernadette* (Dominion Theatre, 22 June 1990; 28) proudly proclaimed itself 'the People's Musical', financed largely by small investors who had never dreamed of funding a West End show. Musical theatre had been democratised! Mrs Kathleen

Hall signed up with £500, convinced that *Bernadette* 'is a very important turning point. So many things in this world are nasty and aggressive, and I believe this is the start of something better.'[10] To think she might have had a new kitchen! Not one professional angel put a hand in its pocket; all 2,500 were amateur angels, convinced that this biomusical about Bernadette Soubirous, who in 1858 at Lourdes had visions of the Virgin Mary, might be a West End hit.

Its authors, piano tuner Gwyn Hughes and his wife Maureen, had no doubts, explaining that 'It has everything you need for big musical themes – drama, conflict, religious ecstasy, mystery and the whole range of emotions you get in human behaviour when people are stirred up by something they don't immedi-ately understand.'[11] What *they* didn't understand was why any of this would make a decent musical. Undeterred, as early as 1979 the Hughes had raised funds to mount an amateur production in Shrewsbury, at which point enthusiasm got the better of them. They ended up selling their house to get the show into London, living in rented accommodation in Windsor while working as teachers in Epsom. Their main qualification was that they had once got a song into the running for the Eurovision Song Contest. Did no alarm bells ring when the director was named as Ernest Maxin, the man who had come a cropper with *Barnardo*? The Vatican sent a much-needed blessing. At a gala preview, the papal Pro-Nuncio, Archbishop Luigi Barbarito, led a ten-minute standing ovation at curtain fall, but against the £250,000 advance booking, the production had cost £1,550,000. Within days of opening, audiences dropped to around 500 a night. Dissension broke out.

With 16-year-old Natalie Wright, daughter of an ice-cream salesman, in the title role, *Bernadette* opened to a torrent of scathing reviews. As one of its charac-ters had asked, 'How can a minor create a major disturbance?' The question critics were asking was how the show had ever got to London in the first place. 'The miracle of *Bernadette* is how it got to a first rehearsal, let alone a first night';[12] 'this marzipan musical with its sack-cloth and ashes filling is aimed at the kind of audi-ence of tiny tots that appreciate a Christmas pantomime';[13] 'It reeks of nauseating, sententious piety [...] Tritely inert melodrama does battle with lyrics and music [...] of thunderous banality [...] the punitive options of Catholic confessors are considerably widened'.[14] The *Independent* headed its notice 'Holy Unacceptable'.

A poll of patrons at the Dominion showed that 70% thought it excellent, 20% good, 3% average and 5% below average. This may only have confirmed the low expectations of the average West End audience, but this information, and com-ments (mainly from the 70% contingent) were prominently displayed outside the theatre. This sort of anti-critic nonsense had already been tried, with no less fatal consequences, during the run of the ballet-musical *The Princess* thirty years earlier. The fellowship with which *Bernadette* was apparently suffused was anyway in dis-array. The Hughes were criticised for not delivering a final script by the agreed date, and for exerting interference and pressure. There were claims that they thought their percentage of profits was not high enough. Producer William Fonfe

('What I did was very dangerous. It was all or nothing. It was suicidal.') mortgaged his house and ended up owing £300,000. London Transport, only one of the show's creditors, was owed £32,637. With assets estimated at a mere £11,329.00, *Bernadette* vanished (just as she had appeared) into voluntary liquidation on 1 October 1990.

No doubt the show had its admirers. Some of these may as well have been those who put their money into it. It is likely that many of those had little or no knowledge of professional theatre, or of the manifold difficulties associated with the production of a musical. The entire *Bernadette* experience was hounded by an almost total lack of sophistication. At one point, the on-stage Bernadette, caught mid-vision, was confronted by an official who asked 'Where is this lady? I don't see her.' 'Please, monsieur,' replied Bernadette, 'you're standing on the Holy Mother's bush.' Which suggests that those involved with *Bernadette* lacked a little in worldliness.

# 1991

*Children of Eden*
*Matador*
*The Hunting of the Snark*

Stephen Schwartz's *Godspell*, a portmanteau American musical based on New Testament parables from the Gospel According to St. Matthew, had flourished in London alongside *Jesus Christ Superstar*, lasting 1,128 performances at Wyndham's Theatre. Schwartz followed up with *Pippin* – a London flop in 1973 – and the Broadway only *The Magic Show*, at which point his luck seemed to run out, landing him with three commercial failures in New York, *The Baker's Wife* – which failed to rise in London – *Working* and *Rags*. By-passing Broadway, his next show (his 'fourth consecutive, monumental disaster', according to Steven Suskin[15]) *Children of Eden* (Prince Edward Theatre, 8 January 1991; 103) returned him to the Bible. John Caird's book took the Book of Genesis as its inspiration, concentrating on the adventures of Adam and Eve, and the fate of Noah's Ark. At almost three hours long, and with an orchestra of 22, *Children of Eden* had a sort of grandeur that was a long way from the more modest *Godspell*, a grandeur accentuated by the impressive designs of John Napier, providing 'a remarkable spectacle', giving 'the impression that in the beginning was not the word, or the music, but the design concept'.[16]

Caird told *Time Out*, 'I am absolutely prepared for *Children of Eden* to be dumped on just like all the other pieces of popular theatre that I have been involved in.'[17] He was right in this. The *Sunday Telegraph* decided it was 'all perfectly competent, and all completely lacking in what you might call the divine spark',[18] while *Time Out* thought that 'Caird's curious interpretation seems closer to a religious version of *The Jungle Book* or a Ladybird guide to anthropology rather than a key into the elemental passions of the Old Testament.'[19] Schwartz's songs yielded several effective, even beautiful, moments, underlining its cry of belief that the sins of fathers are passed down, generation to generation. Among Schwartz's flops, *Children of Eden* is probably the most likely to remain in the repertoire, albeit that in 1991 it seemed little more than a last wheeze of the pop-orientated biblical musical. It was revived in London at the Union Theatre in the autumn of 2016.

Oh long lost happy days gone by, when a musical could be a light bulb moment one morning, and a few weeks later be in rehearsal en route to the West End. There was no delay in holding up the works of many of the most prominent composers and writers of those lost happy days gone by, no endless workshopping of their efforts, no absurdly expensive publicity campaigns pinned to them. Sandy Wilson's little musical, *The Buccaneer*, so small it had to stand on tip-toe to be noticed at all, probably got into London with the help of a few posters and a couple of column inches in the London press, as did many musicals before musicals got above themselves. Julian Slade and Dorothy Reynolds had probably never even heard of a logo, but with many musicals of the future the logo was pretty well all the public got. Did *Mr and Mrs* ever have a concept album? Awful as that show may have been, it never overrated its importance, never pretended it was *relevant*. What associated product merchandise was on sale at the Strand Theatre during the run of the Dr Crippen biomusical *Belle*? A do it yourself Morse code machine that automatically tapped out 'I-L-O-V-E-Y-O-U'? Toothbrushes embossed with the face of the funny little dentist? What thoughts, in those long lost happy days gone by, of a television series mounted by the BBC at peak time, that effectually handed the producers of a musical the opportunity to freely advertise their forthcoming projects to millions of supine viewers? Was there ever a tasteful ceramic miniature of *Hooray for Daisy!*'s very own favourite cow, now cloned as a milk jug, on sale at its performances? By the beginning of the 1990s, the image was so important that it was in danger of becoming a hologram replacing, and standing in for, the show itself.

*Matador* (Queen's Theatre, 16 April 1991; 119) – 'The Musical Story of a Boy from Nowhere' – was yet another biomusical, this time based on the life of El Cordobés, inspired by Larry Collins and Dominique Lapierre's book *Or I'll Dress You In Mourning*. Having the distinguished director Elijah Moshinsky in charge of proceedings suggested this was serious stuff; after all, Moshinsky was more used to working at the Royal Opera than on Shaftesbury Avenue. He endorsed *Matador* as 'the Hemingway musical' (perhaps not the most alluring tag; it didn't work for *Too Close To the Sun*) in which John Barrowman as El Cordobés was 'the James Dean of the bullring'. He apparently didn't bother to ask what use Dean would have been faced with a bull having a temper tantrum, but – again – it was *image* that mattered. Composer Michael Leander and lyricist Edward Seago had always wanted to write a good musical after seeing *My Fair Lady* at Drury Lane, but sadly ended up writing *Matador* instead, in league with book writer Peter Jukes. En route they had successful careers writing songs for such as Cliff Richard and Gary Glitter. A concept album (the sort denied *Mr and Mrs*) was made by Tom Jones.

The £1.5 million production had a first-class company that included Stefanie Powers, Caroline O'Connor, Alexander Hanson and Nicky Henson, but the notices were poor. For the *Independent, Matador* was 'just about recognizable as a musical (albeit of a debased kind)';[20] Jack Tinker expressed surprise that 'the dead hand of mediocrity can still exert so firm a hold';[21] Adam Sweeting in the *Guardian* thought the mock-Spanish accents 'makes you think you're watching *'Allo 'Allo!* in a tapas bar';[22] for Charles Osborne it was all 'quite dreadful [...] even the curtain calls are ludicrous'.[23] The *Daily Mail*'s headline 'Gored To Tears' left no doubt. Powers publicly protested against the critics 'glorifying themselves by saying something witty and cute at someone else's expense', while animal lovers demonstrated and the RSPCA distributed leaflets outside the theatre. Inside, the rock 'n' roll and flamenco entertainment on offer ran out of steam.

Empty seats in the stalls of the Prince Edward Theatre may have been because those interested in the progress and health of the British musical, and the sanctity of English literature, had taken themselves off to Guildford cemetery, put their ears to the ground at lot no. 2213, and listened for sounds of the Revd Charles Lutwidge Dodgson turning in his grave. Lewis Carroll, not especially well known for letting his hair down, would of course never even have known what a musical *was*, although he might have sensed instinctively that whatever a good musical was, *The Hunting of the Snark* (Prince Edward Theatre, 24 October 1991: 60) wasn't. What he would have made of Mike Batt's adaptation – book, music and lyrics – is anyone's guess. The show's journey to the West End was tortuous: a series of semi-staged concerts with Batt conducting in nautical rig and the orchestra togged out as sailors, and – a sign of the times – the concept album. Grinding its way through twenty-six indistinguishable songs was a cast with names that resounded with current West End audiences and beyond, including David McCallum as Carroll, Kenny Everett, and (less known but better) Philip Quast, who had already played the Bellman in an Australian concert version.

The performers paled beside the technology, with 152 computer-linked projectors throwing 12,000 animations, bombarding the audience with images that at least took their mind off the songs and the liberties taken. Batt's numbers had a computer-generated air about them. The *Observer* regretted that 'Carroll's queer poem is sporadically quoted and pushed aside for lyrics, music and staging of unmitigated direness', while 'the score of tired recording blather, mixed with echoes of Barry Manilow's "Copacabana" rhythms and all-purpose soul detergent is devoid of melody, invention and any theatrical excitement'.[24] The *Daily Telegraph* witnessed 'a Turkey dancing towards disaster'.[25] After a few weeks, the hunt for the totally elusive snark was abandoned, over £2 million having been squandered on the hopeless quest. There was some currency in blaming the failure on its creator, whose work, after all, was 'batts', although Batt's attitude to Carroll's poem at least had something in common with Carroll's own opinion of it. When asked what his words meant, Carroll replied that he hadn't the least idea.

# 1992

*Moby Dick*
*Valentine's Day*
*Which Witch?*

A musical from Herman Melville? *Really?* An opera, and you'd be looking out for Britten's follow-up to *Billy Budd*, but … a *musical*? *Moby Dick* (Piccadilly Theatre, 17 March 1992; 127) has somehow escaped obloquy and (for those who like this sort of thing) achieved cult status. In 2016, a production of the much-revised original was staged at the Union Theatre. In 1992, the leaky vessel battled tidal waves of disapproval. *The Times* was disappointed that the 'whale of a yarn drowns in an ocean of pointless mediocrity' within a musical whose 'effect is of a vehicle, whose tyres have gone pop: revving, overheating, going nowhere'.[26] Robert Longden's possibly brilliant idea was to invade Melville's book with St Trinians'-type schoolgirls, beloved from the cartoons of Ronald Searle and a series of increasingly insipid films by Frank Launder and Sidney Gilliat. At first glance, *Moby Dick* seems like *Passion Flower Hotel* of the early 1990s, little more than an excuse for twanging suspender tops. That doesn't account for the tangling with Captain Ahab, played here by the dragged-up headmistress of the St Trinians'-type establishment now called St Godley's (get it?), whose pupils decide to raise funds for the school by doing their own version of Melville's novel under the supervision of the headmistress, played by a man; in true Alastair Sim fashion she/he gets to play Captain Ahab, too. In mixing up so many elements with little regard for sense, Longden faced critics with a puzzle many couldn't bother to work out. The fact that Sim didn't live long enough to be in a British musical was a disadvantage.

Originally staged at Oxford Old Fire Station, the show was taken up and expanded for London, against the advice of some of his staff, by Cameron Mackintosh. There was something about it that vaguely recalled *The Utter Glory of Morrissey Hall*, a delightfully curious piece set around a very St Trinians'-type girls' school with an inventive score by Clark Gesner. Gesner's show sounds utterly British, but isn't; perhaps because it did, it closed on its opening night on Broadway. Faced with initial perplexity, *Moby Dick* might have suffered the same fate. *The Times* complained that it was like 'being sucked into somebody's very silly, very private joke',[27] the *Daily Express* denouncing it as deliberately amateurish, shambolic and bizarre. In all of this, the reviewers might as well have been at a pantomime. Was there now no place for such nonsense? *Moby Dick*'s scatter-shot entertainment, its sense of mindless fun and senseless outrage went back to Grimaldi's time and beyond. In the now torrid environment so familiar to the musicals created for international consumption, *Moby Dick* deserved to be forgiven for turning its back on the fashionable, patently artificial seriousness with which most new musicals were thickly coated. The Piccadilly almost certainly wasn't the right theatre for it, the songs (co-written with Hereward Kaye) perhaps incidental to the general chaos, but *Moby Dick* may yet be one of the few British musicals of its time to enjoy an after-life. Maybe, but for the *Daily Telegraph* critic Chris Bennion, it was 'like a school disco-themed night at Yates's Wine Lodge'.[28] Being set in a school may partially have accounted for the show's immaturity.

Even staged in the Minerva Studio in leafy Chichester, the 'romantic musical comedy' *Valentine's Day* (Globe Theatre, 7 September 1992; 28) seemed dangerously out of time in the inhospitable early 1990s. Adapted from George Bernard Shaw's *You Never Can Tell* by Benny Green and David William, with Denis King setting Green's lyrics, the show didn't sit well in London where, despite much revision between Sussex and the West End, it was greeted with apathy or hostility. The *Evening Standard* headline, 'Valentine Day's Massacre' wasn't helpful. *Pygmalion* had been turned into the superb *My Fair Lady*, and seven years before *Valentine's Day* Green and King had turned *The Admirable Bashville* into the much-admired *Bashville*, but there was less luck now; *You Never Can Tell* may have been one of Shaw's 'pleasant plays' but it seemed resistant to musical adaptation.

Gillian Lynne's production hadn't thrilled everyone at Chichester, not least Lynne, who wanted the piece restructured before London. There seemed no reason why the old play shouldn't cope with being stuffed with songs; the plot, after all, was not too taxing. Mrs Clandon returns to England having brought up her three children overseas. In Torquay, her daughter Gloria falls for the hard-up dentist Mr Valentine, and Mrs Clandon has the misfortune to bump into her long forgotten husband, unleashing romantic entanglements. As recently as 1966 *You Never Can Tell* had achieved 284 performances at the Haymarket with Ralph Richardson as the waiter William. Then, it had succeeded as a well-made play with a top-quality cast, and as late as 2005, a revival with Edward Fox's William enjoyed a decent run.

*Valentine's Day* was not so fortunate. There were several cast alterations between Chichester and London. Edward Petherbridge's rapscallion waiter survived the transfer, but Steven Pacey's Mr Valentine was replaced by Alexander Hanson (who got the best of the notices), the Gloria of Fiona Fullerton was replaced by Teresa Banham, and Judy Parfitt's Mrs Clandon by Elizabeth Counsell. King's score was workmanlike-inoffensive, as in 'The World Was Changed This Morning', but when the curtain went up after the interval the cast found themselves staring out at empty seats where once patrons had sat and stared. In the years following, Green was said to grow apoplectic whenever the show was mentioned.

The *Daily Telegraph* complained that 'Bland tunes, so-so lyrics and Shaw's exhaustingly bright and sexless chatter [not that it had seemed to matter when Lerner and Loewe got their hands on it] makes this an irritatingly arid experience'.[29]

*Midweek* told its readers it was 'one of the direst evenings in town. And to see actors of the calibre of Edward Petherbridge struggle through dated tosh of this order is A-class embarrassment.'[30] 'It's far from clear just what it is Denis King's mildly pleasant but anaemic music and Benny Green's banal lyrics are hoping to do for the play' in 'an evening of virtually non-stop insipidity enlivened only by the odd spasm of acute embarrassment'.[31] As *Valentine's Day* folded, those responsible for it were probably remembering that you never can tell.

In the currently depressing atmosphere of uninteresting failures, worse was to come. Tragically, **Which Witch?** (Piccadilly Theatre, 22 October 1992; 70) has some pretensions of being British, despite its music by the obviously unBritish Benedicte Adrian and Ingrid Bjørnov, the show based on an idea by Ole A. Sørli. Performed as a concert work in Bergen in 1987, it graduated to a concept album, touring concert version, double album in 1990, and thus determinedly on until reaching its apogee in Piccadilly Circus, spruced up for the occasion with a new book by British director Piers Haggard, and lyrics from Kit Hesketh-Harvey, whose *Beautiful and Damned* was yet undreamed of. Claimed by some to be Norway's finest export since Edvard Grieg, *Which Witch?* was oh-so-loosely based on passages from the sixteenth-century *Malleus Maleficarum*, a fact that no doubt excited heated discussion among the average musical-bound coach parties unloading in Shaftesbury Avenue. Now, that fusty old document had been translated into what the producers advertised, covering all eventualities, as 'The Opera Musical' and, no surprise, 'A Powerful Story of a Romantic Passion', involving 'the forbidden love of a beautiful young Italian girl for a handsome German bishop in Renaissance Europe'. For Jack Tinker, the music was 'instantly identified as a combination of Late Naïve and Early Naff', with Hesketh-Harvey's lyrics marrying 'Lower-trite with Middle-turgid'.[32]

King Harald and Queen Sonja of Norway flew in to see the show, which had been given a £1 million loan by the Norwegian government, and sponsored by Norsk Hydro, who had faith in a production that had witches with outsize penises flying over the stalls during a Black Sabbath sequence. Although it was 'no more than, let's say, a tale of social climbing and power politics in a suburb of Plymouth', *The Times* conceded that the score, with bits and pieces of stuff that apparently reminded its critic of Sullivan and Mendelssohn, managed 'tuneful moments amid some pretty numbing recitative'.[33] Closing with a loss of £2 million, *Which Witch?* took with it the now obligatory laundry list of endless songs, one of which was catchily titled '2,665,866,746,664 Little Devils'. No doubt audiences at the Piccadilly filed out of the theatre happily singing that one.

# 1993

*Robin, Prince of Sherwood*
*Leonardo*
*Lust*

Considering that Robin Hood stole from the rich to give to the poor, British musicals did him no favours. In 1965, *Twang!* did little to enhance his reputation. Hood probably did better as the hero of pantomimes up and down the land. In light operatic mood, Hood had done quite well, especially in America where Reginald De Koven's comic opera *Robin Hood* had premiered in 1891 and been persistently revived up to the end of World War II. In Britain, thirty years before De Koven's work, George Alexander Macfarren's sylvan *Robin Hood* was well received; the musicologist Edward Dent found it 'very full of good fun and on the way to Sullivan'. It had the advantage of an agile libretto by John Oxenford, with whom Macfarren had already collaborated on *Allan of Aberfeldy* in 1850. The well-functioning collaboration echoed down the years, but by the 1990s, beyond Andrew Lloyd Webber and Tim Rice, itself a pairing that would not endure, the British public was hard pushed to name any collaborators creating musical theatre. Looking at the author credits for **Robin, Prince of Sherwood** (Piccadilly Theatre, 3 February 1993; 109), the question remains 'who?'

Produced and directed by Bill Kenwright and subtitled in its publicity as 'The Hero That Lives In Us All' [really?], here was 'a new musical adventure', with a top price of £10 for adults, £5 for children. The review headlines were not encouraging: 'Arrowing Stuff';[34] 'The Stinker of Nottingham';[35] 'Sherwood Rings With Jingles as Robin's Merry Men Go Camping'.[36] Here was the prince who put the ham in Nottingham. Jack Tinker pronounced the show 'piffle [...] It is childish without becoming child-like, it is vacuous without being light-footed or light-hearted and it is intense without attaining the least hint of intelligence'.[37] Describing the show as 'lamentable', Charles Spencer found that in the songs 'originality is in woefully short supply. Almost every number sounds like crude pastiche, ranging from heavy metal to power ballads, from Beach Boy harmonies to Madonna-like disco.'[38] Mistakenly, the *Financial Times* thought it 'Corny to the core, and wet behind the ears, [but] this new rock musical might just become a hit.'[39] It didn't.

How many untutored patrons of **Leonardo** (Strand Theatre, 3 June 1993; 44) walked out of the theatre believing, as its book writer John Kane would have them believe, that da Vinci had a love affair with that enigmatic smiling-faced Mona Lisa? It was news to some that he made her pregnant, along the way slapping her playfully on the bottom, and cheekily inviting her to assist him in his research. Kane's cock-eyed distortion overlooked the fact that da Vinci was gay, didn't make his model pregnant, and didn't fill his days by singing absurdly emotional songs. Perhaps audiences expected artists to slap their models on the bottom and smirkingly ask them to help them with their research. Audiences might be forgiven for thinking this so-called 'Portrait of Love' no more than a bad dream thought up by an army of writers who came up with such lyrics as 'mille grazie – up your arzie': lead singer of the pop group Unit 4 Plus 2, Tommy Moeller (to whom some sources credit music and lyrics) Greg Moeller (some sources suggest he wrote the book), the Australian record producer and songwriter Russell Dunlop (unmentioned in some sources), and Duke Minks (some sources credit him with the main crime of having had 'the idea'), one-time road manager for Unit 4 Plus 2, airline owner and vice-president of Citibank. This bewildering list of achievement suggests nothing that equipped these people to write a musical. Minks told the press that *he* had written the show on aeroplanes. After deep thought, he informed the *Independent*, 'What we wanted was a contemporary story, not a heavy Renaissance Hamlet situation.'[40]

It was the involvement of Minks, Liverpudlian financial adviser to the Pacific island of Nauru, that made *Leonardo* possible. His reasons for convincing the Nauru government that it should put £2 million into a spectacular staging of a musical from writers that nobody in musical theatre had ever heard of (or would ever want to hear from again) may have been honourable. Nauru thrived on profits made from the phosphate in bird droppings (guano), making a comfortable living from the fertiliser given gratis by its resident bird population. There were fears that this livelihood was, in a manner of words, drying up. What better solution than putting on a West End musical to swell the coffers? So it was that far away in London town, the curtain rose to show Leonardo on his deathbed, his completed portrait of Mona conveniently placed at his side.

The problems of writing a biomusical about a painter seemed not to occur to its creators, but as painters go, Leonardo was *serious*. Making a musical about da Vinci came close to making a musical of *King Lear*. At its first night after-show party, quite a relief after the almost four-hour-long performance, the President of Nauru exuded confidence, with the slight reservation that 'I don't know myself whether the love aspect is entirely true. But a bit of love, a bit of music, it takes the worries away.' As often happens in politics, his chief secretary to the government toed the official line: 'I think it is beautiful.'[41]

*Leonardo* was laughed out of court, 'a mind-numbingly boring musical [...] based on the touching hypothesis that our Len was not interested in boys but loved a girl [...] The whole thing is the most utter bilge.'[42] Jeremy Kingston thought that 'the whole drift of this show is absurd',[43] in agreement with *Time Out*'s verdict that here was 'a bland, boring musical, innocuous except for its pathetic attempt to rewrite history'.[44]

The self-imposed difficulties created by complex scenic designs in the musical demonstrated the increasing importance of the show's physical appearance; people did indeed expect to come out of a musical whistling the scenery. One of the major aspects that separated *Oliver!* from *Wildest Dreams* (there were many others) was the mechanisation involved. It may have been possible for cast members to push Sean Kenny's sets into its various positions, but the sets were a *concept*; indeed, by 1962 Kenny's sets for *Blitz!* verged on a miracle of engineering, whereas Sally Jacobs' scenery for Cheltenham's *Wildest Dreams*, and Basil Pattison's scenery for the London transfer of *Wildest Dreams*, belonged to the painted front cloth school of design.

Kenny's design for *Stop the World* had the best of several worlds – extreme simplicity, daring originality and (from Kenny) an unexpected nihilism. Its sparse presentation had the advantage of seeming new and daring, with no hint of the mechanical needs demanded by *Blitz!* As London musicals developed and budgets monstrously increased, scenic design became ever more important. By 1984, musicals like *Starlight Express* would have shut down at a mechanical failure, while *Peg* (Peter Rice's sets, pretty enough, never looking much more than an assortment of plywood) told audiences the producers had spent as little as possible. As the price of tickets rose, customers wanted to see what their money was spent on.

*Leonardo* had spent the money and counted the cost. At the previews, for which audiences still had to pay prices that would have seriously alarmed theatregoers of even a decade before, they were greeted by a sheet of paper that informed them: 'The whole purpose of Previews is to put into practice what has been rehearsed and to iron out any bugs in the sound, lighting and set prior to a formal opening.' *Really?* Why, then, was the audience *there*? The idea that previews might be the time to judge audience reaction to the material, or give the writers and producer pause to consider changes, cuts and additions seems to have been forgotten: now, it was problems with that damned scenery. Did it matter that preview audiences at *Leonardo* didn't see the back portals that explained how the hero saw his life as if a series of pictures (a pity the back portals were missing as these showed his painting of the Last Supper); the marketplace's wall had the night off; the rosette window in the cathedral couldn't be lowered; the backdrops and lattice wall divides representing Lisa's house could not be used. There were, too, 'various other minor pieces' that couldn't be shown. Never mind – the information sheet concluded: 'Hopefully you may win the 2 Free Return Tickets to Italy and take the opportunity to visit Florence.' By the time you got back, the show had long closed.

By the end of June ticket prices were halved, and the evening shortened by twenty minutes, but nothing could save one of the silliest biomusicals of the period. People mourning its demise might have drawn comfort from the fact that, in the manner of the London bus, something very similar was already on its way: the 2003 *Lautrec*, whose painter subject had already suffered at the hands of *Bordello*. Anyway, audiences were probably put off by the title *Leonardo*. *Leo* might have struck a much friendlier note. It would certainly have cost less in light bulbs.

The spirits of the musical theatre enthusiast may or may not have been heightened by the arrival of the Heathers brothers' musical *Lust* (Theatre Royal, Haymarket, 19 July 1993; 128) based on William Wycherley's play *The Country Wife*, now redressed as 'a couple of hours of undiluted British smut' according to the

*Sunday Express*.[45] Despite its story about a seventeenth-century rake (played by Denis Lawson) who pretends he has been castrated, the *Mail on Sunday* found it 'About as sexy as a public information film.'[46] 'I wish I could write that *Lust* is a must,' wrote Christopher Tookey (the author of another period musical, *Hard Times*), but 'it smells strongly of Rust. I fear that it will, despite the endeavours of a hard-working cast, shortly be Dust.'[47] Many of the reviews were favourable, but by some chemistry unspecified and indecipherable, *Lust* was one of those musicals that somehow escaped being remembered as such.

# 1994

## Out of the Blue

Wading through the coma-inducing *Out of the Blue* (Shaftesbury Theatre, 4 November 1994; 20) there is, at least, one moment that genuinely thrills. It is the *last* moment, that final confident stroke of the composer's restless pen when, after prolonged slumber, Shun-Ichi Tokura's great big blanc-mange of a score ceases its wobbling and with a few terminal shivers, shudders its last, long-awaited, breath. Dubbed by its cast 'A Flash in Japan', the show opened with very little advance publicity at one of London's unluckiest venues, and with *Out of the Blue* the luck wasn't going to change. Paul Sand's libretto had so complex a plot, moving between 1945 and 1970 and between Nagasaki and Boston, that it is a miracle anyone ever understood it. Apparently, a child is conceived by an American airman after Nagasaki is bombed. Believing the child dead of the radiation sickness that killed his bride, the soldier returns to America and consigns himself to the Catholic church.

Nicky Pope in *Nine To Five* thought the chorus, masked and cloaked, were 'undermined by ludicrous through-sung lyrics' in a score that was 'a bland, forgettable middle-of-the-Pacific cop-out, not capturing the flavour of either Japan or America'.[48] The *Observer* was equally unimpressed, finding 'not a single moment of inspired melody in Shun-Ichi Tokura's score, and the book by Paul Sand is simultaneously confusing and trite'.[49] Not all dismissed the score. 'Earnest But Not an Earner' ran the headline in *The Times*: 'Benedict Nightingale finds that good songs cannot lighten an Anglo-Japanese musical with a too dogged decency of purpose',[50] while Charles Spencer for the *Daily Telegraph* described 'a worthy piece of work, more rock-tinged requiem than a musical'.[51]

That such stuff was now being taken seriously almost beggars belief. As the words hammered out with intense but elusive meaning during *Out of the Blue* insisted, 'Let us be perfectly clear!'

*

# 1995

*Prisoner Cell Block H*

In the dead days of the British musical, *Prisoner Cell Block H* (Queen's Theatre, 30 October 1995; 88) at least guaranteed an evening of low kitsch, and wasn't genuinely British. Adapted from the Australian soap opera created by Reg Watson, long established as a cult favourite on British television, this was a splendid exercise in bad taste, complete with wobbling sets, lesbian warders and troublesome prisoners. The show put up a rag-bag of enjoyably tacky songs by Don Battye and Peter Pinne. The Wentworth Detention Centre in Victoria settled comfortably at the Queen's, where Joan Ferguson (known as the leather-crazy Freak) and Liverpudlian Lily Savage played by Paul O'Grady, imprisoned for, among other offences, stealing a fondue set, vied for attention. For the *Daily Mirror*, 'This panto-style send-up lasts for little more than two hours but feels like a life sentence,'[52] while the *Daily Express* relished 'deliciously low camp in which new depths of tackiness are enthusiastically plumbed'.[53]

# 1996

*The Fields of Ambrosia*
*Disgracefully Yours*
*Voyeurz*

A dismal year for the British musical flop. The most misunderstood, misinterpreted, or perhaps mistaken, *The Fields of Ambrosia* (Aldwych Theatre, 31 January 1996; 23) was either the most daring or the most foolhardy. It had its origin in Garrie Bateson's disturbing screenplay for MGM's *The Travelling Executioner*, a 1970 movie directed by Jack Smight and starring Stacy Keach as Jonas Candide, a sort of part-preacher, part-carnival barker who travels the deep South of America in 1918 with his electric chair 'Reliable', promising his clients 'the prettiest death'. Remember those initials, J. C. – one of the work's many allegorical fancies. MGM's movie trailer assured prospective audiences that J. C.'s clients 'were always satisfied', thanks to Candide's unique style of despatching them. Beguiling them with alluring descriptions of the Elysium landscape for which they were bound – those very fields of ambrosia – they meet their end as if setting out on a new life, full of enchantment, peaches and cream, peace and welcoming women. They are bound for a world of which on earth they have known nothing. Who could fail to be moved by the movie, with Candide's promise of perfection played against the calculated horror of the death he is employed to deliver? As a plea for abolishing death by electric chair, Smight's film has a terrifying potency.

Candide's sympathetic professionalism is shaken when he is commissioned to execute a young woman, Gretchen Herzallerliebst. Entrapped by her sexuality, he contrives the disappearance of his chair, old Reliable, to delay her death, and together they plan her escape. Gretchen is shot attempting the breakout. Candide ends his career sitting in his own version of old Sparky, awaiting his despatch ('Fry me while I'm hot!') to those ambrosian fields, in which, just before the final curtain of *The Fields of Ambrosia*, he is reunited by the already-up-there Gretchen. Musicalising Bateson's work inevitably threw up seemingly insurmountable problems with which only a brave soul would grapple. This man was the American actor Joel Higgins, who turned in book and lyrics and played Candide in the first, American, production at New Brunswick's George Street Playhouse in 1993, with Christine Andreas as Gretchen. Both repeated their roles in the £1.3 million London production of *The Fields of Ambrosia*. It met a wall of critical disdain.

The headlines told the story: 'Cheap and Cheerless';[54] 'Why axing this executioner's tale would be a mercy killing';[55] 'Death and a Midden';[56] 'Tasteless fry-up warrants a death sentence'.[57] For the *Independent*, Paul Taylor recalled how 'The second half of the show left me weak with bliss as it trampled over good taste and political correctness like a herd of bullocks.'[58] Nicholas de Jongh found it 'tasteless [...] I have never seen a more morally unappealing musical than this [...] loathsome'.[59] In the *Daily Telegraph*, Charles Spencer warned 'you would be a fool to miss it. It is one of the all-time *great* bad musicals.'[60]

Despite reservations, the composer and lyricist David Spencer decided that 'all such considerations are overridden by the impression that the focus is tight and assured; that the *right* things, dramaturgically speaking, are being sung about; and that what Higgins and Silvestri have on their hands is an audience pleaser that doesn't cheat.' Spencer went on, 'The performances are as persuasive as the material. There could not be a more charming hustler than Mr. Higgins, nor a more alluring death-row prisoner than Ms. Andreas – who shares with her leading man the dubious distinction of being underrated, underused and underappreciated. But maybe *The Fields of Ambrosia* will change all that.'[61]

It didn't. The critical outrage and sometimes vociferous reaction of its audiences did for Higgins' brave attempt to break some of the barriers that imprisoned the musical. The show sometimes opened itself to ridicule, as when Jonas's young assistant Jimmy sang after being gang-raped, 'If it isn't one thing, it's another'. *The Fields of Ambrosia* was brought down by attacks on its tastelessness, but the show was not without merit. It *looked* and *sounded* bleak (with reason), but Silvestri's score was at the very least interesting and occasionally gorgeous, with Higgins and Andreas giving committed performances. Far superior to many other scores of its period, this had a splendid, hideously inappropriate title song; the truly romantic 'Too Bad' as Jonas and Gretchen carouse to a gramophone in her condemned cell and Jonas advises her to 'think about the rope' as an alterative to his own solution of 'old Reliable'. Ravishingly orchestrated by Harold Wheeler, 'Too Bad' can't be discounted as rubbish, nor can 'Continental Sunday'. The American writer Peter Filichia stood back from critical outburst in London. 'I am ashamed that British theatre critics are so simple. And so mean. I'm flabbergasted that they couldn't respond to one of the most fascinating, fully three-dimensional characters I've ever encountered in the (literally) thousands of musicals I've seen.'

*

In their ways, all three of the year's flops were shocking, but *The Fields of Ambrosia* was way ahead in quality of much that followed. A new rock 'n' roll musical by Richard O'Brien, *Disgracefully Yours* (Comedy Theatre, 18 March 1996; 24), from Edinburgh Festival, moved into Panton Street for a short season. It was a pale shadow of O'Brien's *Rocky Horror Show*, whose potency was unweakened after 21 years. Now assisted by The Fabulous Frockettes and The Black Angels, O'Brien appeared as Mephistopheles Smith (aka The Devil) welcoming audiences to the Club Inferno PLC (aka Hell). Basically a protracted cabaret act badly in need of a show doctor, the show failed to excite much interest. Complaining of its wearying 4/4 rock tempo, Alastair Macaulay thought it brought the West End musical to 'a new low' in 'very probably the dullest show in London'.[62] Complaining that it wouldn't have upset the pensioners in Bexhill-on-Sea, the *Evening* Standard pronounced it 'Diabolical, I'm afraid. And for all the wrong reasons.'[63] A Freudian slip in the theatre programme had a cast member referring to the show as *Disastrously Yours*.

*Was* the West End still shockable? Impresario Michael White, who had managed to shock it in 1970 with his nudie revue *Oh! Calcutta!*, hoped so. Michael Lewis and Peter Rafelson's show (hardly a musical at all), *Voyeurz* (Whitehall Theatre, 22 July 1996; 64), had been 'developed' from a concept album and performance by the all-female band 'Fem2Fem' at the Astoria the previous year. To move it into the Whitehall, where the saintly Phyllis Dixey had bared herself with such British rectitude, was little short of treason. What passed for a plot followed the sexual adventures of Jane, an innocent in New York until she walks through the doors of the lesbian club 'Voyeurz'. Note the use of a French word that the non-French-speaking British could just about make out to mean something naughty to look at. For Rachel Campbell-Johnston in *The Times*, 'The simulated sex was only marginally less embarrassing than watching the vicar's Jack Russell mounting the postmistress's spaniel at a village fete.'[64]

# 1997

*Always*
*Maddie*
*Stepping Out*

Short shrift awaited *Always* (Victoria Palace, 22 May 1997; 76), none shorter than the verdict of a reviewer on BBC radio at the mention of the title: 'Never.' The torrent of abuse seemed almost disrespectful when one considered the subject, but the review headlines refused to bow the knee. 'Wallis and Mr Dopey ... Banality Reigns Supreme in Musical of Royal Love' announced *The Times*; 'Always is a Place To Avoid' cried *Metro*. The tone seemed heartlessly inconsiderate towards a work that its producers billed as 'The Ultimate Love Story ... It is the stuff of fairy tales and legends. It is also a true story.' But what love story *could* be described as 'ultimate'? Tristan and Isolde? Romeo and Juliet? Abelard and Heloise? Popeye and Olive Oyl? Who else but the lovable Edward VIII, aka David, and the adorable Wallis Simpson, aka the Duchess of Windsor.

*Always* was always on a hiding to nothing, but survived being work-shopped in Melbourne three years earlier. The work of William May and Jason Sprague, with additional book material by Frank Hauser who co-directed in London with Thommie Walsh, the show's only real asset was Jan Hartley as the distinctly unappealing Simpson. Saddled with dismal dialogue that regularly sent audiences at the Victoria Palace into gleeful tittering, Hartley somehow overcame the insipidity of the songs to suggest she might be capable of more than a one-dimensional representation of a heroine who, it is rumoured, had learned the skills of *l'amour* in Shanghai. Not a shred of rumour came within a whisker of *Always*. If one didn't know better, one might have thought the Lord Chamberlain had red-pencilled the script to remove anything less than subservient. How much livelier on occasion it would have been for everyone if Wallis had let her hair down and got some of these historical rumours off her chest. No chance of that in *Always*. It was as if the writers and producers were in constant fear of a royal visit to the theatre; the knee was constantly bended.

There have been few more embarrassing sights in London than Clive Carter's unhappy king, forced (at Buckingham as well as Victoria Palace) to sign the abdication. Delivering this speech, *Always* reached one of its apogees of awfulness. One suspected that the writers could not have chosen two characters with whom British audiences in 1997 would sympathise less. That 'ultimate' love story might be a sitting target for satire, even tongue-in cheek if satire was too much of a stretch, but dishing it up as a serious romance – with songs?

Relief was on hand from two supporting players, both of whom got to spend more time in their dressing-rooms than they expected when signing their contracts. Sheila Ferguson probably got through the collected works of Balzac during the run, only having one number, 'Love's Carousel'. It may only have lasted six minutes, but it qualified as one of the most outstandingly absurd moments in British musicals of recent years. Backed by chorus boys disguised as prancing horses, Ferguson went into theatrical legend with a voice that, as one critic put it, could destroy buildings. Then, from the faded shadows of old West End musicals *Wish You Were Here* and *Wonderful Town*, came Shani Wallis as Wallis's (no relation) comforting auntie. Before the Victoria Palace opening, Wallis complained to the press about her role. Like Ferguson, she was mostly confined to barracks, emerging only for a mawkish solo 'Someone Special' (that would be her niece, of course) and a second-act belter 'The Reason For Life Is To Love' with no backlash.

'If always were a place I'd take you there' ran the theme song, but the show headed instead to 1936 Wales where Edward was visiting a Welsh Miners' village, the men doffing their caps with due reverence and extolling their monarch, who probably wouldn't have recognised a pick if one of the miners had hit him over the head with one. It was at this moment that the *Sunday Independent* thought the show 'enters the pantheon of hokiness'.[65] Martin Spence in *Midweek* explained

It is hard to imagine a greater testament to love
than to give up your crown and your country
for the woman you love.
It is the stuff of fairytales and legends.
It is also a true story.

In 1936 Edward VIII chose to abdicate
the throne rather than abandon his true love,
Wallis Simpson. This extraordinary
relationship is brought to life in this remarkable,
exquisite and lavish new musical.

A NEW MUSICAL
*Always*

starring
CLIVE CARTER     JAN HARTLEY
SHANI WALLIS
DAVID McALISTER     CHRIS HUMPHREYS
SHEILA FERGUSON

By WILLIAM MAY and JASON SPRAGUE
Additional Book By FRANK HAUSER

Set Design by                Costume Design by
HILDEGARD BECHTLER          TOM RAND

Lighting Design by           Musical Arrangements
PETER MUMFORD               and Orchestrations by
                            JOHN CAMERON

Production Musical
Direction by                Sound Design by
CHRIS WALKER    TERRY JARDINE for AUTOGRAPH

Musical Staging by THOMMIE WALSH

Directed by
FRANK HAUSER and THOMMIE WALSH

Opening on 10 June 1997 with previews from
20 May 1997, ALWAYS brings together an outstanding
cast and creative team.

**32**  Just how 'ultimate' the love story told by *Always* was remains a mystery

that 'The evening ends with the abdication and Edward proposing with a reprise of "Always", holding a lily in his hand for apparently the next 40 years. No mention is made of Hitler or the strains of marriage and exile.'[66]

It is good to end this section on a note of profundity. The romantic novelist Barbara Cartland would no doubt have attended a royal gala for *Always* had one been arranged (not surprisingly, it wasn't), but was clearly visible at the first night. She breathlessly told the press how she had once met Edward and Simpson in Paris after the abdication, at a restaurant. He was asking for butter and the butter hadn't arrived. 'How sad,' Dame Barbara ruminated. 'This man used to be King of England and now he can't get any butter.' If only such original thought had found its way into *Always*.

\*

The ghostly complications of *Blithe Spirit* were as nothing compared to those of the timid catastrophe that was next to arrive in London. Coward's comedy of manners had just about survived being turned into a musical, *High Spirits*, owing most of its Broadway run to Beatrice Lillie's outrageous Madame Arcati, and some of its West End failure to Cicely Courtneidge's inability to copy Lillie's success. Jack Finney's novel *Marion's Wall* was a tougher proposition, and the show that tried to crack it had a decidedly mixed reaction. 'It cannot be said too often,' reported the *Financial Times*, 'that the modern musical is the cesspit of theatre today: that it is an array of synthetic emotion, synthetic characterisation, synthetic lines, synthetic melodies. The latest to hit the West End – like a soggy cash – is *Maddie*.'[67] In support, the *Evening Standard* headed its review 'Balderdash, babble and baloney leading to a dead end. It's a grim night.'[68] The Lyric's box-office probably went a little quieter when you'd seen the *Independent's* warning of a 'Thoroughly Monotonous Maddie'.[69]

There was, however, in more senses than one, other writing on the wall. Picking up either the *Daily* or *Sunday Telegraph*, you probably wanted to ring the Lyric's box-office before all tickets sold, and didn't bother to telephone because there were sure to be none available, so extraordinary did this new musical sound. If Irving Wardle was to be trusted, here at last was a score in which 'Sondheim rubs shoulders with Jerome Kern', offering 'uproarious scenes of social upheaval' in a 'well carpentered fairy tale' that, on top of all this, offered London a new star.[70] For John Peter in the *Sunday Times*, *Maddie* was 'a real find', 'warmly recommended'.[71] Over at the *Daily Telegraph*, Charles Spencer was throwing hats in the air for 'The Show We've Been Waiting For', hailing a return to 'the traditional values of the musical's golden age'. To which golden age Spencer thought *Maddie* was related must remain a mystery. He went on to praise the score with its 'full-blown showbiz anthems', and the show itself as some sort of antidote to 'overblown mega musicals'.[72] As shows intentionally written as antidotes are rare (Alan Melville's genteel Scots musical of 1959, *Marigold*, was an intentional antidote to such mega musicals as *West Side Story*, and paid for it by quickly collapsing) this merely seemed another good reason for lifting up that telephone and grabbing a ticket.

At least there was nothing overblown about *Maddie*; it was more a case of under-nourishment. Shaun McKenna and Steven Dexter's book understood its proportions: a small show with a small cast and small band; just the sort of show the British had shown no interest in in years. It arrived on Shaftesbury Avenue with decent credits, a by-product of students' work at Oxford under the professorship of Sondheim, although nothing of his influence could remotely be said to have scratched the surface of *Maddie*. McKenna was lyricist to Stephen Keeling's music, and in 1996 a production by Salisbury Playhouse was greeted enthusiastically. For some reason, the *Daily Telegraph* launched a campaign among its readers to get the show into London, inviting them to become investing angels. On the back of such generosity, *Maddie* (Lyric Theatre, 29 September 1997; 48) made the transfer, its publicity promising yet another 'Magical New Musical'.

In 1977 San Francisco, young married couple Jan and Nick Cheyney move into their new apartment, only to discover that it had once been the home of the long-dead 1920s actress Marion (Maddie) Marsh, killed in a car crash en route to a meeting with Cecil B. DeMille. Their landlord, an elderly piano player in vaude-ville, tells them Maddie's story. It isn't long before Maddie herself turns up inside Jan's body, inhabiting her life and creating the problems that take over the show. It's a fascinating if irritatingly muddling concept. The return of Maddie, in spiritual form only (we never see her), is much more dangerous than the disruption Elvira causes in *Blithe Spirit*, and gave the star of *Maddie* a challenging dual role. Summer Rognlie, as Jan and Maddie, had earned raves at Salisbury. In London, Charles Spencer wrote that 'her leather lunged voice and ability to combine the sassy with the vulnerable put me in mind of Liza Minnelli'.[73] Irving Wardle thought her a 'star worthy of Maddie's dreams'.[74]

In the end, there simply wasn't enough about *Maddie* to whet the palette. It had its moments, suggestions now and again that Keeling and McKenna should be encouraged to write more, but an air of uncertainty prevailed. Were the songs good or rotten? Why did so many of them sound unfinished? Why had nobody told the writers? No doubt about Lynda Baron, as the show's baddie wealthy man-eating older star, singing 'Knick Knacks', with a lyric by Anthony Drewe that was the low-point of the night, but the score had its more acceptable moments, best in Rognlie's 'The Time of My Life' and 'Star'. Ultimately, *Maddie* could not escape its dwarfishness, or its hapless pretence to be American. Meanwhile, the reviews left a question mark over the integrity of some of its critics.

The heart-warming play becomes the even more heart-warming musical! Richard Harris's feel-good *Stepping Out* was one of the long runners of the 1980s, lasting three years in London, and turned into Lewis Gilbert's semi-musical 1991 movie with Liza Minnelli. Originally produced eleven months earlier for the Theatre Royal, Plymouth, *Stepping Out: The Musical* (Albery Theatre, 28 October 1997; 142) squeezed the lemon dry. Composer Denis King hated the title. He'd thought it appropriate for an almost entirely female cast that he should work with a female lyricist with whom he'd already collaborated, Mary Stewart-David. The working relationship between Harris and Stewart-David was problematic, but director Bob Tomson and choreographer Kenn Oldfield helped the Plymouth show to success. There was no reason why Harris's artfully artless comedy about a group of dispa-rate women who, each for her own reason, join a tap dance class, along the way sharing their problems, shouldn't work as a musical; in a different milieu, Broad-way had done the same sort of thing in *A Chorus Line*. The difference with Harris's characters was that we felt homey when the women opened up. At final curtain, as in *A Chorus Line*, all came together in a celebration of dance that brought the show to a rousing conclusion. In this way, audiences had always thought that the originally songless *Stepping Out* was a musical anyway, at least for the last five minutes. Making it into one didn't take things any further, only reminding the audience that the straight play had been better all along. The very fact that Harris's play was now a musical made a nonsense of the central idea that none of the dance class was any good when it came to performing.

At Plymouth and in London the tap dance teacher, a disappointed ex-professional, was played by Liz Robertson. When the production was taken up for London by Bill Kenwright, Tomson and Oldfield were dropped, and new director Julia McKenzie, who had directed Harris's original play, and new choreographer Tudor Davies, were brought in. McKenzie wanted the show reworked and recast. Friction between the director and King and others in the production team led to the composer and director not being on speaking terms. King managed to resist plans to drop Robertson, whom he regarded as the show's saving grace, but others fell by the wayside and were replaced.

When *Stepping Out: The Musical* unhappily tapped its way to London, the welcome was nowhere as heart-warming as it had been at Plymouth, although even now the *Sunday Telegraph* applauded, as did *The Times* for 'the last ten minutes' when the company pulled off the public display of tap virtuosity. This had been 'magic'. Of course, it always *had* been in the play; the high spot of the evening was something the musical could not hope to improve on. Rather than stepping out, the *Guardian* decided 'The best thing that can be said [...] is how much it makes you appreciate staying in', regretting that 'trying to turn it into a musical kills the goose stone dead' in a show where 'Every number is like an interval – often an embarrassingly over-extended one.' There was no doubt that 'Harris has well and truly cooked his goose this time around.'[75] For the *Daily Telegraph*, the piece was 'insubstantial and incompetent',[76] while the *Evening Standard*, with its discouraging headline 'A Tap Dance To the Muzak of Mediocrity' pronounced it 'the authentic British musical', 'a quintessentially English, low-key, low-brow entertainment, as easy on the brain as on the ear'.[77] Why hadn't Harris and King decided on an opening out of the original one-set play as in the movie, rather than stuffing the show with numbers whenever a character needed to be brought forward? There seemed little doubt that what *Stepping Out*'s musical lacked was imaginative rethinking of its original source. Which should have been left to rest.

# 1998

*Saucy Jack and the Space Vixens*

From its modest beginnings at the 1995 Edinburgh Festival, a show described by *London Midweek* as 'the most purely enjoyable and outrageous feast of camp this side of *The Rocky Horror Show*', flourished.[78] The *Evening Standard* imagined 'an episode of *Blake's Seven* scripted by Danny La Rue, with some Eurovision songs thrown in, and you will have a fairly accurate picture of this sci-fi musical'.[79] Co-lyricists Charlotte Mann and Michael Fidler were students at the University of Kent when, with Johanna Allitt and Simon Curtis, they came up with the idea for *Saucy Jack and the Space Vixens* (Queen's Theatre, 25 March 1998; 85), with music by Jonathan Croose and Robin Forrest. Fidler was inspired by seeing a musical, *Ilsle, Queen of the Nazi Love Camp*, at Edinburgh: 'It made me think that the first thing you need is a good title, and sometimes that's all you need.' At Saucy Jack's cabaret bar on Frottage III, the Slingback Killer is on the loose, her speciality method of despatch being a stiletto through the heart. The air in space was thick with *double-entendre*. Never mind that when it got to London, some critics thought it had landed in the wrong place. *The Times* found 'its lack of charm, tension and wit and even sense is sadly exposed',[80] but *Saucy Jack* was vibrant entertainment for those who sought it. Was it really only now that 'there are signs that theatre is attracting a different kind of audience, the ones who grew up thinking the theatre was stuffy and dull'?[81] That could only be a good thing. *Saucy Jack* went on to a vigorous after-life that persists up to the present in various revivals, the latest in April 2016 at the King's Head, Islington.

# 1999

*A Saint She Ain't*
*Tess of the D'Urbevilles*

Between Molière's *Le Cocu Imaginaire* and Dick Vosburgh's happy entertainment *A Saint She Ain't* (Apollo Theatre, 22 September 1999; 133) gapes a chasm, but, Molière, no matter how vaguely and how much abused, was the model for this laugh-a-line spoof on 1940s Hollywood musicals, staffed by characters who were in effect impersonations or approximations of the likes of Mae West, W. C. Fields, Rita Hayworth, Gene Kelly and others of the silver screen. Happy go lucky was in the air. Ned Sherrin's production transferred from Islington's King's Head Theatre, where Vosburgh's neat cracks ('By the single blue eye of Veronica Lake') sometimes surely only stirred obsessed cineastes. The gaps were filled by Denis King's pastiche tunes. Best remembered was Pauline Daniels as the Mae West, singing 'The Banana For My Pie', with its inexhaustible *double-entendre*: 'The pen for my inkwell, the brush for my flue.' *Variety* reported 'a series of vague approximations of [their] original inspirations with no personality of their own' in a show that 'makes *Dames at Sea* look and sound like an imperishable masterpiece'.[82]

Vosburgh (*A Day in Hollywood, A Night in the Ukraine* and *Windy City*) and the veteran comedian and writer Barry Cryer kept the performances fresher than most. Nicholas de Jongh awarded one star in the *Guardian*, but for the *Sunday Telegraph* it was a 'funny, tuneful, zestful and gloriously silly show', while the *Pink Paper* found it 'a laugh from start to finish'.[83] Despite its dispensing of easy pleasure, it ultimately joined other such spoofs as *Dames at Sea* and *The Great American Backstage Musical* in failing to get a long life in the West End.

By the end of the 1990s the British musical reached a nadir with ***Tess of the d'Urbevilles*** (Savoy Theatre, 10 November 1999; 77), as flaccid an adaptation of any novel as could be imagined. If it achieved anything, it suggested that provincial critics (who generally approved of it) and cosmopolitan critics (who didn't) seldom agreed. On its pre-London tour, the show was hailed as 'a landmark in musical theatre' by the *Sheffield Telegraph*, perhaps because it sounded nothing like one worthy of the description. A government enterprise scheme and forty novice 'angels' had scraped together the £1.5 million production costs, and – after the pre-London notices – were braced for a triumph when the show reached the Strand, but 'Some things simply should not be made into musical theatre,' decided the *Pink Paper*. 'Steeped in melodrama, and without any of the sexual chemistry of the book, you are bombarded by song after turgid song. I've enjoyed three hours at the dentist more.'[84] According to the *Observer*, Hardy's story had been reduced 'to a bodice-ripper' in which Stephen Edwards' music 'surges unmemorably, and Justin Fleming's lyrics warble unsteadily in search of clunking rhymes'.[85] Hammerstein, Ira Gershwin or Yip Harburg it wasn't: 'Father's close to dying and he won't last long / And we will lose our cottage when he's finally gone' was a fair example.

Before *Tess*, Edwards had been approached by the Tennessee Williams Trust to adapt *A Streetcar Named Desire*, turning down the idea because he felt it would 'destroy' Williams's 'language'. Howard Goodall had already considered the Wessex novel as a subject. Now, Edwards wrote much of the music first, sometimes using Hardy's poems as rhythmic models, to which Fleming added words ('I so want to wed him / Instead I've misled him'). The box-office probably laid staff off after reading the review headlines: 'A Simpering Romance' (*Guardian*); 'Three Hours of Non-Musical Torture' (*Daily Mail*); 'Tess Makes My Brain Soften' (*Sunday Telegraph*). *Tess's* luck ran out as the show began playing to less than thirty patrons per performance. A closing notice was posted for 15 January 2000, but the Official Receiver impounded the costumes and sets and sealed off the theatre on the Monday of its final week. Along the sorry way, someone rechristened the show *Tosh of the d'Urbevilles*.

# 2000–2005

**'I would quite happily have volunteered for death myself to help speed things up'**

*Guardian* on *Behind the Iron Mask*

**2000**

*Lautrec*
*Hard Times*
*Napoleon*

Henri Toulouse-Lautrec hadn't got much of a welcome when in 1974 he turned up surrounded by ladies *de la nuits* in *Bordello*. Back for *Lautrec* (Shaftesbury Theatre, 6 April 2000; 84), he got much the same response, although at least this time the title warned audiences what they might be in for. Then, the painter had been played by Henry Woolf, now it was Sevan Stephan, with Hannah Waddingham as the prostitute Suzanne singing the best number of the night, 'Look Into My Eyes' to Henri's mother, played by the British musical veteran Jill Martin, a survivor from the 1950s through *Joie de Vivre* (when she sang the ballads 'Open Your Eyes' and 'The Kiss Was Very, Very Small'), *Tom Brown's Schooldays*, Frank Loesser's *Where's Charley?*, the revue *Cockie!* and a record-breaking appearance in all three London productions of *My Fair Lady*.

Some of the £3.5 million spent on *Lautrec* was evident in Robert Jones' brilliant designs for *fin-de-siècle* Montmartre, but Rob Bettinson's colourful production couldn't altogether mask the cartoonish nature of the script, with material that sounded weak and was sometimes historically inaccurate, with no mention of Lautrec's syphilis. The book by Shaun McKenna (*Maddie*, *La Cava*) came in for a deal of criticism, 'poorly constructed and woefully underwritten', whether showing how the painter fought with his family, fell in love with a prostitute, drank himself under the table or was thrown into an asylum. All this was 'dealt with in such thinly written short scenes that the pathos and drama are completely lost'.[1] Out of curiosity, many went because Charles Aznavour had written the music, with lyrics by his long-time writing partner Dee Shipman, late of *Someone Like You*. Shipman had already collaborated with Roger Webb on an adaptation of Wolf Mankowitz's *A Kid For Two Farthings* that never reached the stage. Her luck didn't improve. By most accounts, *Lautrec* was 'a bizarre event: lavishly mounted, passionately performed and yet peculiarly empty';[2] 'a collection of resolutely wooden songs' and 'All in all, not so much *Folies Bergère* as a straightforward folly'.[3] *Time Out* concluded: 'Pretty much every salient detail of illustrious composer Charles Aznavour's aesthetically-challenged portrait of the artist as a fun-loving but

emotionally fragile midget fails to satisfy.'[4] Once more, the rising cost of the enterprise proved unbearable, bringing this particular Parisian experience to its speedy
conclusion.

Christopher Tookey, film critic of the *Daily Mail*, had determined to make a
musical from Charles Dickens thirty years before his **Hard Times** (Theatre Royal,
Haymarket, 6 June 2000; 112) reached the West End after its run-in at Windsor's
Theatre Royal. A jollier attempt at making a night out of one of Dickens' darker
novels could hardly be imagined, although David Benedictus in the *Independent*
claimed that 'absolutely nothing happens all evening. It's benign but, I'm afraid,
boring. Except, that is, for the number "Spring Is In the Air" in which the chorus
dress up as flowers and do a tap routine using just their fingers. Don't ask.'[5] With
this number, choreographer Craig Revel Horwood created one of the most memorably silly moments of British musicals, to sit beside Sheila Ferguson's deafening
encounter with a merry-go-round in *Always*.

Tookey's adaptation and music, in collaboration with Hugh Thomas, reached
London with Tookey as co-producer and director, on a shoestring budget of
around £80,000, much of it financed by Tookey himself. He described the show as
'an unpretentious crowd-pleasing romp with a serious side' although 'not in the
Cameron Mackintosh mode'. Its pulling power was its two male stars, Roy Hudd
and Brian Blessed, well cast but by no means compatible, with Blessed sometimes
lapsing into forgetting which character he was playing and Hudd keeping the
evening jogging along with spontaneous or well-tried music-hall fooling. Patsy
Rowlands, whose earlier musicals included the original *Valmouth* and taking
over from Joan Sims in *Instant Marriage*, was third-billed, but withdrew before
opening, replaced by Ann Emery, third-billing denied.

The theatre programme described *Hard Times* as 'a very British musical, which
draws on the music hall, pantomime, operetta and circus traditions. One of its
purposes is to show, in the manner of Dickens himself, that popular entertainment
and art can exist in the same piece.' Who had ever thought it couldn't? Tookey and
Thomas's treatment used the circus elements from the original prose to frame the
action, but with characters arriving as themselves and then taking on the persona
of others, with a cast list that made bewildering reading, confusion, as well as
the smell of sawdust and elephants, was in the air. It was harmless enough, and
tuppence-coloured enough in Gemma Fripp's pleasing designs, but plopped on
stage as a right old muddle: Hudd coming on as circus owner Samuel Sleary but
turning into old Mrs Pegler and a host of other people, and Blessed introduced as
an unexpectedly booming Dickens and changing into a booming Mr Gradgrind.
At the performance I saw, Blessed (much to Hudd's consternation) forgot which
character he was playing.

A host of decent talent got tangled up in the proceedings, but the lack of definition made for a colourful rag-bag of a show, with now and again someone breaking

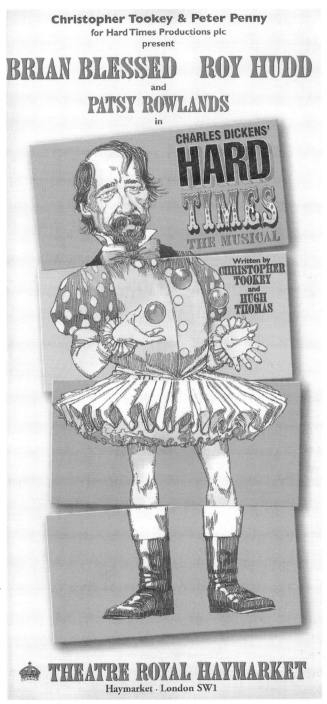

**33**   Some way from *Oliver!* and *Pickwick*, this rethinking of one of Dickens'
darker novels failed to catch on

through with a number that wasn't half bad, as when Jan Graveson sang 'One of These Days'. The ensemble even contained a veteran of the British musical theatre, Ray C. Davis. Ann Emery threw herself into broad comedy sequences, while Blessed had an embarrassing recollection of childhood. For most of the evening, the show assiduously avoided the points that Dickens was trying to make.

Stephen Fay in the *Independent on Sunday* concluded that the writers had let Dickens down. 'Neither the banal lyrics nor the formulaic music are capable of supporting the attack on the cruelty of Victorian capitalism, the need for reconciliation between employers and their workers, or even the feeble love story.'[6] Some of Tookey's fellow critics were more positive. John Gross for the *Sunday Telegraph* thought it 'thoroughly enjoyable if you take it on its own terms. The score is serviceably tuneful, the lyrics are mostly nimble [...] There is colour, energy and exuberance.'[7]

In May, the Gallic assault on the West End continued after *Lautrec* with another international effort, *Notre-Dame de Paris*, based on Victor Hugo's *The Hunchback of Notre-Dame*. Despite or because of some doubting critical Thomases and claims that the show was as much rock concert as musical, *Notre-Dame de Paris* settled into the Dominion Theatre for a healthy 575 performances. The next Gallic show to arrive came via Canada. The failure of *Lautrec* at the Shaftesbury, regardless of other catastrophic musicals at that theatre, seems not to have deterred the producers of *Napoleon* (Shaftesbury Theatre, 17 October 2000; 127) from sending the little French conqueror there for his very own biomusical. Both pieces endured much the same response. Andrew Sabiston and Timothy Williams's show had premiered in Toronto in 1994; they were in their teens when they began work on it. By the time it reached London, *Napoleon* had undergone considerable revision (one of its best numbers, 'Only in Fantasy' hadn't been heard in Toronto), and acquired one of America's most talented directors, Francesca Zambello. Cleverly staged with levitating sets, the appeal was strongly visual. Sheridan Morley somewhat strangely compared the splendours of Michael Yeargan's design to the sets for Novello's *King's Rhapsody* of half a century before.

There was rather less welcome for Paul Baker as Napoleon and the impressively lunged Anastasia Barzee as Josephine. Critics could not be expected to ignore the jokey possibilities around 'Not tonight, Josephine' when it came to writing the generally inhospitable reviews. The impression given was that when musicals turned to historical figures, the treatment was mostly wanting and usually absurd. One of the difficulties was whether the piece concentrated on Napoleon's relationship with Josephine, or with the legendary process of his ambition. As usual, the publicists started by having their cake and eating it, announcing the show as about 'Love, Ambition, Power ... and Betrayal'. But whichever way the writers turned, the critics scoffed. Baker was 'a dopey-looking Napoleon' in a show that had 'the dimensions of a Barbara Cartland romance'.[8]

Complaints that the score was 'dull' with 'naff lyrics' persisted.[9] The blame was laid at the feet of Williams and Sabiston. Kate Kellaway wished 'If only Verdi could rise from his grave and make his way down to the Shaftesbury with a new score under his arm. Then the present score could be vanished to St. Helena [...] This epic story needs thrilling, capacious, heart-stopping music.'[10] Matters were not helped by 'some excruciatingly passionless scenes of love-making' between hero and heroine,[11] but Vanessa Lee and Novello hadn't exactly shocked audiences during the romantic scenes of *King's Rhapsody* either. And so on and on ... here was a 'cartoon history with permanent musical accompaniment that leaves you emotionally and intellectually unstirred';[12] here was 'a production where you come out humming the almost intimidatingly slick and fluent design';[13] here was 'music that often went dum-dum, lyrics that regularly went plonk-plonk, and rhymes that sometimes left me wishing that rhyme hadn't been invented' along with 'several preposterous moments'.[14]

In fact, *Napoleon* was no worse than many other shows that got off lighter. Of course there were preposterous moments; *it was a musical!* It wasn't the epic seven-hour-long 1927 silent movie of Abel Gance: it was a *musical*. With a fifteen-minute interval for an overpriced gin and tonic in the Shaftesbury's bar or a timidly sized tub of inpenetrably frozen ice-cream, it had to entertain and divert, and even here and there instruct (how accurately, who knew?) for the space of two hours. Along the way, some of the stuff first heard in Toronto managed to make it to London six years later, with some attractive numbers: 'The Friend You Were To Me'; Napoleon's cry of ambition, 'The Dream Within', reprised in 'Sweet Victory', and the lovers' great duet 'On That First Night'. During the surrounding dross, there was the luxury of Jonathan Tunick's superb orchestrations, and, for some at least, the splendid Barzee's 'Only in Fantasy'.

# 2002

## *Romeo and Juliet*

Faced with the flood of international musicals washing up in London, it was often difficult for British audiences to work out a show's provenance, with little to alert them that the show had already wandered around every outpost of the empire, and was now ready to soak British audiences for as much money as it could unreasonably ask. The £3 million *Romeo and Juliet – the Musical* (Piccadilly Theatre, 4 November 2002; 112), with Shakespeare's love story transposed (for this occasion only) to present-day Britain, *seemed* British enough. Its composer may have had a French name, but the librettists were British; one, Don Black, was probably the busiest lyricist in British musicals. Gérard Presgurvic's euro-pop-type music had been shunted from country to country, each presumably ignoring the fact that *Romeo and Juliet – the Musical* had already been done somewhat more skilfully as *West Side Story*. Alarmingly, Monsieur Presgurvic's programme note in the Piccadilly programme explained that he 'now lives only for this sort of musical, beamed at an international audience', a statement that clearly indicated the sort of stuff that was now to be expected in and around Shaftesbury Avenue. The very idea that musicals were 'beamed' was indicative of the depressing changes that had by now almost overcome them.

Fifteen-year-old Lorna Want bore the unenviable responsibility of playing Juliet, with Andrew Bevis as Romeo ('They say I'm very young/ I'm going through a phase/ And I must learn to curb/ My adolescent ways'). Penetrating as his psychological understanding of youth might be, Black hoped that purists would not object to the fact that none of Shakespeare's actual lines were used; audiences were probably relieved. 'We've told the identical story, in a different way,' said Black.[15] On hand as the Nurse was the likeable singer Jane McDonald, made popular in a TV fly-on-the-wall documentary, a casting that suggested the show's producers knew the audience they were aiming for, an audience that had never heard of Sondheim or Bernstein. The press reported that everyone at a run-through was in tears. There were probably more tears when the morning papers arrived. 'Just stop shouting and grow up,' pleaded *The Times*.[16] No wonder that at one point of the evening poor Friar Lawrence asked 'How much more can we go through?'

# 2003

## Money To Burn

The very title *Money To Burn* (The Venue, 9 October 2003; 2) perfectly summed up Daniel Abineri's smutty folly, rejected by twenty-one London producers, written, composed, directed and financed by Abineri himself. Could this be the apple-cheeked young innocent who had played the apple-cheeked young Roman Catholic priest opposite Arthur Lowe in a television comedy series *Bless Me, Father*? Abineri had already outraged sections of the British public with his award-winning rock musical *Bad Boy Johnny and the Prophets of Doom*, originally produced in Australia in 1989 with Russell Crowe as Bad Boy. Five years later Abineri mounted the show for a season at the Union Chapel, Islington, but protests from nuns, the *Daily Telegraph* and protests ('offensive and blashphemous') from the Church Council of Great Britain closed it down after 9 performances, bringing Bad Boy's journey to becoming the first rock 'n' roll Pope to an abrupt terminus. Abineri was on equally shaky ground with *Money To Burn*, billed as 'a spanking new musical comedy thriller'. The venue was, at least, unhallowed; a subterranean 320-seater auditorium off Leicester Square, once the crypt of the Notre Dame Church, mainly of interest for its Jean Cocteau frescos.

The plot involved old Etonian Lord Oliver Justin (Peter Blake) planning to murder his wealthy wife Lady Tiggy (Sarah-Louise Young) and pay off his debts. To the accompaniment of Abineri's self-confessed 'jazz pop' score, Justin could be found wearing ladies' underwear and bending over chairs while delivering lines such as 'Absinthe makes the fart blow stronger'. The *Evening Standard* assured readers that 'Connoisseurs of this sub-genre will be heartened to learn that *Money To Burn* is absolutely without merit [...] Abineri aspires to farce, kitsch and camp, but manages to miss each one by a staggering distance.'[17] With the *Financial Times* describing 'a gloop of bad musical farce', including the 'jaw-dropping schoolboy filth of [the] second act's opening chorus',[18] came memories of some of Abineri's lyrics: 'Wank me, spank me / Gag me with a hankie' and 'Your morals may be iffy / But you've given me a stiffy'. Labelling the show as 'a woefully misbegotten enterprise', Michael Billington wondered whether the West End was 'rapidly turning into a garish mausoleum filled with rock and Rat Pack compilation shows, superannuated Americans and Edinburgh Fringe style stand-up [...] *Money To Burn* embodies the current neon sickness.'[19]

At the close of its second performance (the Saturday matinee), the notice went up with immediate effect, and the 9.15 show was summarily cancelled. The management explained that closure was 'due to the devastating reviews in the national papers and the immediate impact these reviews had on our future box office'. The theatre had already been dogged by 'low double-digit attendance'. *Money To Burn* had sidled up to *Oscar Wilde* and the Allon Bacon musical *She Smiled at Me* as one of the shortest runners of all time. It seemed slightly pointless that at curtain fall the audience was asked, à la *The Mousetrap*, not to reveal the denouement.

# 2004

*Beautiful and Damned*
*Murderous Instincts*
*Oscar Wilde*

What had audiences done to deserve *Beautiful and Damned* (Lyric Theatre, 10 May 2004; 112)? This was the British biomusical at its ghastly worst, performed in absurdly artificial American accents. Truly, here was the ersatz musical to end them all. At one point during this tedious, schmaltzy account of the ups and downs (mostly the latter) of the perfectly dreadful F. Scott and Zelda Fitzgerald (at least as shown on stage), one of the characters asked 'Why should they be interesting?' – the very question the audience asked itself all evening. By the end of Act One, the flapping chorines were waving their brassieres in the air and waiters stripped to their essentials, insisting 'We're fabulous people', an opinion with which spectators did not necessarily agree.

Basically, *Beautiful and Damned* followed Zelda's life from an out-of-control brat to a difficult woman plagued by mental illness. In *Marilyn!*, Monroe's mother had confronted the audience at the top of the show by demanding 'Did you know Marilyn Monroe?', going on to detail Mama's condition in a touching ballad 'So Happy To See Me'. For Zelda, the mad scenes (her scenes were mostly mad) outclassed anything in *Lucia di Lammermoor*. From curtain up, a strait-jacket was waiting for Zelda in the wings as Mrs Fitzgerald's psychiatrist ominously proclaimed 'Zelda, we really do have to unlock some of these memories.'

First seen at the Yvonne Arnaud Theatre, Guildford, in June 2003, *Beautiful and Damned* was originally directed by Phil Willmott. Book writer Kit Hesketh-Harvey refashioned the script for London, where Willmott was replaced by choreographer Craig Revel Horwood, whose almost manic direction helped rob the piece of any gravitas it might have had. It seemed extraordinary that Hesketh-Harvey, who had studied musical theatre writing under Stephen Sondheim and won the Vivian Ellis Award for some of his work, should come up with such dialogue, forever sounding like a bad Hollywood biopic: 'The trouble with the Depression is that it's so depressing'; 'I'm so full of confetti I could give birth to paper dolls'; 'We were in love before we were born'.

It would have needed players of the first rank to have a chance of overcoming such material. Michael Praed, about as close as London theatre could get to a matinee idol in 2004, made an unconvincing Fitzgerald ('My plan is to become a novelist', he told us). From the things Hesketh-Harvey made him say, he didn't seem like much of a reader, let alone a major writer, unless he ghosted for Mills and Boon, as one vapid announcement followed another. 'Didn't I just write an epic novel …' he wondered (we wondered with him) '… dwelling in a chateau by the sea?' When he broke into song, we suspected he might be ghosting for Ethel M. Dell as well ('Zelda, you're dancing away with my heart'). Exhausted by such poetry, Praed played the evening in a state of high emotional alert. One could only feel sorry for Helen Anker trapped in impossible circumstances as a Scarlett O'Hara-like Zelda, even when at curtain fall the deceased F. Scott came back to haunt her. A few may have been reminded of a rather more touching return of a ghost at the end of Vincent Youmans' *Through the Years*, but now it was F. Scott's turn to pop back as a well-turned-out cadaver, promising a still demented Zelda 'I love you ee-ee-ee-ee-even now', as magnolias burst out on the backcloth behind them. He was hiding one behind his back, too.

Presumably, as soon as *Beautiful and Damned* finished, F. Scott raced back to his dressing-room and scribbled down Hesketh-Harvey phrases that might come in handy for his next twentieth-century masterpiece. Zelda was always on hand to offer some wishful thinking: 'Centuries later, they'll still be discussing the colour of ma' eyes.' Magnolia? Botanically speaking, magnolias have what might be described as a cream-like sweetness, tempered with nuances of citrus. With this no doubt in mind, F. Scott recommended the plant but skipped the nuances, singing 'Oh beautiful magnolia, You're not as beautiful as she'. This at least gave Zelda the right to reply 'I love magnolias, but beneath their beauty lies the fragmentation of despair.' Precisely.

In a review headed 'Reach For a Sick-Bag or the Bottle', Charles Spencer likened Zelda to 'a pushy assistant behind the cosmetics counter in Boots'. 'Beautiful this show certainly isn't,' he wrote. 'Damned to a short run, with angry recriminations all round, I fear it almost certainly is.'[20] The *Independent on Sunday* remembered 'ludicrous hallucinatory scenes in an asylum' in a book that was 'disappointingly

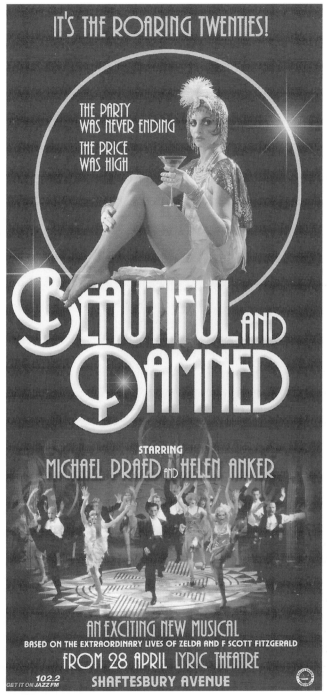

**34** One of the more desperate attempts at biography with songs, *Beautiful and Damned* provided a nightmare vision of the British musical

witless. Pretty damned awful.'[21] 'Beautiful? Absolutely not,' reported the *Independent*; 'Damned? Somebody ought to be.'[22] In a one-star review, Lynn Gardner argued 'You wouldn't even try to get away with this nonsense in any form but that of the West End musical and it is what makes the West End musical into a nonsense that is impossible to take seriously.' She decided that 'it just hasn't got the balls to risk not pleasing the audience with lots of pretty and affecting songs and pretty and affecting emotions. Even the orgy scene looks like a swingers' weekend in Ruislip kitted out by Ann Summers.'[23]

If it hadn't been for the Dobson family that financed the production, *Beautiful and Damned* would never have seen the light of day. They were introduced to it by its producer Laurence Myers. Until that moment, none of the Dobsons had ever even stepped into a theatre. They subsequently seemed to devote their lives to getting the show on, and bringing it to London; one hopes they have recovered from the experience. Myers was in frolicsome mood as he wrote a programme note, 'In Bed with the Producer' for the Lyric production. He assumed that by the time you got round to reading it 'The songs are still going around your head and you have tap danced to bed.' That was a possibility, unlikely as it seems. On stage, only moments after Zelda approached early death in her mad-house, the company was ready for its curtain call, rushing on, forever flapping its way through Horwood's St Vitus-inspired moves, still trying to convince us that here was the epitome of the roaring 1920s. The songs, horrible as they were, were by Roger Cook and Les Reed.

Few musicals can have lived out their agonies so much in the public glare as *Murderous Instincts* (Savoy Theatre, 7 October 2004; 12). Small wonder that along the way someone suggested the more appropriate title *Suicidal Tendencies*; the *Independent* described it as 'a drama full of passion, tears and bitter rows, with colourful and outspoken characters. In fact, it could make a great musical.'[24] Is there another example of a leading lady having gone on to write a coruscating (fictionalised) account of the disastrous goings-on behind the scenes of a musical in the making, *A Fanny Full of Soap*.[25] Nichola McAuliffe's skills as a novelist gave her, as one reviewer pointed out, something to fall back on 'when her parts dry up'. She had already told the *Daily Mail* of the show's troubles, although 'This show always, for no reason I could articulate, felt right [...] we all felt we had something special on our hands.'[26]

There's little doubt that when the show premiered at the Theatre Royal, Norwich, the air was already thick with dissension. The first appointed director, Gregory Thompson from the Royal Shakespeare Company, was not long in post. As the provincial premiere's curtain fell on the first act, producer Manny Fox (who confessed to being 'mad as a box of frogs') berated the current director Bob Carlton. This almost certainly wasn't the first time such drastic action had been taken, but never before had it happened in the stalls of the theatre, in full view of the audience. As it happened, the ensuing review on Radio Norfolk (of which the production team probably took little notice) hit nails on the head. Lynn McKinney wrote that the show 'can't quite decide what it is. Part comedy, part thriller, part musical, this show is struggling for an identity [...] The music is infectious, but the storyline becomes more bizarre by the moment.' The fact that this analysis might as well have applied to countless other productions doesn't detract from its accuracy. By some reckonings, the show was to go through eight directors, a distinct advance on its first, overseas, production where it had only got through six.

In fact, *Murderous Instincts* had already been a hit in 2002, but in Puerto Rico, to whose heart the show belonged. That heart throbbed with salsa; salsa was the show's *raison d'être*, and there were stunning examples of it from Jhesus Aponte and Janet Fuentes Torres. Originally the British production was announced as 'the salsa musical', but the publicity switched to 'The musical to die for'. The work of Manny Fox's wife Cinda Fox, heiress to the Firestone rubber tyre fortune, the music for *Murderous Instincts* was by the Puerto Rican Alberto Carrion. Fox assured the press that the show would take musicals back to 'the old tradition of the great Broadway musicals', in 'an uplifting story of the triumph of the human spirit over adversity'; nothing that hadn't already been done from *The Sound of Music* to *West Side Story*. In fact, *Murderous Instincts* was very far from setting its sights on so average an ambition. Following the death of a Puerto Rican tycoon, his family meet to hear the will, along with his widow (played by McAuliffe. Fox had already made up his mind he wanted Meryl Streep for the Broadway transfer.). The ensuing dramas more closely recalled *Something's Afoot*, a neat and consistently amusing satire on Agatha Christie's *And Then There Were None* (aka *Ten Little Niggers)*, a show that mixed camp with murder.[27] The cocktail wasn't that much different for *Murderous Instincts*, except for the generous dash of salsa that pepped up the proceedings, but did not – perhaps mistakenly – dominate them.

Carlton was probably embarrassed to be publicly criticised by Fox, but Fox repented, rehired him and subsequently sacked him all over again, despite Cinda Fox telling her cigar-chumping husband that if he sacked Carlton their marriage was over. Being sucked into the volcanic financial uncertainties of mounting a musical, it was almost *de rigueur* that, in line with many others in a similar situation, the Foxes remortgaged. Carlton was replaced as director by Michael (son of Mickey) Rooney, who had no work permit. Blacked by Equity, Rooney departed but continued directing by telephone from Paris. Murray Melvin and Sydney Ralph were brought in to salvage operations. After rehearsals at which osteopaths were on call to treat salsa injuries (McAuliffe had earlier been removed 'from all the numbers where serious bottom dislocation was required'[28]) some calm and organisation returned, with Ralph insisting 'Oh no, we don't like Mrs Mary Rude'.[29] Previews at the Savoy were put back two weeks, but the company was heartened by a gala performance for the Facial Surgery Research Foundation, better and now

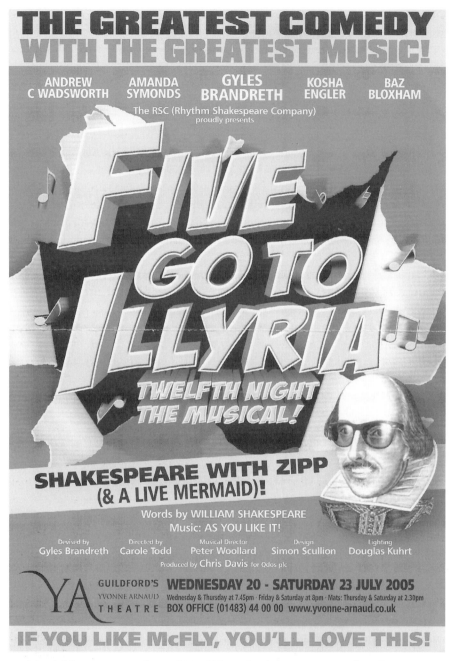

**THE GREATEST COMEDY WITH THE GREATEST MUSIC!**

ANDREW C WADSWORTH    AMANDA SYMONDS    GYLES BRANDRETH    KOSHA ENGLER    BAZ BLOXHAM

The RSC (Rhythm Shakespeare Company) proudly presents

**FIVE GO TO ILLYRIA**

*TWELFTH NIGHT* THE MUSICAL!

**SHAKESPEARE WITH ZIPP (& A LIVE MERMAID)!**

Words by WILLIAM SHAKESPEARE
Music: AS YOU LIKE IT!

Devised by Gyles Brandreth    Directed by Carole Todd    Musical Director Peter Woollard    Design Simon Scullion    Lighting Douglas Kuhrt

Produced by Chris Davis for Qdos plc

YA GUILDFORD'S YVONNE ARNAUD THEATRE    **WEDNESDAY 20 - SATURDAY 23 JULY 2005** Wednesday & Thursday at 7.45pm · Friday & Saturday at 8pm · Mats: Thursday & Saturday at 2.30pm BOX OFFICE (01483) 44 00 00 www.yvonne-arnaud.co.uk

**IF YOU LIKE McFLY, YOU'LL LOVE THIS!**

**35**  Adding songs to bits of *Twelfth Night* did not a musical make. Some vague echo of Enid Blyton did nothing to help *Five Go to Illyria*, a 2005 show devised by Gyles Brandreth. Wherever else they went, this Five didn't go to London

more appropriately known as Saving Face. In turn, four public relations companies attempted to promote the faltering production.

By opening night, the Foxes had decamped to Puerto Rico, Fox explaining that 'We have been through hell, pure unadulterated hell.' The doubts expressed at its Norwich premiere persisted. The review headlines divided the verdict 'A Lumbering Lack of Wit, Humour or Camp Flair in This Vanity Production: Ghastly Musical is Murder Most Foul';[30] 'It's a Shambles, it's mad, it's a hit'.[31] Sam Marlowe for *The Times* described a show with 'all the heat of a frozen margarita and all the suspense of Cluedo [...] crude, predictable and not sufficiently daft to entertain even in the most superficial way'.[32] Flipping the coin, Charles Spencer thought it 'one of the most fabulously bonkers musicals I have ever witnessed, and infinitely more fun than those deeply disappointing heavyweight contenders, *The Woman in White* and *Brighton Rock*'[33] and that *Murderous Instincts* 'could well become the surprise hit of the season'.[34] John Gross agreed, proposing that audiences should 'Approach it as you might an over-the-top soap opera or a copy of *Hello!*, and it has considerable entertainment value [...] One way and another, the show might yet prove to be the stuff of legend.'[35] The legend was to be witnessed by very few onlookers; on the first Monday of the second week of the £2 million show, only 130 of the Savoy's seats were filled. It is perfectly possible that, encouraged by the British public's passion for the BBC's *Strictly Come Dancing*, and very possibly starring some of its stars, we have not seen the end of *Murderous Instincts*. McAuliffe subsequently told the press 'Manny Fox had the most expensive top-of-the-range Hornby train set and he put his foot right through it.'[36]

A quick and fatal blow to the British biomusical, **Oscar Wilde** (Shaw Theatre, 19 October 2004; 1) sneaked into London under the radar of the West End. Written, composed and directed by disc jockey and writer Mike Read, it marked the reopening of its revamped venue with a first night glittering with such luminaries as Cliff Richard (for and of whom Read had already penned a musical) and Alvin Stardust. Wilde's grandson, Merlin Holland, gave the stamp of approval that suggested the piece had literary value, explaining that now Wilde was seen as a simple man who wanted to spend more time with his family, and introducing 'a new aspect to the story'. Thus, we were to learn how Bosie pleaded in song with Oscar 'Think of me when the sun goes down'. It was time to make Wilde cuddly. The Shaw proved a bad venue, with no booking facilities and microphones that died on stage on opening night but picked up off-stage conversations, which were possibly more interesting than Read's cloth-eared dialogue. The script sometimes slipped into rhyming couplets ('Rhyming couplets did not do Shakespeare or Gilbert and Sullivan much harm,' he later said). Some of these had a dying fall. 'I am going to stand my ground and fight,' the Marquess of Queensberry told his son Bosie, 'The things you two do just can't be right.' 'Your barbaric ways,' complained Bosie, 'leave me amazed.' The lyrics had just as much depth: 'Grief never grows old,' lamented Wilde in Reading Gaol, 'it never dies, It's fresh as the flowers, as clear as the skies.' This made the rhyming couplets of *Queenie* sound like Walt Whitman. By some cruel theatrical stroke of fate, Wilde was played by Peter Blake, still in recovery having survived *Money To Burn* the year before.

The notices for this 'grim evening'[37] were derisory. 'In 1895 Oscar Wilde was sentenced to two years hard labour. A more cruel and unusual punishment has been devised by Mike Read – a musical of exquisite awfulness.'[38] The *Sunday Telegraph* had no doubt who was to blame: 'To say the result of his labours is dire would be an understatement. The storyline is all over the place, with production values to match. Characterisation is grotesque, and the sense of period is wonky.'[39] When Wilde left England for France, he departed to the strains of 'La Vie en Rose', a song composed in 1945. Read's vision of a dangerously over-emotional martyr did not appeal to Benedict Nightingale, for 'Whatever else he was, he wasn't a sentimental prat.'[40]

Only five tickets had been sold for *Oscar Wilde*'s second night, and a decision was taken to close the show immediately. A musing Read insisted that 'Had we staged it at any proper theatre, West End or otherwise, it would have worked.' After all, 'Every time Charles Dickens published something, *The Times* shredded him.' With a loss of around £80,000, this 'bilge', this 'pitiful vanity project'[41] went into British musical theatre history records for the wrong reasons. One of its numbers, 'Grief Never Grows Old' had some sort of after-life through recordings by Cliff Richard and the Bee Gees. The show was revived at the Above the Stag Theatre in 2012.

# 2005

*Acorn Antiques*
*The Far Pavilions*
*Behind the Iron Mask*

It didn't signify that *Acorn Antiques* (Theatre Royal, Haymarket, 10 February 2005; 116) wasn't much of a musical. It didn't become one until after a badly overstretched first half. Victoria Wood's music, book and lyrics extended her popular sketches satirising the popular TV soap-opera *Crossroads*. The result was unmitigated joy for fans of Noele Gordon and Wood and the show's real star, Julie Walters, whose characterisation of Mrs Overall (parodying actress Ann George) was already much loved. With a top ticket price of £65, the limited season ran with 96% audience capacity, only closing because Walters had other commitments and it would have been impossible to recast satisfactorily, although Wood took on her role at certain performances. The ridiculousness of its second half salvaged it, but musically it was of negligible interest. Somewhat oddly, Dominic Cavendish, writing of the original Salford production, thought it 'a pretty trenchant satire on the decline of the English high street',[42] but Kate Bassett in the *Independent* noted how it 'merrily burlesques every shoddy West End musical you've ever seen [...] This spoof is really Wood's jovial answer to *The Producers*.'[43] Having its cake (or a Mrs Overall's macaroon) and eating it, *Acorn Antiques* was as intent on sending up the medium it hoped to find success in as repeating the jolly idiocies of Wood's TV series. The director was Trevor Nunn.

Come and gone and never much missed, *The Far Pavilions* (Shaftesbury Theatre, 14 April 2005; 180) reached the stage at a cost of £4.5 million with a top ticket price of £47.50. The delights of the piece were predominantly visual. It was a question of location. M. M. Kaye's mammoth novel, a protracted romance that ranged across the 1857 uprising in Sepoy to the second Afghan war, followed the fortunes of a handsome army officer, Ashton (Ash) Pelham-Martyn, brought up originally in India as Ashok. In childhood Ash swears a sort of *Half a Sixpence* allegiance to his childhood sweetheart the princess Anjuli, but moves to England. Inculcated with British values, he returns to India as an adult, where his enduring passion for Anjuli exposes the cultural differences between the two cultures. The stern features of a seriously overweight Queen Victoria dominated the front-cloth as the audience prepared themselves for curtain up at the Shaftesbury; when the time came, blood ran over her face, making way for what seemed to be a critique of the bloodiness of the British Raj that in so many ways, and with considered intent, *The Far Pavilions* musical wanted to be. The difficulty was how to deliver the message alongside the entertainment, the uneasy relationship between the sets of values, the shackling of Victorian beliefs to India's age-old beliefs, the noisy distance between the differing ethics. The commercial temptation must have been to turn *The Far Pavilions* into yet another lush, overromantic, oversung, overwrought British musical; to make it fashionable, to fit it into what writers and producers imagined the public would tolerate.

Of opulence there was no shortage: in Andreane Neofitou's fabulous costume designs, perfectly set against Lez Brotherston's shifting sets. Philip Henderson's score had an easy richness about it, listed in the credits above the equally essential contribution by Kuljit Bhamra of 'Indian music and lyrics', with John Cameron responsible for 'orchestral score' and David Braun-White for 'musical arrangements and supervision'. There had been no lack of attention to detail, no sense that, as with so much else of the period, the show had been patched together. Producer Michael E. Ward had pursued the project for many years, and was credited with 'original adaptation'. Nevertheless something was lacking, and the source was such a bulky book, problems that both versions of *Gone With the Wind* were faced with, problems already faced by Harold Rome in *Fanny*.

There was also a disconnect between the collision of the opposing cultures, and the music used to define it. Paul Taylor felt that 'the story cries out for a musical tussle between English and Indian music, between stiff-backed Victorian vernacular and the churning splash of sitars, between the regimented and the organised'.[44] In 1928, Emmerich Kálmán's score for *Die Herzogin von Chicago* ('The Duchess of Chicago') was effectively a battle between the melodies of the old operettas, notably the Viennese waltz, and the interloping modern strains of the Charleston as brought over by young ladies of America. Rarely played today outside Hungary, where Kálmán's works are still revived with splendid assurance at the Budapest Operetta House, *Die Herzogin von Chicago*'s trick is to use a device that the creators of *The Far Pavilions* might have considered: treat the music as a central plot device defining the differing cultural attitudes. Henderson and his team (were the two parts of the score composed in unison or by Henderson and Bhamra sitting, as it were, in separate rooms?) do creditable things with the music, but seem not to be working in concert or against one another.

Had librettist Stephen Clark ever heard a Kálmán score? Kálmán wasn't a man to waste material. What need had he of waste, when most of his scores haven't any spare meat on them? Kálmán's approach is economical, his melodies used sparingly but exploited and firmly placed in the audience's mind by the end of the night by their repetition in musical climaxes and finales. Turn to the list of numbers for *The Far Pavilions*, and one of the problems is all too apparent: there are forty of them. Quite apart from harnessing a composer to the hapless task of setting so much that might better have been achieved in dialogue, it needed Mr Memory from *The Thirty-nine Steps* to remember even one of them by the time he got back to the theatre foyer.

There is another component missing in *The Far Pavilions*, and one that was increasingly in short supply in British musicals and their flops: fun. At least it wasn't so rare for musicals of an earlier age to create excellent comedy alongside the human tragedy in which, by 2005, musicals were all too frequently drenched. Kálmán, Lehár and their like could manage a touching love story within a more emotionally restrained context, underpinned with fun. Among British composers, Novello was perhaps the exception, emotional restraint not being apparent in his armoury of pulsing romanticism, but even the most luscious of his scores never over-reach themselves, although they climb high, almost reaching the excesses of the Lloyd Webber school. Christopher Hassall's lyrics give Novello's work that essential coolness; overlooked and in some quarters disdained as he now may be, Hassall's words remain poetry, giving the music the excuse to do what it does. On the evidence of *The Far Pavilions*, Clark, and some may say it to his advantage, was no Hassall. Perhaps this is a contributing reason why Henderson's musicianly score doesn't stick in the mind. Some preferred Bhamra's Indian contribution, and meanwhile most of the audience probably didn't mind one way or the other, sat back and watched what they vaguely thought of as a sort of beautifully costumed Asian version of *Les Misérables* as it paraded its beauties.

Mark Shenton for the *Stage* saw 'a galumphing great Asian white elephant of a musical', 'sustained on a tide of bland anthemic statements and syrupy ballads'.[45] In the *Sunday Telegraph*, Tim Walker explained how 'Kaye's themes of national identity [honour, and forbidden love] can seem trite and vacuous if not downright

**36** Proving that gorgeous costumes, luxurious orchestration and ravishing spectacle is never enough, *The Far Pavilions* was a lush extravagance with no particular reason

comical',[46] while the *Observer* recalled 'a joyous outpouring of storytelling, an uplifting evening for the soul'.[47] Business was not helped by the spate of bombings in London during the summer, for which the producers blamed *The Far Pavilion*'s closure.

A Folly of the Year award would easily have gone to **Behind the Iron Mask** (Duchess Theatre, 2 August 2005; 23), the brainchild of John Robinson, who also wrote its music and lyrics. According to the theatre programme, Robinson was a seasoned composer, having set to music Shakespeare, Tolkien, Carroll, Betjeman, Hardy, Longfellow and Madeleva, and authored two musicals, *Lorna Doone* and *Shipperbottom's Rocking Horses*. Now, Colin Scott and Melinda Walker's book told the seventeenth-century story of Eustache Dauger, imprisoned in the Bastille and elsewhere for 34 years. According to Voltaire, Dauger was a relative of Louis XIV, or (according to Dumas) the king's identical twin. Fictionalised via Dumas' *The Three Musketeers* and countless other works, a musical titled *Behind the Iron Mask* hinted at a psychological approach, even an explanation, of the prisoner's plight. In the event, the audience was not only made to watch the suffering of the prisoner all over again, to the accompaniment of a six-piece band, but to suffer the musical itself. To stage it, Robinson formed his own production company, recorded a demo version of the songs performed by Robert Fardell, who six years later got the part of the man behind the mask, and persuaded private investors to part with £500,000. With a tight rehearsal period, and two days of technical adjustments, the show's premiere in the middle of London's silly season already boded ill.

Director Tony Craven had a cast of three, Fardell, Mark McKerracher as the jailor and Sheila Ferguson as the Gypsy, to enact his 'powerful tale of confinement, passion and freedom'. Beneath the headline 'Lock 'em up and throw away the key', Charles Spencer thought it 'merely unendurable. There's no insane flourish to its mediocrity, no sublimity to its awfulness. It is just relentlessly, agonizingly third-rate [with a cast that] perform as if they have been on a prolonged Mogadon bender.'[48] Lynn Gardner was no more impressed: 'John Robinson's music would not bother you were it being piped into a lift, but his lyrics would [...] I would quite happily have volunteered for death myself to help speed things up.'[49] For *The Times*, 'The music sometimes has a pleasant Lloyd-Webbery lilt, but the lyrics are mostly vile and the sudden twists of behaviour would take platoons of psychologists to unravel.'[50] There was no better from the *Daily Express*:

> A man in an iron mask is not best placed to sing for more than two hours some of the most leaden lyrics devised. To suggest it is plain terrible does not do justice to its sheer, gothic, relentless awfulness, from the refusal of the score to lift off into a memorable ballad to the bizarre gay ending which suggests the gypsy, the prisoner's one true love, has been his jailer.[51]

# 2006–2016

## 2007

*Bad Girls*

A prison full of women? The possibilities of making something musical out of it had already been exploited in *Prisoner Cell Block H*. At least that show proved that having the stage crammed with women didn't make a feminist musical. I'm not sure if that claim would be made by the creators of **Bad Girls: The Musical** (Garrick Theatre, 16 August 2007; 86). Firstly, it was an adaptation based on a long-running television series, created by Maureen Chadwick and Ann McManus, who had also written for *Footballer's Wives* and *Waterloo Road*; Kate Gotts wrote its incidental music. The encouraging news was that Chadwick and McManus wrote the book for the musical, and Gotts the music, a follow-through that encouraged expectation. Still, this was a musical made up from television, and musicals from television were seldom good news: think *Acorn Antiques* (not even fully qualified to call itself a musical), *Budgie* and – as big a disaster as any – *I Can't Sing*.

Gotts saw *Bad Girls* as 'an indictment of our penal system', insisting that the musical was 'not a piss take. It is serious and it is funny. You go on a real voyage of emotions.'[1] The prison was the all-female HMP Larkhall, whose officers included warder Jim Fenner (David Burt) and Sylvia 'Bodybag' Hollamby (Helen Fraser, repeating her television role). A lesbian romance between the newly appointed wing governor Helen Stewart and long-term prisoner Nikki Wade ran alongside the sleazy behaviour of screw (in more sense than one) Fenner.

The notices were mixed. Susannah Clapp in the *Observer* heard 'unflaggingly vivacious music and lyrics';[2] Nicholas de Jongh heard 'not very tuneful songs', although the dialogue 'crackles and snaps convincingly with lush vulgarity, innuendo and violence'.[3] Under the headline 'Bad's the Word', Tim Walker in the *Daily Telegraph* denounced 'a profoundly immoral piece of work', accusing the writers of having created 'a rotten and hideous thing. The show might well come to be seen as the apogee of yob culture',[4] although one would have thought several other apogees of that manifestation had happened long before. *Bad Girls* may well have been merely 'an enjoyable piece of sentimental melodrama'.[5] Recognising the show as in the line of *Blood Brothers*, *Spend Spend Spend* and *Billy Elliot* (and *Made in*

*Dagenham* wasn't far ahead), Mark Shenton praised 'a story that embraces strong social issues with punchy songs'.[6] The Union Theatre staged a revival in 2016.

Alongside *Bad Girls,* Gotts' other musicals mark her as a composer worth watching. *Crush,* 'a romantic musical comedy' produced at Coventry in 2015, describes the goings-on in a 1960's girls' school; it's Elinor Brent-Dyer on acid. In contrast, *The Realness* (2014) is a grit-crunching description of young people's street-life. The pity is that these works are not reaching beyond their origin. As *Bad Girls* suggests, it is to composers like Gotts and to her collaborators, seriously employed in trying to contribute to a vibrant school of British music theatre, that our respect and gratitude should be extended. Too often, the names that come and go in the writing credits of the mega-musicals have no afterlife. Where are the managements willing to risk good writers?

# 2008

**Gone With the Wind**
**Marguerite**
**Imagine This**

*Gone With the Wind*? Choose your model: Broadway through and through's Harold Rome London version of 1972, or the Margaret Martin (who?) 2008 model. Thereby hangs a cautionary tale for anyone intent on musicalising a source that someone has already had a go at. How many of the 2008 company had ever even *heard* of their predecessor? How many of the artists ever bothered to listen to the original 1972 cast recording of Rome's (quite good in the circumstances) songs? I suspect none. If they had, they would surely have reconsidered their positions and signed on again at the Labour Exchange. Most actors, after all, have little knowledge of the history of their art, of the performers or the techniques that made them. Many in the musical theatre world regard whatever they happen to be appearing in at the time as simply another job. Perhaps this is inevitable, and understandable, and perhaps it's how it should be. Unlike frustrated theatrical historians trying to make sense of their past, they are themselves on stage making theatrical history, sometimes for the wrong reason.

Nevertheless, the 'Gone With the Winders' of 2008 would have been well advised to look over their shoulders at what musicals had done to Margaret Mitchell's blockbusting novel almost forty years earlier, and at the notices the show had attracted. There were good portents for Rome's 1972 production: the *Evening News* proclaimed that it would run for ever. In the *Sunday Times,* J. W. Lambert praised the 'brilliant vulgarity' of Davis Hays and Tim Goodchild's sets, and the burning of Atlanta, in a production that was 'a heartwarming piece of showmanship, a brave, ebullient gesture in a frightened world' in an evening that 'unfolded with immaculate precision'. With a top price of £25, an estimated budget of £160,000, and contracts in waiting for other international productions, Rome and Fielding's *Gone With the Wind,* although running less long than forecast, should not be classed a failure.

Harold Rome was better known in his native America than he was in London, where he wasn't better known for anything. He also wasn't a Rodgers or Hammerstein. He wasn't a Jule Styne or even a Hugh Martin, but something of each. Rome sprang to Broadway prominence via American revues of the 1930s into shows such as the holiday camp extravaganza *Wish You Were Here*, which London had just about tolerated in 1953, despite those in the front stalls nightly getting soaked when the cast dived into the on-stage swimming pool. Three years later, *Fanny*, a Gallic romance adapted from Marcel Pagnol, wasn't much appreciated at Drury Lane, partly because it was stupidly cast, but listening to its score today it's a gem compared to some that played there. If the West End wanted more of Rome's songs (there was no sign that it did) it had to wait until the 1972 *Gone With the Wind*, London already having missed out on his *Destry Rides Again* and *I Can Get It For You Wholesale*. Now, Fielding's production threw everything at this melodramatically spectacular retelling of Mitchell's epic, adapted by Horton Foote. With *Fanny*, Rome had already shown he embraced the epic challenge. They produced the best of his scores.

The 1972 London production should have made a star of its Scarlett O'Hara, June Ritchie, giving one of the finest performances in a West End musical for years, but being the leading lady of a (in part) British musical, her chances of achieving stardom were negligible. Nevertheless, Rome's show lasted a year without ever becoming a popular hit. It was 'not an entertainment for critics or those choosy, hardcore metropolitan audiences who read them [...] But,' as Layton [Joe Layton, the director] informed the *Guardian*, 'people will go to it anyway, out of curiosity, nostalgia or camp mockery. It has something for most of them. As a business epic if not a musical one, it should be unstoppable as Sherman's armies.'[7] Everything was in place. Ritchie's performance was lauded, America had sent a handsome leading man in Harve Presnell, the show had extraordinary sets that recalled the Lane's reputation for melodramatic illusion, and the not-always-brilliant score held the night together without too much embarrassment, and the thematic 'Tara' even survived the tinny orchestra.

The idea of mounting *another* version of Mitchell's book prompts the question: why? For some reason, someone somewhere thought it worthwhile. Now, **Gone With the Wind** (New London Theatre, 4 April 2008; 79) appeared in much more costly garb, approximately £4.5 million, directed by the man who many saw as the saviour of the British musical, the man whose very presence gave the modern musical a claim to intellectual consideration, Trevor Nunn. His name alone was enough to propel the publicity campaign. What else, after all, was there to propel it? Rome was no household name, so what hope for the newcomer Margaret Martin, writing music, book and lyrics without any help other than having Nunn credited alongside her. There was even some doubt that Martin was a qualified composer, described by some of the press as 'an American public health expert'. At first run-through, her original script ('adapted' by Nunn) ran five hours. John

Napier's panoramic set was meant to encompass every aspect of the saga, but roused nothing like the excitement felt in 1972. The casting simply wasn't on the level of Rome's show, with little hurrahing for its Scarlett, Jill Paice, or Darius Danesh as not-giving-a-damn Rhett.

Susannah Clapp reported that 'On press night, Jill Paice's Scarlett was sweet though reedy; Darius Danesh's Rhett – growly and smugly disdainful – was dominating, if occasionally disarming; instead of snogging Scarlett, he gnawed her.' In all, 'Margaret Martin has done a rotten job.'[8] Having taken on Scarlett's misplaced optimism, Kate Bassett in the *Independent* wrote 'Tomorrow is another day, but this musical might not see it [...] The American Civil War has a great set, it's just a shame about the lousy songs, weak leads and inept characterisation.'[9] 'Connoisseurs of big, bad musicals must rush to catch *Gone With the Wind*,' wrote Nicholas de Jongh, 'in case it's blown away on gales of ridicule.'[10] The best that may be said of the second London *Gone With the Wind* is that it showed how much more grateful everyone should have been for the first.

*Marguerite* (Theatre Royal, Haymarket, 20 May 2008; 135) might with justification have billed itself as 'The Tragic Musical'. An honourable affair, it came with credentials flying: a book by Alain Boublil and Claude-Michel Schönberg and director Jonathan Kent, loosely based on Dumas' 1848 novel *La Dame aux Camélias*, on which Verdi had based *La Traviata*. Boublil and Schönberg had scored heavily with *Miss Saigon*, a sort of updating of *Madame Butterfly*, *Martin Guerre* and the seemingly indestructible *Les Misérables*, with lyrics by Herbert Kretzmer (*Our Man Crichton*, *The Four Musketeers*) who now provided them for *Marguerite*. The composer was Michel Legrand, whose outstanding score for *The Umbrellas of Cherbourg* had been heard in two West End stage versions, both quick flops.

In occupied Paris in 1942, Marguerite (Ruthie Henshall), the mistress of Nazi officer Otto (Alexander Hanson), falls in love with jazz musician Armand (Julian Ovenden, playing piano as well as singing) with devastating and (for Marguerite) fatal consequences. Staged by Kent with stately theatricality, the show was never less than professionally sound, with Henshall proving her worth as a serious musical actress. The score was tasteful, but came in swathes of intensity that seldom excited; the interesting, sometimes unexpected trajectories of the music generated an unsettling atmosphere, perhaps appropriate to the time and setting of the piece but inclining to the monotonous. With so many downbeat numbers, a general coolness prevailed, but *Marguerite* held on to its integrity. Other tragic love stories (take *West Side Story*) didn't feel the necessity to stay po-faced all night as *Marguerite* did from curtain up to curtain down. 'Gee Office Krupke' and 'America' lightened Bernstein and Sondheim's load, in just the way that Shakespeare knew when to bring on the clowns.

*Marguerite* was probably wise to keep a straight face, and Verdi was never going to write comedy numbers for his adaptation from Dumas. With the Gestapo

always at the musical's back, it's no place for an easy laugh; considering the awfulness of the comedy material in most British musicals, this is just as well. The raw
end of the deal was that, at the end of the night, there was probably only one
number the audience might have picked up on, 'The Face I See', around which
swam a good deal of gloopy gloom.

Critical reaction was mixed. Tim Walker for the *Daily Telegraph* praised 'A great
night at the theatre [...] Sex, songs and swastikas – who could ask for anything
more?'[11] Was he, perhaps, muddling *Marguerite* with *The Producers*? It seemed
'a cut above your average West End musical' to Kate Bassett, for whom 'many of
the songs have gently haunting tunes with a touch of mournful ballad about them',
and 'such moments go a long way to compensate for the banalities of the lyrics and
the book by Boublil, Schönberg and Kent'.[12] Regretting that the insights of Dumas'
novel could not easily be translated to the stage, Christopher Hart nevertheless
heard music that was 'listenable, but only a couple of songs strike you as being
truly catchy – you can't help thinking of Verdi'. Ultimately, 'despite weaknesses,
this is still a musical with real integrity, intent and substance',[13] probably the very
things most West End musical theatre-minded audiences were least in search of.
Good as Henshall was, she was hampered by having to play a woman for whom
one felt little sympathy. This was no Rodgers and Hammerstein heroine, and *Marguerite* probably paid the price.

That price was certainly paid by **Imagine This** (New London Theatre, 19 November 2008; 37), originally tried out at Plymouth the previous year. If Nazis had got
into British musicals in *The Dancing Years*, had more of an offstage presence in
*Yours, Anne*,[14] had a somewhat lethargic role in *The Sound of Music*, stayed largely
out of mind in *Out of the Blue*, were the source of much political incorrectness
in *The Producers*, and cast a threatening shadow over *Marguerite*, they were now
centrestage at the New London Theatre, from which *Gone With the Wind* (Mark
II) had long been blown away. 'Could it get worse at the New London than *Gone
With the Wind*?' asked Michael Coveney. 'It could. And it just did. This is a Holocaust musical that makes *Springtime for Hitler* look like *The Sound of Music*.'[15]
Really? Others looked askance at the very idea of *Imagine This*, 'manipulative and
morally dubious' according to the *Daily Telegraph*,[16] 'something nobody should
have imagined' according to *The Times*.[17]

In an abandoned locomotive train depot inside Warsaw's Jewish ghetto, a
struggling company is rehearsing *Masada*, a play set in AD 70, in which a Roman
general falls in love with the daughter of a Jewish rebel. Against the backdrop of
this ancient drama, the Jewish company endure the terror of the Nazi regime.
Glenn Berenbeim's book demanded respect, if only for the concept. In the theatre,
*Imagine This* could be an emotionally draining experience as it ominously unfolded
from the opening recollection of 'The Last Day of Summer', but the experience was
far from comfortable. David Benedict identified 'a fundamental mismatch between

the need for the bombast of a hit musical and the opening number that introduces us to a sweetly struggling theatre troupe with almost no resources', while 'The resulting Masada musical they stage has such wildly overblown production values and sentiments that the evening tips over into being *Les Misbegotten*.'[18]

The gallows humour struck a sour note. 'You Nazis will love it,' actor-manager Daniel tells the Gestapo officers. 'There's singing, dancing and all the Jews die in the end.' Although this, mercifully, was not true of *Imagine This*, audiences knew the facts. The problem may simply have been that these were musical theatre actors representing a holocaust. Inevitably, Israeli composer Shuki Levy's music and David Goldsmith's lyrics couldn't always bear the weight of history and situation, but for some there was no doubting the theatrical potency. How to convey the cruelty of those AD Romans and twentieth-century Nazis? Inevitably, they ran the danger of becoming little more than cartoons, a trap that Timothy Sheader's direction could not always avoid.

'No one can fault the nobility of intention,' wrote Claudia Pritchard, with authors that 'head into deep waters at a time when many stick to the shallows of pop nostalgia and shows of the film of the book of the recipe.' Ultimately, and with some justification, Pritchard considered that 'The deaths are too many, the memories too painful, the cruelty too unspeakable to be borne by this art form.'[19] For Susannah Clapp, 'it could hardly have been better done. Shuki Levy's score, which begins with a roundabout waltz before if gets to the point, is sweetly sung and fervent.' 'Imagine this,' she continued. 'That the most doomed of subjects for a musical, the most dopey of scenarios, turns out to be if not a swan at least not a turkey.'[20] *Variety's* verdict was that 'even those able to overlook its *longueurs* and weaknesses are being asked to watch a feel-bad show just as a recession starts to bite'.[21]

# 2009

## *Too Close To The Sun*

Did he or didn't he? The mystery of Ernest Hemingway's death remained unsolved by the fictionalised retelling of the last 48 hours of his life in *Too Close To the Sun* (Comedy Theatre, 24 July 2009; 19). There had already been five suicides in the Hemingway family before the *New York Times* headline of 3 July 1961 announced 'Wife says he was cleaning weapon'. Helen Dallimore, playing Wife No. 4 Mary in Roberto Trippini and John Robinson's musical, based on a play by Ron Read, told a journalist before the show's opening 'The truth is that Mary had the keys to the gun cabinet.' In character, Mary sang 'He always knew all there was to know about guns and how to handle them in the right way.' Charles Spencer wondered 'whether a sickening premonition of this terrible show' hadn't been responsible for Hemingway's self-destruction.[22] If Hemingway's suicide didn't inspire the writers of *Too Close To the Sun* maybe the 1980 Broadway *One Night Stand* did. Herb Gardner's non-starter script had the hero greeting the audience with the news that he would be killing himself at 10 pm, but not until they had listened to some not-so-good Jule Styne songs. *One Night Stand* closed during previews; in view of the derision heaped on it, *Too Close* might sensibly have followed suit.

The West End Whingers recognised its qualities at once: 'It's up there with the greats: *Leonardo, Which Witch?*, *Fields of Ambrosia, Bernadette, Jean Seberg* and *Behind the Iron Mask*.' The latter had been the first Trippini–Robinson fiasco four years earlier and, once again, a Robinson musical sneaked into one of London's snuggest theatres to fill out a summer lack of decent product. Launching out on an eight-week run, it managed two, every night of its bear-garden reception bedevilled with giggling, audience walk-outs, no applause at the end of numbers, and punters aptly replying to such gift-horse lines as 'Enough of this bullshit', and a character 'looking for a decent script'. James Graeme's Hemingway was telling no lie when interviewed before opening night, promising that the show was 'unique in its own way ... The music is of its own style. It's unusual.'

It was; unusually tuneless, wayward, and misshapen, with some ludicrous responses to the lyrics, which were 'squirmingly snigger-inducing' according to *Metro*. Letting the audience into the secrets of his writing life, Hemingway sang 'I always choose telling detail over long effect / I find the right place for the moral accent mark.' Prior to opening, Dallimore was upbeat: 'I think anyone who knows Hemingway is going to be fascinated by this piece.' Yes, but the fascination was one of horror, with such added delights as Dallimore one night falling through a wicker table.

The last days of Hemingway's life were played out on a revolve set of his ranch in Ketchum, where his scheming young secretary Louella plans to oust Wife No. 4, becoming Wife No. 5 and heir to the writer's estate. Just as unpleasantly, an old down-on-his-luck friend arrives to get the writer's permission to make a biopic of his life. Ridding himself of both secretary and old friend, Hemingway kills himself. He would have been proud of Mary's last thoughts, which veer to the philosophical: 'I didn't know life would turn out that way / But I'm behind him for his final hooray.' In the circumstances, perhaps it wasn't advisable for Hemingway to stare out at the Duchess's audience and sing 'Do I make a certain kind of sense?' Most nights, audiences didn't think the question rhetorical, although they should have sympathised with an anti-hero who at one moment informed them that 'My kidneys are avoiding their use.'

The notices above a string of one-star reviews spelled disaster for *Too Close To the Sun*. Sample the headlines: 'Drab Tale of Hemingway's Final Days Wilts on Stage';[23] 'Folly of Being Ernest';[24] 'As Dead as Hemingway';[25] 'A Trite, Unrealistic Portrayal of What Might Have Been'.[26] In the circumstances, many of the notices seemed reticent, with Dominic Maxwell for *The Times* finding that 'for the most part, Robinson and Trippini skip rhymes in favour of a sort of sub-Sondheimy recitation [...] Bar by bar, it's not that awful, but the cumulative effect, as musical phrase crashes into musical phrase, is banal, borrowed and clumsy.'[27] Then, of course, there was the dialogue: 'I'm not going to stop living till I'm totally dead' and 'My wang bang doodle-hammer needs a kick-start.'

# 2010

*Wolf Boy*
*Love Story*

Two mini-musicals provided the British musical flops of 2010. Of the first, one critic considered it 'not a show for kids, or even for squeamish adults';[28] another 'a harrowing mass that only awkwardly can be described as entertaining'.[29] *Wolf Boy* (Trafalgar Studios, 6 July 2010; season) reached central London via its debut at Chiswick's Tabard Theatre and a season at Edinburgh Fringe Festival. Based on Brad Fraser's play *Love and Human Remains*, director Russell Labey's book promised an uncompromising confrontation with mental and sexual distress, violence and gay issues, mixed into a musical. In an institution for the seriously disturbed, adolescent David (possibly a wolf) and suicidal Bernie build a friendship based on the mutual wreckage of their childhoods, involving all sorts of abuse and unhappiness, in what was widely promoted as 'the psycho-sexual musical thriller'. Composer Leon Parris accompanied a story of devastating woe. As Louise Gooding wrote, the music 'is surprisingly catchy [...] If you're into misery set to music, it could be one for you,'[30] while Sandra Giorgetti decided that the show 'has moments as gripping as any thriller but musically it is less adept'.[31] Having no star names in its cast, separated from the West End by Trafalgar Square (although the theatre had in the past thrived as the White-hall), having no interval, using pre-recorded music in an acoustic where some of the performers could not be easily heard, and sending the audience home with a blood-curdling climax, *Wolf Boy* tried to break new ground.

Death was stalking through the British musical. Alexander Walker described Paramount's 1970 movie of Erich Segal's novelette as 'Camille with bullshit'; forty years on, librettist Stephen Clark and composer Howard Goodall musicalised it for **Love Story** (Duchess Theatre, 6 December 2010; 96). The story was enacted by Emma Williams and Michael Xavier, who inevitably lacked the Hollywood glamour of the silver screen's Ryan O'Neal and Ali MacGraw almost half a century before; this was only one of the problems in changing a weepie movie into a starless chamber musical that offered wisps of classical erudition and a cookery demonstration, with fresh spaghetti bolognese made on stage eight times a week. Clark's libretto served *Traviata* with pasta. Was this a gimmick?

Clark's credits included lyrics for the much-revised *Martin Guerre*[32] (a true flop by any other name), work on *The Far Pavilions* and *Zorro*, and a translation for English National Opera of *Traviata* that probably marked him out as the natural choice for getting rhymes out of Segal's tale of young love interrupted by the heroine's death. Michael Coveney was admiring, but 'I'm not sure that, in tampering

– or not tampering enough – with the famous 1970 movie, the adapters haven't drained it of tragic validity. It's still just a weepie.'[33] Originally staged at Chichester's Minerva Theatre, *Love Story* was probably at its happiest in that space; once removed to London, it looked and sounded too alone and small to be a commercial success. Paul Vale for the *Stage* found that 'The characters remain only mildly engaging, with scenes and time passing so swiftly that you end up not really caring about anyone.'[34]

In its way, Goodall's musical, like the film on which it was based, belonged in the 1970s, when a little off-Broadway show could sneak into London (nowhere else to go, as there was no off-West End) for a couple of weeks. *Love Story* arrived, putting people off (and not too popular with the theatre management) by being played without an interval, and making do with a tasteful instrumental ensemble, piano and a few strings, on stage. Matt Wolf noted Goodall 'displacing his gift for harmony and the occasional choral interlude to a landscape usually associated with Lloyd Webber [...] But in going down the art musical route, this *Love Story* also proves oddly unexciting; a little bit of vulgarity, as it happens, might have come in handy.'[35] Wolf's reservations were not shared by many critics, who heaped praise on a show that has gone on to a considerable afterlife. In the shadow of mightier musical successes, *Love Story* has probably benefited from its economical conception.

A deal of delicacy had gone into *Love Story*, but even tear-jerking must be leavened, and with no hint of the blatant lushness that Lloyd Webber would have brought to it, the show was too easily dismissable as budget or bijou or chamber, and inevitably mentioned in the same breath as *The Fantasticks, All in Love, Cindy, Romance!*, the sometimes affecting *Maddie*, Monty Norman's *So Who Needs Marriage?* or, more desperately, John Robinson's *Behind the Iron Mask* and *Too Close To the Sun.*

In 1970, Paramount's production manager was warned that the insistently old-fashioned romanticism of Segal's story held no mass appeal to a movie audience. He was wrong. It scooped the biggest box-office profit of that year. Goodall and Clark's musical too often sounded hymn-like, as if Goodall was never quite willing to embrace the musical play as a specific genre with its particular distinctions and exclusions. Beyond all this, there was no denying the writers' skill in fashioning a lithe score that made use of Francis Lai's theme music for the movie. Musically, the show was clearly superior to many other British musical flops and successes of the decade, even if the competition was thin.

# 2011

*Betty Blue Eyes*
*Lend Me a Tenor*

There was much to celebrate about *Betty Blue Eyes* (Novello Theatre, 13 April 2011; 189). As the British musical reduced its critics to ever-increasing despair, up popped a charmingly nostalgic piece with a talking pig that few critics could resist. This was 'popular entertainment at its very best', according to Charles Spencer; it left him 'grunting and snorting with pleasure'.[36] The day after opening night the papers were full of oinking and congratulatory comments about bringing home the bacon. Presented and promoted with boundless enthusiasm by Cameron Mackintosh, based on a film written by Britain's most popular playwright Alan Bennett, starring one of ITV's most loved ex-soap stars Sarah Lancashire, with a score by Britain's most prominent musical play collaborators George Stiles and Anthony Drewe, directed by Richard Eyre, and with the voice of Betty provided by Kylie Minogue, what was there not to attract an audience?

More emphasis on Bennett's contribution might have made a difference, but once in the theatre it seemed not to matter: Bennett's (and Malcolm Mowbray's) script for *A Private Function*, best remembered for Maggie Smith's performance, got lost in a musical that might as well have been by Victoria Wood, although it had been written by Cincinnati writer Ron Cowen and Baltimore's Daniel Lipman, who may or may not have had a clue about what a genuine British musical was. The play was very northern, which probably helped explain the presence of Sarah Lancashire (the clue is in the name), who got excellent notices but wasn't Imelda Staunton. At times, Lancashire seemed to be giving a showcase rather than a performance; one minute Margaret Thatcher, the next a leggy Ethel Merman, but always with songs that worked well enough on stage before fading from the memory. Most of the charm came from Reece Shearsmith as the timid chiropodist Gilbert Chivers. Exaggeration and artificiality stretched the evening, while the obvious delight engendered by Ann Emery's music-hall Mother Dear and the constant farting of poor old Betty proved that low comedy could still detract an audience's attention from a play's deficiencies.

Was this really the way to prove that British musicals of the 2010s were alive and kicking? The much-publicised pig certainly wasn't. What was the point of *Betty Blue Eyes*, a musical about a pig (mixed up rather uncomfortably with the 1947 honeymoon period of the Duke of Edinburgh and Princess Elizabeth) that had to pitch itself somewhere between the 1940s and 2011? Neither period seemed especially keen to be harnessed to a jolly and supposedly old-fashioned musical. Sandy Wilson had exploited the 1920s with *The Boy Friend*, and the 1930s with *Divorce Me, Darling!*, but said he would never do the same for the 1940s, for which he felt no attraction. Living through the 1940s probably wasn't that much fun, and a certain glumness was never far away from *Betty Blue Eyes*. The show's sense of period never got beyond the land of pretence beloved by many stage musicals. The authentic note was never struck.

**37**  One of the major new musicals based on movies that tried to assert themselves at the end of the period, *Betty Blue Eyes*, set in 'Austerity Britain', hoped to thrive in a cash-strapped age

If this was supposed to be the 1940s, we needed to hear it. We didn't need to be listening to the songs of Stiles and Drewe when we needed Noel Gay, we might have had Cicely Courtneidge or Gracie Fields instead of the perfectly professional Lancashire, Arthur Askey instead of Shearsmith. Much fun was expected from the animatronic porcine heroine of the piece, but on stage Betty seemed curiously arthritic, lacking the same charm (a quality that doesn't radiate from many musicals after 1960) as the production that busied about her. Despite its many admirers, not all audiences seemed especially interested to learn if Betty managed to avoid ending up on a plate of ham, preferring to see it handed out with more assurance at other long-running London musicals. 'This little piggy limps all the way home,' wrote Kate Bassett in the *Independent on Sunday*,[37] in a book that 'falls flat' and was 'all a bit lame'.

*Lend Me a Tenor: the Musical* (Gielgud Theatre, 2 June 2011; 76) started life well before its London opening. Ken Ludwig's farce was a West End hit in 1986, and also played at the Gielgud, then called the Globe. Librettist Peter Sham and composer Brad Carroll, unknown to Broadway or London, collaborated on a musical adaptation premiered as a reading at the Utah Shakespeare Festival in 2006; it was seen on stage at Utah the following year. Redressed and much revised, the British production opened at Plymouth in 2010 before reaching London the next year. There was no doubting the professionalism at work. Director Ian Talbot's association with the piece went back to its London run as a straight play when he played Max (Damien Humbley in the musical), the self-effacing assistant (who just happens to know every note of Verdi's *Otello*) to the director of the Cleveland Grand Opera (Matthew Kelly). By default, Max becomes the real hero of the night when the world-famous tenor Tito Merelli (Michael Matus) is so indisposed that Max has to black up as the substitute Moor.

The well-rehearsed dilemma of turning a tightly plotted farce into a musical (think *Popkiss*, messing about with Ben Travers, or the successful Ray Cooney farce *Move Over, Darling* tiresomely turned into *Once More Darling*[38]) by breaking its verbal rhythm with song and dance, couldn't be avoided, and the score, workmanlike enough in the theatre, wasn't good enough to disguise the interruptions. After a promising curtain-raiser with a chorus courtesy of Signor Verdi, the night immediately sagged with 'Fling' and 'How 'Bout Me?', to be rescued eventually by the snappy ensemble of 'For the Love of Opera' with its madly dancing bellboys. The high spot of the evening (apart from an effective First Act curtain) was Merelli and Max's impassioned 'Be Yourself', which never failed to raise the audience. There was enthusiasm for Sophie-Louise Dann's man-eating diva with a potted history of operatic exaggeration (the sort of stuff Anna Russell once did) in 'May I Have a Moment?' Fun as it was, it was a classic example of the sort of number that belongs only in a flop and, like almost everything else on show, didn't seem quite finished. Too often, Carroll's score was out of tune with the play, at its most

**38** Glowing reviews (and the less glowing ones the publicists didn't mention) couldn't save the amiable *Lend Me a Tenor*

redundant when faced with the songs for Merelli and his temperamental wife (Joanna Riding).

Reviews were mixed. For the *Guardian*, Michael Billington complained that 'it misses a trick in not doing more to satirise operatic conventions',[39] and there was little more encouragement from Dominic Cavendish: 'The songs – with flip, throwaway lines, are barely memorable, the dance sequences fine but infrequent, and emotions are brought to the boil with all the sophistication of 4-minute pasta.'[40] With no stars considered starry enough to put above the title, punters were left to wonder if this was indeed 'the most accomplished musical comedy opening in the West End this season'.[41] *Lend Me a Tenor* had quality components (not least Paul Farnsworth's gilded sets) that attracted faithful devotees, but wasn't helped by the public's increasing antipathy when it came to unproved product. While customers poured out of coaches for *Phantom* and *Les Misérables*, it wasn't long before 'a tenner [£10] for a tenor' became a glib and unwelcome indication of the show's inability to attract paying customers.

# 2013

*From Here To Eternity*
*Stephen Ward*

If you wanted to spend three hours watching a British musical pretending to be American, *From Here To Eternity* (Shaftesbury Theatre, 23 October 2013; 208) was just the ticket.

In tune with several other papers, the *Daily Express* discovered that 'as a dark, sprawling tale that avoids obvious emotional button-pushing, lazy juke-box numbers or ear worm tunes running through the whole score, it's a commendably ambitious work',[42] but even as the show broke out, the headline banner reviews used for promotion spelled trouble. 'This is one sexy show – brave, explicit, startlingly powerful … see it' roared *All About You*, and 'The musical magic is sealed with lyrics by Tim Rice whose famous writing talent is in full force' trumpeted *Blouin Artinfo*, described as 'The Premier Global Online Destination'. It's a wonder there wasn't a review from somebody's Auntie Gladys. Who or what was or were *All About You* or that 'Premier Global Online Destination'? Perhaps the producers were sideswiped by that word: global. When all is said and done, global was certainly the musical *Eternity*'s intended destination, but what prospective customer was going to be inveigled into spending a small fortune on a ticket to experience Rice's 'famous writing talent'? If that was the flagship banner, something was up.

With Lloyd Webber's *Stephen Ward* turning the corner for London, it was as if the two Goliaths of the British musical, joined at the creative hip and unchallenged for over forty years, were gathering for one last reunion (or tussle), the only trouble being that their partnership had ended years before. Now, they rode into the West End as figureheads of two competing productions. It was inevitable that the fate of *Eternity* would be linked to that of *Stephen Ward*. Rather like a long-estranged couple turning up at a 'do' wearing identical outfits, each with a new partner, the collision of Webber's socially aware biomusical and Rice's World War II epic assumed almost biblical proportions in a theatrical milieu very different from that in which their partnership had dominated British musical theatre four decades before.

The musicalisation of James Jones's 1951 novel set in Hawaii around the time of the Japanese bombing of Pearl Harbor in December 1941 threw up two fundamental problems. Jones's canvas stretches across almost 900 pages of text, involving three story strands; coherently working these into a two-and-a-half-hour show was never going to be easy. Anyone contemplating making a musical from a prose epic has Rome's adaptation of Margaret Mitchell's *Gone With the Wind*, Rome's *Fanny* and Slade's *Vanity Fair* already flashing up a warning; all had fallen foul of the critics. Worse, in 1953 Fred Zinnemann directed a movie version of Jones's book that locked Burt Lancaster and Deborah Kerr in a sea-lapped embrace on a beach, worming its way into cinema history. With a back history like this, any staging looked like being done by stand-ins. Being a musical, of course that very scene had to be pivotal ('Let's bring the curtain down on Act I right then!'). Darius Campbell, best known from a TV talent programme *Pop Idol*, had the unenviable task of succeeding Lancaster; he had already (working as Darius Danesh) had the misfortune to stand in for Clark Gable in the mark II *Gone With the Wind*. Of course such substitution couldn't work; it just proved night after night how much better American movies of the 1950s were than British musicals pretending to be American musicals in the 2010s.

Try as it might, Bill Oakes' adaptation was left juggling the elements against the necessity of introducing musical numbers that too often seemed superfluous or unmemorable or both. *Variety* noticed that 'Oakes never solves the problem of how best to drive the stage story, not to mention: Which story?'[43] Audiences were moved from one to another along a conveyor belt as 'the "inaction" keeps flitting between stories rather than building a head of steam'.[44]

The focal point should have been Stuart Brayson's score. Already credited with the music for *The Boy Who Wanted More* and *Mata Hari*, Brayson emerged with more credit than either of his collaborators. With British musical theatre almost denuded of composers, Brayson perhaps promised more than he delivered, but in the present climate it seems a promise unlikely to be fulfilled. In happier days, a composer like Brayson would have been busier, but what hope now of anyone achieving quality through quantity of product? In the 1930s, Vivian Ellis wrote for 16 major shows. Between 1935 and 1951 Novello put his name to eight. Bart scored six between 1959 and 1965. The Slade and Reynolds partnership wrote seven between 1952 and 1961, not counting Slade's new score for Sheridan's *The Duenna*. Against these totals, Brayson will count himself lucky to reach two.

Mark Shenton saw one of *Eternity*'s dilemmas, that Brayson and Rice 'are not the new Lloyd Webber and Rice, let alone the new Rodgers and Hammerstein,

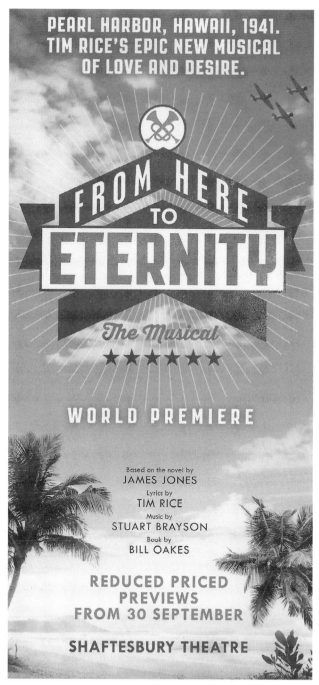

**39**   Unkindly nicknamed *From Here To November*, Tim Rice's Pearl Harbor
musical, along with Andrew Lloyd Webber's *Stephen Ward*, seemed to book-
mark the end of a certain sort of British musical

whose *South Pacific* this regularly reminds us of, but can't come near to matching'.[45] Michael Billington cited 'a musical based on skilled professionalism rather than expressive need'.[46] In a story that vibrated with passions (straight, gay, violent, personal and political) the passions never drove the reason to do the show in the first place. The gay brothel sequence had been cut from Jones's book before its first publication, and reinstated by Penguin Books in 2013, but on stage it fell as flat as the orgy scene in *Stephen Ward*. When Campbell and Rebecca Thornhill made use of a wooden table only a couple of minutes after being introduced, it seemed more comic than erotic.

No doubt passions had gone into the making of the show, but they barely registered with an audience. Brayson had been plying Rice with songs for years before Rice, slowly and perhaps a little unwillingly, went for total immersion. If hearts really can be involved in the making of musicals, perhaps Rice's wasn't properly in it. Trying to help, Lee Menzies, co-producer with Rice, announced the show as 'a grown-up musical', whatever that meant. Audiences were not fooled. When the curtain came down for the interval just as Thornhill was about to succumb on that far-off beach (not very well recreated on the Shaftesbury's stage), the Lord Chamberlain of long ago might as well have been standing in the wings, keeping things decent. There seemed no end of ways in which this show couldn't do what it wanted. The most successful component was undoubtedly the ultra-macho drilling of the soldiers' choreography by Javier de Frutos, but even this was diluted by the same male dancers having to adapt much less successfully to the gay brothel sequence.

By December, Rice was regretting 'rather a ghastly experience because we haven't had the numbers of audience that we'd hoped for'.[47] The show had already outlived one wag referring to it as *From Here To November*, although it was proving to be another notch on the Shaftesbury Theatre's gravestone of musical flops. Rumours surrounding the show's problems were not helped by Quentin Letts' backhanded opinion that it was 'A ridiculous musical which could become a cult classic … harmless nonsense … a hoot, not necessarily by intention'.[48] Despite its better moments, Christopher Hart for *The Times* thought the show 'a pointless, reheated rehash of an old, dated Hollywood movie', 'full of missed opportunities and blind alleys, and above all it makes you feel how crude and blunt an instrument musical theatre can be for exploring or dramatizing the finer human emotions'.[49]

In declaring itself during its opening number as being 'pro-Macmillan', Alan Melville's 1963 London revue *All Square* was sticking its neck out, for a much bigger scandal than that involving John Vassall[50] was about to engulf the Conservative Party, letting loose the gutter and more respectful press in a screeching defence of British morality at an affair threatening the very stability of the government. Secretary of State for War John Profumo had been introduced to Christine Keeler by the osteopath Stephen Ward at Lord Astor's home in the summer of 1961. Rumours of a sexual relationship between Profumo and Keeler grew, provoked by Keeler's sexual liaison with a Soviet agent.

A crisis was reached in March 1963, when Profumo told a ministerial deputation that he had not had a sexual relationship with Keeler. In June, he told the House of Commons he had lied, and resigned. Ward was charged with living on immoral earnings (a charge for which there was no evidence), and after taking an overdose died in August towards the end of his trial. John Osborne, Joe Orton, Kenneth Tynan and others sent a wreath of roses to his funeral bearing the message 'To Stephen Ward, a victim of British hypocrisy'.

So much associated with the Profumo affair lifted the veil of respectability from Britain's Establishment, to which *All Square* had fixed its colours. The scandal precipitated Macmillan's resignation in October, making way for Alec Douglas-Home, an epitome of upper-class gentlemanliness, to replace him as Prime Minister, and giving Home's brother, the playwright William Douglas-Home, the opportunity to write a topical entertainment about his brother's change of life.[51] Home's play naturally bypassed the protean activities of Keeler, Mandy Rice-Davies and company, but the pack of cards that collapsed with such devastating results pointed a way towards the sexual liberation that now galloped forward.

Macmillan selected another Establishment figure, Lord Denning, to undertake the inquiry arising from Profumo's difficulties. His lordship set about the task with saturnalian relish. He tactfully overlooked the known sexual entanglements of various prominent politicians, including the Minister of Transport Ernest Marples who associated with prostitutes, at the same time peppering his report with sub-headings ('The Man in the Mask') worthy of a *News of the World* exposé. Leaving nothing unturned, Denning arranged for the penis of government minister Duncan Sandys to be examined by a doctor as a means of eliminating him from identification as 'The Headless Man'.[52] On the day of publication, the sale of some 100,000 copies of Denning's report recalled the hysteria that had greeted the appearance of Penguin Book's unexpurgated *Lady Chatterley's Lover*. The British public of 1963, hopeful of lubricious entertainment, acted like Victorian housemaids frantic to obtain Marie Corelli's latest literary orgasm. Many had the satisfaction of discovering that Denning had done nothing to advance social acceptance of sexual diversity or freedom.

The many-faceted complexities of what came to be known as the 'Profumo scandal' presented a formidable challenge to the creators of **Stephen Ward** (Aldwych Theatre, 19 December 2013; 116). What use would they make of the vast amount of documentary evidence; what attitude would the musical strike; how would the composer of *The Woman in White* and *Love Never Dies* respond? This would not be the first British musical to centre on a popular scandal: *The Stiffkey Scandals of 1932* told the story of the Revd Harold Davidson's association with the working girls of Soho, and *Belle* the saga of Dr Crippen. In fact, there are similarities to Monty Norman's account of the Crippen case in *Stephen Ward*. Andrew Lloyd Webber's snake-charm music introduces his anti-hero in a Blackpool waxworks where Ward is displayed between Hitler and the Acid Bath murderer. *Belle*, too, opens in a waxworks where Crippen is on show. Both shows share another trick: not for nothing is *Belle* subtitled *The Ballad of Dr Crippen*, for Norman's piece has a simple Weill-like tune that threads the scenes. *Stephen Ward* uses the same device. There, the similarity ends. *Belle*, despite outraging the 1961 critics, manifests on several levels: as fable, as satire, as black comedy, as documentary, as polemic against capital punishment, as broad comedy, as absurd sentimentality. *Belle* fires off in all these ways, although it must be left to others to decide if it *works* in these ways (it didn't for those 1961 critics). One of the principal problems with *Stephen Ward* was that it failed to resolve its disparate elements, failed to see the possibilities of the story's telling or settle on a style of its own. Meanwhile, the political and moral aspects of Ward's downfall had to rub alongside Lloyd Webber's inappropriate score, which perhaps suffered further from his self-orchestration.

Christopher Hampton and Don Black's libretto laboured under the necessity of having to explain an enormous number of facts to its audience (it needn't have done if its approach had been fundamentally different), with scant characterisation. Centrally, Ward remained nebulous. Never mind the hope that this drama might at last bring him understanding; its reception suggested that the British public no longer, if it ever had, cared. A braver piece might have reinvented him as an amoral trailblazer, exaggerating his relevance for theatrical effect. The show might still have flopped (even more quickly) but at least would have set its sights higher than a dreary linear retelling.

Despite sound performances from Charlotte Spencer as Keeler and Charlotte Blackledge as Rice-Davies, the women remained uninteresting, but the whole musical might have been written from their point of view; their own stories were potentially as interesting as Ward's. In stretching the ambition of its book, lyrics and music, much might have been achieved, although the central predicament of dealing with Ward's morality would have remained. Such issues had not been a problem for *Pal Joey*'s fornicating charmer, or the hero of *The Beggar's Opera*.

Hampton's work was hampered by Lloyd Webber insisting on long passages of musical recitative, when nothing could disguise the paucity of ideas and clumsy rhymes. What would Lorenz Hart or Oscar Hammerstein have made of such stuff? When Ward and Rice-Davies engage in a very British tea party conversation, the music is reduced to something mercifully left out of *The Woman in White*, dainty and sterile and merely serving to point up the empty casualness of the lyrics. The mood shifts gear noisily, and in the second act tedium sets in with the wrangling of press reporters (crudely represented as various species of pond life). Having the reporters performed in patently artificial 'cockney' voices by small part players underestimates the intelligence of audiences: these reporters might as well have been imported en masse from the laughable newspaper reporter scenes in *Always*.

An orgy scene was another opportunity for more embarrassing lyrical and musical moments, topped by the dubious coupling of 'You've never had it so good' (Macmillan's phrase) with 'You've never had it so often'. Here, one might as well be listening to some bad British musicals of the 1960s, which were generally better served, or a smarter one from the 1950s, *Expresso Bongo*, where some of the issues with which *Stephen Ward* hopelessly tussles were dealt with more skilfully. Despite the references to flogging, sex, prostitution, and the occasional use of a four-letter word, *Stephen Ward* was prim; its very artificiality guaranteed it. Nevertheless, the show offered two ballads in the Lloyd Webber manner, 'This Side of the Sky' and, sung by Profumo's wife Valerie Hobson, 'I'm Hopeless When It Comes To You'.

Richard Eyre directed the £2.5 million production, but the show met with lukewarm response, and after weeks of playing to poor houses announced its early closure. Michael Billington reported that 'the show undeniably belongs to (Alexander) Hanson as Ward. And it is not his fault if we feel that this story of the breaking of a social butterfly on a wheel needs a melodic astringency that is not exactly Lloyd Webber's forte.'[53] Swimming against the tide, Charles Spencer's hunch was that 'those who like Lloyd Webber best when he's doomy-gloomy won't warm to this show, but that those who have previously found him overwrought will find this sharp, funny – and, at times, genuinely touching – musical highly enjoyable'.[54]

Discontent continued, with Dominic Maxwell for *The Times* complaining of 'an irate but over-informative attempt to precis the Profumo affair into a two-hour show',[55] and Paul Taylor's opinion that 'in the process of laudably trying to clear Ward's name, the show runs the risk of sanitising him. His platonic relationship with Keeler is romanticised in a way that downplays the seedy voyeurism and his use of the girl as bait.'[56] *Time Out* found little to satisfy: 'There's much huffing and puffing about establishment nastiness and Ward's blamelessness, but the manner in which this man – a prime candidate for a good Yewtree-ing[57] if e'er there was one – is presented as some sort of saint is borderline offensive [...] Ward is a fascinating figure, but far too complex and human to bear up to this brash analysis, no more credible or rounded than that waxwork Hitler.'[58]

Following his unfrocking in Norwich Cathedral, the Revd Harold Davidson (Ward's compatriot in disgrace) attempted to convince the British public of his innocence by appearing as a carnival geek in a barrel on Blackpool promenade. He was subsequently mauled to death by a lion (female, appropriately) while appearing at Skegness Amusement Park as a Daniel in the den. Ward's posthumous appearance in a Blackpool waxworks seems sadly apt as a comment on his immortality. In its specifics, *Stephen Ward* misfired. A musical based on the story of John Vassall might have proved altogether more interesting. The saga of a not very distinguished civil servant, trapped by the fact that homosexual acts were illegal, propelled to national notoriety, imprisoned and then cast out into society again might have provided a much more interesting evening. As leading men go, Vassall at least seemed not unpleasant or ambiguous, and might have been just as an effective, and more challenging, inspiration for a picture of British society in the 1960s. *John Vassall* would have involved Hampton and Lloyd Webber in an exploration of issues around the official attitudes to gay sex and sexual equality, which were still relevant in 2013 in a way that the sexual issues around Ward were not.

What did it matter that nobody would have recognised the name of John Vassall?; apparently, not many people remembered Stephen Ward. Did passers-by at the Prince Edward Theatre in 1996 look up and cry 'How wonderful! They've made a musical about Martin Guerre!'? That one, of course, had been revised in a second edition, as had *Jeeves*; no such luxury awaited *Stephen Ward*. *John Vassall* probably needed a more imaginative approach than those responsible for *Stephen Ward* would have brought to it, but what a very much braver choice it might have been. It may have been the associated gloss (Macmillan and his crew, Keeler and Rice-Davies, the upper-class set) of the Stephen Ward case that helped attract its adaptors, but what justice did they restore to Ward, who certainly deserved it? What justice to Keeler, or to Mrs Profumo? Giving her the soppiest song of the night didn't answer. Working through the fog that swirled around *Stephen Ward* somehow deterred the public. Ultimately, the collapse of Lloyd Webber's political 'biotuner', married in the public's mind with the early demise of Tim Rice's *From Here To Eternity*, looked like a defining moment in the history of the British musical flop.

# 2014

*I Can't Sing*
*Made in Dagenham*

Harold Fielding knew a thing or two about flops, surviving many and once turning one of the most critically mauled shows into a box-office record-breaker (*Charlie Girl*). The flops got him in the end: *Man of Magic* about Harry Houdini, *Phil the Fluter* (an attempt to repeat the template casting of *Charlie Girl*: one elderly leading lady of the charm school, one pop singer, one comic actor), *Gone With the Wind* (losing money despite a year's run at Drury Lane), and the switch to bijou productions in the 1980s with *The Biograph Girl* and *Peg*, before losing £3 million on *Ziegfeld*, and going into liquidation at the collapse of the even more bijou than most *Someone Like You*. There had been substantial successes too, not least *Half a Sixpence* and some American musicals for which he managed to sign up significant names (Ginger Rogers in *Mame*). These, as the West End must, depended on the volume of customers paying for product, precious to Fielding as the coach trade.

David Green of the Dorset Theatre-Goers Club knows all about the coach trade. His 500 members are offered a tempting choice of productions to visit, including West End musicals. These are always oversubscribed, with one recent exception. Despite having bought 100 tickets in expectation of overwhelming demand for *I Can't Sing* (London Palladium, 26 March 2014; 53), the tickets languished. Shortly after, Green was relieved to receive a call from the Palladium box-office informing him that a refund was on its way as the show was closing. If the Dorset Theatre-Goers acted on instinct, so had composer Steve Brown (*Spend Spend Spend*) and director Sean Foley. When told of the idea of making a musical around a TV talent show, both thought it one of the worst ideas for a musical they had ever heard. Somewhere in the troubled history of *I Can't Sing*, someone must have whispered the words *Jerry Springer: the Opera*. That may have obliterated any doubts: that show had been a sensation in London, even with 'opera' attached to it. Victoria Wood had pastiched a popular and much-discussed TV show (*Crossroads*); why shouldn't comedian and writer Harry Hill do the same with this 'X Factor Musical'? And what better send-off than previewing two of the numbers in the 2013 Royal Variety performance?

*Acorn Antiques: the Musical* had never (so far as we know) involved the participation, guidance or philanthropy of anyone linked to the soap opera. The £6 million *I Can't Sing* did. The presiding genius of the TV show was Simon Cowell, whose links with the musical have never been fully understood, although he gave his approval and put money into the production, which would have him as its central character with messianic appeal to television viewers. Linking himself to such a parody did nothing to help the box-office for a show that was 'undermined by a flimsy plotline and parody that doesn't dig deep enough to reveal anything new'.[59] West End Whingers agreed, wondering if Hill had 'gone off the boil. And the whole *X Factor* parody thing is way too late and has already been overdone. The moment has passed!'[60]

*I Can't Sing* opened cold at the 2,286-seater London Palladium without any provincial try-out, cancelling its first two previews because of technical difficulties. Two weeks into the previews, Foley was sending the audience home after an interval of 50 minutes because of a 'major electrical malfunction'. Grist to the mill, the ongoing technical problems found their way into Hill's script. The auditorium couldn't be filled for opening night. The upper circle was closed (never a good sign). At £87.50 a ticket, although good seats could soon be got for £20, perhaps *I Can't Sing* was never going to appeal to people who preferred to keep their slippers on, sag into the sofa and watch the telly, or even those who remembered the glaring insincerities of Hughie Green's *Opportunity Knocks* talent show doing the same thing in the 1960s. They could love or loathe Cowell in comfort at home and nip out of the room for a quick cup of tea rather than paying to see a satirical, or at least preposterous, impersonation of him on stage. As Hill wryly admitted at the show's last night, the prices put people off coming too: 'The prices!' he said, '£3 for a tub!'

The critics were amused but divided. The *Evening Standard* reported that 'at the heart of the enterprise is Hill's perennially wacky sensibility, abetted by the song-writing of composer Steve Brown, whose default setting is exuberant pastiche [...] a cheeky surreal and anarchic piece of entertainment, keenly aware of its own tackiness and triviality'.[61] Not wishing to be misunderstood, the *Sunday Times'* verdict was 'witless, infantile, noisy. Embarrassing, derivative, shamelessly money-grubbing tripe',[62] while Charles Spencer considered that 'The show may be too raucous and vulgar for some, but *I Can't Sing* strikes me as a big popular hit blessed with real heart and great theatrical panache.'[63]

There was so much going for *I Can't Sing*, with its host of eccentric no-hopers longing for fame, an axe-murderer, nun or hunchback likely to turn up for an audition, Foley's tirelessly inventive direction, Es Devlin's complex and witty designs, Brown's consistently energetic and appealing score that beat anything in either *Stephen Ward* or *From Here To Eternity*, Cynthia Erivo's superb singing of the title song with Hill's great lyrical twists ('I can't sing / Open my throat and windows start to crack / I thought a quaver was a cheese-based snack'), the singing dog who acted as Greek chorus to the show, a flying pig, Cowell (excellently smooth Nigel Harman), the auditionees in line pleading approval in 'Please Simon'. None of it was enough. Just as Cowell often told the more hopeless of his disciples, the public's reaction was 'It's a no from me.' It was a pity, for ultimately sweetness, innocence and one or two souls had been poured into *I Can't Sing*, and the West End was the poorer for its passing. In a long catalogue of joyous woe, it seemed to occupy a special place in the last days of the true British musical flop, on which the ghostly remains of so many misunderstood or misconceived musicals sympathetically gazed down.

Unlike most other British musical flops of its time, *Made in Dagenham* (Adelphi Theatre, 5 November 2014; 212) attracted more praise than brickbats. If many of the critics were to be believed, here was an adaptation from a 2010 movie that survived the switch, unlike *From Here To Eternity*, *Mrs Henderson Presents* and *The Go-Between*. The writing team could hardly have been stronger. Composer David Arnold had four James Bond film scores to his credit. The lyricist was Richard Thomas, librettist for Mark-Anthony Turnage's *Anna Nicole* and creator of *Jerry Springer: the Opera*. Book writer Richard Bean, author of the successful *One Man, Two Guvnors*, was asked before opening night if working on the musical had encouraged him to write another. Bean was doubtful. 'I wouldn't choose to. And let's face it, if the show goes down in history, it wouldn't be because of the book. Everyone else will be Lennon and McCartney and I'll be Ringo on drums.' Director Rupert Goold told the BBC: 'We know that the British musical is in a challenged position at the moment.[It had been in a challenged position for as long as anyone could remember.] We do have a tradition from Lionel Bart onwards of a particular kind of musical theatre.'[64]

What that tradition was, or whether he considered the new work to be in that tradition, Goold did not go on to explain, but there was no doubt that *Made in Dagenham* had musical theatre antecedents: *Strike a Light!* and more significantly *The Match Girls*. At the head of the Dagenham biteback, Rita (Gemma Arterton) is the direct descendant of *The Match Girl's* heroine Kate. Those girls were the forebears of the workers that made car seat covers at Ford's Dagenham plant. In 1968 the female sewing machinists downed tools, demanding equal pay to male employees and proper recognition of their skills. As a rebellion against the male-dominated bosses this was clearly in the line of the Bryant and May strikes. As an example of working-class solidarity among an unlikely group, this was 'a saga well worth making a song and dance about'.[65] It not only set *Made in Dagenham* back down the Victorian path, but aligned it with other feel-good shows that evinced the mood captured in so many Ealing films of the mid twentieth century, just as in more recent times in *Billy Elliot*, played out against the panorama of striking miners; *The Full Monty* and the musical *Girls* based on *Calendar Girls* that opened in London in 2017. Verismo, perhaps, was back, mirroring a social fabric of our own times (a decade or so late). There had scarcely been a hint of this in British musicals since the end of the 1950s; looking back, one could justly sing a verse or two of 'Fings Ain't Wot They Used T'Be'. There were now, after all, even more coffee houses than the ones mentioned in that song half a century before, when 'frothy' was considered a speciality.

In its way, *Made in Dagenham* threw the 1960s and the accumulated unhappiness and dilemmas of its characters back at us, its language toughened enough to put over Sophie-Louise Dann's 'Ideal World' and the gold-dust theatricality of Isla Blair's 'Connie's Song'. Whatever it was, at least it tried to show real people the like of which we might have passed in the street. The Dagenham girls' action would lead to the Equal Pay Act of 1970, although it was another fourteen years before the women won recognition as skilled workers, and even in 2016 the disparities continue. There was no doubt that here was a spunky musical with fire in its belly, with an integrity and sense of purpose that was highly commendable. It may be, as the *Daily Telegraph* observed, that 'like the cause of equal pay itself, there's an air of unfinished business about it all. Despite celebrating how a bunch of workers found their voice, the evening lacks a truly compelling one of its own.'[66] Following poor ticket sales, the closure of the show coincided with the ending of Arterton's contract. Henry Hitchings was not far wrong in describing a show 'broad, occasionally crass and a little too manipulative [...] But it also manages to be robustly likeable.'[67] Standing up for womens' rights was always an essential thing, but having 'Stand up' constantly bawled out by the cast in the show's finale made it almost obligatory to give the show a standing ovation, a mark of gratitude given to very few of the shows that crowd these pages.

# 2016

*Mrs Henderson Presents*
*The Go-Between*

Few musical flops can have got off to so limp a start as *Mrs Henderson Presents* (Noel Coward Theatre, 16 February 2016; 142) with a front-curtain comic. This immediately missed a trick: why not bring on one of the many famous comics who had honed their skills at the Windmill, the theatre where the nudes never moved? How much more convincing had the show been linked, not by this nameless comic whose pathetic material wouldn't have lasted two minutes into his audition, never mind the 30 years he ridiculously assured the audience he'd been treading the Windmill boards. Using the comic to give the show some cohesion was the clumsiest of devices, but *Mrs Henderson Presents* suffered from a lack of imagination in most departments. How much better if that comic had been one of the real ghosts of the Windmill: having the continuity done by Tony Hancock or Jimmy Edwards or Bruce Forsyth would have given the show an imaginative twist.

Terry Johnson's book mistakenly clung limpet-like to its film origins while lacking the advantage of the 2005 movie's stars, Judi Dench and Bob Hoskins. Such faithfulness was misguided. A more intelligent concept would have broken free, but what might have been something along the line of Sondheim's *Follies* never emerged. If Johnson had started from scratch things might have been better; he would have been freed from the constraints established by the film's linear treatment. Confining the musical to the war years corseted it; why couldn't it have told the *whole* story of the Windmill birth to death, the Sheila van Damm years, the changes in British society that eclipsed it? As it was, this show wasn't in the least concerned with social history, only about showing parts of the female body and making ineffective and protracted jokes about it, and plucking vague, sentimental strings about World War II.

What, anyway, was *Mrs Henderson Presents* (musical version) supposed to be *about*? It trod its territory with precipitous uncertainty. Was it about a tacky old theatre or about women taking off their clothes? Was it about the war that raged above and around the theatre as the girls' robes slipped from their shoulders? Was it about old age? Heaven knows, there were enough songs about getting on. Mrs Henderson's opening salvo, 'Whatever Time I Have', Vivian Van Damm's 'Now Is Not the Time', and their duet 'Anything But Young' suggested it had been written for OAPs. Was it about the war? The spectre of the conflict hovered over all, interrupting the soppy romance between Maureen (Emma Williams) and Eddie (Matthew Malthouse), but against this backcloth their relationship wasn't in the least affecting. The inclusion of the peculiarly morose 'Innocent Soldier' was no more than an intrusion. *Mrs Henderson Presents* wasn't the place for a pallid attempt at mourning a lost generation. Whenever the show moaned about the war – there was more of it in 'He's Got Another Think Coming' – you longed for someone to start up a chorus of 'Who's This Geezer Hitler?' Suddenly, you realised that Bart's song for *Blitz!* was a masterpiece. Even so, the best thing about *Mrs Henderson Presents* was George Fenton and Simon Chamberlain's intermittently excellent music, best in 'Living In a Dream World' and 'If Mountains Were Easy To Climb', but too much of the evening wound around Don Black's lengthy lyrics, with a seemingly unending title song and a number for the Lord Chamberlain that recalled 'Hush-Hush' from *Salad Days*, being basically a string of weak rhyming jokes about female body parts. Somehow, it came over as yet another idea among several that should have been resisted.

*Mrs Henderson Presents* covered too much too weakly, turning po-faced after the interval, just as so many shows – from *Funny Girl* to *Tom Brown's Schooldays* – had before it. Another missing ingredient was the sheer seediness that imbued the sort of shows the Windmill and the little army of touring nudie revues, so that the production never for a moment *looked* convincing, never *smelled* right. There were difficulties, too, with the constant shifting of emphasis as the evening rolled on, first highlighting Mrs Henderson herself (gamely over-acted by Tracie Bennett in a manner that should have been reined in), then the intellectual major-domo of the Windmill, Mr Van Damm (the excellent Ian Bartholomew), then chorine Maureen (Emma Williams) in the process of turning from Little Miss Nobody into assertive Miss Somebody, presumably having gained her confidence by stripping off, then the theatre itself, then the war, then the death of soldiers.

The show had a mixed reception. In the 'for' camp was Michael Arditti, hailing 'a gloriously old-fashioned "book musical", its style perfectly suited to its subject. The score is beautifully varied, ranging from pastiche revue numbers worthy of Sandy Wilson, through a defiant anthem for Mrs Henderson, destined to become a cabaret standard, to poignant wartime choruses.'[68] The original Theatre Royal, Bath production had been much praised by Michael Billington as a 'shot in the arm for the British musical' displaying 'a defiant Britishness',[69] but there were many detractors, with the *Observer* awarding it only two stars, and the *Financial Times* three, Sarah Hemming writing that it exposed 'the troubling question of whether stripping off constitutes empowerment or exploitation for the women'.[70] The sexual politics disturbed by the essential nudity coloured many of the reviews, notably those by female critics. There were many dissenting voices. Gerald Berkowitz found it 'unpretentious, unmemorable and unnecessary [...] the overpowering atmosphere is an odd glumness, with more focus on the two partner's ageing and the Home Front pains of wartime than on the putting-on-a-show adventure'.[71] Faced with this feminine riposte to *The Full Monty*, West End Whingers decided 'It's not the nudity that exposed the cast, it's the weak material they are forced to make something of.'[72] For the *Review Hub*, Scott Matthewman reported that 'ultimately the story that hangs [the songs] together struggles. Despite the wartime setting, the stakes never feel quite high enough; the risk of losing it all is always too far away.'[73]

If he wanted to make a musical about the Windmill, Johnson would have done better to look elsewhere than the Dench–Hoskins movie, moving from the Windmill to the Whitehall Theatre, where the great Phyllis Dixey – deservedly known as the First Lady of British Striptease – reigned supreme, famously in a show called *Peek-a-Boo*. In 1978, Thames TV produced Philip Purser's play *The One and Only Phyllis Dixey*, starring Lesley-Anne Down. This, together with Purser and Jenny Wilkes's biography of the most unlikely of strippers, should by now have alerted some creator of musicals to set to work. Dixey's is a tale of extraordinary fortitude, faithfulness and, ultimately, tragedy. Of course, this would be in better hands with Sondheim than with Johnson, for Dixey's story demands focus, a sharp intelligence, the ability to bring depth rather than the artificial poignancy that spasmodically erupted in *Mrs Henderson Presents* like air-raid searchlights over London. Sadly, *Mrs Henderson Presents* has made it all the more unlikely that anyone will write that Phyllis Dixey musical, which would surely have featured the sad heroine as she posed twice nightly in 'Aphrodite's Triumph Over Psyche' against a tastefully draped Grecian colonnade.

Any West End production, in 2016, using only a piano (*one* piano) to accompany an almost entirely sung-through two-and-a-quarter-hour-long British musical deserved some sort of award; even *Salad Days* and *Hooray for Daisy!* and *Wildest Dreams* had *two* pianos (the composer himself had the courtesy to sit at one of them night after night – no such personal appearance for *The Go-Between*) and – the luxury! – a drum kit. Not so **The Go-Between** (Apollo Theatre, 27 May 2016; 162), straining to be an opera, music and lyrics by Richard Taylor, book and lyrics by David Wood from Leslie Poles Hartley's novel.

Beckoning from the posters was one of Britain's best-known musical actors, Michael Crawford, making a West End return and perhaps singing a swan-song. The role of the elderly Leo Colston, on stage throughout as he recalls and watches his younger self propelled into the psychological despair that disfigured Hartley's adult life, was an endurance test for the 75-year-old actor. With Crawford as an Alan Bennett lookalike, the emotionally desiccated Leo stumbled through Roger Haines' relentlessly restless staging, the production intent on hoping we would forget there was one set, already on view when the audience arrived, making do for everything. *One* set, and *one* piano. This clearly wasn't going to be much of a party. Hartley's novel isn't high on energy, but musicals that turn their back on it do so at their peril. In a story of such cumulative and impending trauma this is a difficulty. Hartley's book has a very particular 'inwardness', having no need to be other than static.

It probably didn't help that audiences at the Apollo knew the Joseph Losey movie of 1971: Michael Redgrave solemnly crumpled as Hartley's stand-in; Alan Bates as Ted; Julie Christie as Marian; Margaret Leighton as Mrs Maudsley. For many, those images were unshiftable, along with the sheer heat coming off the screen from the Norfolk locations. No matter how capably the stage actors played, they were no more than stand-ins for those the public remembered. Competently professional as it all was, this company couldn't rip the skin off Hartley's rice-pudding of personal disillusion. That would have required actors of an altogether different class.

The show was appropriately discreet. Among the general gentility of which Hartley's sister Norah, ever the guardian of her brother's reputation, would have approved (although she would have dismissed the very idea of a musical out of hand), the moments of high drama lacked impact – the discovery by Mrs Maudsley and young Leo of Ted and Marian having sex (shown here by the cast putting its umbrellas up and down; one of the best comic bits – perhaps unintentional – of business of the night), and Ted's suicide.

As for a sense of place – there was nothing at the Apollo to suggest the open skies of Norfolk, the Edwardian laze. No; here, we had a ghostly, silvery segment of a country house (with *one* piano in the background), with weeds creeping up the chair legs, and enough jigging and jogging by the actors to keep things on the move. The feelings that Hartley inspires, his straight, uncluttered line of contact to the reader, was gone. Assiduously (but disappointingly) avoiding using Hart-ley's most famous opening sentence, Wood used half of it – 'The past is a foreign country.' Which reminds us, wouldn't a different title have been better for the show? *The Go-Between: the Musical* made it sound like just another project by people wanting to squeeze the lemon even harder.

As for the score, as genteel and flowing as you like, we must look back to those earlier composers and writers who knew a thing or two about what made musicals tick, and, more importantly if they were to survive, stick. Now, a wisp of a tune might pass by, but it was gone before you had a chance to take it, with no orches-tral weight but the constantly tinkling, and very solitary, piano to disguise it. The theatre programme listed no songs, presumably because none were discernible in the stream of notes from which some might manage to identify elderly Leo's plaintive 'Butterfly', in truth a number so fragile and momentary that it might have been written by a passing lepidopterist.

Over all hung a bargain-basement atmosphere – *one* set, *one* piano, *one* tune. Crawford convinced us that we should be bothered, but his conviction couldn't mask the unsatisfactory elements. As they rolled out into Shaftesbury Avenue, did customers realise they'd sat through a chamber opera? Did they think they might have witnessed a work that somehow advanced the British musical, now shrink-wrapped into something so modest and manageable that shone a light to the future? With *one* piano? We were back to the 1950s, the British musical stripped back to its bare essentials, without any of the essentials that had seemed to promise so much in the past.

Paul Taylor for the *Independent* welcomed 'this enthralling, beautifully tex-tured chamber musical' that 'fleshes out a dialogue between present and past' in a piece that had 'a striking imaginative integrity in its own right'.[74] For the *Londonist*, 'the subtlety and emotional intelligence of Hartley's novel is reduced to saccharine melodrama in musical form'.[75] Depressingly, *Time Out* suggested that 'it feels like the perfect exemplar of how little the Brits have done to advance the musical genre', with 'a lack of big, stirring numbers; the period garb and small cast contributes to a general air of safeness; the excessive gloom feels misjudged'.[76] Dominic Cavendish had much admired the piece when premiered at Leeds five years earlier (when the elderly Leo had much more to the point been played by an actor-*doppelgänger* of Hartley), but now regretted the 'bare-bones chamber aesthetic' had been retained, with the *one* piano 'at which Nigel Lilley heroically thunders away, like an over-worked secretary forced to touch-type the entire novel'.

It would be a hard nut that left the theatre unmoved, but the thanks were due to Hartley's story, the only book in which he dared move too close to the sun. Sadly, you didn't come out of the theatre thinking 'I can't imagine it ever being done better', but 'Why didn't they do it differently?' How many times such sad reflections have dawned on the thresholds of Shaftesbury Avenue late at night when the usherettes are eager to get you back onto the street, or after matinees where tea and Fullers' cake were once plentifully available? How many times have flops made us wonder? There are, of course, many kinds of wonder in this world. For all any of us know, the musical of *The Go-Between* may well have been one of them; perhaps the greatest of all time. Progress has always had its ups and downs. If now we can relish the all-moving pig that seemed to excite many in *Betty Blue Eyes*, let us not forget that in the apparently dreadful *Happy Holiday* of 1954, a *live* piglet was brought on stage. What was more, it proceeded to drink a full bottle of milk. The British musical flop has always had its surprises.

# British Musical Flops in London 1960–2016

*Key to production details*
**Title**
**Main author credits:** Music, lyrics and book, with any details of adaptation
**London**: Theatre, date of first performance
**PC:** Principal cast members
**MN:** Musical numbers. This information is taken primarily from the original
theatre programme of the relevant production
**Number of performances**

## ACORN ANTIQUES
Music, book and lyrics by Victoria Wood
Theatre Royal, Haymarket, 10 February 2005
PC: Julie Walters (Victoria Woods substituted at matinees), Celia Imrie, Duncan
Preston, Josie Lawrence, Neil Morrissey, Sally Ann Triplett
MN: No musical numbers listed in theatre programme
116 performances

## ALWAYS
Music, lyrics and book by William May and Jason Sprague
Victoria Palace, 22 May 1997
PC: Clive Carter, Jan Hartley, Shani Wallis, Sheila Ferguson
MN: Long May You Reign; Someone Special; I Stand Before My Destiny; Why?;
Love's Carousel; If Always Were a Place; This Time Around; It's the Party of the
Year; Hearts Have Their Reasons; The Reason For Life Is To Love; Montage;
Invitation For Two; Always
76 performances

## AMBASSADOR
Music by Don Gohman; lyrics by Hal Hackaday; book by Don Ettlinger, based on
Henry James' novel *The Ambassadors*
Her Majesty's Theatre, 19 October 1971
PC: Howard Keel, Danielle Darrieux, Isobel Stuart, Richard Heffer, Margaret
Courtenay, Ellen Pollock, Blain Fairman
MN: A Man You Can Set Your Watch By; It's a Woman; Lambert's Quandary; Lilas;
The Right Time the Right Place; Surprise; Charming; All of My Life; What Can
You Do With a Nude?; Love Finds the Lonely; Tell Her; La Femme; Young With

Him; I Thought I Knew You; What Happened To Paris?; La Nuit D'Amour; Am I Wrong?; Mama; That's What I Need Tonight; You Can Tell a Lady By Her Hat; This Utterly Ridiculous Affair; Not Tomorrow; Thank You, No!
86 performances

*ANDY CAPP*
Music and lyrics by Alan Price; book and lyrics by Trevor Peacock
Aldwych Theatre, 28 September 1982
*PC:* Tom Courtenay, Alan Price, Val McLane, John Bardon, Nicky Croydon
*MN:* On My Street; We're Waiting; Good Evening; I Should Be Ashamed of Myself; Good Old Legs; I Have a Dream; Oh Gawd, Men … Beasts!; Poor Old Head; Points of View; Spend Spend Spend; Don't Tell Me That Again; Frozen Moments; I Could Never Have Dreamed Him; Goin' To Barcelona; Hermione; When You've Lived In Love With Someone; Mr Scrimmett; The Trouble With People; It's Better To Be In Simple Harmony; The Wedding
99 performances

*ANN VERONICA*
Music by Cyril Ornadel; lyrics by David Croft; book by Frank Wells and Ronald Gow, based on the novel by H. G. Wells
Cambridge Theatre, 17 April 1969
*PC:* Arthur Lowe, Hy Hazell, Mary Millar, Peter Reeves, Charles West, Simon Kent
*MN:* A Whole Person; I Don't See What Else I Could Have Said; Ann Veronica; Maternity; Opportunity; Sweep Me Off My Feet; One Man's Love; Chemical Attraction; I Couldn't Do a Thing Like That; Why Can't I Go To Him?; They Can't Keep Us Down Anymore; Rococo Trot; Stand In Line; Home Sweet Home; Glad To Have You Back; If I Should Lose You; You're a Good Man; Too Much Meat
44 performances

*AT THE SIGN OF THE ANGEL*
Book and lyrics by Dudley Stevens; music by Geoffrey Brawn
Players' Theatre, 24 September 1975
*PC:* John Bailey, Robin Hunter, Clifton Todd, Larry Drew, Christopher Wren
*MN:* No musical numbers listed in theatre programme
Season

*BAD GIRLS*
Music and lyrics by Kath Gotts; book by Maureen Chadwick and Ann McManus
Garrick Theatre, 16 August 2007
*PC:* Helen Fraser, Nicole Faraday, David Burt, Laura Rogers, Caroline Head, Emily Aston, Maria Charles
*MN:* I Shouldn't Be Here; Guardian Angel; Jailcraft; One Moment; A Life of Grime;

The A-List; The Key; That's the Way It Is; Freedom Road; The Future Is Bright; Sorry; Every Night; All Banged Up; The Baddest and the Best; First Lady
108 performances

### BAR MITZVAH BOY
Music by Jule Styne; lyrics by Don Black; book by Jack Rosenthal, based on his play
Her Majesty's Theatre, 31 October 1978
*PC:* Joyce Blair, Harry Towb, Barry Angel, Ray C. Davis, Leonie Cosman, Vivienne Martin
*MN:* Why?; If Only a Little Bit Sticks; The Bar Mitzvah of Eliot Green; This Time Tomorrow; Thou Shalt Not; The Harolds of This World; We've Done Alright; Simchas; You Wouldn't Be You; The Bar Mitzvah; Rita's Request; Where Is the Music Coming From?; The Sun Shines Out of Your Eyes; I've Just Begun
78 performances

### BARNARDO
Music, lyrics and book by Ernest Maxin
Royalty Theatre, 22 May 1980
*PC:* James Smillie, Fiona Fullerton
*MN:* London's East End; Oy Vey; The Midnight Waltz; Lovely 'ot Pies; There's a First Time; Snuggle Up; What Children Will Do; You're the Man; Tosh; Welcome To Dreamland; Girls; Cor!; I Feel Sorry For You; I'm a Winner; My Son; Why Don't We Try Again?; Who Needs a Man?; Am I Running Out of Time?
43 performances

### BASHVILLE
Music by Denis King; lyrics and book by Benny Green, based on the play *The Admirable Bashville* by George Bernard Shaw
Open Air Theatre, Regent's Park, 2 August 1983
*PC:* James Cairncross, Christina Collier, Joan Davies, Douglas Hodge, Vincenzo Nicoli, Donald Pelmear, Peter Woodward, Ewart James Walters
*MN:* Fancy Free; Eight, Nine, Ten; Lydia; One Pair of Hands; A Gentleman's True To His Code; Because I Love Her; Take the Road To the Ring; Hymn To Law and Order; Black Man's Burden; He Is My Son; Bashville; Boats Are Burned
Season: closed 24 August 1983

### BEAUTIFUL AND DAMNED
Music and words by Les Reed and Roger Cook; book by Kit Hesketh-Harvey; original concept by Roger Cook and Les Reed; additional material by Laurence Myers
Lyric Theatre, 10 May 2004
*PC:* Michael Praed, Helen Anker, David Burt, Susannah Fellows
*MN:* I'm Dancing; No Can Figure; Beautiful Magnolia; Refuse To Be a Girl; Little

Miz Alabama; Tomorrow Won't Happen; The Letters; Beautiful and Damned; Living Well's the Only Way; The Old World Shines Again; Trouble; Over the Top; Dream Ballet; Golden Days; The Queen of Babylon; Tender Is the Night; Save Me the Waltz; Being a Woman; Even Now
112 performances

### BEHIND THE IRON MASK

Music, lyrics and original idea by John Robinson; book by Colin Scott and Melinda Walker
Duchess Theatre, 2 August 2005
*PC:* Sheila Ferguson, Robert Fardell, Mark McKerracher
*MN:* Listen; Antiphonal Madness; There Is Sweet Music; Do You Look For Love?; Pearls, Pearls, Pearls; I've Got a Secret; Darkness; You'll Never Leave Here!; The Enigma; Possession; Can't You See?; Turmoil; Who's the Prisoner Here?; Touch Me; Take Me As I Am; I'm a Lady; Shadowland of Life; In a Single Moment; Tristesse; Where Are You?; If All This Means Love
23 performances

### BELLE, or THE BALLAD OF DR CRIPPEN

Music and lyrics by Monty Norman; book by Wolf Mankowitz, based on a play by Beverley Cross
Strand Theatre, 4 May 1961
*PC:* George Benson, Rose Hill, Virginia Vernon, Nicolette Roeg, Davy Kaye, Jerry Desmonde
*MN:* The Ballad of Dr Crippen [recurring]; Fifty Years Ago; Mister Lasherwood and Mighty Mick; Bird of Paradise; Meet Me At the Strand; You Are Mine; Colonies; The Devil's Bandsman; Hyoscine; Pills, Pills, Pills; Ain't It a Shame; The Surgery Recitative; Song of Our Future; Lovely London; Posthorn Medley; A Pint of Wallop; Mother Song [There's Nobody Like a Fairy Godmother]; The Bravest of Men; Waltzing With You; Belle; I Can't Stop Singing; Policeman's Song; Coldwater, Michigan; Don't Ever Leave Me; The Dit-Dit Song; The Minstrel Show [comprising: I Do Not Wish To Know That; Mister Robinson and Master Jack; Ah Got So Much Trouble]; You Can't Beat a British Crime
44 performances

### BERNADETTE

Book, music and lyrics by Gwyn and Maureen Hughes
Dominion Theatre, 22 June 1990
*PC:* Natalie Wright, Nikki Ankara, Meredith Braun, Terry Mitchell, William Pool, Chris Van Cleave
*MN:* You Are the Reason; Vespers; Lourdes; I Only Want To See a Light; Poor Soubirous Soubirous; Only Fools Ignore a Child; Who's the Other One?; I'm Trying; Who Are You?; Only Time; Don't Turn Away; One Day; Bernadette's a

Liar; Idle Minds; Watch Me Begin; Like a Child; Have Another; Eternally; What Is the World?; Where You Are (I Will Be); So Beautiful; It Was An Illusion; Bernadette; God Answer Me; Love Goes On; A Corner In Your Heart

28 performances

### BETTY BLUE EYES

Music by George Stiles; lyrics by Anthony Drewe; book by Ron Cowen and Daniel Lipman

Novello Theatre, 13 April 2011

*PC:* Sarah Lancashire; Reece Shearsmith; David Bamber; Jack Edwards; Ann Emery; Mark Meadows; Adrian Scarborough

*MN:* Overture: Austerity Britain; Fair Shares For All; A Place On the Parade; Magic Fingers; Painting By Heart; Nobody; A Private Function; Betty Blue Eyes; The Riot; Lionheart; Steal the Pig; Entr'acte: The Pignap; Another Little Victory; Kill the Pig; It's An Ill Wind; Pig No Pig; The Kind of Man I Am; Since the War; Finale Ultimo: Confessions; Goodbye Austerity Britain; Jitterbug

189 performances

### BIG SIN CITY

Music, book and lyrics by Neil, Lea and John Heather

Roundhouse, 30 May 1978

*PC:* Jack Wild, Michael Price, Su Pollard, Nicholas Chagrin

*MN:* Big Sin City; Jailhouse Bop; They're Sending Us Down; I'm a Dic; It Must Be Love; Ponzie; Freeze; Twenty Four Hours; Rumble; The Pleasure Pit; Down Under; Sin City Fever; Hots For Louise; K.I.D.S; Without You Here By My Side; Everything Money Can Buy; It'll Be Me; You; Revenge; The Knife Fight

6 performances

### THE BIOGRAPH GIRL

Music by David Heneker [with Warner Brown*]; lyrics by David Heneker and Warner Brown

Phoenix Theatre, 19 November 1980

*PC:* Bruce Barry, Sheila White, Guy Siner, Kate Revill, Jane Hardy

*MN:* The Moving Picture Show; Working In Flickers; That's What I Get All Day; The Moment I Close My Eyes; Diggin' Gold Dust; Every Lady Needs a Master*; I Just Wanted To Make Him Laugh*; I Like To Be the Way I Am In My Own Front Parlor [*sic*]; Beyond Babel; A David Griffith Show; More Than a Man; The Industry; Gentle Fade; Nineteen Twenty-Five; The Biograph Girl; One of the Pioneers; Put It In the Tissue Paper

57 performances

### BLOCKHEADS

Music by Alexander Peskanov; book by Michael Landwehr, Kay Cole and Arthur Whitelaw; lyrics by Hal Hackady

Mermaid Theatre, 17 October 1984

*PC:* Mark Hadfield, Kenneth H. Waller

*MN:* Have We Still Got It?; Playin' the Halls; Star Quality; Is This Where the Rainbow Ends?; Rumons [sic] From Rome; Sad Happy; Goodbye, Mae; Timing; Nothin' Personal; Laugh; Starting From Now; Blockheads; G.A; That Man Up There; Makin' Movies; One Cuff Link

Season

### BORDELLO

Music by Al Frisch; book by Julian More; lyrics by Julian More and Bernard Spiro

Queen's Theatre, 18 April 1974

*PC:* Henry Woolf, Stella Moray, Angela Easterling, Cristina Avery, Lynda Bellingham, Judy Cannon, Norma Dunbar, Paddy Glynn, Brenda Kempner, Angela Ryder, Liz Whiting, Jacquie Toye

*MN:* A Place Like This; Bordello; Yourself; A Country Bride; Apache Dance; Morality; Business Tango; Simple Pleasures; Art Should Be Art; Can-Can; Family Life; If You Should Leave Me; Madame Misia; All the Time In the World; I Love Me; The Girl In Cabin 54; The Way I See It; Belly Dance; Hallucination; What Does It Take?

41 performances

### BUDGIE

Music by Mort Shuman; lyrics by Don Black; book by Keith Waterhouse and Willis Hall

Cambridge Theatre, 18 October 1988

*PC:* Adam Faith, Anita Dobson, John Turner

*MN:* They're Naked and They Move; Thank You, Mr Endell; There Is Love and There Is Love; If You Want To See Palermo Again; In One of My Weaker Moments; I'm Sure We Won't Fall Out Over This; Mary, Doris and Jane; Why Not Me?; If It Wasn't For the Side Effects; Old Compton Street; If That Baby Could Talk; Winners and Losers; I Like That In a Man; Budgie

110 performances

### CALL IT LOVE?

Songs by Sandy Wilson; book by Robert Tanitch

Wyndham's Theatre, 22 June 1960

*PC:* Lally Bowers, Derek Waring, Ann Saker, Terence Knapp, Nicholas Meredith, Norman Warwick, Richard Owens, Karin Clair

*MN:* Love Play; Love Song In Rag; I Know, Know, Know; Hate Each Other Cha-Cha; Call It Love?

5 performances

## THE CARD
Music and lyrics by Tony Hatch and Jackie Trent; book by Keith Waterhouse and
  Willis Hall, based on the novel by Arnold Bennett
Queen's Theatre, 24 July 1973
*PC:* Jim Dale, Millicent Martin, Marti Webb, Dinah Sheridan, John Savident, Joan
  Hickson
*MN:* Hallelujah!; Nine Till Five; Lead Me; Universal White Kid Gloves; Nobody
  Thought of It; Moving On; Come Along and Join Us; That's the Way the Money
  Grows; The Card; Opposite Your Smile; I Could Be the One; Nothing Succeeds
  Like Success; The Right Man
130 performances

## CHILDREN OF EDEN
Music and lyrics by Stephen Schwartz; book by John Caird
Prince Edward Theatre, 8 January 1991
*PC:* Ken Page, Martin Smith, Richard Lloyd-King, Shezwae Powell, Kevin Colson
*MN:* Let There Be; The Naming; The Spark of Creation; In Pursuit of Excellence; A
  World Without You; The Expulsion; Wasteland; Lost In the Wilderness; Close
  To Home; Children of Eden; Generations; Degenerations; Shipshape; The
  Return of the Animals; Stranger To the Rain; In Whatever Time We Have; The
  Flood; What Is He Waiting For? The Hardest Part of Love; Ain't It Good?; In
  the Beginning
103 performances

## THE CLAPHAM WONDER
Music, lyrics and book by Sandy Wilson, based on the novel *The Vet's Daughter* by
  Barbara Comyns
Marlowe Theatre, Canterbury, 26 April 1978
*PC:* Jan Todd, Anita Dobson, George Parsons, Liz Bagley
*MN:* The Clapham Wonder; The Vet's Daughter; Someday; A Lot More To Life
  Than That; The Waterfall; The Strumpet From the Trumpet; Eh, Rosa?; Any
  Time; You Know What; Everything, London; 'Ow Do You Know If You Like It
  (Till You've Tried It)?; My Little Tin Trunk and Me; Mrs Gowley's First Round;
  Don't Change, Lucy; Alice's Ball; Mrs Gowley's Second Round; Come For a
  Spin; Our Golden Afternoon; A Wine-Coloured Suit (and a Feather Boa)
Season

## COLETTE
Music, lyrics and book by John Dankworth
Comedy Theatre, 24 September 1980
*PC:* Cleo Laine, John Moffatt, Kenneth Nelson
*MN:* You Can Be Sure of Spring; He's a Captain!; I'm Special; Ambitious; Paree!;
  Our Relationship; Alone With Myself; Attention Will Wander; You've Got To

Do (What You've Got To Do); We'll Stick Together; I Never Make the Same Mistake; Little Girl; Nothing Special; A Little Touch of Powder; Love With Someone Younger; Will He Ever Be Back?; Little Red Room
47 performances

### THE DANCING HEIRESS
Music and lyrics by Murray Grand; book by Jack Fletcher and Murray Grand
Lyric Opera House, Hammersmith, 15 March 1960
*PC:* Millicent Martin, Irving Davies, Jill Ireland, Lally Bowers, Pamela Strong
*MN:* The Lady Is News; We're Out For Money; Life Is Peaches and Cream; You're a Tonic; I'm Going To Wind-Up With You; Youth and Beauty; Under-Tow of Love; Marion's On the Make; The Internashnal [*sic*]; Zig-Zag; Morning, Noon, Evening and Night; That Same Old Sensation; You; Song of the Shadows; Agua Caliente
Season: 15 performances

### THE DANCING YEARS
Music and book by Ivor Novello; lyrics by Christopher Hassall
Saville Theatre, 6 June 1968
*PC:* June Bronhill, David Knight, Moyna Cope, Cathy Jose, Enrico Giacomini
*MN:* Dawn Prelude; Uniform; Waltz of My Heart; The Wings of Sleep; Lorelei; My Life Belongs To You; I Can Give You the Starlight; My Dearest Dear; Chorale and Tyrolese Dance; Primrose; In Praise of Love; Rainbow In the Fountain; Leap Year Waltz; Finale
52 performances

### A DAY IN HOLLYWOOD, A NIGHT IN THE UKRAINE
Music by Frank Lazarus; book and lyrics by Dick Vosburgh
Mayfair Theatre, 28 March 1979
*PC:* John Bay, Sheila Steafel, Frank Lazarus, Paddie O'Neil, Maureen Scott
*MN: A Day In Hollywood*: All God's Chillun Got Movie Shows; Movie Fan's Love Song; Goldwyn and Warner and May'r and Zanuck and Zukor and Cohn; Movies Are Your Best Entertainment; A Night In the Ukraine; I Love a Film Cliché [music by Trevor Lyttleton]. *A Night In the Ukraine*: Samôver the Lawyer; Just Like That; Again; Sing Me a Sensible Song; Natasha; A Night In the Ukraine
168 performances

### DEAN
Music by Robert Campbell; book and lyrics by John Howlett
Casino, 30 August 1977
*PC:* Glenn Conway, Murray Kash, John Blythe, Anna Nicholas, Betty Benfield
*MN:* The Ballad of James Dean; Sounds of New York; What Price Gold?; I Scream; Say Hello To Your Mother; Lullaby; Gonna Make Him a Star; I Didn't Mean You;

Girl In Times Square; Just One Knock On That Door; Lost in L. A.; Running Out of Time; Happy New Year Kid; Hollywood Dreams; Play That Song Again; That Boy; Misery, Mystery; Texas

35 performances

*DEAR ANYONE*
Music by Geoff Stephens; lyrics by Don Black; book by Jack Rosenthal
Cambridge Theatre, 8 November 1983
*PC:* Jane Lapotaire, Peter Blake, Stubby Kaye, Stephanie Voss
*MN:* Everything's Terrific – Help!; I'll Put You Together Again; Sure Is Hard Talking To a Lady; Sure Is Hard Keeping it From Warren; Shortcomings; Don't Stop Him If You've Heard It; Thank You World, You're All Heart; You'd Be Amazed; What About Us?; I Don't Know the Answer; How Lucky We Are; Radio Jingle; All Rocked Out; Why the Panic?; When You See Your Loretta Again; Dear Anyone; Ain't Coming Down From This Mountain

65 performances

*DISGRACEFULLY YOURS*
Music, book and lyrics by Richard O'Brien
Comedy Theatre, 18 March 1996
*PC:* Richard O'Brien, Brother Michael Dalton, The Fabulous Frockettes, The Black Angels
*MN:* Must Be Mephistopheles Smith; Welcome To One Hell of a Party; Ain't That To Die For; Rhythm of the Heartbeat; Let's Get To the Heart of It; The Best Has Yet To Come For Me; Incubus of Love; It's Up To You 'Which Cup You Brew'; Tulip Baker; Heart On Fire; The Dance of Love; The Angel In Me; Disgracefully Yours

Season: 24 performances

*DIVORCE ME, DARLING!*
Music, lyrics and book by Sandy Wilson
Globe Theatre, 1 February 1965
*PC:* Joan Heal, Patricia Michael, Philip Gilbert, Anna Sharkey, Cy Young, Geoffrey Hibbert, Maria Charles
*MN:* Here We Are In Nice Again; Someone To Dance With; Challenge Dance; Whatever Happened To Love?; Lights! Music!; Back To Nature; On the Loose; Maisie; The Paradise Hotel; No Harm Done; Together Again; Divorce Me, Darling!; Here Am I (But Where's the Guy?); Out of Step; Fancy Forgetting; You're Absolutely Me; Back Where We Started; Blondes For Danger; Swing-Time Is Here To Stay

87 performances

*DRAKE'S DREAM*
Music and lyrics by Lynne Riley and Richard Riley; book by Simon Brett
Shaftesbury Theatre, 7 December 1977; revised version by Ken Hill transferred to
    Westminster Theatre, 1 February 1978
*PC:* Paul Jones, Donald Scott, Janet Shaw, David Burt, Caro Gurney
*MN:* Listen All You Seadogs; At the Court of Elizabeth; I've Always Had a Dream;
    She Plays a Dangerous Game; Let's Get Going!; Take a Little Time; When the
    Winds Command Us Away; Weaving Our Webs; Between Today and Tomor-
    row; Sedition; Gold; Waiting Isn't Easy; Nova Albion; God of the Waters; The
    Telephone Song; Spice of Life; Fa La La!; Aground; Sailing Around
82 performances

*EASTWARD HO!*
Music by Nick Bicât; lyrics by Howard Schuman; book by Ben Jonson, Robert
    Chetwyn and Howard Schuman, based on Jonson's play
Mermaid Theatre, 7 July 1981
*PC:* Philip Sayer, Anita Dobson, Prue Clarke, Mark Rylance, Trevor T. Smith
*MN:* Humours of 1605; Eastward Ho!; Lady Flash; Thrifty Sentences; Hunger and
    Thirst; The Carnal Jig; Young Wives; When a Citizen Rides Out of Town; The
    Virginia Song; What Slitgut Saw; For the Good of Their Souls; Transparent
    Castles; In the Counter; The Song of Repentance
45 performances

*ENRICO*
Music by Renato Rascel; lyrics and book by Garinei and Giovannini (English
    version in collaboration with Peter Myers and Ronald Cass)
Piccadilly Theatre, 3 July 1963
*PC:* Renato Rascel, Roberta D'Esti, Julia Carne, Roger Delgado, Frank Coda, Gloria
    Paul, Clelia Matania
*MN:* Buona Sera; Just Round the Corner; Varieta; Bon Giorno; Socialist Anthem;
    Strike; Com'e Bello; Theresa; The Boater; My Son; The Furlana; Arriverderci
    Not Addio; The Song of Rome; Ballad; Resistance Song; Boogie Woogie; Made
    In Italy
86 performances

*'ERB*
Strand Theatre, 7 April 1970
Music, lyrics and book by Trevor Peacock, based on the book by W. Pett Ridge
*PC:* Trevor Peacock, Bridget Turner, Deborah Grant, Malcolm Rennie, Peter
    Childs, Nickolas Grace
*MN:* Saturday Night; Southwark Park; Everything I've Got; Here's Alf, Here's Ron;
    Very Nice To Meet You; Lovely; I'm an Ordinary Bloke; Love Is a Bubble; Got Me
    Name In the Paper; Ten Trees; 'Ave a Good Time; Off On Holiday; Salt and Sand;

Too Big For His Boots; World Full of Wonders; He Is a Man; When I Was a Boy
38 performances

*THE FAR PAVILIONS*
Music by Philip Henderson; Indian music and lyrics by Kuljit Bhamra; book and
   lyrics by Stephen Clark, based on the novel by M. M. Kaye
Shaftesbury Theatre, 14 April 2005
*PC:* Kabir Bedi, David Burt, Hadley Fraser, Kulvinder Ghir, Simon Gleeson,
   Sophiya Haque, Gayatri Iyer
*MN:* Two Worlds Collide; Hawa Mahal; I Promise You; Chances We Take; There
   Is a Secret; Torn In Two; Dream of Me Tonight; The 'Pindi Club Ball; Look In
   the Mirror; Gabbru Put Punjab De; Memsahibs!; Raat Guyi – Oy Shava; Who
   Do You Think You Are?; Love Will Reign; Where Do I Turn?; Afghanistan; Who
   Could Have Known?; The Fathers of India; Haunted By Voices; It Takes Time;
   Trust Your Heart; Love, Let Me Go; Blood Red Bride; We Have To Be Gods;
   Do and Die; Born To the Battle; Gentle Light; Freedom and Honour; Chak De!;
   Prayer; I See Myself; Hari Bol; Mercy of the Gun; An Honour To Die; Free At
   Last; Our Love Is Not the Only Love; A Woman Like You; The Siege; Journey of
   Our Hearts; The Far Pavilions
180 performances

*THE FIELDS OF AMBROSIA*
Music by Martin Silvestri; book and lyrics by Joel Higgins, based on an original
   screenplay by Garrie Bateson
Aldwych Theatre, 31 January 1996
*PC:* Joel Higgins, Christine Andreas, Marc Joseph, Marc Heenehan
*MN:* Ball and Chain; Hubbub; The Fields of Ambrosia; How Could This Happen?;
   Nuthin'; Who Are You?; Reasonable Man; Step Right Up; Too Bad; That Rat Is
   Dead; Hungry; Continental Sunday; Alone; The Card Game; The Gallows; Do It
   For Me; All In This Together; The Getaway; The Breakout
23 performances

*FIRE ANGEL*
Music by Roger Haines; book and lyrics by Paul Bentley, from William Shake-
   speare's play *The Merchant of Venice*
Her Majesty's Theatre, 24 March 1977
*PC:* Gaye Brown, Helen Chappelle, Anthony Wood, Linda Kendrick, C. T. Wilkin-
   son, Derek Smith
*MN:* Don Piranha's Boys; Daddy's Girl; My Body's Weary; African Ice; Satan Baby;
   Morning Psalm; Moonlight Quartet; Carnival; Shining Moon; Diarrhoea Dave;
   Sun Man; Ell Nekomoss; Fire Angel; Brother, Be Bright; Getting Together; The
   Mercy Song
42 performances

*FOLLOW THAT GIRL*
Music by Julian Slade; lyrics and book by Dorothy Reynolds and Julian Slade
Vaudeville Theatre, 17 March 1960
*PC:* Susan Hampshire, Peter Gilmore, Marion Grimaldi, Patricia Routledge,
    Newton Blick, James Cairncross
*MN:* Tra La La; Where Shall I Find My Love?; I'm Away; Follow That Girl; Solitary
    Stranger; Life Must Go On; Three Victorian Mermaids; Doh, Ray, Me; Song and
    Dance; Taken For a Ride; Shopping In Kensington; Waiting For Our Daughter;
    Lovely Meeting You At Last; Victoria! Victoria!; One, Two, Three; Evening In
    London
211 performances

*FOUR THOUSAND BRASS HALFPENNIES*
Music by Kenny Graham; book adapted by Bernard Miles from John Dryden's play
    *Amphitryon*; lyrics by Gerald Frow
Mermaid Theatre, 8 July 1965
*PC:* James Bolam, Freddie Jones, Esmond Knight, Sally Miles, Denise Coffey,
    Timothy Bateson, Jennifer Clulow
Repertory season

*FROM HERE TO ETERNITY*
Music by Stuart Brayson; lyrics by Tim Rice; book by Bill Oakes, based on the
    novel by James Jones
Shaftesbury Theatre, 23 October 2013
*PC:* Darius Campbell, Siubhan Harrison, Robert Lonsdale, Ryan Sampson,
    Rebecca Thornhill
*MN:* G Company Blues; Thirty Year Man; Another Language; Don'cha Like Hawaii;
    You Got the Money; Marking Time; Fight the Fight; Run Along Joe; More Than
    America; Love Me Forever Today; I Love the Army; Ain't Where I Wanna Be
    Blues; Maybe; Something In Return; The Boys of '41; Almost Perfect Lie
208 performances

*THE GAMBLER*
Music by Peter Brewis; book and lyrics by Peter Brewis, Bob Goody and Mel Smith
Comedy Theatre, 2 July 1986
*PC:* Mel Smith, Bob Goody, Peter Brewis, Philip Davis, Paul Bown
*MN:* Get Yer Life; Loach's Song; Horse Race; Barmaid's Song; Ten Thousand Quid;
    Danny's Song; I've Sailed Through Hell; Craps; Easy; Shaking In the Shadows;
    Poker Song
45 performances

*GIRLFRIENDS*
Music and lyrics by Howard Goodall; book by Howard Goodall and John Retallack
Playhouse Theatre, 6 October 1987

*PC:* Hazel O'Connor, David Easter, Clare Burt, Tracey Halsey
*MN:* Prologue; We Can Take It; Somewhere In England; The Lecture; The Chances
   Are; The Debriefing; Not Heroes Here; Not One of Us; What a Place; I See Him
   Everywhere; With Men; I Don't Feel Guilty; Shy Girls; Jump; The Darkness Is
   Now My Friend; Bloomin' Cap; Some Nights; Nothing Could Be Too Harsh;
   The Pack Drill; Wake Me O Wake Me; Stay Don't Go; I Dream of So Much
   More; The Real War; Just Once More; The Chances Are [2]; The Final Flight;
   Talk of Victory; Epilogue: Before the War
43 performances

### THE GO-BETWEEN
Music and lyrics by Richard Taylor; book and lyrics by David Wood, based on the
   novel by L. P. Hartley
Apollo Theatre, 27 May 2016
*PC:* Michael Crawford, Gemma Sutton, Stuart Ward, Issy van Randwyck
*MN:* No musical numbers listed in theatre programme
162 performances

### THE GOLDEN TOUCH
Music, lyrics and book by James Gilbert and Julian More
Piccadilly Theatre, 5 May 1960
*PC:* Sergio Franchi, Gordon Boyd, Evelyne Ker, Cec Linder
*MN:* Isles of Greece; Way Out; Athens In My Blue Suit; High Life; Hard To Get; It's
   a Deal; Whisky A' Go' Go; Funny Thing; Art For My Sake; Beatnikology; Lemon
   On a Tree; Trust; You're So Like Your Father; Battle Hymn of the Colony; Not
   Enough of Her To Go Round
12 performances

### GONE WITH THE WIND
Music by Margaret Martin; book and lyrics by Martin, adapted by Trevor Nunn,
   based on the novel by Margaret Mitchell
New London Theatre, 22 April 2008
*PC:* Darius Danesh, Jill Paice, Madeleine Worrall, Edward Baker-Duly
*MN:* Born To Be Free; On Your Land; Ellen's Prayer; Gentle People; She's No Lady;
   Always In My Mind; Come Join the Troop; The Very Best People; I'm Your
   Man; Scarlett O'Hara Again; Can This Be All?; Gone With the Wind; Desperate
   Times; Nobody Knows You; I'm Gonna Find My Own; Wings of a Dove; Recon-
   struction Bounty; Just Two!; Once Upon a Time; Every Child; Alone
79 performances

### GOOD TIME JOHNNY
Music by James Gilbert; lyrics by Julian More and James Gilbert; book by Julian
   More

Birmingham Repertory Theatre, 16 December 1971
*PC:* Ronnie Barker, Eric Flynn, Colette Gleeson, Joan Sims
*MN:* Bed; A Crackerjack; Crackerjack Dance; Above Below; One For a Win, One
   For a Place; Well, Isn't That Nice; Come a Little Closer, Rosa; Big Lover; Why
   Should the Devil Have the Best Songs?; Another One For the Poor; Sigmund;
   Good-Time Johnny [*sic*]; What Have I Got To Lose?; Don't Come Any Nearer,
   Vera; Never Have a Clever Idea; That Indefinable Something; Riverside Rag;
   The Laugh's On Me
Season

*GOODBYE MR CHIPS*
Music and lyrics by Leslie Bricusse; book by Ronald Starke, based on the novel by
   James Hilton
Chichester Festival Theatre, 11 August 1982
*PC:* John Mills, Colette Gleeson, Nigel Stock
*MN:* Roll Call; Would I Have Lived My Life Then; Fill the World With Love; School-
   days; That's a Boy; Where Did My Childhood Go?; Boring; Take a Chance; Walk
   Through the World; When I Am Older; The Miracle; A Day Has a Hundred
   Pockets; You and I; What a Lot of Flowers; When I Was Younger; Goodbye Mr
   Chips
Season

*HARD TIMES*
Music, lyrics and book by Christopher Tookey and Hugh Thomas, based on the
   novel by Charles Dickens
Theatre Royal, Haymarket, 6 June 2000
*PC:* Roy Hudd, Brian Blessed, Peter Blake, Susan Jane Tanner, Malcolm Rennie,
   Helen Anker, Ann Emery
*MN:* The Greatest Show On Earth; Fact!; That's What Made Me a Man; Wond'ring
   Again; Another Town Tomorrow; One of These Days; People Can!; Factory
   Town; I've Never Heard the Last of It; What Do You Know About Love?; A
   Modern Marriage Pact; Father of the Bride; Haven't We Met?; A Boy Must Do;
   Spring; Better Things Shall Be; Mrs Sparsit's Staircase; Ask of Me Anything;
   When I Was a Boy; My Bounderby Alphabet
112 performances

*HIGH DIPLOMACY*
Music by William L Reed and George Fraser; book and lyrics by Alan Thornhill
   and Hugh Steadman Williams
Westminster Theatre, 5 June 1969
*PC:* Muriel Smith, Donald Scott, Patricia Bredin, John Moore, Kalman Glass, Matt
   Zimmerman, Madhav Sharma, Donald Simpson
*MN:* High Diplomacy; What They Say and What They're Meaning; Efficiency;

Hail To the Precarious Isles!; Reading People; No Strings Attached; X Marks the Spot; Give 'em What They Want – Tell 'em What To Do; Everything That He Does; Is She On Our Side – Or Theirs?; For Everyone, Everywhere; Just Between You and Me; For Certain; It May All Depend On You; If I Don't Do It, Nobody Else Will; Will There Be a Street In the Future?; It's Crazy – It's Mad!; The Oldest Au Pairs In the Business; The Operator; Children In the Dark
172 performances

## THE HIRED MAN
Music by Howard Goodall; book and lyrics by Melvyn Bragg, based on his novel
Astoria Theatre, 31 October 1984
*PC:* Julia Hills, Christopher Wild, Billy Hartman, Clare Burt
*MN:* The Hiring; Work; Crossbridge; The Hunt; After the Hunt; The Pub; The Fight; May and Harry; Whitehaven; The Union Meeting; Before the War; The War; Crossbridge Club Walk; The Pit; The Rehiring
164 performances

## HIS MONKEY WIFE
Music, lyrics and book by Sandy Wilson, based on the novel by John Collier
Hampstead Theatre Club, 20 December 1971
*PC:* Robert Swann, June Ritchie, Bridget Armstrong, Sally Mates, Jeffry Wickham, Myvanwy Jenn, Roland Curran
*MN:* Emily's Waltz; Home and Beauty and You; Marriage; In Boboma Tonight; Haverstock Hill; Don't Rush Me; Who Is She?; Dear Human Race; Leave It All To Smithers; Mad About Your Mind; His Monkey Wife; A Girl Like You; Doing the Chimpanzee; Live Like the Blessed Angels
Season

## HOORAY FOR DAISY!
Music by Julian Slade; lyrics and book by Dorothy Reynolds and Julian Slade
Lyric Opera House, Hammersmith, 20 December 1960
*PC:* Eleanor Drew, Robin Hunter, Dorothy Reynolds, Angus Mackay, Joe Greig, Edward Hardwicke
*MN:* She's Coming On the 4.48; I Feel As If I'd Never Been Away; No Lullaby; Nice Day; Soft Hoof Shuffle; If Only You Needed Me; How, When and Where; See You On the Moon; Going Up; Wine Is a Thing; Ting-a-Ling; He's Got Absolutely Nothing; Madame, Will You Dine?; It Won't Be the Same; I'm Sorry; Let's Do a Duet; Personally
51 performances

## HOUSE OF CARDS
Music by Peter Greenwell; lyrics and book by Peter Wildeblood, based on David Magarshack's translation of Alexander Ostrovsky's play *Even a Wise Man*

*Stumbles*
Phoenix Theatre, 3 October 1963
*PC:* Patrick Mower, Geoffrey Hibbert, Stella Moray, Barbara Evans, Barbara Couper, Douglas Byng, Robin Palmer
*MN:* Give Us the Money; You've Only Got To Ask; If You Were Not So Beautiful; The Mashenka Waltz; I Don't Remember At All; The End of Summer; Thé Dansant; Charity Begins At Home; The Secret With Women; The Delectable Life; Somewhere There's Someone; Down the Mountainside; A Marriage Has Been Arranged; I Didn't Even Ask Her; Easy To Please; The Political Situation
27 performances

*THE HUNTING OF THE SNARK*
Music, book and lyrics by Mike Batt
Prince Edward Theatre, 24 October 1991
*PC:* David McCallum, Kenny Everett, Philip Quast, Mark McGann, David Firth, Veronica Hart
*MN:* Prologue; Opening Titles; Children of the Sky; Hymn To the Snark; The Storm and Arrival; Who'll Join Me On This Escapade?; The Way We Think; The Departure; The Bellman's Speech; Midnight Smoke; The Trouble With You; Dancing Towards Disaster; The Banker's Fate; The Hunting; Nursery Pictures; Waiting For a Wave; The Butchery Waltz; Snooker Song; The Pig Must Die; More Trouble; The Dismal and Desolate Valley; A Delicate Combination; As Long As the Moon Can Shine; Yet More Trouble; The Vanishing; Whatever You Believe
60 performances

*I AND ALBERT*
Music by Charles Strouse; lyrics by Lee Adams; book by Jay Allen
Piccadilly Theatre, 6 November 1972
*PC:* Polly James, Sven-Bertil Taube, Lewis Fiander, Aubrey Woods
*MN:* It Has All Begun; Leave It Alone; I've 'eard the Bloody 'Indoos 'as It Worse; The Victoria and Albert Waltz; This Gentle Land; This Noble Land; I and Albert; His Royal Highness; Enough!; Victoria; This Dear Paradise; All Glass; Draw the Blinds; The Widow At Windsor; No One To Call Me Victoria; When You Speak With a Lady; Go It, Old Girl!
120 performances

*I CAN'T SING*
Music and lyrics by Steve Brown; book by Harry Hill
London Palladium, 26 March 2014
*PC:* Nigel Harman, Ashley Knight, Victoria Elliott, Cynthia Erivo, Simon Bailey, Alan Morrissey
*MN:* If That's Not Entertainment; It Could Be Me; Life Is Lovely; Please Simon;

All Woman; I Can't Sing!; Better Than That; The Hugging Song; Missing You Already; X Factor Fever; Here Come the Judges; Uncomplicated Love; Falling In Love With Myself; Make a Wish … It Happens; Fabulous; A Song I Wrote For You; X-Tasy; Journey To a Dream; You Can Sing!
53 performances

## IMAGINE THIS
Music by Shuki Levy; book by Glenn Berenbeim; lyrics by David Goldsmith
New London Theatre, 19 November 2008
*PC:* Leila Benn Harris, Peter Polycarpou, Bernard Lloyd, Simon Gleeson, Gary Milner, Michael Matus
*MN:* The Last Day of Summer; Imagine This; Masada Prologue; Rufus's Letter To Caesar; Free; When He Looked In My Eyes; Salome's Lament; Hail; No More; Rebel's Prayer; Masada; I Am the Dove; Far From Here, Far From Now; To Touch a Cloud; The Last Laugh; Don't Mind Me; Writing On the Wall; I Surrender; Passover Prayer; The Choice
37 performances

## THE IMPORTANCE
Music, book and lyrics by John Hugh Dean, adapted from *The Importance of Being Earnest* by Oscar Wilde; additional lyrics by Lorna Read
Ambassadors Theatre, 22 May 1984
*PC:* Sheila Bernette, Judy Campbell, Robert Dorning, David Firth, Karen Lancaster, Ruth Mayo, Patrick Ryecart
*MN:* London Society; Bunburying; The Importance of Being Earnest; Your Engagement; I Must Write That Down Before I Forget; Every Flower In the Garden; Bring His Luggage Down; Sincerely Yours; I Am Never Wrong; Tea Ballet; Yes For a Woman He Will; One Vital Question; My Ward; Born In a Handbag
29 performances

## INNOCENT AS HELL
Music, book and lyrics by Andrew Rosenthal
Lyric Theatre, Hammersmith, 29 June 1960
*PC:* Hy Hazell, Patricia Laffan, Totti Truman Taylor, Barbara Evans, Griffith Jones, Barbara Couper
*MN:* [for *Two of Everything*] Yes, Virginia; I'd Rather Stay At Home With You; When I Asked For a Match; I Want That; Small Streak of Gray; The First Time; I'm Going Away For a While; In Vino Veritas; The Best of Friends; The Hard Core Gang's All Here; I'd Go Home To My Mother; How Nice For You; Two of Everything; Ne'er Do Well; Hamburger Heaven; That's How the Whole Thing Began; Time and Tide; Samedi Soir; As Long As You Live
*MN:* [for *Best of Friends*, included] Saturday Song; The First Time; Innocent As Hell

*Numbers included in the London production but not heard in the American production*: Breakfast Dance; A Damned Good Man At the Bar; My Place; You Never Had It So Good

*Note: Innocent As Hell* was previously presented in 1947 as *Best of Friends* for a season at the Navy Recreation Park, Norfolk, Virginia, and subsequently presented off-Broadway in an altered form as *Two For Everything* at Marymount Manhattan Theater, 14 October 1976 for 10 performances

13 performances

## ISABEL'S A JEZEBEL

Music by Galt MacDermot; book and lyrics by William Dumaresq

Duchess Theatre, 15 December 1970

*PC:* Rosemary McHale, Carl Rigg, Joan Geary, Howard Wakeling, Peter Farrell, Maria Popkiewicz

*MN:* More Than Air; The Fisherman and His Wife; Down By the Ocean; On the Sands By the Sea; Isabel's a Jezebel; O Fish In the Sea; In Another Life; Nothing; Sand; I Love You Isabel; The Language and the Music; Oh Mummy Darling; Clinging Can Tell You; Mummy, Mummy, Mummy; Oh God, It Matters Now; The Saddest Moon; All She Wants Is; What Can He Do Other Than What He Does?; These Are the Things; Mama Don't Want No Baby; Stanley Your Irritability [sic]; Did You Hear Something, Isabel?; Use My Name; My God When I Think; She Was a Little Angel; Daddy, Daddy, Daddy; Where Do They Really Come From?; The Moon Should Be Rising Soon; The Weeds In the Wind; I Never Wanted a Baby; It Just Can't Be That Bad; Love Knows No Season; So Ends Our Night

61 performances

## JACK THE RIPPER

Music by Ron Pember; lyrics and book by Ron Pember and Denis de Marne

Players' Theatre, 25 June 1974 for a season, transferred to Ambassadors Theatre, 17 September 1974, and subsequently to the Cambridge Theatre, 17 February 1975

*PC:* Terese Stevens, Eleanor McCready, Peter Spraggon, Charles West, Howard Southern, Roy Sone

*MN:* Saturday Night; Sing Sing; I'm the Girl You All Know; God Bless; Goodbye Day; What a Life; Love; Ripper's Going To Get You; Charlie and Queenie; Half a Dozen Pints; There's a Boat Coming In; There Ain't Any Work Today; Look At Her; Suspects; Policeman's Chorus; Step Across the River; Montage

228 performances

## JEAN SEBERG

Music by Marvin Hamlisch; lyrics by Christopher Adler; book by Julian Barry

National (Olivier) Theatre, 15 November 1983

*PC:* Elizabeth Counsell, Joss Ackland, Kelly Hunter, John Savident

*MN:* Life In America; Movie Show; Dreamers; Let Me Ride the Wind; If I Knew Then; It Wouldn't Work Out; You Heard It Here; Gotta Get a Partner; My Lips Are Sealed; Secrets; It's the Least We Could Do

Repertory season

## JEEVES

Music by Andrew Lloyd Webber; book and lyrics by Alan Ayckbourn

Her Majesty's Theatre, 22 April 1975

*PC:* David Hemmings, Michael Aldridge, Gabrielle Drake, Gordon Clyde, Bill Wallis

*MN:* Banjo Boy; Code of the Woosters; Literary Men; My Sort of Man; Travel Hopefully; Female of the Species; Today; When Love Arrives; Jeeves Is Past His Peak; Half a Moment; S.P.O.D.E.; Summer Day; Eulalie; 'Tis Nature's Plan

38 performances

## JOEY JOEY

Music, lyrics and story by Ron Moody; book by Keith Waterhouse and Willis Hall

Saville Theatre, 11 October 1966

*PC:* Ron Moody, Vivienne Martin, Gordon Rollings, Joe Baker, Peter Pratt, Teddy Green, Ann Hamilton

*MN:* Typitywitchet; Where You Been Joe?; Friend; Our Place; You My Son; Flowers; Softly and Secretly; Mary; When You Dance With Me; Harlequinade; My Fault; The Life That I Lead; Get Your Coat On Joey; Let's Think About Me For a Change; Hot Codlins; Run Across London; You Can't Keep a Good Clown Down; Basket Dance; Darkly Handsome; Winter Harlequinade; Father and Son

23 performances

## JOHNNY THE PRIEST

Music by Antony Hopkins; lyrics and book by Peter Powell, based on the play *The Telescope* by R. C. Sherriff

Princes Theatre, 19 April 1960

*PC:* Jeremy Brett, Stephanie Voss, Bunny May, Hope Jackman, Frances Buckeridge, Phillada Sewell

*MN:* Doin' the Burp; The Maybury Story; The Little Box; Hellfire; Johnny the Priest; Vicarage Tea; Be Not Afraid; I'm Your Girl; Beyond These Narrow Streets; Rooftops; The Foggy Foggy Blues; He'll Let You Down; Bound Over; Ping Pong; Johnny Earn Peanuts; A Tanner's Worth of Tune; Charge Me; A Boy Called Johnny; Stormy Night; Farewell Johnny

14 performances

## JOIE DE VIVRE

Music by Robert Stolz; lyrics by Paul Dehn; book by Terence Rattigan, based on his play *French Without Tears*

Queen's Theatre, 14 July 1960
*PC:* Donald Sinden, Joan Heal, Joanna Rigby, Robin Hunter, Jill Martin
*MN:* Opening Chorus; Why?; There'll Always Be a Navy; Give Me!; Grab It While You Can; Open Your Eyes; Leave the Building; How Can I Tell the Other Man?; Fraternity!; 'Allo, Beeg Boy!; Scottish Can Can; Another Day; The Girl I'm Intending To Marry; The Kiss Was Very, Very Small; Le West End; I'm Sorry But I'm Happy
4 performances

*JORROCKS*
Music and lyrics by David Heneker; book by Beverley Cross, based on the books of R. S. Surtees
New Theatre, 22 September 1966
*PC:* Joss Ackland, Thelma Ruby, Cheryl Kennedy, Paul Eddington, Bernard Lloyd, Willoughby Goddard
*MN:* Ask Mr Jorrocks; Belinda; The Happiest Man Alive; Fresh Bloomin' Health; We'd Imagined a Man; Toasts of the Town; The Midsummer Fox; I Don't Want To Say Goodnight; The Opening Meet; The Hounds of John Jorrocks; Love Your Neighbour; A Little Bit Individual; You Can Depend On Me; I Well Recall the Day; I Don't Want To Behave Like a Lady; Once He's In He'll Never Get Out; The Sport of Kings; Jorrocks
181 performances

*KING*
Music by Richard Blackford; lyrics by Maya Angelou and Alistair Beaton; adaptation by Lonne Elder III
Piccadilly Theatre, 7 April 1990
*PC:* Simon Estes, Cynthia Haymon, Clarke Peters, Godfrey James, Shezwae Powell, Ray Shell
*MN:* Cotton's My Momma; I'm the One They're Gunning For; The Nameless of the Earth; Welcome To Atlanta; Equal Rights; My America; Don't Tell Me; Midnights, Mornings and Moonlight; Everything To Win; We're Coming To Get You; Ain't Gonna Let Nobody Turn Me Round; No More Sorrow; The Price of Freedom; We Are On the Move Now; So It Was At Lexington; They're After Your Vote; The Ultimatum; Drum Major Instinct; Only Love Lasts; Safe In Your Arms; Sacrifice; Always the Young; There's Another Way; My America; Rejoin the Battle; I Have a Dream
58 performances

*KINGDOM COMING*
Music by Bill Snyder; lyrics by Stanley Baum; book and additional lyrics by David Climie and Ronnie Cass
Roundhouse, 21 May 1973
*PC:* Antonia Ellis, John Bluthal, Michael Howe, Aubrey Morris

*MN:* [order of songs from second night on] Wanderin'; The Provider; The House That Rex Built; Wild Oat; Is There Someone?; A Real Warm Human Being; It Might Have Been; A Woman's Way; Why Not Now?; Kingdom Coming; Uncommon Cold; Woman To Woman; Lend An Ear; A Man Alone; Give Or Take a Hundred Years
14 performances

*KINGS AND CLOWNS*
Music, lyrics and book by Leslie Bricusse
Phoenix Theatre, 1 March 1978
*PC:* Frank Finlay, Elizabeth Counsell, Dilys Watling, Maureen Scott, Anna Quayle, Colette Gleeson, Sally Mates, Ray C. Davis
*MN:* Kings and Clowns; Henry Tudor; Good Times; To Love One Man; Get Rid of Her!; I'm Not!; The Grape and the Vine; A Woman Is a Wonderful Thing; In Bed; My Son; Young Together; Tomorrow With Me; Could Anything Be More Beautiful?; Bitch!; The Perfect Woman; Is Sad; Ten Wishes; The End of Love; A Man Is About To Be Born; Sextet
34 performances

*THE LADY OR THE TIGER*
Music by Nola York; lyrics by Michael Richmond; book by Jeremy Paul and Michael Richmond, based on the short story by Frank Stockton
Fortune Theatre, 3 February 1976
*PC:* Kate Crutchley, Vernon Joyner, Gordon Reid, John Morton, Keith Strachan, Martin Elliott
*MN:* Ours Is the Kingdom; The Bow Song; Daddy's Little Girl; Childish Things; Sophistication; Money In My Hat; The Lady Or the Tiger; Lady Evadne; Everything Around Me; You Know What I Mean; Sing It Along; Light a Convenient Candle; Minstrel Music; Chariot Wheels; Angelo; Good Goodbye; Here's Gold; What Would You Do?; Better Than a Man
52 performances

*LAUTREC*
Music and lyrics by Charles Aznavour; English lyrics by Dee Shipman; book by Shaun McKenna
Shaftesbury Theatre, 6 April 2000
*PC:* Sevan Stephan, Jill Martin, Nigel Williams, Martin Fisher, Hannah Waddingham, Peter Gallagher
*MN:* The Honour of the Family; Can Can; The Child Inside the Man; Questions; Painting; Let's Drink; Love Is a Pain; When You Love Me; The Exhibition; How Many Days?; Doing It; Souvenirs of Second Best; Me and You; Look Into My Eyes; Let Him Be Free Now
84 performances

## LEND ME A TENOR

Music by Brad Carroll; lyrics and book by Peter Sham, based on the play by Ken Ludwig

Gielgud Theatre, 2 June 2011

*PC:* Matthew Kelly, Damian Humbley, Sophie-Louise Dann, Michael Matus, Joanna Riding, Cassidy Janson

*MN:* Verdi's *Otello*; Where the Hell Is Merelli?; Fling; How 'bout Me?; For the Love of Opera; Facciamo L'Amor; The Last Time; Be Yourself; Before You Know It; Il Stupendo; Lend Me a Tenor; May I Have a Moment?; Knowing What I Know

76 performances

## LEONARDO

Music and lyrics by Tommy Moeller, Greg Moeller, Russell Dunlop and Duke Minks; book by John Kane

Strand Theatre, 3 June 1993

*PC:* Jane Arden, James Barron, Paul Collis, Hal Fowler, Lisa Hollander

*MN:* Kyrie; Who the Hell Are You?; Firenza Mia; Part of Your Life; Eye To Eye; Ti Amo; Goodbye and No One Said a Word; She Lives With Me; Forever Child; Just a Dream Away; Commonsense; Her Heart Beats; Endless As My Love; Just One More Time; La Gioconda; Genius; Be Too Close To Me; What She Sees In You; Francesco's Torment; Portrait of Love

44 performances

## LIE DOWN, I THINK I LOVE YOU

Music, lyrics and book by Ceredig Davies

Strand Theatre, 14 October 1970

*PC:* Ray Brooks, Ray Davis, Vanessa Miles, Tim Curry

*MN:* No musical numbers listed in theatre programme

13 performances

## THE LILY WHITE BOYS

Music by Tony Kinsey and Bill Le Sage; lyrics by Christopher Logue, Lindsay Anderson, Charles Fox and Oscar Lewenstein; book by Harry Cookson

Royal Court Theatre, 27 January 1960

*PC:* Albert Finney, Philip Locke, Monty Landis, Georgia Brown, Sally Ann Field, Ann Lynn, Willoughby Goddard, Ronnie Stevens

*MN:* The Opening Lament; The Song of Reasonable Ambition; The Committee's Point Number; The Young Hero Sings a Song of Self-Understanding; A Youth Leader Advises Neutrality and Respectfulness; The Boys' Spare Chorus; The Solicitor's Song; The Song of Natural Capital; The Girls' Spare Chorus; The Sentimental Number; The Song of the English Salesmen; The Song of Innocent Prosperity; The Song of Practical Values; The Bag of Gold Song; The Quartet; Jeannie On the Price of Ethics; The Song of Good Adjustment By the Company

Analyst; The Destiny Duet; The Chorale
45 performances

*LIONEL*
Music and lyrics by Lionel Bart; book by John Wells, conceived by Allan Warren
New London Theatre, 16 May 1977
*PC:* Avis Bunnage, Todd Carty, Marian Montgomery, Hugh Futcher, Adrienne
   Posta, Aubrey Woods, Clarke Peters
*MN:* Mirror Man; Down the Lane; Jellied Eels; Who Will Buy?; Business As
   Usual; What Makes a Star?; Big Times; It's Yourself; I'd Do Anything; Consider
   Yourself; When Does the Ravishing Begin?; Sparrers Can't Sing; You've Gotta
   Pick a Pocket Or Two; Butterfingers; In the Land of Promises; Do You Mind?;
   Rock With the Cavemen; Livin' Doll; To Be a Performer; Puttin' Out the Flags;
   Easy Going Me; Opposites; Unseen Hands; Fings Ain't Wot They Used T'Be;
   Handful of Songs; The Day After Tomorrow; There's Only One Union; Who's
   This Geezer Hitler?; Where Is Love?; Living In Dreamland
40 performances

*LIZA OF LAMBETH*
Music by Cliff Adams; lyrics and book by William Rushton and Berny Stringle,
   based on the novel by W. Somerset Maugham
Shaftesbury Theatre, 8 June 1976
*PC:* Angela Richards, Christopher Neil, Patricia Hayes, Bryan Marshall, Michael
   Robbins, Eric Shilling
*MN:* Husbands; Liza; Gawd Bless Her; I Come Down From Wigan; Liza of Lam-
   beth's Mum; Liza Ballet; Prince of Wales; Is This All?; Watch It; Red Jollop;
   Good Bad Time; Who In His Right Mind?; Dirty Bertie; Tricky Finish; Going
   Down To Chingford On a Chara; Whatever Happens To a Man; Liza Outing;
   Beautiful Colours; What's the Use of Killing Yourself?; Gilbert and Sullivan;
   Why Can't We Choose?; I Know I Shouldn't Like It; Between Ourselves; A Little
   Bit On the Side
110 performances

*THE LONDONERS*
Music and lyrics by Lionel Bart; book by Stephen Lewis, based on his play *Sparrers
   Can't Sing*
Theatre Royal, Stratford East, 27 March 1972
*PC:* Martine Howard, Ray Hoskins, Yootha Joyce, Stephen Lewis, Philip Davis,
   Rita Webb, Valerie Walsh, Bob Grant, Brian Murphy
*MN:* No musical numbers listed in theatre programme
63 performances

*LOST EMPIRES*

Music by Denis King; lyrics and book by Keith Waterhouse and Willis Hall, based on the novel *Lost Empires* by J. B. Priestley

Darlington Civic Theatre, 15 May 1985 and tour

*PC:* Brian Rawlinson, Angela Richards, Peter Adamson, Julia Chambers, Leslie Randall, Peter Ledbury

*MN:* Till Ready; He's a Shy Boy; You're So Different; The Bill; Quite the Gentleman; Actors; Success; Nice Girls Don't; The Show Must Go On; Twice Nightly; If Autumn Met Spring; Where Is My Love Tonight?; 'Ows Abaht?; A Prediction; Lost Empires; Gag-Time Rag; It Will All Be Over By Christmas

Tour

*LOVE ON THE DOLE*

Music by Alan Fluck; lyrics by Robert Gray; book by Terry Hughes based on the novel by Walter Greenwood and the play by Ronald Gow and Walter Greenwood

Nottingham Playhouse, 21 July 1970

*PC:* Eric Flynn, Angela Richards, Vilma Hollingbery, Neil Fitzwilliam, Lila Kaye, Maureen Pryor

*MN:* Is It Always To Be Tomorrow?; Hanky Park; My Favourite Music; Long Trousers; What's There To See At the Seaside?; Pawnshop Song; Who Can You Trust If You Can't Trust Your Bookie?; Beyond the Hill; Up On the Moors; Some Other Day; The Spirits; This Life of Mine; I'm On Your Side; There May Never Be a Next Time; Love On the Dole; A Little Piece of Paper; Clogging; Sal and Sam; Was She Once Young?

Season

*LOVE STORY*

Music and additional lyrics by Howard Goodall; book and lyrics by Stephen Clark, based on the novel and screenplay by Erich Segal

Duchess Theatre, 6 December 2010

*PC:* Emma Williams, Michael Xavier, Peter Polycarpou

*MN:* What Can You Say?; Jenny's Piano Song; Winter's Night; The Recital; What Happens Now; Nocturnes (pre-echo); Phil's Piano Song; Summer's Day; Pasta; Everything We Know; The Tide Has Turned; Nocturnes; Clapping Symphony

96 performances

*LUST*

Music, book and lyrics by the Heather Brothers, based on *The Country Wife* by William Wycherley

Theatre Royal, Haymarket, 19 July 1993

*PC:* Denis Lawson, Paul Leonard, Sophie Aldred, Judith Paris, Anthony Dawes, Julian Curry

*MN:* Lust; The Art of Deceiving; Serve the Dog Right; I Live For Love; A Pox On

Love and On Wenching; Somewhere Out There; Ladies of Quality; Husbands Beware; Come Tomorrow; What a Handsome Little Fellow; The Captain's Jig; Wait and See; Dear Sir; Ode To the One I Love; China; A Little Time In the Country; The Master Class; One of You; Vengeance; We Thank You
128 performances

## MADDIE
Music by Stephen Keeling; lyrics by Shaun McKenna; book by Shaun McKenna and Steven Dexter
Lyric Theatre, 29 September 1997
*PC:* Summer Rognlie, Graham Bickley, Lynda Baron, Kevin Colson
*MN:* Don't Look Back; Maddie Dancing; Knick Knacks; Ghost; I'll Find Time For You; Easy; I'll Have My Way; The Time of My Life; Star; One More Day; I've Always Known; Suzi's; From Now On; Afraid; At the Gates; If Not For Me
48 performances

## MADE IN DAGENHAM
Music by David Arnold; lyrics by Richard Thomas; book by Richard Bean
Adelphi Theatre, 5 November 2014
*PC:* Gemma Arterton, Adrian Der Gregorian, Isla Blair, Sophie-Louise Dann
*MN:* Busy Woman; Made In Dagenham; This Is What We Want; Union Song; Wossname; Always a Problem; Payday!; I'm Sorry, I Love You; School Song; Connie's Song; Everybody Out; This Is America; Storm Clouds Montage; Cortina!; The Letter; In An Ideal World; We Nearly Had It All; Viva Eastbourne; Stand Up
212 performances

## MAGGIE
Music, book and lyrics by Michael Wild, adapted from *What Every Woman Knows* by J. M. Barrie
Shaftesbury Theatre, 12 October 1977
*PC:* Anna Neagle, Anna Sharkey, Peter Gale, Briony McRoberts, Leonard Fenton, Barry Sinclair
*MN:* Charm; I Never Laughed In My Life; Three Hundred Pounds; Scottish Lullaby; Shand; Maggie; The London Waltz; If I Ever Really Love; Do You Remember?; Till the End of Time; I Can See the Stars; Dougal Drummond's Railway; Soliloquy; Just An Idea; I Just Took a Look At Me
42 performances

## THE MAID OF THE MOUNTAINS
Music by Harold Fraser-Simson and James W. Tate; lyrics by Harry Graham and others; additional lyrics by F. Clifford Harris and 'Valentine'; book by Frederick Lonsdale

Palace Theatre, 29 April 1972

*PC:* Jimmy Edwards, Lynn Kennington, Gordon Clyde, Jimmy Thompson, Janet Mahoney

*MN:* [music by Fraser-Simson and lyrics by Harry Graham unless otherwise stated. Lyric revisions by Harold Purcell and Emile Littler] Friends Have To Part; Live For Today; My Life Is Love [music: James W. Tate; lyric: F. Clifford Harris and (Arthur) Valentine]; Farewell; Dividing the Spoil; Song of the Vagabonds [music: Rudolf Friml; lyric: Brian Hooker]; We're Gathered Here; Love Will Find a Way; Save Us; Bachelor Gay [music: James W. Tate; lyric: F. Clifford Harris and (Arthur) Valentine]; Dirty Work; Husbands and Wives; When Each Day; Pedro the Fisherman [music: Harry Parr Davies; lyric: Harold Purcell]; When You're In Love [music: James W. Tate; lyric: F. Clifford Harris and (Arthur) Valentine]; Over There Over Here (sic); Paradise For Two [music: James W. Tate; lyric: F. Clifford Harris and (Arthur) Valentine]

96 performances

## MAN OF MAGIC

Music by Wilfred Wylam; lyrics and book by John Morley and Aubrey Cash

Piccadilly Theatre, 15 November 1966

*PC:* Stuart Damon, Judith Bruce, Stubby Kaye, Doris Hare, Colin Welland, Gaye Brown

*MN:* Floral Sisters; Man In the Crowd; Fantabulous; The Man Who Captures My Heart; Suddenly; Sling the Gin; Conquer the World; Man of Magic; Don't Bother Me Bub; The Earth Is the Lord's; Like No Other Man; Kester's Crystal Cabbage; You Can't Keep a Good Man Down; This He Knows; Say Your Name

135 performances

## MANDRAKE

Music by Anthony Bowles; book and lyrics by Michael Alfreds, based on the play *Mandragola* by Machiavelli

Criterion Theatre, 16 April 1970

*PC:* Margaret Burton, Roy Kinnear, Paul Shelley, Sarah Atkinson, Julia McCarthy, Ian Paterson, Sandra Michaels, Edward Caddick

*MN:* The Chase; Song of Exposition; Whose Baby Are You?; Waiting; To Give a Helping Hand; She Never Knew What Hit Her; To Get It Off My Chest; The Waters of the Spa; Mandrake; Chaperone's Lament; The Means To An End; Sostrata's Testament; Never Be the Servant To a Master With a Mistress; If Things Go Awry; The Situation Changes Overnight; Hymn To Mandrake

12 performances

## MARDI GRAS

Music and lyrics by Alan Blaikley and Ken Howard; book by Melvyn Bragg

Prince of Wales Theatre, 18 March 1975

*PC:* Lon Satton, Nicky Henson, Pepsi Maycock, Dana Gillespie, Gaye Brown, Aubrey Woods

*MN:* Mardi Gras (Breeze From the River); Everything About You; From Now On (Immortal, Invisible); Isn't It a Nice Sensation?; I Call the Tune; That's That; The Second Line; That's the Trick*; New Orleans; Love Keeps No Season; I Can See It All; Everybody's Moving; One In a Million*; Make Jazz; Celandine's Blues; When I Feel the Spirit Move Me; The Calinda; Love's Fool; Ash Wednesday * [*listed in the theatre programme at some point during run]

212 performances

## MARGUERITE

Music by Michel Legrand; lyrics by Herbert Kretzmer; book by Alain Boublil, Claude-Michel Schönberg and Jonathan Kent

Theatre Royal, Haymarket, 20 May 2008

*PC:* Ruthie Henshall, Julian Ovenden, Alexander Hanson, Simon Thomas, Andrew C. Wadsworth

*MN:* Come One Come All; Let the World Turn; Jazz Time; China Doll; The Face I See; Time Was When; The World Begins Today; Waiting; Intoxication; Day By Day [recurring]; I Am Here; Take Good Care of Yourself; Dreams Shining Dreams; I Hate the Very Thought of Women; The Letter; What's Left of Love; How Did I Get To Where I Am?

135 performances

## MARILYN!

Music by Mort Garson; lyrics and book by Jacques Wilson

Adelphi Theatre, 17 March 1983

*PC:* Stephanie Lawrence, John Christie, Judith Bruce, John Bennett, David Firth, Bruce Barry, Margaret Burton

*MN:* Did You Know Marilyn Monroe?; I Am Camera; Somebody Will Love Me; What Do We Do With the Girl?; Can You Hear Me Mama?; The Most Beautiful Girl of Them All; 8 x 10 Glossies; Where Do You Want Me?; I Never Knew a Girl Like Her Before; Seeing Other Men; Come and Get It Girl; It Happens; The Man Has Got An Eye; I Can See Myself Very Clearly; To Love Somebody; Then the Town Comes Down On Your Head; I'm Going Public; So Happy To See Me; Who's That Girl?; How Do You Like It?; Bigger Than Life; A Girl Like You Needs a Little Protection; There's So Much To Do In New York; Dumb Blonde; The Wedding: The Scene Will Play; Beautiful Child; It Was Not Meant To Be; Somewhere a Phone Is Ringing

156 performances

## MATADOR

Music by Michael Leander; lyrics by Edward Seago; book by Peter Jukes from the book by Seago and Leander

Queen's Theatre, 16 April 1991

*PC:* John Barrowman, Stefanie Powers, Caroline O'Connor, Alexander Hanson, Nicky Henson, Jackie Dunn

*MN:* Panama Hat; No Way Out of This Town; Moon In the Sky; Manolete, Belmonte, Joselito; I Was Born To Be Me; This Incredible Journey; A Boy From Nowhere; I'll Take You Out To Dinner; I'll Dress You In Mourning; What Is There More Than Love?; Paseo; Corrida; To Be a Matador; Only Other People; Children of the Sun; Child of the Sun; I Can Get By; I'm You, You Are Me

119 performances

## THE MATCH GIRLS

Music by Tony Russell; lyrics and book by Bill Owen

Globe Theatre, 1 March 1966

*PC:* Vivienne Martin, Gerard Hely, Marion Grimaldi, Cheryl Kennedy, Ray C. Davis

*MN:* Phosphorus; 'Atful of 'ope; Look Around; Me; Men; Something About You; Mind You Bert; Dear Lady; We're Gonna Show 'em; Cockney Sparrers; This Life of Mine; The Hopping Dance; I Long To See the Day; Comes a Time; An Amendment To a Motion; Waiting

119 performances

## MAYBE THAT'S YOUR PROBLEM

Music by Walter Scharf; lyrics by Don Black; book by Lionel Chetwynd

Roundhouse, 10 June 1971

*PC:* Harold Kasket, Douglas Lambert, Andee Silver, Al Mancini, Elaine Paige, Liz Whiting

*MN:* Maybe That's Your Problem; Something Must Have Happened; That's What Makes My Country Great; Rainbow Hopping; The Lazy Rock; Rock, Rock, Rock; McDougall Street; The Silver Spoon Symphony; What's a Few Years?; A Night To Remember; What Will Become of Me?; Tips; Head Shrinker's Lament; The Restless Years; Thick As Thieves; Feminine Freedom Or Die; Time For More Commandments

18 performances

## METROPOLIS

Music by Joe Brooks; book and lyrics by Dusty Hughes and Joe Brooks, with additional material by David Firman

Piccadilly Theatre, 8 March 1989

*PC:* Brian Blessed, Judy Kuhn, Graham Bickley, Jonathan Adams, Paul Keown

*MN:* 101.11; Hold Back the Night; The Machines Are Beautiful; He's Distant From Me Now; Elitist's Dance; Children of Metropolis; One More Morning; It's Only Love; Bring On the Night; You Are the Light; The Sun; There's a Girl Down Below; Futura; Nothing Really Matters; This Is My Time; Listen To Me;

Learning Song; The City's On Fire; When Maria Wakes; Futura's Promise; Haven't You Finished With Me?; Let's Watch the World Go To the Devil; One of Those Nights; Metropolis
214 performances

## THE MITFORD GIRLS

Music by Peter Greenwell and others; book and lyrics by Caryl Brahms and Ned Sherrin and others
Globe Theatre, 8 October 1981
*PC:* Patricia Hodge, Lucy Fenwick, Colette Gleeson, Patricia Michael, Gay Soper, Julia Sutton, Oz Clarke
*MN:* [all original songs by Greenwell, Brahms and Sherrin, in a score that also used existing material] Imagination; Why Do People Fall In Love?; Why Fall For Love?; The Controversial; I'll Fall In Love; Think of Being Rich; Find Your Partner and Dance; Why Love?; Strange Forces; Travelling Light
105 performances

## MOBY DICK

Music by Hereward Kaye and Robert Longden; book and lyrics by Robert Longden, based on the novel by Herman Melville
Piccadilly Theatre, 17 March 1992
*PC:* Tony Monopoly, Jackie Crawford, Earl Tobias, Hope Augustus
*MN:* Hymn; Parents' Day; Forbidden Seas; In Old Nantucket; A Man Happens; Gypsy Dancer; Love Will Always; Primitive; Punish Us; People Build Walls; Pequod; Sign Up; At Sea One Day; Building America; Mr Starbuck; Heave; Deck Dance; Can't Keep Out the Night; Whale of a Tale; Ship Ahoy; Shadows of the Deep; Storm; Save the Whale
127 performances

## MONEY TO BURN

Music, book and lyrics by Daniel Abineri
The Venue, 9 October 2003
*PC:* Peter Blake, Tony Kemp, Sarah-Louise Young, Camilla, Perry Benson
*MN:* Money To Burn; In the Red (and Feelin' Blue); Broadway Show; Piggy Dead, Bacon Saved; Never Gonna Quit (While I'm Ahead); That's What I Like (Whack Me, Smack Me); Ain't No Shame In Fame; Bankrupt; Lustin' For Justin (The Asset Strippers); (We're Going) Offshore; The Dirty Dagger of Deceit; (Fight) Fire With Fire
2 performances

## MR AND MRS

Music, lyrics and book by John Taylor; 'adaptation' by Ross Taylor, based on Noel Coward's plays *Fumed Oak* and *Still Life*

Palace Theatre, 11 December 1968

*PC:* John Neville, Honor Blackman, Hylda Baker, Alan Breeze, Liz Edmiston, Leslie Meadows

*MN:* 'Mr' – Millions of People; Other People's Husbands; Happy Family; I Feel I Want To Dance; And So We Got Married; No More Money; Big Wide World 'Mrs' – If the Right Man Should Ask Me; Father of Two, Mother of Three; Give Us a Kiss; Come Thursday; I Want To Wet My Whistle; Before Today; The Electric Circus; I'll Be Always Loving You; Mr and Mrs

44 performances

## MR BURKE M.P.

Music, book and lyrics by Gerald Frow

Mermaid Theatre, 6 October 1960

*PC:* Wally Whyton, Raf De La Torre, John Turner, Sally Miles, Peter Clegg, Edward Rees

*MN:* It's a Rat Race; Marriage of Convenience; Inanimate; Father Figure; Get a Cause; I'd Move To the Jungle; Underneath the Skin; 95% of Me Loves You; Wear a Smile; It's All Yours; You're Going To Be Caught

114 performances

## MRS HENDERSON PRESENTS

Music by George Fenton and Simon Chamberlain; lyrics by Don Black; book by Terry Johnson

Noel Coward Theatre, 16 February 2016

*PC:* Tracie Bennett, Ian Bartholomew, Emma Williams, Jamie Foreman, Matthew Malthouse

*MN:* Everybody Loves the Windmill; Mrs Henderson Presents; Whatever Time I Have; Lord Chamberlain's Song; What a Waste of a Moon; Rubens and Renoir; Ordinary Girl; It Starts With a Dream; Perfect Dream; Living In a Dream World; He's Got Another Think Coming; Women at War Medley; Now Is Not the Time; Anything But Young; We'll Never Close; Innocent Soldier; If Mountains Were Easy To Climb

142 performances

## MRS WILSON'S DIARY

Music by Jeremy Taylor; lyrics by John Wells; book by Richard Ingrams and John Wells

Criterion Theatre, 24 October 1967

*PC:* Bill Wallis, Myvanwy Jenn, Bob Grant, Peter Reeves, Sandra Caron

*MN:* Here I Kneel; Who?; Who Are the Bastards Now?; The Terrible Mr Brown; Why Should I Worry?; What Would They Say?; Harold and Me; One Man Band

175 performances

*MURDEROUS INSTINCTS*
Music by Alberto Carrion; book and lyrics by Cinda Fox
Savoy Theatre, 7 October 2004
*PC:* Nichola McAuliffe, Arvid Larsen, Kevin Colson, Sara Ingram
*MN:* No musical numbers listed in theatre programme
12 performances

*NAPOLEON*
Music by Timothy Williams; book by Andrew Sabiston and Timothy Williams;
  lyrics by Andrew Sabiston
Shaftesbury Theatre, 17 October 2000
*PC:* Paul Baker, Anastasia Barzee, David Burt
*MN:* Cape Diem (The Victim's Ball); The Rest of My Life; Seven Days; The Road
  To Glory; The Dream Within; Cut Throat Game; Only In Fantasy; Billiards;
  A Gentleman's Agreement; The Journey Begins; Eighteenth of Brumaire; On
  That First Night; The Royal Chorus of Disapproval; The Republic Ball; I Am the
  Revolution; Calm Before the Storm; Timor Mortis; Sweet Victory Divine; Saint
  Napoleon's Day; The Needs of France; The Last Crusade; The Friend You Were
  To Me; The Hunt; Russia; Waiting and Hoping; Gates of Paris; Rhapsody of the
  Turning Tides; Exile of the Heart
127 performances

*NELL!*
Music and lyrics by John Worth; book by John Worth and Philip Mackie
Richmond Theatre, 8 April 1970 and tour
*PC:* Jackie Trent, Hermione Baddeley, Stuart Damon, Gerard Hely
*MN:* Tickle 'n Slap; It's a Bargain; China Oranges; I Can Do It; I Must Choose;
  Bring Out Your Dead; Pretty Witty Nell; Around the Corner; No More; Charley
  the Second; Old Rowley; The King Must Be Fed; I'll Be Near You; 'E 'ad a Drink
  With Me; My Little Girl; Funeral Music; It's a Boy; Nell!
Tour

*NITE CLUB INTERNATIONAL*
Original music and lyrics by Dennis Deal and Albert Evans
Playhouse, 9 March 1988
*PC:* Ruth Madoc, Kathryn Evans, Stuart Milligan, Philip Gould, Peter Bishop
*MN:* [by Deal and Evans; score also included standard works] Nite Club; Circe
  [Deal]; The Canarsie Diner; He Never Leaves His Love Behind; Bonjour; Paris;
  You're My Big Affair; Crazy New Words; The Long Goodbye; All Man; Club Au
  Revoir / The Strip; Dressed To Kill; Dead End Street
29 performances

*ON THE LEVEL*
Music by Ron Grainer; lyrics and book by Ronald Millar
Saville Theatre, 19 April 1966
*PC:* Barrie Ingham, Angela Richards, Gary Bond, Sheila White
*MN:* G.C.E.; You Can Take It; Strangely Attractive; Thermodynamically Yours;
Chaos; A Very Good Friend; Peaceful; Bleep-Bleep; My Girl At the Dance; Let's
Make the Most of Now; Where the Action Is; Nostalgia; Love Gets Younger
Every Year; On the Level; And Then I'll Go; Chorale
118 performances

*ONCE MORE DARLING*
Music by Cyril Ornadel; lyrics by Norman Newell; book by Ray Cooney and John
Chapman, based on their play *Not Now, Darling*
Churchill Theatre, Bromley, 5 June 1978 and tour
*PC:* Norman Vaughan, Jack Douglas, Lynda Baron, Leon Greene, Jan Hunt,
Yvonne Marsh
*MN:* We've Got To Get This Show On the Road; Actually / Claudette; My Wife
Doesn't Understand Me; Get 'em Off; Have a Good Time; If You Sit Around
and Wait; I Was Bored; You; Infidelity; Men; What a Team; Remember Monte
Carlo; We Might As Well Be Strangers; Once More Darling
Tour

*ONE NIGHT STAND*
Music, book and lyrics by Mike Harding
Apollo Theatre, 21 July 1981
*PC:* Jeffrey Longmore, Cliff Howells, Andrew Hay, Richard Platt, Linda Jean-Barry
*MN:* Babbling Brook; One Night Stand; Bad Acne; … End Away; Fancy Him; Sweet
Saturday Night; Punch Up; We're Gonna Be Stars; Eggs and Chips Medley; How
Far Can You Go?; Marks and Spencer's Saraband; Fumble and Grope; Goodbye
Cleckheaton; Can Ye Twist John Peel; When Tomorrow Comes
47 performances

*OUR MAN CRICHTON*
Music by Dave Lee; lyrics and book by Herbert Kretzmer, based on the play *The
Admirable Crichton* by J. M. Barrie
Shaftesbury Theatre, 22 December 1964
*PC:* Kenneth More, Millicent Martin, Patricia Lambert, David Kernan, George
Benson, Dilys Watling, Anna Barry
*MN:* Tweeny!; Yes, Mr. Crichton; Down With the Barriers; Were I As Good; Our
Kind of People; Let's Find An Island; London, London – My Home Town;
Doesn't Travel Broaden the Mind?; Yesterday's World; I Tries; The Hairpin;
Little Darlin'; Oh! For a Husband, Oh! For a Man; I Never Looked For You;
Nobody Showed Me How; My Time Will Come
208 performances

## OUT OF THE BLUE
Music by Shun-Ichi Tokura; lyrics and book by Paul Sand
Shaftesbury Theatre, 4 November 1994
*PC:* Meredith Braun, Simon Burke, David Burt, Greg Ellis, James Graeme, Paulette Ivory, Michael McCarthy
*MN:* No musical numbers listed in theatre programme. Original cast recording gives titles as follows: Let Me Go; Kyrie; Is This a Test?; You Are All I See; Only Believe; Something To See Me Through; No Sound; On Your Side; Trio; Last Time We Met; The Magic Spell; I Think We're All Present; Spirit Clears; Suddenly Now, Out of the Blue; Tell Him; How Dare You? / What Is That?; Hana My Love; The Enemy Machine; Nothing At All; I Know Hideko, I Know; Message From a Dark Day; What Can I Hope For? I Don't Know; At Sunrise; Let Us Be Perfectly Clear; Help Me To See This Through; Hot Summer's Day; Finale
20 performances

## PASSION FLOWER HOTEL
Music by John Barry; lyrics by Trevor Peacock; book by Wolf Mankowitz, based on the novel by Rosalind Erskine
Prince of Wales Theatre, 24 August 1965
*PC:* Pauline Collins, Francesca Annis, Jane Birkin, Karin Fernald, Jean Muir, Nicky Henson, Bill Kenwright, Bunny May, Jeremy Clyde
*MN:* School Song; A Little Hammer; What a Question; What Does This Country Need Today?; The Syndicate; Naughty, Naughty; Tick Which Applies; Bully-Off; Passion Flower Hotel; How Much of the Dream Comes True; A Great Big Nothing; I Love My Love; Beastly, Beastly; Something Different; Don't Stop the Show
148 performances

## PEG
Music and lyrics by David Heneker [original theatre programme lists no librettist, but the book was based on the play *Peg o' My Heart* by J. Hartley Manners]
Phoenix Theatre, 12 April 1984
*PC:* Siân Phillips, Ann Morrison, Martin Smith, Patricia Michael, John Hewer, Julia Sutton, Edward Duke, David McAlister
*MN:* A Matter of Minutes; That's My Father; Pretty Dresses; Three of a Kind; Peg and Jerry; Come Away With Me; Ethel's Waltz; The Steamers Go By; Peg o' My Heart [by Alfred Bryan and Fred Fisher]; There's a Devil In Me; The Fishing Fleet; How Would You Like Me?; I Want To Dance; Manhattan Hometown; Who Needs Them?; Easy; When a Woman Has To Choose; A Genuine Hall-Marked Alpha-Plus Little Brick
146 performances

*PHIL THE FLUTER*
Music and lyrics by David Heneker and Percy French; book by Beverley Cross and
    Donal Giltinan
Palace Theatre, 15 November 1969
*PC:* Evelyn Laye, Stanley Baxter, Mark Wynter, Sarah Atkinson, Caryl Little
*MN:* If I Had a Chance; Abdul Abulbul Amir [French/Cross]; Mama; A Favour
    For a Friend; They Don't Make Them Like That Anymore; Good Money;
    How Would You Like Me?; Phil the Fluter [French/Heneker]; The Mountains
    of Mourne [French/Heneker]; I Shouldn't Have To Be the One To Tell You;
    Follow Me; Where Is She? [Moorhouse/Heneker]; You Like It; Are You Right
    There Michael? [French/Heneker]; That's Why the Poor Man's Dead [French/
    Heneker]; Wonderful Woman
123 performances

*PILGRIM*
Music by Carl Davis; book and lyrics by Jane McCulloch, adapted from John Bun-
    yan's *The Pilgrim's Progress*
Roundhouse, 15 October 1975
*PC:* Paul Jones, Peter Straker, John Bowe, Ken Bones, Geoffrey Burridge, Ena
    Cabayo, Joanna Carlin
*MN:* Make It While You Can; Am I Damned?; Keep On Travelling; I'm a Pilgrim;
    Why Must You Leave?; I Must Find a Way To Be Saved; How To Be a Proper
    Man; The Way Is Hard; Thy Sins Be Forgiven; I'm Glad That I Was Born To Die;
    There Is No True God; Because You're a Man; Prepare Yourself For a Bloody
    War; To Be a Pilgrim; Soon Born To Die; Jesus Gives Us All His Love; Brothers
    Can You Listen?; How Fair, How Pleasant; Who Can Find a Virtuous Woman?;
    You'll Find Your Soul At Vanity Fair; Can I Go?; Catechism; Follow the River;
    Come Gentle Pilgrim; All Things Go Out In Mystery; New Joy To Fill All Your
    Days; There Is a Way To Hell; To Everything There Is a Season
Season: closed 8 November 1975

*POCAHONTAS*
Music, lyrics and book by Kermit Goell, based on his book
Lyric Theatre, 14 November 1963
*PC:* Anita Gillette, Terence Cooper, Isabelle Lucas, Michael Barrington, Christene
    Palmer
*MN:* Prologue; The First Landing; Gold; She Fancied Me; Free As a Bird; You Have
    To Want To Touch Him; Too Many Miles From London Town; Eagle Dance;
    London Bridge Is Falling Down; I Love You Johnnie Smith; Things; Virginia;
    Oranges and Lemons; I Want To Live With You; I Have Lost My Way; Give Me
    a Sign; Like My True Love Grows; Yes, I Love You; Fit For a Princess; You Can't
    Keep a Good Man Down; Masque of Christmas
12 performances

*POPKISS*
Music by John Addison and David Heneker; lyrics and book by Michael Ashton,
   based on the play *Rookery Nook* by Ben Travers
Globe Theatre, 22 August 1972
*PC:* Daniel Massey, Patricia Hodge, John Standing, Isla Blair, Joan Sanderson,
   Mary Millar
*MN:* The Trouble With You; The Girl From Up the Road; Tonight Was On the
   Way; Cheer-O, Mr Popkiss; I'm Not Going Back To Him; You Are Who?; Up the
   Stair; Clara; Something Must Have Happened To Me; A Rumour Gets Around;
   The Life of a Wife; I Know You; Wrong All Along; Doing My Bit
60 performances

*POPPY*
Music by Monty Norman; lyrics and book by Peter Nichols
Barbican Theatre, 25 September 1982
Revised version: Adelphi Theatre, 14 November 1983
*PC:* Nichola McAuliffe, David Firth, Janet Shaw, Geoffrey Hutchins, Alfred Marks,
   Antonia Ellis
*MN:* The Emperor's Greeting; Dunroamin-on-the-Down; Whoa, Boy; The Good
   Old Days; Why Must I?; In These Chambers; If You Want To Make a Killing;
   Nostalgie de la Boue; John Companee; Poppy; China Clipper; The Bounty of the
   Earth; The Emperor's Lament; China Sequence; They All Look the Same To Us;
   The Blessed Trinity; Sir Richard's Song; Rock-a-Bye Randy; The Dragon Dance;
   Rat-Tat-Tat-Tat
97 performances

*THE PRINCESS*
Music and lyrics by Mario Braggiotti; story and choreography by Jo Anna
Strand Theatre, 23 August 1960
*PC:* Violette Verdy, Pierre Lacotte, Jo Anna, Claudia Cravey, Keith Beckett
*MN:* No musical numbers listed in theatre programme
44 performances

*PRISONER CELL BLOCK H*
Music, lyrics and concept by Don Battye and Peter Pinne, based on the TV series
   created by Reg Watson; additional dialogue and songs by Lily Savage
Queen's Theatre, 30 October 1995
*PC:* Lily Savage, Maggie Kirkpatrick, Liz Smith, Penny Morrell, Terry Neason,
   Emma Kershaw, Alix Longman, Jeffrey Perry
*MN:* Trouble At Wentworth; The Freak [music and lyric by Alix Longman]; Life
   On the Inside [music by Winston Eade; lyric by Lily Savage]; Top Dog; Gimme
   a Man [additional lyric by Emma Kershaw]; Twinset and Pearls [music and
   lyric by Jeffrey Perry]; Feel I Wanna Boogie [additional lyric by Alix Longman];

Stir Crazy Blues [music by Simon Lee; lyric by Alix Longman]; Gloves; Teddy [music and lyric by Sara Stephens]; I Never Told Him I Loved Him; I'm Innocent [music by Winston Eade; lyric by Lily Savage]; Love Will Set Us Free [music and lyric by Lesley Hayes]; Style [music by Winston Eade; lyric by Don Battye]; Why Not For Me

88 performances

*PULL BOTH ENDS*
Music and lyrics by John Schroeder and Anthony King; book by Brian Comport
Piccadilly Theatre, 18 July 1972
*PC:* The Young Generation, Christine Holmes, Gerry Marsden, Judy Bowen, Susan Toogood, Michael Cotterill
*MN:* Every Morning; After All (We're Only Women); The Cracker Song; A Tiny Touch; What About People; Particular Woman; Some Kind of Love; Decisions; Put a Little Smile; If You Knew the Way I Feel; Wallflowers; Cayo; Get the World To Dance; Here Am I; Henry and Liza; Strike!; Little Leather Book; Something About Her; Can This Be Love?; Oh Joe (A Tiny Touch); Handshakes and Promises; We're Ready; Pullin' Together

36 performances

*QUEENIE*
Music by Ted Manning and Marvin Laird; lyrics and book by Ted Willis
Comedy Theatre, 22 June 1967
*PC:* Vivienne Martin, Paul Eddington, Kevin Colson, Simon Oates, Cheryl Kennedy, Neil Fitzwilliam
*MN:* Ballad; Here Is the Key of the Door; Bill; Birthday Dance; I Can't Help Remembering; Queenie; We're Gonna Be Dead and Gone; Bill's Dance; Special Kind of Man; Starting From Now; Poor Poor Man; This Is the Meaning of Love; That's Beautiful; How Does He Look In the Morning?; Now That the Kissing Has Started; Young People; I Feel Fabulous Tonight; Excuse Me For Speaking My Mind

20 performances

*RESTORATION*
Music by Nick Bicât; book and lyrics by Edward Bond
Royal Court, 21 July 1981
*PC:* Simon Callow, Irene Handl, Philip Davis, Nicholas Ball
*MN:* No musical numbers listed in theatre programme
62 performances

*RIDE! RIDE!*
Music by Penelope Thwaites; lyrics and book by Alan Thornhill
Westminster Theatre, 20 May 1976

*PC:* Gordon Gostelow, Caroline Villiers, Brendan Barry, Richard Owens
*MN:* Have You Heard?; He's Just a Little Man; Riding Song 1; Deep In the Black-
ness; London Street Cries; London Town; Strange City; The Lord Jehovah
Reigns [lyric by Isaac Watts]; The Whole Wide World Is My Parish; Audrey's
Conversion; The Garden of England; Why Me?; He Knows My Name; Enthu-
siasm; A Nice Little Change of Air; Say What You Mean; One By One; Let the
Enemies of the Lord; Everyone Is Needed; What Thou Hast Done [lyric by John
Wesley]; Riding Song 2; The Travellers' Blessing; Ride Out
76 performances

### ROBIN, PRINCE OF SHERWOOD
Music and lyrics by Rick Fenn and Peter Howarth
Piccadilly Theatre, 3 February 1993
*PC:* Mike Holoway, Peter Howarth, Liz Curnick
*MN:* Prologue; Robin Hood; King Richard; The Devil's Contract; The Market Song;
The Sheriff and Loxley; A Bridge Across Forever; Little John; Hanging Around;
Robin and Marion; Morgana's Bar; Friar Tuck; Call Me Robin Hood; The Sheriff
of Nottingham; Robin, Prince of Sherwood; The Robbery; Sisters of Sodom; The
Sheriff, Marion and Loxley; It's Raining Gold; The Wedding Train; The Wholey
[*sic*] Bible; I Believe In My Dreams; The Light Grows Dim; The Hanging
109 performances

### ROMANCE!
Music and lyrics by Charles Ross; book by John Spurling
Duke of York's Theatre, 28 September 1971
*PC:* Bill Simpson, Joyce Blair, Jess Conrad, Roberta D'Esti, John Blythe
*MN:* Rush Hour; Another Day; Dear Sirs; Dear Old Dad; Something's Missing;
The Lady and the Gamekeeper; Something's Happening; Lovely To See You,
Darling; Every Thursday; Where Is the Mystery?; I Want To Know; Romance!; I
Believe In Love; Nothing Left To Say.
6 performances

### ROMEO AND JULIET
Music by Gérard Presgurvic; lyrics by Don Black; book by David Freeman and
Don Black
Piccadilly Theatre, 4 November 2002
*PC:* Andrew Bevis, Lorna Want, Jane McDonald, Sevan Stephan, James Graeme,
David Bardsley
*MN:* Verona; Born To Hate; All Days Are the Same; Without Love; The Marriage
Proposal; You Must Marry; Kings of the World; The Ball [1]; Born To Love; The
Ball [2]; She Can't See Me; Two Different Worlds; All For Love; Ugly and Beau-
tiful; And Now She Is In Love; These Are My Rivers; Word Is On the Street; It's
Today; Live; Dying In the Dust; Revenge; Fools; No Place Too Far; He's Yours;

She Came From Me; All Days Are the Same Without You; I Can't Do This; God Knows Why; Where Rivers Keep Flowing; Empty Sky; Guilty
112 performances

*A SAINT SHE AIN'T*
Music by Denis King; book and lyrics by Dick Vosburgh, based on Molière's play *Le Cocu Imaginaire*
Apollo Theatre, 22 September 1999
*PC:* Barry Cryer, Pauline Daniels, Brian Greene, Gavin Lee, Michael Roberts, Corrina Powlesland
*MN:* My Molière; Start-the-Day-Tune; The Navy's In Town; My All-American Gal; A Saint She Ain't!; I Love To Hold Rose With the Rolled Hose and the Shing-Shing-Shingled Hair; I Only Dig That Jive; You're the Only Star In My Heaven; Manitowoc; There Ought To Be a Way; The Joke's On Me; A Beautiful Lady; Can't Help Dancing; The Banana For My Pie
133 performances

*SAUCY JACK AND THE SPACE VIXENS*
Music by Jonathan Croose and Robin Forrest; book and lyrics by Johanna Allitt, Simon Curtis, Michael Fidler and Charlotte Mann
Queen's Theatre, 25 March 1998
*PC:* David Scholfield, Catherine Porter, Johanna Allitt, David Ashley, Natasha Bain, Adam Meggido, Mark Oxtoby, Hannah Waddingham, Daniel Wexler
*MN:* Saucy Jack's; Plastic Leather and Love; All I Need Is Disco; Glitter Boots Saved My Life; Park My Bike; Thrill Me; Nowhere To Run; I'm Just a Tortured Play-thing; Cheer Up Bunny; Crime Fighting Mamas; Living In Hell; Fetish Number From Nowhere; Let's Make Magic; Space Trucking
85 performances

*SCAPA!*
Music, lyrics and book by Hugh Hastings, based on his play *Seagulls Over Sorrento*
Adelphi Theatre, 8 March 1962
*PC:* David Hughes, Pete Murray, Edward Woodward, Timothy Gray
*MN:* Scapa; Don't Give a Damn; I Like It Here; Never Volunteer; Napoli; Seagull In the Sky; Give It All You've Got; Some Voice; Trouble; Nocturne; Bella; Wakey-Wakey; She Had Such a Beautiful Touch; The Sound of Bagpipes; I Wish I Was An Orchestra; A Girl In Every Port; One Woman; A Letter To Mum; Squares Dance
44 performances

*THE SECRET GARDEN*
Music by Steven Markwick; book and lyrics by Diana Morgan, based on the novel by Frances Hodgson Burnett

King's Head Theatre Club, 12 January 1987
*PC:* Lucinda Edmonds, Michael G. Jones, Richard Gauntlett
*MN:* Lillian; Tregaron Hall; Get Up Miss Mary; Wales; Other Little Girls; Wales
   Lullaby; The Telwyth Ted; The Secret Garden; You Got Friends; A Little Piece
   of Earth; The Boy Rajah; Dai and I; My Love Is a Rose; That's Spring; Money;
   Nightfolk
Season: closed 22 February 1987

## SHERLOCK HOLMES

Music, book and lyrics by Leslie Bricusse, based on characters created by Arthur
   Conan Doyle
Cambridge Theatre, 24 April 1989
*PC:* Ron Moody, Liz Robertson, Derek Waring, Julia Sutton
*MN:* Sherlock Holmes; Without Him, There Can Be No Me!; London Is London;
   Vendetta; Look Around You; Anything You Want To Know; Her Face; Men Like
   You; A Lousy Life; I Shall Find Her; No Reason; Halcyon Days; The Lord Abides
   In London; Down the Apples 'n' Pears; He's Back!; A Million Years Ago – Or
   Was It Yesterday?; The Best of You, The Best of Me
97 performances

## SING A RUDE SONG

Music by Ron Grainer; lyrics and book by Caryl Brahms and Ned Sherrin, with
   additional material by Alan Bennett
Garrick Theatre, 26 May 1970
*PC:* Barbara Windsor, Denis Quilley, Maurice Gibb
*MN:* That's What They Say; 'Ang Abaht; Happiness; Whoops Cockie!; I'm In a
   Mood To Get My Teeth Into a Song; Only a Friendly Kiss; Tattenham Corner;
   I've Been and Gone and Done It; Haven't the Words; You Don't Know What It's
   Like To Fall In Love At Forty; Waiting On the Off Chance; Waiting For the Royal
   Train; I'm Nobody In Particular; One of Nature's Ladies; Wave Goodbye!; Sing
   a Rude Song; Leave Me Here To Linger With the Ladies. [Score also included
   two original Lloyd songs: My Old Man (Don't Dilly Dally); The Boy I Love (The
   Boy In the Gallery).]
71 performances

## SMILIN' THROUGH

Music and Lyrics by John Hanson; book by Hanson and Constance Cox, based on
   the play and film by Jane Murfin and Jane Cowl
Prince of Wales Theatre, 5 July 1972
*PC:* John Hanson, Lauverne Gray, Tony Adams, Carole Doree, Glyn Worsnip,
   Freddie Eldrett
*MN:* Ragged Feet Rag; When You're Young; Smilin' Through; Why Did I Leave
   Ireland?; If You Really Loved Me; You, Who Have Never Known Love!; Set 'em

Up Landlord!; Poor Old John!; Who Wants To Be Free?; We're Not Going Home Tonight; With Sweet Louise; There's Nothing Like a Wedding!; The Best Man!; Something Old, Something New!; The Luckiest Girl In the World; Will You Love, Honour and Obey?; Aren't You Glad?; The Time Will Come; Why Must I Leave You?; The Best Man; Give Me Your Hand

28 performances

*SO WHO NEEDS MARRIAGE?*
Music, lyrics and book by Monty Norman
Gardner Centre, Brighton, 8 May 1975 and tour
*PC:* Diana Coupland, Jon Pertwee, June Ritchie, Eric Flynn, Elizabeth Power, John Gower
*MN:* Do I Want a Divorce?; Welcome To the Club; You've Got Everything To Fight For; Theobald's Ponderings; Picking Holes; How Can I Make You Understand?; Live My Life; Before It's Too Late; Our Yesterday Tune; Nothing Would Please Me More; D.I.V.O.R.C.E.; Fast Approaching the Point of No Return; The Improved Permeosonic Decoder; You Just Can't Win; Don't Shut Me Out; So Who Needs Marriage?; For Want of a Word
Tour

*SOMEONE LIKE YOU*
Music by Petula Clark; lyrics by Dee Shipman; book by Robin Midgley and Fay Weldon, based on an original idea by Petula Clark and Ferdie Pacheco
Strand Theatre, 22 March 1990
*PC:* Petula Clark, Dave Willetts, Clive Carter, Jane Arden, Joanne Campbell
*MN:* Home Is Where the Heart Is; Look Where the Journey Led; Empty Spaces; Picking Up the Pieces; Liberty; What Can One Person Do?; Someone Like You; What You Got!; Amen; All Through the Years; Soldiers' Blues; So Easy; Getting the Right Thing Wrong; I Am What You Need; It's a Big Big Country; Young 'Un; Without You; The Women's Credo; The Fight
44 performances

*SONGBOOK (A Tribute to Moony Shapiro)*
Music, lyrics and book by Monty Norman and Julian More
Globe Theatre, 25 July 1979
*PC:* David Healey, Gemma Craven, Diane Langton, Anton Rodgers, Andrew C. Wadsworth
*MN:* Landin' Headfirst On My Feet; Songbook; East River Rhapsody; Your Time Is Different To Mine; Such Sweet Poison; Mr Destiny; Pretty Face; Je Vous Aime, Milady; Les Halles; Olympics Song; Nazi Party Pooper; I'm Gonna Take Him Home To Momma; Bumpity Bump; Das Mädchen am Fenster; The Girl In the Window; Victory V; April In Wisconsin; Freddie Fox; Happy Hickory; When a Brother Is a Mother To His Sister; Climbin'; Don't Play That Love Song Any

More, Marvin; Lovely Sunday Morning; Rusty's Dream Ballet; The Pokenhasset Public Protest Committee; I Accuse; Messages; I Found Love; Don't Play That Love Song Any More; Golden Oldie; Nostalgia
208 performances

*SPIN OF THE WHEEL*
Music and lyrics by Geoff Morrow; book by Timothy Prager
Comedy Theatre, 7 April 1987
*PC:* Neil McCaul, Maria Friedman, Teddy Kempner, Erin Donovan
*MN:* Spin of the Wheel; That's a Long Story; It's Only a Game Show; He Likes the Girl; Lucky; What Would You Do Without Me?; One More Postcard; He Loves the Girl; Life Is a Citrus Tree; Life Is a Carousel; The Largest Known Butterfly; He Hates the Girl; Minding the Store; Dirty Work; If; When I Came Out of the Cellar; Imagine This; Daly Is the Name
36 performances

*STAND AND DELIVER*
Story, music and lyrics by Monty Norman; book by Wolf Mankowitz
Roundhouse, 24 October 1972
*PC:* Nicky Henson, Anna Dawson, Elizabeth Mansfield, Derek Godfrey, Pamela Cundell
*MN:* Jack Sheppard Theme; Our Humble Thanks; Dance On Nothing; What a Strange Life; Jill of All Trades; Look No Further; Do Unto Husbands; The Wheel; Fool To Fall In Love; Jack's Escape; Runaway Jack; When a Woman's In Love; He's Mine; It's Wearing; Tra'lah, Tra'lah; Six Men's Shoulders; By Hook or By Crook; Hanging Day; Stand and Deliver
Season: 14 performances

*STEPHEN WARD*
Music by Andrew Lloyd Webber; book and lyrics by Christopher Hampton and Don Black
Aldwych Theatre, 19 December 2013
*PC:* Alexander Hanson, Joanna Riding, Charlotte Spencer, Charlotte Blackledge, Daniel Flynn
*MN:* Human Sacrifice; Super-Duper Hula-Hooper; When You Get To Know Me; You're So Very Clever To Have Found This; This Side of the Sky; Manipulation; He Sees Something In Me; You've Never Had It So Good; Black-Hearted Woman; Mother Russia; While We Can; Love Nest; Freedom Means the World To Me; 1963; Give Us Something Juicy; Profumo's House; The Police Interview; I'm Hopeless When It Comes To You; The Arrest; The Trial; Too Close To the Flame
116 performances

*STEPPING OUT*
Music by Denis King; lyrics by Mary Stewart-David; book by Richard Harris, based on his play
Albery Theatre, 28 October 1997
PC: Liz Robertson, Helen Bennett, Helen Cotterill, Barbara Young, Carolyn Pickles, Sharon D. Clarke, Colin Wakefield, Rachel Spry, Felicity Goodson, Gwendolyn Watts
MN: One Night a Week; Quite; Don't Ask Me; Love To; What Do Men Think?; Too Much; Never Feel the Same Again; Definitely You; Not Quite; Just the Same; What I Want; Once More; Loving Him; Stepping Out
134 performances

*THE STIFFKEY SCANDALS OF 1932*
Music and lyrics by David Wood; book by David Wright
Queen's Theatre, 12 June 1969
PC: Charles Lewsen, Annie Ross, Terri (Terese) Stevens
MN: Dear Lord and Father of Mankind; 1932; Girls!; Don't Judge By Appearances; I Can't Understand You; The Lament of Ingelbert Ralph Thole; Pestering; The Prostitutes' Padre; Playthings; What a Scoop; 3 Maybe; When My Dreamboat Comes Home; The Church of England; The Fight Goes On; Simple Gifts [traditional, arranged by Carl Davis]
12 performances
Originally staged as *A Life In Bedrooms* (1967) and subsequently as *The Prostitutes' Padre* (1997)

*STRIKE A LIGHT!*
Music by Gordon Caleb, with additional songs by John Taylor*; lyrics and book by Joyce Adcock
Piccadilly Theatre, 5 July 1966
PC: Jean Carson, John Fraser, Evelyn Laye, Charles West, Josephine Blake
MN: Come the Revolution; It's a Fight; Bit of It Now; Everything*; Pawnshop Doorway; Up In the World*; Scandalous; Another Love; When I Read; Let's Make a Night of It; Strike a Light; Summer Evening; Private Enterprise; Dear Lady; Girls Who Go With Sailors; Making Friends*; Vesta Girls; Near Me; Teach Me; I Don't Know the Words
30 performances

*THE SWAN DOWN GLOVES*
Music by Nigel Hess; lyrics by Billie Brown and Nigel Hess; book by Billie Brown
Aldwych Theatre, 22 December 1981
PC: Michael Fitzgerald, Terry Wood, Richard Pasco, Julia Tobin, Derek Godfrey
MN: With the Sun Arise; Everything's Going To Be Fine; Catastrophe; Lost!; Let's Be Friends; Make Your Own World; How's the Way; Going To Town; Stuck In

a Muddle; Best Foot Forward; Demewer [sic] But Dangerous; Any Old Rose; Muck; Spuds; Brave New World
Season

*SWAN ESTHER*
Music by Nick Munns; book and lyrics by J. Edward Oliver
Young Vic, 17 December 1983
*PC:* Sam Kelly, Amanda Redman, James Coombes, Stephen Lewis, David Henry, Christina Nagy
*MN:* A Far Outpost of Persia; Bow Down; The Queen's Party; The Emperor's Wrath; Haman's Advice; Take Away My Crown; A Bright Idea; I've Neglected To Mention; We All Need; Country Girl; My Love Is Like a Dream; The Beauty Contest; A Strange Girl; Persia Is Stable; Kill the King; The Emperor's Memoirs; Treason; I Am Great; I Don't Trust Haman; Nothing To Lose; Esther; Evil Haman; The King Can't Sleep; Prize Surprise; Haman's the One; Ahasuerus Repents; Esther and Mordecai
Season

*TESS OF THE d'URBEVILLES*
Music by Stephen Edwards; lyrics by Justin Fleming; book by Karen Louise Hebden
Savoy Theatre, 10 November 1999
*PC:* Philippa Healey/Poppy Tierney, Jonathan Monks, Maxine Fone
*MN:* Who's Spinning the Wheel?; Do I Love Her?; Guide, Philosopher and Friend; Save My Soul; Leaving the Past Behind; I Have Your Love; Water Meadows; I'd Marry Him Tomorrow Morn; Can I Trust Him?; In the Twilight of the Morning; The Wedding; I Fear His Gaze; Chaseborough Market; The Old Chase Wood; Sorrow; Birds of the North Star; Threshing Field; Come Back To Me; River of Regret; Angel Returns; Stonehenge
77 performances

*THOMAS AND THE KING*
Music by John Williams; lyrics by James Harbert; book by Edward Anhalt
Her Majesty's Theatre, 16 October 1975
*PC:* Richard Johnson, James Smillie, Dilys Hamlett, Caroline Villiers
*MN:* Processional; Look Around You; Am I Beautiful?; Man of Love; The Question; What Choice Have I?; We Shall Do It!; Improbable As Spring; Power; Consecration; 'Tis Love; Sincerity; The Test; Replay the Game; A New Way To Turn; Will No One Rid Me?; Civilisation; So Many Other Worlds
20 performances

*THE THREE CASKETS*
Music by Peter Greenwell; book and lyrics by Gordon Snell
Players' Theatre, 1 March 1961

*PC:* Margaret Burton, Denis Martin, Laurie Payne, Robin Hunter, Patsy Rowlands, Karin Clair, Jean Burgess
*MN:* Hurrying and Scurrying; This Is the Day; The Game of Love; I'm Paddy O'Larragon; O'Larragon's Choice; O'Larragon's Farewell; Lady Disdain; I Wanna Carry You Back; Joe's Choice; Miss Portia; I Know; Soon, Soon, Soon; Bassanio's March; Love Will Find a Way; Forever and a Day; What a Lovely Plot; Bassanio's Choice; Now You're Mine; On Such a Night
Season

### TOM BROWN'S SCHOOLDAYS
Music by Chris Andrews; lyrics and book by Joan and Jack Maitland, based on the novel by Thomas Hughes
Cambridge Theatre, 9 May 1972
*PC:* Roy Dotrice, Judith Bruce, Ray C. Davis, Trudi van Doorn, Adam Walton, Richard Willis, Christopher Guard, Leon Greene
*MN:* Petticoat Government; I Like My Children Around; Head Up; In the Swim; My Way; Three Acres and a Cow; Where Is He?; What Is a Man?; Six of the Best*; The Ballad of the Great White Horse; Young Tom; Have a Try; If I Had a Son*; A Boy's Point of View; Vision of Youth; Warwickshire Home; One For Your Nose; Hold Me [*lyric by Joan Maitland]
76 performances

### TOO CLOSE TO THE SUN
Music and lyrics by John Robinson and Roberto Trippini; book by Roberto Trippini, based on a play by Ron Read
Comedy Theatre, 24 July 2009
*PC:* James Graeme, Helen Dallimore, Tammy Joelle, Christopher Howell
*MN:* Prologue; Just Relax – Think Good Thoughts; The Ketchum, Idaho Walk; Do I Make a Certain Kind of Sense?; I Do Like To Be Liked; Make Yourself One With the Gun; Sentimental Small-Towner That I Am; Super-Eager Little Her; Illusion Lyrique; All Will Be Well; Hollywood! Hollywood!; Havana; Too Close To the Sun; In the World's Face; Alabama – the Queen of Them All; Waiting In the Shadows; Just Gimme Half of Half a Chance; Strong and Silent Types; Can't Think of It Without Wanting To Cry; Stormy Weather, Boys; Poor Little Silly Young Me; Forgive Me Wife, You'll Understand; The Regret; I Did My Best; Character Gives You the Man
19 performances

### TRELAWNY
Music and lyrics by Julian Slade; book by Aubrey Woods, based on the play *Trelawny of the Wells* by Arthur Wing Pinero, adapted by Slade, Woods and George Rowell
Sadler's Wells Theatre, 27 June 1972, transferring to the Prince of Wales Theatre

3 August 1972

*PC:* Ian Richardson, Max Adrian, Gemma Craven, Joyce Carey, Elizabeth Power, Teddy Green, David Morton, John Watts

*MN:* Pull Yourself Together; Walking On; Ever of Thee; Trelawny of the Wells; On Approval; Rules; Back To the Wells; Old Friends; The One Who Isn't There; We Can't Keep 'em Waiting; The Turn of Avonia Bunn; Hail To Aladdin; Arthur's Letter; Two Fools; Life; This Time

177 performances

## *TROUBADOUR*

Music by Ray Holder; lyrics and book by Michael Lombardi

Cambridge Theatre, 19 December 1978

*PC:* John Watts, Kim Braden, Andrew C. Wadsworth

*MN:* Vendors' Cries; The Wife Beating Song; Troubadour; One Only Rose; Woman Is a Cheat; Can Anyone Assist Me?; Panic In the Palace; The Loneliness of Power; Ave Maris Stella; If There Is Love; Aubade; Onward To Jerusalem; We Must Have Jerusalem; Mary's Child; Kalenda Maya

[Original cast recording includes numbers not listed in theatre programme: O Admirabile; Melancholy Lover; Islamic Prayer; Mime Dance Interlude; Woman, Whoever You Are]

76 performances

## *TWANG!*

Music and lyrics by Lionel Bart; book by Lionel Bart and Harvey Orkin

Shaftesbury Theatre, 20 December 1965

*PC:* James Booth, Barbara Windsor, Toni Eden, Long John Baldry, Bernard Bresslaw, Ronnie Corbett, Elric Hooper

*MN:* May a Man Be Merry; Welcome To Sherwood; Wander; What Makes a Star?; Make An Honest Woman [of Me]; Roger the Ugly; To the Woods; Dreamchild; With Bells On; Sighs; You Can't Catch Me; Living a Legend; Unseen Hands; Writing On the Wall; Who's Little Girl Are You?; Follow Your Leader; I'll Be Hanged; Tan-Ta-Ra! [A title song heard on the original cast recording is not listed in the original theatre programme.]

43 performances

## *TWO CITIES*

Music by Jeff Wayne; lyrics by Jerry Wayne; book by Constance Cox, based on Charles Dickens' novel *A Tale of Two Cities*

Palace Theatre, 27 February 1969

*PC:* Edward Woodward, Kevin Colson, Nicolette Roeg, Elizabeth Power, Leon Greene

*MN:* The Best of Times; Street Prologue; Tender Love and Patience; Independent Man/What Would You Do?; Look Alike; And Lucie Is Her Name; Golden-Haired

Doll; Suddenly; The Time Is Now; Let 'em Eat Cake; The Bastille; Two Different People; The Machine of Doctor Guillotine; Only a Fool; Carmagnole; Will We Ever Meet Again?; Knitting Song; Quartet; Long Ago; It's a Far, Far Better Thing
44 performances

*VALENTINE'S DAY*
Music by Denis King; lyrics by Benny Green; book by Benny Green and David William, based on George Bernard Shaw's play *You Never Can Tell*
Globe Theatre, 7 September 1992
*PC:* Edward Petherbridge, John Turner, Edward de Souza, Elizabeth Counsell, Alexander Hanson
*MN:* Professional Man; All For One (and Both For Me); Answer All Your Children's Questions; I've Noticed This Before; Step By Step; Nice Morning; You Never Can Tell; Luncheon Chorale; The World Was Changed This Morning; Don't Tell Me – Let Me Guess; Gloria's Soliloquy; Affairs of the Heart; He Is Nothing To Me Now; Brighten Up the Night; Bohun's Song; Who Would Have Dreamed?; Valentine's Day
28 performances

*VANITY FAIR*
Music by Julian Slade; lyrics by Robin Miller; book by Robin Miller and Alan Pryce-Jones, based on the novel by William Makepeace Thackeray
Queen's Theatre, 27 November 1962
*PC:* Frances Cuka, Sybil Thorndike, Eira Heath, Gordon Boyd, Michael Aldridge, Naunton Wayne, George Baker, Joyce Carey, Gabriel Woolf, John Stratton
*MN:* Vanity Fair; I'm No Angel; Impressed; There He Is; Dear Miss Crawley; Mama; Love, Honour and Obey; Farewell; Advice To Women; Waterloo Waltz; Where Is My Love?; How To Live Well On Nothing a Year; Someone To Believe In; Rebecca; Forgive Me; I Could Be Good; Poor Dear Girl
70 performances

*THE VICAR OF SOHO*
Music by Tony Russell; additional music by Iwan Williams; book and lyrics by Stuart Douglass
Gardner Centre, Brighton, 2 August 1972
*PC:* George Benson, James Bolam, Anna Barry, Cristina Avery, Sammie Winmill
*MN:* Hymn: I Heard the Voice of Jesus; Call It a Trade; There's a New World Coming; God Made the Little Red Apple; Zambuk; Excuse Me, Dear; Strike!; London Is a Cruel Town; Give Me a Little Man; A Normal Point of View; Oratorio: The Trial; Glebe Fruits; Mr. Blackpool; Everyone's the Same Beneath the Cloth; I Am Much Older; I Am Much Wiser; Change It; Entertain Us; Daniel
Season

## VIRTUE IN DANGER

Music by James Bernard; lyrics and book by Paul Dehn, based on the play *The Relapse* by John Vanbrugh

Mermaid Theatre, 10 April 1963, transferred to Strand Theatre, 3 June 1963

*PC:* John Moffatt, Patricia Routledge, Barrie Ingham, Jane Wenham, Richard Wordsworth, Lewis Fiander, Gwen Nelson, Alan Howard

*MN:* Don't Call Me Sir!; Fortune Thou Art a Bitch!; Stand Back, Old Sodom!; I'm In Love With My Husband; Hurry Surgeon!; Let's Fall Together; Hoyden Hath Charms; Nurse, Nurse, Nurse!; Why Do I Feel What I Feel?; Fire a Salute!; Put Him In the Dog House; Wait a Little Longer, Lover; O Take This Ancient Mansion; Say the Word; I Shall Have To Cuckold Someone

121 performances

## VOYEURZ

Music, book and lyrics by Michael Lewis and Peter Rafelson

Whitehall Theatre, 22 July 1996

*PC:* Fem 2 Fem [L.D. (sic), Chris Minna, Lala Hamparsomian, Christine Salata]; Sally Anne Marsh, Krysten Cummings, Natasha Kristie

*MN:* Introduction; Dreamtime; Come To Me; Sin; Reflections; Sex On a Train; Out In Style; The Hole; Xtropia; Swing; Kinda Slow Now; Insatiable; Go For the Kill; Cruel and Unusual; Until the Dawn; Tantric Trance (Animus); I'd Die For You; Stand Back; Dark Dance; I'm So Sorry; Compulsive Jane; Evil; Worship

64 performances

## THE WATER BABIES

Music, book and lyrics by John Taylor, adapted from Charles Kingsley's novel

Royalty Theatre, 24 July 1973

*PC:* Jessie Matthews, Hope Jackman, Richard Willis, David Morton, Eleanor McCready, Yvonne Marsh

*MN:* Come Read Me My Riddle; Chimneys! Chimneys!; My Name Is Tom; I'm Grimes; Harthover Hall; There's Nobody Like Her; After Him!; I've Never Been So Far From Town Before; Song of the Stream; Poor Tom; I've Never Been a Water Babe Before; The Wibble-Wobble Walk; Have You Seen the Water Babies?; The Water Babies; Mrs Doasyouwouldbedoneby; I Like To Cuddle Little Babies; The Doasyoulikes; The Other-End-of-Nowhere; The Way To the Shiny Wall; The Underwater Glide; When All the World Is Young; There's Hope

67 performances [matinees only]

## THE WAYWARD WAY

Music by Lorne Huycke; lyrics by Bill Howe; based on the play *The Drunkard* by W. H. Smith and 'A Gentleman'

Vaudeville Theatre, 27 January 1965

*PC:* Jim Dale, Cheryl Kennedy, David Holliday, John Gower, Roberta D'Esti, Stella Courtney
*MN:* Haven That Is Graven On My Heart; It's Old To Some But New To Me; Oh Sweet Revenge; Nobody's Making Sense; Everybody On Earth Loves a Wedding; Molly; Brotherhood; Goodbye For Good; A Curlicue; He's Wayward In a Way; The Foul D. T.'s; Every Soul You Save
36 performances

*WHICH WITCH?*
Music by Benedicte Adrian and Ingrid Bjørnov; lyrics by Kit Hesketh-Harvey; book by Piers Haggard, based on an original manuscript by Ole A Sørli
Piccadilly Theatre, 22 October 1992
*PC:* Graham Bickley, Vivien Parry, Benedicte Adrian, Gay Soper, Billy Hartman, Stig Rossen, Leo Andrew, Jahn Teigen
*MN:* Malleus Maleficarum [The Hammer of Witches]; The Marriage Contract; Confession; The Blessing; Scandal; You Are My Love; True Believers; Yours; Bad Omens; Daniel's Prayer; Spin the Wheel; Love Me, Love Me Not; Bad Omens II; Spectral Evidence; The Ducking; Maria's Curse; If This Should Fail; Midsummer Night; Eternally; Black Mass; The Witches; Queen of Dark; The Invocation; How Do You Feel?; Possessed; The Executioner; Daniel Do Not Die; Little Witch; Cardinal Gonzaga; The Exorcism; 2,665,866,746,664 Little Devils; Gertrude's Arrest; She Devil; Testimony; She's Guilty; The End; Rescue; Almighty God; Reunion; Burn the Witches; Hallelujah
70 performances

*WILDEST DREAMS*
Music by Julian Slade; lyrics and book by Dorothy Reynolds and Julian Slade
Vaudeville Theatre, 3 August 1961
*PC:* Dorothy Reynolds, Angus Mackay, Anna Dawson, John Baddeley, Edward Hardwicke
*MN:* Nelderham; Mrs. Birdview's Minuet; Please Aunt Harriet; Till Now; Girl On the Hill [reprised as 'Man On the Hill']; Zoom, Zoom, Zoom; Here Am I; Wildest Dreams; Red Or White; You Can't Take Any Luggage; A Man's Room; I'm Holding My Breath; Quite Something; Green; Oxblood Hill; There's a Place We Know; When You're Not There; This Man Loves You
76 performances

*WILD, WILD WOMEN*
Music by Nola York; book and lyrics by Michael Richmond
Astoria Theatre, 15 June 1982
*PC:* Susannah Fellows, Steve Devereaux, Gordon Reid, Lesley Joseph, Mark Barratt
*MN:* Aggroville; Peaceable Haven; Lucky For Lovers; The Earps; A Man Alone; Bundle of Joy; Wild, Wild Women; The Vow; Dancin' Backwards; Ooh La La

Love; The Stars Already Know; Full o' Love; Madame de Pompadour; The Ballad of Romeo and Juliet; Seventeen and a Bit
29 performances

*WINDY CITY*
Music by Tony Macaulay; book and lyrics by Dick Vosburgh, based on *The Front Page* by Ben Hecht and Charles MacArthur
Victoria Palace, 20 July 1982
*PC:* Dennis Waterman, Anton Rodgers, Diane Langton, Amanda Redman, Victor Spinetti, Robert Longden
*MN:* Hey, Hallelujah!; Wait 'Til I Get You On Your Own; Waltz For Mollie; Saturday; Long Night Again Tonight; No One Walks Out On Me; Windy City; Round In Circles; I Can Just Imagine It; I Can Talk To You; Perfect Casting; Bensinger's Poem; Circles Round Us; Water Under the Bridge
250 performances

*WINNIE*
Music by Cyril Ornadel; lyrics by Arnold Sundgaard; book by Robin Hardy
Victoria Palace, 21 May 1988
*PC:* Robert Hardy, Virginia McKenna, Lesley Duff, Toni Palmer, Frank Thornton, Charles West
*MN:* The Colonel's Complaint; Winnie; Did You Call Me, Darling?; In Distant Tomorrows
63 performances

*WOLF BOY*
Music and lyrics by Leon Parris; book by Russell Labey, based on the play *Love and Human Remains* by Brad Fraser
Trafalgar Studios, 8 July 2010
*PC:* Paul Holowaty, Daniel Boys, Emma Rigby, Gregg Lowe, Annabel Howitt
*MN:* No musical numbers listed in theatre programme. A published recording of the score has four tracks: The Visit; One Wall Away From Your Dreams; 1 Seven, 2 Jacks and an Ace; Come Home
31 performances

*WREN*
Music by David Adams and Chuck Mallett; lyrics and book by David Adams
May Fair Theatre, 25 June 1978
*PC:* Steven Grives, Richard Tate, Donna Donovan
*MN:* In Praise of Man; Will You Build a Little Church For Me?; Turn Ye To Me; Invention; Saints and Soldiers; Wit; A Country To Love; Monarchy Madness; The Corn Hop Dance; As I Make Love To Thee; Love For All; I Will Arise; Keep a Watch On My Heart; Out of Our Minds; Dreaming Spires
34 performances [Sundays only]

*THE YOUNG VISITERS*

Music by Ian Kellam; lyrics and book by Michael Ashton, based on the novel by
   Daisy Ashford; additional songs* by Richard Kerr and Joan Maitland
Piccadilly Theatre, 23 December 1968
*PC:* Alfred Marks, Jan Waters, Anna Sharkey, Vivienne Ross, Frank Thornton,
   Barry Justice
*MN:* Daisy Ashford's Written a Book; Prettiest In the Face; If I Can Wait; You'll
   Be Mine*; First and Last Love; Rickamere Hall; My Young Visiters and Me;
   Near You*; That's What a Visiter's For; An English Gentleman; Twice the Man;
   Crystal Palace; Belted Earl; Quite a Young Earl; What Does a Gentleman Ware?;
   Up the Ladder*; The Girl I Was; I'm Not Beautiful; She Is Me; I Will Keep My
   Righteous Anger Down; Better For Marrying You; In Love With the Girl I See
63 performances

# Notes to the Text

*Preface and Acknowledgements, pages xi–xx*
1  Lionel Bart in conversation with John Cunningham, *Guardian*, 16 May 1977.
2  *Daily Mail*, 2 July 1960.
3  *Evening Standard*, 17 January 1964.
4  *Daily Mail*, 2 July 1960.
5  Philip Hope-Wallace, *Guardian*, 4 July 1960.
6  Robert Muller, *Daily Mail*, 1 July 1960.
7  *Tatler and Bystander*, 27 July 1960.
8  Like *Oh! My Papa!*, Julian Slade and Dorothy Reynolds's *Salad Days* had been transferred into London from the Bristol Old Vic.
9  Extracts from Ronald Barker's review of *The Ghost Train* in *Plays and Players*, February 1955, p. 20.
10 *Sunday Telegraph*, 24 October 2004.

*1960, pages 1–20*
1  'Song of the Underprivileged' from *England, Our England*, produced at the Princes Theatre, 7 May 1962. It flopped. The music was by Dudley Moore.
2  Peter Roberts, *Plays and Players*, March 1960, p. 13.
3  Alan Pryce-Jones, *Observer*, 31 January 1960.
4  *The Times*, 28 January 1960.
5  Frances Stephens, *Theatre World*, March 1960, p. 6.
6  *Daily Mail*, 16 March 1960.
7  *Observer*, 20 March 1960.
8  Audrey Williamson and Charles Landstone, *The Bristol Old Vic: The First Ten Years* (J. Garnett Miller, 1957), pp. 117–18.
9  *Sunday Dispatch*, 20 March 1960.
10 *Tatler*, April 1960.
11 Robert Muller, *Daily Mail*, 18 March 1960.
12 Robert Muller, *Daily Mail*, 20 April 1960.
13 Irving Wardle, *The Times*, 20 April 1960.
14 Milton Shulman, *Evening Standard*, 20 April 1960.
15 Bernard Levin, *Daily Express*, 6 May 1960.
16 Robert Muller, *Daily Mail*, 6 May 1960.
17 *Sunday Dispatch*, 8 May 1960.
18 *The Times*, 6 May 1960.
19 *Guardian*, 6 May 1960.
20 Bill Lester, *Plays and Players*, June 1960, p. 17.
21 Peter Jackson, *Plays and Players*, August 1960, pp. 17–18.
22 Miss Laffan's role in the 1954 bargain-basement Danziger brothers' movie *Devil Girl from Mars* alone ensures that she will never be forgotten.
23 Lisa Gordon Smith, *Plays and Players*, August 1960, p. 31.
24 Robert Muller, *Daily Mail*, 15 July 1960.

25  Kenneth Tynan, *Observer*, 17 July 1960.
26  *The Times*, 15 July 1960.
27  Theatre programme for *The Princess*.
28  Robert Muller, *Daily Mail*, 24 August 1960.
29  Peter Roberts, *Plays and Players*, October 1960, p. 13.
30  *Daily Telegraph*, 7 October 1960.
31  *Evening Standard*, 7 October 1960.
32  *Daily Mail*, 7 October 1960.
33  *The Times*, 7 October 1960.
34  Bill Lester, *Plays and Players*, November 1960, p. 17.
35  Lisa Gordon Smith, *Plays and Players*, February 1961, p. 33.
36  *Stage*, 29 December 1960.
37  Peter Lewis, *Daily Mail*, 21 December 1960.
38  *Daily Telegraph*, 21 December 1960.

*1961–1964, pages 21–39*
1   Sir Melville Macnaghten, *Days of My Years* (Edward Arnold, 1914).
2   In conversation with the author.
3   *Daily Express*, 5 May 1961.
4   J. W. Lambert, *Sunday Times*.
5   *Daily Express*, 5 May 1961.
6   Robert Muller, *Daily Mail*, 5 May 1961.
7   *Daily Telegraph*.
8   Caryl Brahms, 'Go To Belle!', *Plays and Players*, June 1961, p. 11.
9   Philip Hope-Wallace, *Guardian*, 4 August 1961.
10  Ibid.
11  Anthony Cookman, *Tatler*, September 1961.
12  David Pryce-Jones, *Financial Times*, 9 March 1962.
13  The now-forgotten *Carissima*, a Venetian romance with book and lyrics by Eric
    Maschwitz and music by Hans May, had run for over a year at the Palace Theatre
    in 1948.
14  Set to the music of Dvořák, Eric Maschwitz's *Summer Song* played for 148 perfor-
    mances at the Princes Theatre in 1956.
15  Letter from Hugh Hastings to author.
16  Ibid.
17  *Queen*, April 1962.
18  Irving Wardle, *The Times*, 9 March 1962.
19  Anthony Cookman, *Tatler*, April 1962.
20  Robert Muller, *Daily Mail*, 9 March 1962.
21  *Not To Worry*, a revue written exclusively by Stanley Daniels, played for 20 perfor-
    mances at the Garrick Theatre from 22 February 1962. Its principal players were
    Alec McCowen and Prunella Scales.
22  Bernard Levin, *Daily Express*, 9 March 1962.
23  David Pryce-Jones, *Financial Times*, 9 March 1962.
24  Gerard Fray, *Guardian*, 28 November 1962.
25  *The Times*, 28 November 1962.
26  Bernard Levin, *Daily Express*, 28 November 1962.
27  *Gramophone*, July 1963.
28  *The Times*, 11 April 1963.
29  W. A. Darlington, *Daily Telegraph*, 11 April 1963.

30  *The Times*, 4 July 1963.
31  Milton Shulman, *Evening News*, 4 July 1963.
32  *Theatre World*, August 1963, p. 10.
33  *Illustrated London News*, August 1963.
34  Peter Lewis, *Daily Mail*, 4 July 1963.
35  Jeremy Rundall, *Plays and Players*, September 1963, p. 47.
36  *Theatre World*, August 1957, p. 5.
37  John Percival, *Plays and Players*, December 1963, p. 43.
38  B. A. Young, *Punch*, 9 October 1963.
39  Maureen Cleave, *Evening Standard*, 4 July 1963.
40  Gordon Langford in conversation with the author.
41  Hugh Leonard, *Plays and Players*, January 1964, p. 42.
42  Ibid.
43  In fact, written by composer Joseph Tunbridge and librettist Jack Waller.
44  *Evening Standard*, 23 December 1964.
45  *The Times*, 23 December 1964.
46  Philip Hope-Wallace, *Guardian*, 23 December 1964.

*1965–1966, pages 40–61*
1   Tod Slaughter, the inimitable actor specializing in moustachioed villains, whose film versions of melodrama remain a timeless delight. Produced by George King, they include *The Face at the Window*, *Maria Marten*, *Sweeney Todd* and *Crimes at the Dark House*, a vastly entertaining adaptation of Wilkie Collins' *The Woman in White*, with Hay Petrie as Count Fosco easily outmatching Michael Crawford's interpretation in Andrew Lloyd Webber's musical version.
2   *Daily Telegraph*, 28 January 1965.
3   *Daily Mail*, 22 February 1965.
4   *The Times*, 2 February 1965.
5   *Stage*, 11 February 1965.
6   *Our Man Crichton* (1964), based on J. M. Barrie's *The Admirable Crichton*, music by Dave Lee, book and lyrics by Herbert Kretzmer, ran for 208 performances at the Shaftesbury Theatre.
7   *Daily Mail*, 3 February 1965.
8   Ibid.
9   Bernard Levin, *Daily Mail*, 2 February 1965.
10  *Illustrated London News*, March 1965.
11  *Theatre World*, August 1965, p. 13.
12  *Queen*, March 1965.
13  Ibid.
14  Hugh Leonard, *Plays and Players*, October 1965, p. 35.
15  *Daily Telegraph*, 25 August 1965.
16  *The Times*, 25 August 1965.
17  *Illustrated London News*, 1 January 1966.
18  *Queen*, January 1966.
19  The most informative information about the making of *Twang!* is Jon Bradshaw's 'Truth About *Twang!!*' in the April and May 1966 issues of *Plays and Players*.
20  Jeremy Kingston, *Punch*, 9 March 1966.
21  Bernard Levin, *Daily Mail*, 2 March 1966.
22  *Queen*, 16 March 1966.
23  *Illustrated London News*, 12 March 1966.

24 *The Times*, 20 April 1966.

25 *Daily Mail*, 17 March 1966.

26 *Daily Mail*, 20 April 1966.

27 *Evening Standard*, 20 April 1966.

28 *Punch*, 27 April 1966.

29 *Illustrated London News*, 22 April 1966.

30 J. Roger Baker, *London Life*, 7 May 1966.

31 *Dearest Dracula* might have done better than *Strike a Light!* but never got to London. John Gower stood in for Bela Lugosi. Mary Millar was one of his singing victims.

32 Note in theatre programme.

33 Carson had understandably fled from Britain, after being trapped in the London show *Love from Judy* that established her as a true British star. Emigrating to America, she made an entertaining TV comedy series, *Hey, Jeannie*, in which she frequently, and totally disarmingly, burst into song.

34 Terry Coleman, *Guardian*, 6 July 1966.

35 *Plays and Players*, December 1966, p. 25.

36 Milton Shulman, *Evening Standard*, 6 July 1966.

37 Peter Roberts, *Plays and Players*, November 1966, p. 13.

38 *The Times*, 23 September 1966.

39 *Sunday Times*, 25 September 1966.

40 *Evening News*, 23 September 1966.

41 *Illustrated London News*, 30 September 1966.

42 *Guardian*, 23 September 1966.

43 *Sunday Express*, 16 October 1966.

44 *Theatre World*, February 1963, p. 42.

45 *The Love Doctor*, taken from Molière, starred Ian Carmichael and Joan Heal at the Piccadilly Theatre, running for 16 performances in 1959.

46 The 1992 British production of *Grand Hotel* at the Dominion Theatre failed to repeat the long-running success of the Broadway original.

47 Richard Findlater, *Grimaldi, King of Clowns* (MacGibbon and Kee, 1955), p. 211.

48 W. A. Darlington, *Daily Telegraph*, 12 October 1966.

49 *Guardian*, 12 October 1966.

50 *Plays and Players*, December 1966, p. 25.

51 *Illustrated London News*, 19 October 1966.

52 *Evening News*, 12 October 1966.

53 *The Magic of Houdini* by Gyles Brandreth and John Morley (Pelham, 1978).

54 *Daily Mail*, 17 November 1966.

55 *Financial Times*, 17 November 1966.

56 *Evening News*, 17 November 1966.

57 W. A. Darlington, *Daily Telegraph*, 17 November 1966.

58 *Financial Times*, 17 November 1966.

*1967–1969, pages 62–80*

1 *Lady*, 29 June 1967.

2 *Guardian*, 23 June 1967.

3 Henry Raynor, *The Times*, 23 June 1967.

4 *Illustrated London News*, 1 July 1967.

5 *Punch*, 28 June 1967.

6 Leslie Halliwell, *Leslie Halliwell's Film Guide*, 6th ed. (Paladin, 1988), p. 237.

7   Philip Hope-Wallace, *Guardian*, 7 June 1968.
8   *Punch*, 12 June 1968.
9   *Sunday Times*, 9 June 1968.
10  Jessie Matthews was originally offered the two roles taken by Hylda Baker in *Mr and Mrs* for £250 a week. She subsequently played Mrs Doasyouwouldbedoneby in John Taylor's musical *The Water Babies*, adapted from Charles Kingsley's novel, at the Royalty Theatre in 1973.
11  Felix Barker, *Evening News*, 12 December 1968.
12  Philip Hope-Wallace, *Guardian*, 12 December 1968.
13  *Sunday Times*, 15 December 1968.
14  Michael Billington, *The Times*, 12 December 1968.
15  Felix Barker, *Evening News*, 12 December 1968.
16  Philip Hope-Wallace, *Guardian*, 12 December 1968.
17  *Daily Telegraph*, 24 December 1968.
18  Jeremy Kingston, *Punch*, 1 January 1968.
19  *The Times*, 24 December 1968.
20  *Illustrated London News*, 29 December 1968.
21  Milton Shulman, *Evening Standard*, 28 February 1969.
22  A reference to the recent Palace production of *The Desert Song*.
23  *The Times*, 28 February 1969. John Martin Harvey first appeared on stage as Sidney Carton in *The Only Way* in 1899; a film version followed in 1927.
24  Philip Hope-Wallace, *Guardian*, 28 February 1969.
25  *Illustrated London News*, 8 March 1969.
26  John Barber, *Daily Telegraph*, 28 February 1969.
27  The 'belles' of *The Bells of St Martin's* (seen at the St Martin's Theatre in 1952) were headed by the unlikely partnership of Douglas Byng and Hattie Jacques.
28  *Star Maker* toured in 1956 but failed to get a London booking. Courtneidge's next, and last, London musical was the unsuccessful *High Spirits* (1964).
29  *Guardian*, 18 April 1969.
30  *Lady*, 24 April 1969.
31  *Illustrated London News*, 26 April 1969.
32  *Daily Express*, 18 April 1969.
33  *Guardian*, 18 April 1969.
34  Cyril Ornadel, *Reach For the Moon: A Portrait of My Life* (Book Guild, 2007), p. 232.
35  Theatre programme for *High Diplomacy*.
36  Peter Roberts, *The Times*, 6 June 1969.
37  *Lady*, 12 June 1969.
38  *Evening Standard*, 6 June 1969.
39  The revue played for 44 performances at the Comedy Theatre in 1964.
40  R. B. Marriott, *Stage*, 26 March 1964.
41  *Daily Mail*, 20 March 1964.
42  *Queen*, 18 June 1969.
43  *Illustrated London News*, 21 June 1969.
44  *Lady*, 19 June 1969.
45  *Guardian*, 13 June 1969.
46  *Daily Telegraph*, 13 June 1969.
47  *Stage*, 5 June 1969.
48  The recent failures at the Palace Theatre since the closure of *The Sound of Music* were the American *110 in the Shade* and *Mr and Mrs*.
49  *Punch*, 19 November 1969.

50 *Daily Telegraph*, 14 November 1969.
51 *Evening Standard*, 14 November 1969.
52 *Tatler*, 19 November 1969.

*1970–1972, pages 81–108*
1 Braham Murray, *The Worst It Can Be Is a Disaster* (Methuen, 2007), p. 105.
2 J. C. Trewin, *Illustrated London News*, 18 April 1970.
3 John Barber, *Daily Telegraph*, 8 April 1970.
4 Philip Hope-Wallace, *Guardian*, 8 April 1970.
5 John Barber, *Daily Telegraph*, 17 April 1970.
6 Philip Hope-Wallace, *Guardian*, 17 April 1970.
7 Ibid.
8 Quotation from the programme note in Helen Wicks' review in *Plays and Players*, April 1960, p. 17.
9 *Guardian*, 27 June 1970.
10 *Daily Telegraph*, 27 May 1970.
11 *Sunday Express*, 31 May 1970.
12 *Daily Mail*, 27 May 1970.
13 *Daily Telegraph*, 27 May 1970.
14 Milton Shulman, *Evening Standard*, 27 May 1970.
15 *Guardian*, 27 May 1970.
16 *All of Me* by Barbara Windsor (Headline, 2000), p. 129.
17 *Guardian*, 15 October 1970.
18 *Sunday Telegraph*, 20 December 1970.
19 *Guardian*, 19 December 1970.
20 *The Times*, 19 December 1970.
21 *Daily Telegraph*, 19 December 1970.
22 *Daily Telegraph*, 17 June 1971.
23 *Guardian*, 17 June 1971.
24 Ibid.
25 *Daily Telegraph*, 18 September 1971.
26 Irving Wardle, *The Times*, 29 September 1971.
27 Felix Barker, *Evening News*, 29 September 1971.
28 *Daily Mirror*, 2 October 1971.
29 Irving Wardle, *The Times*, 20 October 1971.
30 *Tatler*, December 1971.
31 Colin Frame, *Evening News*, 28 March 1972.
32 Michael Billington, *Guardian*, 28 March 1972.
33 Hugh Leonard, *Plays and Players*, June 1972, pp. 28–30.
34 Ibid.
35 J. P. Wearing, *The London Stage 1940–49* (Rowman and Littlefield, 2014), p. 69.
36 John Barber, *Daily Telegraph*, 1 May 1972.
37 Milton Shulman, *Evening Standard*, 1 May 1972.
38 *Tatler*, June 1972.
39 *Plays and Players*, July 1972, p. 55.
40 *Sunday Telegraph*, 14 May 1972.
41 Irving Wardle, *The Times*, 10 May 1972.
42 *Illustrated London News*, July 1972. A revival of *The Maid of the Mountains* with Lynn Kennington as the Maid had opened at the Palace Theatre in April.
43 *Plays and Players*, July 1972, p. 55.

44 Theatre programme for *Tom Brown's Schooldays*.
45 *Daily Mail*, 4 August 1961.
46 *The Times*, 4 August 1961.
47 John Russell Taylor, *Plays and Players*, August 1972, pp. 42–3.
48 Irving Wardle, *The Times*, 19 January 1972.
49 *Tatler*, August 1972.
50 Charles Lewsen, *The Times*, 28 June 1972.
51 *Plays and Players*, September 1972, pp. 47–8.
52 *Evening Standard*, 19 July 1972.
53 *Sunday Telegraph*, 23 July 1972.
54 *Evening News*, 19 July 1972.
55 Gerald Bordman, *Days To Be Happy, Years To Be Sad: The Life and Music of Vincent Youmans* (Oxford University Press, 1982), p. 148.
56 Philip Hope-Wallace, *Guardian*, 6 July 1972.
57 Felix Barker, *Evening News*, 6 July 1972.
58 George Baxt, *Plays and Players*, September 1972, p. 50.
59 Charles Lewsen, *The Times*, 6 July 1972.
60 Eric Johns, *Theatre Review '73* (W. H. Allen, 1974), p. 181.
61 *Plays and Players*, October 1972, p. 48.
62 *Lady*, 7 September 1972.
63 *Daily Telegraph*, 23 August 1972.
64 *Guardian*, 23 August 1972.
65 E. Victor, *Tablet*, 2 September 1972.
66 *Theatre Review '73* (W. H. Allen, 1973), p. 168.
67 Irving Wardle, *The Times*, 25 October 1972.
68 Other misfiring orgies seem to have occurred in *Passion Flower Hotel*, *From Here To Eternity* and *Stephen Ward*.
69 *Evening Standard*, 25 October 1972.
70 John Percival, *Plays and Players*, December 1963, p. 43.
71 *Plays and Players*, December 1972, pp. 48–9.
72 *The Times*, 7 November 1972.
73 *Guardian*, 7 November 1972.
74 *Daily Telegraph*, 7 November 1972.
75 Charles Strouse, *Put On a Happy Face: A Broadway Memoir* (New York: Union Square Press, 2008), p. 200.

*1973–1976, pages 109–128*
1 Charles Lewsen, *The Times*, 22 May 1973.
2 *Guardian*, 22 May 1973.
3 *Reader's Companion to the Twentieth Century Novel*, edited by Peter Parker (QPD, 1994), p. 45.
4 Jack Tinker, *Daily Mail*, 25 July 1973.
5 *Evening Standard*, 25 July 1973.
6 *Sunday Telegraph*, 29 July 1973.
7 John Barber, *Daily Telegraph*, 25 July 1973.
8 *Guardian*, 25 July 1973.
9 Irving Wardle, *The Times*, 26 July 1973.
10 Dominic Cavendish, *Daily Telegraph*, 25 April 2014.
11 Kieran Johnson, *Whatsonstage*, 30 April 2014.
12 Kate Bassett, *The Times*, 25 April 2014.

13  *The World's the Limit* was produced at the Royal Theatre, Windsor, 7 June 1955. On this occasion, More and Gilbert collaborated with Ronnie Hill, and additional dialogue was contributed by Patrick Cargill and Ronnie Wolfe. The cast included Beryl Reid, Patrick Cargill and Peter Graves.

14  Andy Boyle, *Plays and Players*, May 1974, p. 45.

15  *Sunday Telegraph*, 21 April 1974.

16  Irving Wardle, *The Times*, 19 April 1974.

17  *Sunday Times*, 21 April 1974.

18  Richard O'Keefe, *Plays and Players*, November 1974, p. 32.

19  John Barber, *Daily Telegraph*, 18 September 1974.

20  *Opera*, 19 March 1965, p. 19.

21  John Barber, *Daily Telegraph*, 18 September 1974.

22  *Over 21*, December 1974.

23  Gibbons' novel was in effect a satire on Mary Webb's novel *Precious Bane. Something Nasty In the Woodshed* had a book by its director Adrian Rendle, music by Nick Transem and lyrics by Irving Manley. Its leading players included Philip Gilbert, Bernard Lloyd, Jennifer Jayne and Rosemary Nicols. It had a prescribed run at Stratford East from 18 October 1965. Hugh Leonard considered it 'a hideously tuneless show' (*Plays and Players*, December 1965, p. 41).

24  A musical that seemed content to exist at the most basic level, greatly to the taste of the British public who kept it going for 366 performances. One of the most basic scores of the period, the music was by Laurie Holloway, with book and lyrics by the Joan Littlewood 'nut' Bob Grant.

25  Tom Sutcliffe, 'Wooster Sauce', *Guardian*, 22 April 1975.

26  Irving Wardle, *The Times*, 23 April 1975.

27  *State of Emergency*, a musical by Adam Fergusson and others, originally played at the Civic Theatre, Ayr in1960. It was subsequently presented at the Pembroke Theatre, Croydon, with a company that included Aldridge, Millicent Martin, Madeleine Christie, Roberta D'Esti, Kevin Scott and Martin Dell, but there was no West End transfer.

28  *Keep Your Hair On* had a dismal reception when it opened at the Apollo Theatre in February 1958. Book and lyrics were by John Cranko, with music by John Addison. Its three female leads were Marsden, Barbara Windsor and Rachel Roberts. *Theatre World* (March 1958, p. 9) was unimpressed by 'this rather tasteless trifle', with its central romance 'singularly depressing', a chorus 'hideously garbed and bewigged' and choreography by Cranko that was 'never more than mediocre'. It thought Marsden ('superb technique and vitality') the one bright spot of the evening.

29  Vivian Ellis, letter to *Daily Telegraph*, 7 May 1975.

30  Jack Tinker, *Daily Mail*, 23 April 1975.

31  J. C. Trewin, *Birmingham Post*, 24 April 1975.

32  Michael Billington, *Guardian*, 23 April 1975.

33  Milton Shulman, *Evening Standard*, 23 April 1975.

34  Gary O'Connor, *Financial Times*, 24 September 1975.

35  Milton Shulman, *Evening Standard*, 24 September 1975.

36  *The Times*, 25 September 1975.

37  *Daily Telegraph*, 17 October 1975.

38  Nicholas de Jongh, *Guardian*, 17 October 1975.

39  *Daily Telegraph*, 19 June 1976.

40  *Guardian*, 17 October 1975.

41  *Observer*, 19 October 1975.

42  *Sunday Telegraph*, 19 October 1975.
43  *The Times*, 17 October 1975.
44  Sheridan Morley, *Punch*, 11 February 1976.
45  Felix Barker, *Evening News*, 4 February 1976.
46  John Barber, *Daily Telegraph*, 4 February 1976.
47  Felix Barker, *Evening News*, 4 February 1976.
48  Harold Hobson, *Sunday Times*, 21 March 1976.
49  J. C. Trewin, *Birmingham Post*, 22 March 1976.
50  *Sunday Telegraph*, 21 March 1976.
51  *Observer*, 21 March 1976.
52  Milton Shulman, *Evening Standard*, 19 March 1976.
53  *Daily Express*, 30 February 1976.
54  *Sadie Thompson*, book by Howard Dietz and Rouben Mamoulian; lyrics by Howard Dietz; music by Vernon Duke. June Havoc played the prostitute Sadie. There were 60 performances.
55  *The Moon and Sixpence*, with music by John Gardner, played 9 performances at Sadler's Wells. Critical enthusiasm was muted.
56  *Guardian*, 9 June 1976.
57  *Punch*, 16 June 1976.
58  *Evening Standard*, 9 June 1976.
59  *Sunday Telegraph*, 13 June 1976.
60  John Barber, *Daily Telegraph*, 9 June 1976.

*1977–1979, pages 129–144*
1  Michael Billington, *Guardian*, 17 May 1977.
2  *Sunday Telegraph*, 22 May 1977.
3  B. A. Young, *Financial Times*, 17 May 1977.
4  Opening December 1958, the London run of *West Side Story* (1,039) out-ran the original 1957 Broadway run of 734 performances.
5  The first London visit of *The Boys from Syracuse* didn't receive a warm welcome at Drury Lane when it opened in November 1963, closing after a meagre 100 showings, despite the superb Rodgers and Hart songs and a sterling cast that included Bob Monkhouse, Ronnie Corbett, one of Australia's happiest exports Maggie Fitzgibbon, the glorious Lynn Kennington (the magnificent 'Maid of the Mountains' in 1971) and Denis Quilley.
6  *Two Gentlemen of Verona* (New York, 1971) was a Broadway success in 1971. The British production opened in London April 1973 for a run of 237 performances, with the much-employed Ray C. Davis as Proteus and Samuel E. Wright as Valentine. *Swingin' the Dream* was a Broadway-only 13-performance disaster in New York in 1939. Its music was by Jimmy Van Heusen, with choreography by Agnes de Mille.
7  Seen at the Roundhouse in 1970.
8  *Your Own Thing* had an epic run off-Broadway, but failed to please London when it opened in February 1969, closing after 42 performances.
9  The strong cast included Eric Flynn, Joan Sims and Colette Gleeson.
10  'The greatest comedy with the greatest music' promised the flyer for this follow-up to Gyles Brandreth's revue *Zipp!* Unlike its predecessor, *Five Go To Illyria* didn't go to London.
11  Just qualifying as a failure, *The Kid from Stratford* ran for 235 performances in London, beginning 30 September 1948. The music was by the now largely forgotten

Manning Sherwin and Joseph Tunbridge. An amusing libretto from Basil Thomas and Barbara Gordon concerned the discovery of a musical comedy, *I'm Telling Thee*, written by Shakespeare. *Theatre World* (November, 1948, p. 8) noted a score 'lacking in catchy tunes', thinking it 'a great pity that a show of such undoubted possibility should depend so entirely for its success upon the personality of its – admittedly irresistible – star'.

12 Was *No Bed for Bacon* one of the worst titles ever? Two well-cast provincial productions were staged in 1959 and 1963, but it never looked like a winner. The music was by Malcolm Williamson.

13 Braham Murray, *The Worst It Can Be Is a Disaster: The Life Story of Braham Murray and the Royal Exchange Theatre* (Methuen, 2007), p. 154.

14 *Sunday Telegraph*, 27 March 1977.

15 *Punch*, 13 April 1977.

16 *Punch*, 14 September 1977.

17 *Daily Telegraph*, 31 August 1977.

18 *Evening Standard*, 31 August 1977.

19 *Sunday Times*, 4 September 1977.

20 *Daily Telegraph*, 9 November 1977.

21 Irving Wardle, *The Times*, 13 October 1977.

22 *Evening News*, 13 October 1977.

23 *Observer*, 16 October 1977.

24 *Punch*, 19 October 1977.

25 *The Times*, 13 October 1977.

26 *Sunday Times*, 16 October 1977.

27 Irving Wardle, *The Times*, 8 December 1977.

28 *Illustrated London News*, February 1978.

29 J. W. Lambert, 'London Theatre', *International Theatre Annual*, edited by Harold Hobson (John Calder, 1958), p. 30.

30 A genuinely original musical, *Stop the World – I Want To Get Off* starred Anthony Newley and Anna Quayle in a circus-bound allegory of the ordinary man's humdrum life. The strange mix of drama, song and mime may not have been to everyone's taste, but the songs, rare for a British musical, became popular outside the show. A London run of 485 performances from July 1961 was trumped by the Broadway transfer (with its two British stars) of 555. Warner's 1966 movie version replaced them with Newley's understudy Tony Tanner and Millicent Martin. It successfully enervated the stage production.

31 *The Roar of the Greasepaint – The Smell of the Crowd* toured Britain in 1964 with Norman Wisdom (goodie) as Cocky, playing opposite the baddie of Willoughby Goddard's Sir. The tour didn't make it to London, but the show was remounted on Broadway the following year, with Newley as Cocky and Cyril Ritchard as Sir. Sally Smith as Kid was retained from the London production. Wisdom must have been worth seeing, having impressed the London critics as Charley Wykeham in the 1958 *Where's Charley*. Wisdom hadn't long to wait for his moment of Broadway musical fame in the 1966 *Walking Happy*, an agreeable musical version of *Hobson's Choice* that might have fared better in London.

32 For the 1972 *The Good Old Bad Old Days* Newley repeated his Littlechap/Cocky persona for a London run of 309 performances, but the Bricusse–Newley well was beginning to run dry.

33 Hilton could hardly be expected to approve Roland Starke's book and Bricusse's music that had turned his novel into a piece with song titles that included 'A Day

Has a Hundred Pockets' [really?] and 'Fill the World With Love'.

34  Irving Wardle, *The Times*, 2 March 1978.
35  A late musical collaboration between Richard Rodgers, book writer Sherman Yellen and lyricist Sheldon Harnick, *Rex* had a brief run on Broadway in 1976.
36  John Barber, *Daily Telegraph*, 2 March 1978.
37  Milton Shulman, *Evening Standard*, 2 March 1978.
38  Steve Grant, *Plays and Players*, May 1978, pp. 22–3.
39  *Sunday Telegraph*, 4 June 1978.
40  The Broadway-only *Sugar*, an adaptation of Billy Wilder's film *Some Like It Hot*, was a substantial hit of 1972. A 1992 London production starring Tommy Steele reverted to the film's title, but closed after three months.
41  The great Shirley Booth's last Broadway musical, following *A Tree Grows in Brooklyn*, *By the Beautiful Sea* and *Juno*, the 1970 *Look To the Lilies* had a fabulous title song with Sammy Cahn lyrics, and only 25 performances.
42  *Daily Telegraph*, 25 August 2006.
43  *Guardian*, 22 May 2003.
44  B. A. Young, *Financial Times*, 1 November 1978.
45  Robert Cushman, *Observer*, 5 November 1978.
46  John Barber, *Daily Telegraph*, 1 November 1978.
47  *Daily Telegraph*, 20 December 1978.
48  Milton Shulman, *Evening Standard*, 20 December 1978.
49  B. A. Young, *Financial Times*, 20 December 1978.
50  In 1972, Vosburgh provided the book for *Liberty Ranch*, a musical based on Goldsmith's *She Stoops To Conquer*, with 'concept' and lyrics by Caryl Brahms and Ned Sherrin, and music by John Cameron. Directed by Gillian Lynne, it had a brief run at Greenwich.
51  At the Gielgud Theatre, with Caroline O'Connor and Mark Adams in the leads. The two musicals were 'The Little Comedy' and 'Summer Share', librettist Barry Harman and composer Keith Herrmann.
52  Yearning for an off-Broadway location in London, *The Great American Backstage Musical*, 'an epic for six performers', successfully hid itself at the Regent Theatre in Upper Regent Street. Bill Solly and Donald Ward's diverting piece had a superb company in Judith Bruce, Martin Smith, Larry Dann, Brian Protheroe, Marti Webb and American Bess Motter. Despite far from negligible reviews (for the *Sunday Telegraph* its lyrics had 'more elegance than those for *Evita*', its music 'more bite than that for [the American] *Annie*'), the show was a quick flop.
53  Nicholas de Jongh, *Guardian*, 30 March 1979.

*1980–1983, pages 145–166*
1  Clive Hirschhorn, *Sunday Express*, 25 May 1980.
2  J. C. Trewin, *Lady*, 12 June 1980.
3  *Punch*, 18 June 1980.
4  B. A. Young, *Financial Times*, 23 May 1980.
5  David Gordon, *Gazette*, 27 June 1980.
6  Originally produced at Cambridge Arts Theatre in July 1986, *Now We Are Sixty* featured Aled Jones as Christopher (Robin). Slade wrote music for six Milne lyrics: You Ask For a Poem; Is It Raining?; There Comes a Day; Reverie; The Guides' Anthem. The rest of the music was by Fraser-Simson. The result was unsatisfactory.
7  *Observer*, 28 September 1980.

8   *Punch*, 8 October 1980.
9   Ibid.
10  *Sunday Times*, 28 September 1980.
11  The 1995 London production of *Mack and Mabel* starring Howard McGillin and Caroline O'Connor managed a decent run of 270 performances, against the 66 performances of the original Broadway production of 1974.
12  Unattributed newspaper clipping in Jane Hardy's scrapbook for *The Biograph Girl*.
13  Wendy Trewin, *Lady*, 22 November 1980.
14  Michael Billington, *Guardian*, 20 November 1980.
15  Milton Shulman, *Evening Standard*, 20 November 1980.
16  Francis King, *Sunday Telegraph*, 12 July 1981.
17  *Country Life*, 23 July 1981.
18  Clive Hirschhorn, *Sunday Express*, 26 July 1981.
19  Sheridan Morley, *Punch*, 29 July 1981.
20  *Daily Mail*, 22 July 1981.
21  *Evening Chronicle*, 22 July 1981.
22  Waldemar Januszczak, *Guardian*, 23 July 1981.
23  *Lady*, 6 August 1981.
24  *Financial Times*, 9 October 1981.
25  Ned Chaillet, *The Times*, 9 October 1981.
26  *Lady*, 29 October 1981.
27  Robert Hewison, *Sunday Times*, 26 July 1981.
28  *Punch*, 29 July 1981.
29  Ian Stewart, *Country Life*, 13 August 1981.
30  Antony Thorncroft, *Financial Times*, 17 June 1982.
31  *Sunday Telegraph*, 20 June 1982.
32  *Punch*, 23 June 1982.
33  Presented at Stratford East for 68 performances in 1973, *Is Your Doctor Really Necessary?* had an excellent cast including Maxwell Shaw, Brian Murphy, Diane Langton (the Molly of *Windy City*), Toni Palmer, Larry Dann and Avis Bunnage as the Minister of Health.
34  Ian Armit also provided music for the 1974 *Gentlemen Prefer Anything*, produced at Stratford East for 34 performances.
35  Sheridan Morley, *Punch*, 28 July 1982.
36  *Daily Telegraph*, 21 July 1982.
37  *Daily Express*, 21 July 1982.
38  Michael Billington, *Guardian*, 21 July 1982.
39  *New Statesman*, undated cutting at Theatre and Performance Collections, Victoria and Albert Museum.
40  *Financial Times*, 29 September 1982.
41  *Evening Standard*, 29 September 1982.
42  *Daily Telegraph*, 29 September 1982.
43  *Punch*, 13 October 1982.
44  *The Times*, 29 September 1982.
45  This fascinating adaptation, following on where Ibsen's play ended, was a 5-performance flop in New York in 1982. With book and lyrics by Betty Comden and Adolph Green (unusually involved in a darker subject than in their other works), *A Doll's Life* had music by Larry Grossman, whose distinctive scores included *Minnie's Boys*, *Snoopy!!!* and *Grind*.
46  Ned Sherrin, *Plays and Players*, May 1983, p. 28.

47 Milton Shulman, *Evening Standard*, 3 August 1983.
48 *Daily Telegraph*, 3 August 1983.
49 *Guardian*, 3 August 1983.
50 *Punch*, 7 September 1983.
51 *Financial Times*, 9 November 1983.
52 Irving Wardle, *The Times*, 10 November 1983.
53 *Sunday Telegraph*, 13 November 1983.
54 *Sunday Times*, 13 November 1983.
55 *Financial Times*, 9 November 1983.
56 Michael Coveney, *Financial Times*, 2 December 1983.
57 James Fenton, *Sunday Times*, 4 December 1983.
58 Bernard Levin, 'The Iceberg That Snowballed', *The Times*, 4 April 1984.
59 *Evening Standard*, 25 November 1983.
60 *Times Literary Supplement*, 23 December 1983.
61 *Daily Mail*, 23 November 1983.
62 John Barber, *Daily Telegraph*, 23 November 1983.
63 Martin Hoyle, *Financial Times*, 22 December 1983.

*1984–1989, pages 167–182*
1 Martin Hoyle, *Financial Times*, 19 October 1984.
2 *Sunday Times*, 21 October 1984.
3 *Evening Standard*, 18 October 1984.
4 *The Mitford Girls* musicalised the story of the Mitford sisters. Seen in London in 1981, its book and lyrics were by Caryl Brahms and Ned Sherrin, with music by Peter Greenwell supplementing existing numbers.
5 *Peg* 'A Romantic Brochure', Message from the Producer.
6 Brian Masters, *Evening Standard*, 17 April 1984.
7 Martin Hoyle, *Financial Times*, 13 April 1984.
8 *Sunday Telegraph*, 15 April 1984.
9 The little-remembered Bacon's *She Smiled at Me* managed only 4 performances at the St Martin's Theatre in February 1956. An adaptation of T. W. Robertson's play *Caste*, it gave audiences the rare opportunity to see Jean Kent (her only other West End musical, *Marigold*, was another failure), Peter Byrne (best remembered as Andy Crawford in the BBC's *Dixon of Dock Green*) and Hugh Paddick, in musical theatre.
10 The cast of *Half in Earnest* also included Bryan Johnson as Algernon Moncrieff, Brian Reece as John Worthing, and Stephanie Voss as Cecily Cardew.
11 *Financial Times*, 2 June 1984.
12 *The Times*, 2 June 1984.
13 *Daily Mail*, 11 June 1954. *After the Ball* had its problems: a once magnificently voiced leading lady whose voice had gone (Mary Ellis), another leading lady (Vanessa Lee) whose role had been sidelined by Coward in favour of Mrs Erlynne, a musical director that Coward sacked (Norman Hackforth), and a score drastically cut because of Ellis's inability to sing it. The pairing of Wilde and Coward didn't help either.
14 Michael Coveney, *Financial Times*, 1 November 1984.
15 Anthony Masters, *The Times*, 1 November 1984.
16 John Barber, *Daily Telegraph*, 2 November 1984.
17 *Financial Times*, 11 July 1986.
18 Jack Tinker, *Daily Mail*, 3 July 1986.

19 Miles Kington, *The Times*, 7 August 1986.

20 Valerie Grove, *Evening Standard*, 19 January 1987. The original collaboration had involved Geoffrey Wright as composer.

21 Nicholas de Jongh, *Guardian*, 19 January 1987.

22 *Listen To the Wind* – Vivian Ellis wrote both music and lyrics for this 1954 musical for and from the nursery. Its very particular soundscape is something quite rare in British musical theatre. The book was by Angela Ainley Jeans. The songs, including 'Timothy's Under the Table', 'When I Grow Up', and 'Whistle Down the Chimney', are perfect examples of Ellis's mix of simplicity and sophistication.

23 *Independent*, 19 January 1987.

24 Jeremy Kingston, *The Times*, 9 April 1987.

25 Martin Hoyle, *Financial Times*, 9 April 1987.

26 *Evening Standard*, 19 October 1987.

27 *Independent*, 19 October 1987.

28 Michael Coveney, *Financial Times*, 19 October 1987.

29 Jack Tinker, *Daily Mail*, 19 October 1987.

30 Milton Shulman, *Evening Standard*, 10 March 1988.

31 *Daily Telegraph*, 15 March 1988.

32 *Observer*, 13 March 1988.

33 Mark Steyn, *Independent*, 11 March 1988.

34 Francis King, *Sunday Telegraph*, 24 July 1988.

35 Ibid.

36 Martin Hoyle, *Financial Times*, 1 June 1988.

37 Mark Steyn, *Independent*, 21 July 1988.

38 W. F. Deedes, *Daily Telegraph*, 21 July 1988.

39 Michael Coveney, *Financial Times*, 19 October 1988.

40 Mark Steyn, *Independent*, 20 October 1988.

41 Michael Billington, *Guardian*, 19 October 1988.

42 *City Limits*, undated newspaper clipping.

43 Peter Holland, *Times Literary Supplement*, 17 March 1989.

44 *Time*, 18 March 1989.

45 Ornadel's comments on *Sherlock Holmes* are taken from his autobiography, *Reach for the Moon* (Book Guild Publishing, 2007). Ornadel's detailed recollections, and informative listings, give interesting insights into several London musicals, including *Wish You Were Here* and *Ann Veronica*.

46 *Independent*, 26 April 1989.

47 *Guardian*, 26 April 1989.

48 *Daily Mail*, 25 April 1989.

49 *Daily Telegraph*, 25 April 1989.

50 Charles Spencer, *Daily Telegraph*, 25 April 1989.

51 Martin Hoyle, *Financial Times*, 25 April 1989.

52 Mark Steyn, *Independent*, 26 April 1989.

*1990–1999, pages 183–00*

1 Milton Shulman, *Evening Standard*, 23 March 1990.

2 Lynn Gardner, *Independent*, 23 March 1990.

3 Milton Shulman, *Evening Standard*, 23 March 1990.

4 Lynn Gardner, *Independent*, 23 March 1990.

Michael Billington, *Guardian*, 24 March 1990.

y Milnes, *Financial Times*, 24 April 1990.

7　*Midweek*, 19 April 1990.

8　*Guardian*, 21 April 1990.

9　Jack Tinker, *Daily Mail*, 8 April 1990.

10　*Daily Telegraph*, 22 June 1990.

11　Theatre programme note for *Bernadette*.

12　Sheridan Morley, *International Herald Tribune*, undated clipping.

13　Milton Shulman, *Evening News*, 23 June 1990.

14　Unidentified newspaper cutting at V & A Theatre Collection.

15　Steven Suskin, *Show Tunes*, 4th ed. (Oxford University Press, 2010).

16　Peter Hepple, *Stage*, 17 January 1991.

17　*Time Out*, 2 January 1991.

18　*Sunday Telegraph*, 13 January 1991.

19　*Time Out*, 11 January 1991.

20　Paul Taylor, *Independent*, 17 April 1991.

21　Jack Tinker, *Daily Mail*, 17 April 1991.

22　Adam Sweeting, *Guardian*, 17 April 1991.

23　Charles Osborne, unidentified newspaper cutting.

24　Michael Coveney, *Observer*, 27 October 1991.

25　*Daily Telegraph*, 25 October 1991.

26　*The Times*, 18 March 1992.

27　Ibid.

28　Chris Bennion, *Daily Telegraph*, 19 October 2016.

29　*Daily Telegraph*, 8 September 1992.

30　Bill Williamson, *Midweek*, 8 October 1992.

31　Paul Taylor, *Independent*, 18 September 1992.

32　Jack Tinker, *Daily Mail*, 23 October 1992.

33　Benedict Nightingale, *The Times*, 24 October 1992.

34　*Nine to Five*, 1 March 1993.

35　*Daily Telegraph*, 5 February 1993.

36　*Evening Standard*, 4 February 1993.

37　Jack Tinker, *Daily Mail*, 4 March 1993.

38　Charles Spencer, *Daily Telegraph*, 5 February 1993.

39　Alastair Macaulay, *Financial Times*, 5 February 1993.

40　*Independent*, 10 March 1993.

41　*Independent*, 3 June 1993.

42　John Peter, *Sunday Times*, 13 June 1993.

43　*The Times*, 4 June 1993.

44　Jane Edwards, *Time Out*, 11 June 1993.

45　Clive Hirschhorn, *Sunday Express*, 25 July 1993.

46　William Cook, *Mail on Sunday*, 25 July 1993.

47　Christopher Tookey, *Daily Mail*, 20 July 1993.

48　*Nine To Five*, 5 December 1994.

49　*Observer*, 27 November 1994.

50　*The Times*, 25 November 1994.

51　*Daily Telegraph*, 25 November 1994.

52　*Daily Mirror*, 24 October 1995.

53　*Daily Express*, 24 October 1995.

54　*Financial Times*, 1 February 1996.

55　*Daily Mail*, 1 February 1996.

56　*The Times*, 2 February 1996.

57  *Evening Standard*, 1 February 1996.
58  Paul Taylor, *Independent*, 2 February 1996.
59  Nicholas de Jongh, *Evening Standard*, 1 February 1996.
60  Charles Spencer, *Daily Telegraph*, 2 February 1996.
61  *aislesay.com*.
62  Alastair Macaulay, *Financial Times*, 22 March 1996.
63  Max Bell, *Evening Standard*, 21 March 1996.
64  Rachel Campbell-Johnston, *The Times*, 24 July 1996.
65  *Sunday Independent*, 15 June 1997.
66  *Midweek*, 26 June 1997.
67  Alastair Macaulay, *Financial Times*, 1 October 1997.
68  *Evening Standard*, 30 September 1997.
69  *Independent*, 4 October 1997.
70  Irving Wardle, *Sunday Telegraph*, 5 October 1997.
71  John Peter, *Sunday Times*, 5 October 1997.
72  Charles Spencer, *Daily Telegraph*, 30 September 1997.
73  Ibid.
74  Irving Wardle, *Sunday Telegraph*, 5 October 1997.
75  Lyn Gardner, *Guardian*, 1 November 1997.
76  Charles Spencer, *Daily Telegraph*, 30 October 1997.
77  *Evening Standard*, 29 October 1997.
78  *London Midweek*, undated clipping.
79  Nick Curtis, *Evening Standard*, 27 March 1998.
80  Benedict Nightingale, *The Times*, 27 March 1998.
81  Veronica Lee, *The Times*, 20 March 1998.
82  Markland Taylor, *Variety*, 8 March 2015.
83  *Pink Paper*, 15 October 1999.
84  *Pink Paper*, 19 November 1999.
85  Susannah Clapp, *Observer*, 14 November 1999.

*2000–2005, pages 207–224*
1  *Financial Times*, 7 April 2000.
2  Ibid.
3  *Sunday Times*, 9 April 2000.
4  *Time Out*, undated clipping.
5  David Benedictus, *Independent*, 7 June 2000.
6  Stephen Fay, *Independent on Sunday*, 11 June 2000.
7  John Gross, *Sunday Telegraph*, 11 June 2000.
8  John Gross, *Sunday Telegraph*, 29 October 2000.
9  Ibid.
10  Kate Kellaway, *Observer*, 29 October 2000.
11  Marcus Field, *Independent on Sunday*, 29 October 2000.
12  Michael Billington, *Guardian*, 18 October 2000.
13  Paul Taylor, *Independent*, 19 October 2000.
14  Benedict Nightingale, *The Times*, 18 October 2000.
15  *Daily Telegraph*, 28 September 2002.
16  *The Times*, 5 November 2002.
17  *Evening Standard*, 10 October 2003.
18  Ian Shuttleworth, *Financial Times*, 10 October 2003.
19  Michael Billington, *Guardian*, 10 October 2003.

20  Charles Spencer, *Daily Telegraph*, 11 May 2004.
21  Kate Bassett, *Independent on Sunday*, 16 May 2004.
22  Robert Hanks, *Independent*, 13 May 2004.
23  Lynn Gardner, *Guardian*, 11 May 2004.
24  Terry Kirby, *Independent*, 14 September 2004.
25  *A Fanny Full of Soap* by Nichola McAuliffe (Oberon Books, 2008).
26  *Daily Mail*, 9 September 2004. Manny Fox generously described McAuliffe's article as 'the best piece of journalism by an artist during the creative process'.
27  Music, book and lyrics by James McDonald, David Vos and Robert Gerlach, with other music by Ed Linderman. *Something's Afoot* was a small American musical that was essentially British, being a spoof of the works of Britain's queen of mystery, Agatha Christie. Tony Tanner's production opened at the Ambassadors Theatre in 1977, when the excellent cast was headed by pint-sized Sheila Bernette as Miss Tweed (a Margaret Rutherford–Miss Marple type, with brogues). The show had previously played Broadway for 61 performances, with Tessie O'Shea as Tweed. The company had good reason to join Tweed in singing 'We Owe It All To Agatha Christie'. There were 232 performances in London.
28  *Daily Mail*, 9 September 2004.
29  *Evening Standard*, 5 October 2004.
30  *Evening Standard*, 8 October 2004.
31  *Daily Telegraph*, 9 October 2004.
32  *The Times*, 9 October 2004.
33  John Barry (*Passion Flower Hotel*, *Billy*) wrote the music for the adaptation of Graham Greene's novel, with lyrics by Don Black and book by Giles Havergal, at the Almeida Theatre in 2004. It was directed by Michael Attenborough, son of the 1947 movie's Pinkie, Richard Attenborough. Describing the piece as 'feeble', Michael Billington (*Guardian*, 6 October 2004) thought the novel's 'spiritual content and its rancid seediness' were 'diminished by musicalisation'. Sheridan Morley praised it as 'a rare throwback to that great tradition' of the golden age of British musicals. For *British Theatre Guide*, Kevin Catchpole reported that the music 'fails to add to the drama', asking 'Where are the sounds of the pier, the racecourse or the murky sea and pebbles?' There was no transfer.
34  *Daily Telegraph*, 9 October 2004.
35  *Sunday Telegraph*, 10 October 2004.
36  *Evening Standard*, 15 October 2004.
37  Elisabeth Mahoney, *Guardian*, 21 October 2004.
38  *Evening Standard*, 21 October 2004.
39  John Gross, *Sunday Telegraph*, 24 October 2004.
40  Benedict Nightingale, *The Times*, 21 October 2004.
41  Dominic Cavendish, *Daily Telegraph*, 21 October 2004.
42  Dominic Cavendish, *Daily Telegraph*, 11 January 2005.
43  Kate Bassett, *Independent*, 13 February 2005.
44  Paul Taylor, *Independent*, 14 April 2005.
45  Mark Shenton, *Stage*, 18 April 2005.
46  Tim Walker, *Sunday Telegraph*, 17 April 2005.
47  *Observer*, 24 April 2005.
48  *Daily Telegraph*, 17 July 2005.
49  Lynn Gardner, *Guardian*, 17 July 2005.
50  *The Times*, 17 July 2005.
51  *Daily Express*, 17 July 2005.

*2006–2016, pages 225–253*

1   *Independent*, 28 August 2007.
2   Susannah Clapp, *Observer*, 16 September 2007.
3   Nicholas de Jongh, *Evening Standard*, 14 September 2007.
4   Tim Walker, *Daily Telegraph*, 16 September 2007.
5   Benedict Nightingale, *The Times*, 14 September 2007.
6   *Stage*, 14 September 2007.
7   Ronald Bryden, *Plays and Players*, June 1972, pp. 24–6.
8   Susannah Clapp, *Observer*, 27 April 2008.
9   Kate Bassett, *Independent*, 27 April 2008.
10  Nicholas de Jongh, *Evening Standard*, 5 April 2008.
11  Tim Walker, *Daily Telegraph*, 25 May 2008.
12  Kate Bassett, *Independent on Sunday*, 25 May 2008.
13  Christopher Hart, *The Times*, 21 May 2008.
14  *Yours, Anne*, book and lyrics by Enid Futterman, music by Michael Cohen. Following its off-Broadway run in 1985, this chamber musical was produced at the Library Theatre, Manchester, in 1990, with Siân Reeves as Anne Frank, and a cast that included Thelma Ruby, Judith Bruce, Peter Reeves and Emile Belcourt, directed by Roger Haines. There was no London transfer.
15  Michael Coveney, *WhatsOnStage*, 23 November 2008.
16  *Daily Telegraph*, 20 November 2008.
17  *The Times*, 20 November 2008.
18  David Benedict, *Variety*, 19 November 2008.
19  Claudia Pritchard, *Independent on Sunday*, 23 November 2008.
20  Susannah Clapp, *Observer*, 23 November 2008.
21  David Benedict, *Variety*, 19 November 2008.
22  Charles Spencer, *Daily Telegraph*, 25 July 2009.
23  *The Times*, 25 July 2009.
24  *Evening Standard*, 27 July 2009.
25  *Daily Telegraph*, 27 July 2009.
26  *Independent*, 25 July 2009.
27  Dominic Maxwell, *The Times*, 25 July 2009.
28  Louise Gooding, *What'sOnStage.com*.
29  Sandra Giorgetti, *britishtheatreguide.info*.
30  Louise Gooding, *What'sOnStage.com*.
31  Sandra Giorgetti, *britishtheatreguide.info*.
32  *Martin Guerre* would be closed down after its London opening in July 1996, reopening in a much-altered production, going on to an impressive 675 performances. The book was by Claude-Michel Schönberg (also composer) and Alain Boublil (also lyricist), Edward Hardy and Stephen Clark.
33  *What'sOnStage.com*.
34  *Stage*, 9 December 2010.
35  *artsdesk.com*.
36  *Daily Telegraph*, 14 April 2011.
37  Kate Bassett, *Independent on Sunday*, 17 April 2011.
38  *Once More Darling* was a sad little musical, or 'farce with music' by Ray Cooney and John Chapman, with music by Cyril Ornadel and lyrics by Norman Newell. It had a brief tour in 1978. The eight-strong cast included Norman Vaughan, Lynda Baron and Jack Douglas.
39  *Guardian*, 16 June 2011.

40 *Daily Telegraph*, 16 June 2011.

41 *Stage*, 9 June 2011.

42 *Daily Express*, 24 October 2013.

43 *Variety*, 23 October 2013.

44 Ibid.

45 *londontheatre.co.uk*, 24 October 2013.

46 *Guardian*, 23 October 2013.

47 BBC News, 28 February 2014.

48 *Daily Mail*, 23 October 2013.

49 Christopher Hart, *The Times*, 27 October 2013.

50 In October 1962 John Vassall, a civil servant at the Admiralty, was detained by two Scotland Yard officers in mackintoshes, and charged with having spied for the KGB. 'We have arrested a man who is a bugger,' the Lord Chief Justice, who would refer to Vassall as 'a known pervert', informed the Prime Minister. Macmillan, sensing troubles ahead, replied 'Why the devil did you catch him?' Vassall's trial and conviction licensed the McCarthy-like persecution by the British popular press, politicians and the judiciary. The potential seriousness of Vassall's betrayal (although nothing he passed to the Russians was ever proved to be of major importance) was emphasised by the Cuban Missile crisis, which erupted on 22 October 1962, the very day that Vassall was sentenced at the Old Bailey to eighteen years' imprisonment.

51 William Douglas-Home's play, *The Reluctant Peer*, was produced at the Duchess Theatre in 1964, running longer than Alec Douglas-Home.

52 Richard Davenport-Hines, *An English Affair: Sex, Class and Power in the Age of Profumo* (Harper, 2013): an exemplary account of the scandal engulfing Ward.

53 *Guardian*, 19 December 2013.

54 *Daily Telegraph*, 24 December 2013.

55 *The Times*, 20 December 2013.

56 *Independent*, 19 December 2013.

57 Operation Yewtree, a British police investigation into sexual abuse, was originated in 2012.

58 Andrzej Lukowski, *Time Out*, 19 December 2013.

59 Sarah Hemming, *Financial Times*, 27 March 2014.

60 *West End Whingers*.

61 Henry Hitchings, *Evening Standard*, 15April 2014.

62 Christopher Hart, *Sunday Times*, 30 March 2014.

63 *Daily Telegraph*, 27 March 2014.

64 BBC News, 17 June 2014.

65 *Independent*, 10 October 2014.

66 Dominic Cavendish, *Daily Telegraph*, 6 November 2014.

67 *Evening Standard*, 10 November 2014.

68 Michael Arditti, *Sunday Express*, 21 February 2016.

69 Michael Billington, *Guardian*, 26 August 2015.

70 Sarah Hemming, *Financial Times*, 26 August 2016.

71 Gerald Berkowitz, *www.theatreguide.london*.

72 West End Whingers, 16 February 2016.

73 Scott Matthewman, *Review Hub*, 16 February 2016.

74 Paul Taylor, *Independent*, 8 June 2016.

75 Lettie McKie, *Londonist*, 15 July 2016.

76 Andrzej Lukowski, *Time Out*, 8 June 2016.

# Select Bibliography

Billington, Michael, *State of the Nation: British Theatre Since 1945* (London: Faber and Faber, 2007)

Codron, Michael and Strachan, Alan, *Putting It On: The West End Theatre of Michael Codron* (London: Duckworth Overlook, 2010)

Davenport-Hines, Richard, *An English Affair: Sex, Class and Power in the Age of Profumo* (London: Harper, 2013)

Drabble, Margaret (editor), *The Oxford Companion to English Literature* (Oxford: Oxford University Press, 5th ed., 1995)

Everett, William A., and Laird, Paul R., *The Cambridge Companion to the Musical* (Cambridge University Press, 2nd ed., 2008)

Findlater, Richard, *Grimaldi: King of Clowns* (London: Macgibbon and Kee, 1955)

Gammond, Peter, *The Oxford Companion to Popular Music* (Oxford: Oxford University Press, 1991)

Ganzl, Kurt, *The British Musical Theatre, Volume 2: 1915–1984* (London: Macmillan, 1986)

Green, Jonathon, *All Dressed Up: The Sixties and the Counter-Culture* (London: Jonathan Cape, 1998)

Green, Stanley, *Encyclopaedia of the Musical* (London: Cassell, 1977)

Hughes, Gervase, *Composers of Operetta* (London: Macmillan, 1962)

Jackson, Arthur, *The Book of Musicals: From Show Boat to A Chorus Line* (London: Mitchell Beazley, 1977)

Johns, Eric (editor), *Theatre Review '73* (London: W. H. Allen, 1973)

King, Denis, *Key Changes: A Musical Memoir* (Ledgewood Press, 2015)

Littlewood, Joan, *Joan's Book: Joan Littlewood's Peculiar History As She Tells It* (London: Methuen, 1994)

Morley, Sheridan, *Spread a Little Happiness: The First Hundred Years of the British Musical* (London: Thames and Hudson, 1987)

Murray, Braham, *The Worst It Can Be Is a Disaster: The Life Story of Braham Murray and the Royal Exchange Theatre* (London: Methuen, 2007)

Ornadel, Cyril, *Reach for the Moon* (Brighton: The Book Guild, 2007)

Parker, Derek and Julia, *The Story and the Song: A Survey of English Musical Plays, 1916–78* (London: Chappell, 1979)

*Plays and Players* monthly magazines

Rankin, Peter, *Joan Littlewood: Dreams and Realities* (London: Oberon, 2014)

Roper, David, *Bart!: The unauthorized life and times ins and outs ups and downs of Lionel Bart* (London: Pavilion, 1994)

Rust, Brian, and Bunnett, Rex, *London Musical Shows on Record 1897–1976* (Middlesex: General Gramophone Publications Ltd, 1977)

Seeley, Robert, and Bunnett, Rex, *London Musical Shows on Record 1889–1989* (Middlesex: General Gramophone Publications Ltd, 1989)

Stage *Yearbooks*

Staveacre, Tony, *The Songwriters* (London: British Broadcasting Corporation, 1980)

Steyn, Mark, *Broadway Babies Say Goodnight: Musicals Then and Now* (London: Faber and Faber, 1997)

*Theatre World* monthly magazine and annuals

Traubner, Richard, *Operetta: A Theatrical History* (London: Victor Gollancz, 1984)

Williamson, Audrey and Landstone, Charles, *The Bristol Old Vic: The First Ten Years* (London: J. Garnett Miller, 1957)

Wilson, Sandy, *Ivor* (London: Michael Joseph, 1975)

Wright, Adrian, *A Tanner's Worth of Tune: Rediscovering the Post-War British Musical* (The Boydell Press, 2010)

# Index of Musical Works

# General Index